INDONESIA ETC.

Also by Elizabeth Pisani

The Wisdom of Whores:
Bureaucrats, Brothels and the Business of Aids

Elizabeth Pisani

Indonesia Etc.

Exploring the Improbable Nation

W. W. Norton & Company
New York • London

For information about permission to reproduce selections from this book, write to
Permissions, W. W. Norton & Company, Inc., 500 Fifth Avenue, New York, NY 10110

For information about special discounts for bulk purchases, please contact
W. W. Norton Special Sales at specialsales@wwnorton.com or 800-233-4830

Manufacturing by RR Donnelley, Harrisonburg, VA
Production manager: Anna Oler

Library of Congress Cataloging-in-Publication Data

Pisani, Elizabeth.
Indonesia etc. : exploring the improbable nation / Elizabeth Pisani. — First edition.
pages cm
Summary: "An entertaining and thought-provoking portrait of Indonesia: a rich,
dynamic, and often maddening nation awash with contradictions. Jakarta tweets more
than any other city on earth, but 80 million Indonesians live without electricity and
many of its communities still share in ritual sacrifices. Declaring independence in
1945, Indonesia said it would 'work out the details of the transfer of power etc. as
soon as possible.' With over 300 ethnic groups spread across 13,500 islands, the world's
fourth most populous nation has been working on that 'etc.' ever since. Bewitched by
Indonesia for twenty-five years, Elizabeth Pisani recently traveled 26,000 miles around
the archipelago in search of the links that bind this impossibly disparate nation. Fearless
and funny, Pisani shares her deck space with pigs and cows, bunks down in a sulfurous
volcano, and takes tea with a corpse. Along the way, she observes Big Men with child
brides, debates corruption and cannibalism, and ponders 'sticky' traditions that
cannot be erased"—Provided by publisher.
Includes bibliographical references and index.
ISBN 978-0-393-08858-8 (hardcover)
1. Indonesia—Description and travel. 2. Pisani, Elizabeth—Travel—Indonesia.
3. Indonesia—Social life and customs. 4. Indonesia—Social conditions. I. Title.
DS620.2.P57 2014
915.98—dc23
2014013536

W. W. Norton & Company, Inc.
500 Fifth Avenue, New York, N.Y. 10110
www.wwnorton.com

W. W. Norton & Company Ltd.
Castle House, 75/76 Wells Street, London W1T 3QT

2 3 4 5 6 7 8 9 0

For Mark

INDONESIA, showing the location of further maps

Contents

Prologue

'Miss! Come in and meet my granny!' The invitation came some twenty years ago from a smiley young man who had spotted me tramping along a dirt road in the obscure south-eastern Indonesian island of Sumba. It was skillet hot and ashtray dusty, and I was very thirsty. His granny probably had tales to tell, and she'd certainly be good for a glass of tea or two. Why not? I had clambered up a ladder onto a bamboo veranda where other youngsters were making unrestful noises with gongs and drums, then ducked through the low doorway and blinked into a windowless darkness. Eventually, by the tiny grains of light that sprinkled through the bamboo-weave of the walls, I made out a poster of Jesus and the Sacred Heart. There was a bag of dirty laundry on a bamboo chair. But the room was otherwise deserted; no sign of granny.

'Just a second!' The young man fiddled around with the laundry bag, untying it and peeling back the napkin on top to reveal Granny. She had died the previous day, and would be receiving guests each day until her funeral four days later, as was the local custom. 'It's an honour for her to meet you,' he said. And we sat and drank tea.

Indonesia is full of such improbable moments. In Indonesia, a presidential candidate who doubles as a sultan and moonlights as the head of the national chamber of commerce keeps a posse of albino dwarves at his court for good luck. In Indonesia, a local police chief will explain how crocodiles are called together so that the innocent reptiles can point out the man-eater for capture. It's a country where it is possible to share a beer with a

1

general who cheerfully admits to prolonging a guerrilla war to inflate his budget, and to take tea with a corpse.

Indeed the nation itself is improbable — a string of 13,466 islands inhabited by people from over 360 ethnic groups, who between them speak 719 languages.* It exists today because its combination of volcanic ash and sea air produced spices, and spices drew Europeans. Not content to trade with local princes and sultans as their Arab, Indian and Chinese predecessors had, the Europeans introduced monopolies that led to conflict, colonization, kleptocracy and a war of independence. The modern state of Indonesia was cobbled together out of the wreckage of all of that.

When the country's founding fathers declared independence from Dutch colonists in 1945, the declaration read, in its entirety:

'We, the people of Indonesia, hereby declare the independence of Indonesia. Matters relating to the transfer of power etc. will be executed carefully and as soon as possible.'

Indonesia has been working on that 'etc.' ever since.

Many countries have struggled to find a *raison d'être* that goes beyond lines drawn on a map by former colonists. But few have had to mash together as many elements as Indonesia. Modern Indonesia runs around the girdle of the Earth, covering the distance from London to Tehran, or from Anchorage in Alaska to Washington DC. At the north-western extreme on the tip of Sumatra is Aceh, peopled by Muslim Malays with a dash of Arab etched into their features who are proud to call their land 'the Veranda of Mecca'. Some 5,200 kilometres to the south-east is the province of Papua, which makes up much of the western half of the giant island of New Guinea, home to black-skinned people many of whom, when I first visited, went naked but for penis-gourds, and who had developed some of the most

---

* These numbers are all hard to nail down. In 2012, the Indonesian Bureau of Statistics reported 17,504 islands based on government listings. However, a GIS survey in 2011 conducted in collaboration with the United Nations that excluded atolls that only appear at low tide in reported 13,466 islands. Between 6,000 and 7,000 are thought to be inhabited year-round.

sophisticated farming techniques in the archipelago. The people of Papua and those of Aceh eat different food, pray to different gods, play different music and are of different races. In between, a riot of other cultures is adapting ancient traditions to modern times in wildly different ways.

Today's Indonesia is home to one in every thirty of the people on this planet – 240 million at the last count. That makes the country the fourth most populous in the world. Jakarta tweets more than any other city on earth, and around 64 million Indonesians use Facebook – that's more than the entire population of the UK. But 80 million live without electricity (all of Germany), and 110 million live on less than two dollars a day (all of Mexico). Hundreds of thousands live without electricity on less than two dollars a day *and* are on Facebook.

The list of 'world's biggest', 'tens of millions' and 'fastest growing' statistics from Indonesia is long. And yet as Indonesian entrepreneur John Riady said recently: 'Indonesia is probably the most invisible country in the world.'

Certainly when I was first posted to Indonesia by Reuters news agency in 1988, I knew virtually nothing about the country. I had backpacked my way through Java and Bali in 1983, when I was nineteen, and had once dropped in to North Sumatra to visit orang-utans. That gave me a set of images to work with: Indonesia was a friendly place, but somewhat schizophrenic. Daily life was shambolic and unpredictable, but on top of the generalized chaos sat a painfully refined culture, all ponderous dancers in delicate batiks twirling their hands to the sounds of gamelan orchestras in the shadow of exquisite temple complexes.

Those images were firmly Javanese. In my mind at the time, as in the minds of most foreigners who think about it at all, Indonesia maps on to Java. In a way, that makes sense. Though it takes up just 7 per cent of Indonesia's land mass, Java is home to 60 per cent of all Indonesians. That's 140 million people in an area the size of Greece. The nation's capital Jakarta is in Java of course; Javanese rulers have spread their influence through the many other kingdoms of the islands with varying degrees of success ever since the twelfth century. When Reuters told me, with just ten days' notice, that I would be moving from New Delhi to Jakarta, I knew virtually nothing of the hundreds of other cultures that make up the nation. I could call up an image of Hindu Bali – women swaying gracefully under the weight of the temple offerings they bore on their heads – or the odd image of a coral reef (Eastern Indonesia), a steamy jungle (Sumatra or Kalimantan) or a perfect surf break (the far west). Nothing more.

For the next two and a half years, whenever I could escape from the tyranny of daily stock market reporting, I wandered the country trying to get my head around 'Indonesia'. I hunted orang-utans and separatist rebels, visited illegal gold miners and illegal immigrants. In Jakarta itself I lunched with bankers, film stars and former political prisoners. As my Indonesian grew more fluent, the conversations grew more interesting. But everything I learned made me more aware of how unknowable the country was. Indonesia is forever curdling the expectations.

I left Indonesia in 1991, following several differences of opinion with the military about the accuracy of my reporting, particularly around the unfolding civil war in the north-western province of Aceh. After I left, the military spokesman, Brigadier General Nurhadi Purwosaputro, sent me a note handwritten on personalized notepaper from the Sheraton Towers hotel in Brisbane:

> *I suppose our relationship has always been rather official (professional) because of your position as a journalist. That being the case, I should let you know, with respect and as the Armed Forces spokesman, that you've worked and done your job very well. You've shown a profound understanding of the people, the state, the government and the real problems facing Indonesia.*
>
> *Now your position has changed. You are an ordinary person who I think has a great fondness for Indonesia.*

He went on to invite me to stay at his home when I visited Jakarta. This was a man who told brazen lies about the brutality that his colleagues were visiting on Indonesian citizens in the quarrelsome provinces of Aceh, Papua and East Timor and in other parts of Indonesia too. He did it reluctantly, almost clumsily; sometimes he left his office by the back door to avoid having to face our questions. He once called me long after my deadline to apologize for not being able to give a timely comment on some minor massacre. His excuse: a sacred dagger belonging to his Commander-in-Chief had, of its own accord, made its way back to the head man's birthplace. The Brigadier General had been busy arranging for the dagger to be brought back to Jakarta, and didn't have time to speak to journalists.

This sort of obfuscation was maddening. But I also found it vaguely charming, the idea that a senior military figure would tell a foreign correspondent stories about magic daggers to avoid having to tell more direct lies about the cruelty of his colleagues. While I often wanted to wring Brigadier General Nurhadi's neck, I couldn't help liking him. And he was right. Despite the bad behaviour of many of its leaders, I did have a great fondness for Indonesia.

That fondness brought me back to the country in 2001, three years after protesting students had seized the parliament building, ending Suharto's thirty-two years in power. In the decade I had been away from Indonesia I had retrained as an epidemiologist, specializing in HIV. Now my job was to help Indonesia's Ministry of Health track the spread of an epidemic it would have preferred to ignore among people that it wished didn't exist: drug injectors, transgenders, women and men who sold sex, gay men, prisoners. I still travelled a lot, but over the following four years I saw a rather different Indonesia. Half my time I was locked up with minor civil servants in workshops in three-star hotels in provincial cities. It was a world of protocol, PowerPoint presentations, and endless boxes of sticky cakes. From the inside, the Indonesian bureaucracy seemed less incompetent than I had previously thought, but no less self-serving.

Much of the rest of my time I seemed to spend in back alleys with drug injectors, tripping the pavements with transgender prostitutes or in the blinged-up clubs of the country's embryonic gay scene. I had unlikely encounters. A tattooed junkie I was talking to on a dingy train platform once treated me to a Fanta. 'We were going to rob you, miss, but actually you're quite funny,' he said. I formed unlikely friendships: to this day I get online advice about photography from a ladyboy who used to be one of the capital's most celebrated sex workers.

I left the country for the second time in 2005. But every year, I somehow contrived to go back to Indonesia for a few weeks, staying in the same house, using the same cell phone, borrowing back the same motorbike, then wandering the provinces with the same old friends. I began to feel that the country was one giant Bad Boyfriend. It tickles the senses and elasticates the thinking. It prompts laughter, produces that warm fuzzy feeling that goes with familiarity and slightly embarrassing shared intimacies. Then it forgets important anniversaries, insults friends, and tells endless low-grade lies. Just when you think you are really getting to know it, it reveals some hidden secret, or reinvents itself completely. With Bad Boyfriends you know full well it will all end in tears, and yet you keep coming back for more.

Another thing about the Bad Boyfriend: however much you sometimes want to slap him, you always want other people to admire this wild and exotic beast, to wish they knew him better. And yet over the years I had become used to seeing a mildly panicked look in people's eyes when I mentioned Indonesia at a drinks party in London or New York. I can see them thinking: 'Oh God, Indonesia . . . is that the new name for Cambodia, Vietnam, those places near Thailand . . . ?'

In late 2011 I decided to try to introduce my Bad Boyfriend to the world. A book about Indonesia would give me an excuse to spend more time in the country, to get to know it better, to try to understand how it has changed over the years of my sometimes frustrated devotion. I put the day job running a public health consultancy in London on ice, and made for the islands.

I'd start in the south-east of the country, I thought, and travel in a vaguely anti-clockwise direction up through the eastern islands. In the best of all possible worlds, I'd then turn left and head across to Sulawesi, Borneo and Sumatra. I'd close the circle by trailing south-east through Sumatra. I'd leave Java, the island where nearly two-thirds of Indonesians lived, the template for most people's thoughts about the nation, until the very end.

I had a vague idea that I'd like to track down some people that I had met in my earlier incarnations and travels – maybe even the young man who invited me to tea with his dead granny. I was also keen to visit parts of the country that no Indonesian I knew had ever been to. That was the extent of my planning. Because in Indonesia, planning is a mug's game. Boats come three days late or not at all, flights change destinations mid-air, new visa regulations send you dashing unexpectedly for borders, serendipitous encounters sweep you wildly off course.

There was another reason not to plan. I knew that I could never hope to give a full account of this kaleidoscope nation, a nation whose multicoloured fragments seem to settle into different patterns with every shake of history and circumstance. Though I wanted to capture the essence of 'Indonesianness', to try to find the *benang merah*, the 'red thread' that binds these different islands and cultures into a single nation, I knew the country would change even in the time it would take me to travel it. I was trying to paint a portrait of a nation on the move, and I could only see one fragment of it at any given time.

So I fell back on one of the core principles of my day job as an epidemiologist, the principle of random selection. This holds that if you can't study everyone, the best way to get a picture of what's going on in a large population is to draw a sample at random. Rather than planning where I would go and who I would talk to in advance, I simply trusted that if I got out there and looked through the eyes of enough people in enough places, I'd be able to piece the fragments together into a portrait of the nation as a whole, to understand better the threads that tied the glorious disparity together. I hoped, too, that some of those threads would bind the present snapshot into a larger historical album, revealing some of Indonesia's deep and lasting qualities.

I only had one rule: 'Just say yes'. Because Indonesians are among the most hospitable people on earth, this made for a lot of yesses. Tea with the Sultan? *Lovely!* Join a wedding procession? *Yes please!* Visit a leper colony? *Of course!* Sleep under a tree with a family of nomads? *Why not?* Dog for dinner? *Uuuuh, sure.* This policy took me to islands I had never heard of. I was welcomed into the homes of farmers and priests, policemen and fishermen, teachers, bus drivers, soldiers, nurses. I travelled mostly on boats and rickety-but-lurid buses that blared Indo-pop and had sick-bags swinging from the ceiling. Sometimes, though, I lucked into a chartered plane or rode cocooned in a leather car-seat behind tinted glass. I can count on one hand the number of times I was treated with anything but kindness. I can also count on one hand the number of days that I did *not* have a conversation about corruption, incompetence, injustice and the slings and arrows of outrageous fortune.

In the end, I spent just over a year travelling the archipelago. I occasionally brushed against parts of the country most frequented by visitors – a beach bar in Bali crowded with well-preserved but slightly leathery white men and honeyed Balinese boys, a Jakarta restaurant catering to bankers and stockbrokers fitting in a quick drink before Wall Street opened and their BlackBerries started buzzing. But as I trekked 21,000 kilometres by motorbike, bus and boat, and covered another 20,000 kilometres by plane, I found these encounters were vanishingly rare. Overall, I visited twenty-six of the country's then thirty-three provinces. Though this book starts with an account of some of the archipelago's previous incarnations, and some of my own early encounters with the Bad Boyfriend, it is largely the story of the Indonesia I discovered on this recent journey. More dizzying in its diversity, but also bound more tightly together in ways that I had not expected, it is a nation quite different from the one I thought I knew.

1

Improbable Nation

When the flamboyant nationalist leader Sukarno proclaimed the independence of Indonesia, he was liberating a nation that didn't really exist, imposing a notional unity on a ragbag of islands that had only a veneer of shared history, and little common culture. The haphazard declaration, with its 'etc.' and its 'as soon as possible', was blurted out just two days after Japan's unexpected surrender in the Second World War. Japan had invaded the Netherlands East Indies in 1942, kicking the Dutch colonists out of the islands. This was a cause for celebration among Indonesian nationalists; 350 years of Dutch kleptocracy left them deeply distrustful of white rulers. But the Japanese turned out to be just as bad, though in different ways. The hasty declaration by Sukarno and his fellow nationalists was designed to keep the islands out of the hands of any other grasping outsiders.

'They were unforgettable, the Japanese.' This came from the mother of a fisherman who I stayed with in Eastern Indonesia in early 2012. Though her face had shrivelled in on itself like a dried sour-plum, she must have been a great beauty in her youth. 'Soooooo cruel,' she said. 'All they wanted was to take away the unmarried girls.'

The subject had come up when I asked the woman how old she was. She didn't know exactly, she said, but she was 'already grown when the Japanese were here'. I asked her what those times were like. She shook her head. 'They made the men dig a pit. Then they stood two men at the edge of the pit.' The old

9

lady struggled arthritically to her feet to demonstrate. 'They tied a cloth around their eyes, a white cloth,' she mimed the blindfolding of seventy years earlier, her own eyes still bright with the memory of what she had seen. 'And then from behind, crack, crack,' she chopped at the back of her neck with a wizened hand, then tottered back into her chair. 'Their heads fell into the pit, and one of the bodies sort of hung there, until a Japanese solider pushed it, and then it was in the pit too.'

Several decades later, a Japanese company set up a pearl farm near the old lady's house; a group of executives from Tokyo were taken on a tour to see a bit of local colour. 'I was sitting in the market selling fish. And I greeted them in Japanese and started bargaining; they were so surprised. This granny in the market selling fish in Japanese. They bought all my fish.' She grinned. 'I made them pay four times the normal price.'

The Europeans who preceded the Japanese came to these islands in large part because of the pearls and other riches found in the marketplaces; today's Indonesia was melded together by the cupidity of Dutch merchants. But for centuries before the Europeans arrived, Arab and Asian traders did business in the independent fiefdoms of the archipelago, without feeling the need to bind them into a whole. They were helped along by the winds, which have driven long-distance trade for most of human history. Around the equator, the winds change direction mid-year. That provided a convenient conveyor belt between China and India, the two powerhouses of production and consumption at the time. They blew south from China between December and March, and provided a fast passage up to India from June to September. Anyone who wanted to ship silk and muslin, ceramics and metalwork, tea and silver between India and China had either to climb the Himalayas or to pass through what are now Indonesian waters.

In the interim months, the islands sat in the fickle-winded Doldrums. During these months, traders stayed in the bustling ports that grew up to meet their needs. They unloaded and reloaded, they refitted and provisioned ships, they married local girls in each port and left them to source cargo for their next visit. From the eastern islands of Maluku came nutmeg and cloves. From the other end of the island chain, the Sultanates of Aceh and Sumatra, came pepper. Local rulers competed to attract traders and sea captains to their own particular patch. This port offered the best access to stocks of pepper, that one was known for secure warehousing. Here harbour charges were low, there you were less likely to get robbed. Marco Polo, who is said to have been floating around these waters on his way home from China in around 1290, describes the bustle of Java's ports: 'This Island is frequented by a vast amount of shipping, and by merchants who buy and sell costly goods from which they reap great profit. Indeed the treasure of this Island is so great as to be past telling.'

Wander through any market in an Indonesian trading town today and you'll probably find much the same sights and smells as Marco Polo would have found more than seven centuries ago. Rickety stalls crowd in on one another, cobbled together out of old packing cases, discarded furniture, stray planks and (these days) last season's election banners. No one cares what their stall looks like, it's the goods on the table that count. On one stall, a giant volcano of red chilli peppers is piled simply on white sackcloth. Next to that is a Rubik's cube of wooden boxes, one stuffed with nutmeg, another with pepper, a third with cloves, the other twenty-two in the grid filled with turmeric and ginger, galangal and coriander seeds, with all manner of spices that you might recognize more easily on the tongue than in the raw. On a stone slab, crabs bubble at the mouth, their claws tied with raffia. At the corner stands the equivalent of the old general store. Palm-leaf hats to keep the sun off hard-working rice farmers hang from a pole. There are brooms made of bamboo and coconut fibre, round-bellied terracotta pots balanced on little braziers for tomorrow's soup.

These days, country markets also come with a full complement of patent medicine sellers, who peddle their wares surrounded by props too modern for Marco Polo's days. At one market I visited, a rapt audience listened to a quack promote a cure-all herb over a crackly disco sound-system. They were watched by a model human head, split down the middle, half good-looking youth, half muscle, sinew and popping eyeball. Not far away, a woman sat quietly over sliced circles of what looked like mud, riddled with holes and threaded through with fibre. I guessed it was some kind of tuber, but no, it was indeed mud: an ants' nest. Cooked up in a soup, a slice of quality ants' nest will cure diabetes and high blood pressure, she assured me. Next to her, an old guy with ears like cup-handles and an intermittent moustache had split his stall in two. On one side, he was selling Coke bottles full of *raja gunung*, 'the king of the mountains', a viscous black potion made of roots of plants that grow high on the slopes of the volcanoes that towered over us. This, he explained between hacking cough and gobby spit, is a cure for lung cancer. The other side of his stall was given over to little mounds of tobacco, and dried palm leaves in which to roll it.

The traders spoke to me and their other potential customers in the national, rather than the local language. Born again as 'Indonesian' for political reasons in 1928, the lingua franca of these islands is actually a form of Malay which has been used by traders for millennia. Foreign merchants moved through the polyglot communities of the straits in waves; the Persians dominated in the seventh century, but were later eclipsed by the Arabs. They in turn were challenged by Indians from Gujarat on the west coast and Coromandel on the east, while the Chinese began a strong showing from the 1100s. What they had in common was a passion for trade; then, as now, people of all colours and races from these islands and much further afield haggled in Malay over baskets of mother-of-pearl, cords of sandalwood, cases of birds of paradise, sacks of pepper, rubbery mountains of tripang sea-slugs. Their legacy is handy for travellers today; though private conversations usually take place in the hundreds of local languages spoken throughout the islands, virtually everyone can speak Indonesian; it's the language of public discourse and is used in day-to-day life in the large cities where Indonesians of different backgrounds congregate.

Commerce shaped the archipelago's religion, as well as its language. From the seventh century, scholars travelling with Indian merchants began to spread the Hindu and Buddhist religions to the southern Sumatran kingdom of Sriwijaya, which went on to become the region's first indigenous empire. The rulers of Sriwijaya grew rich enough on trade to build up armies and conquer neighbouring islands, spreading their religions across the water to Java (and recruiting vassal states as far away as southern Thailand and Cambodia). The plains and hills of central Java began to sprout glorious temples. Borobudur, the largest Buddhist temple in the world, was built in the ninth century. A rival dynasty answered with the breathtaking Prambanan complex, at which Hindus worshipped.

The next wave of traders were Muslims from South Asia, southern China and the Middle East. Because a shared religion greased the wheels of commerce – men could eat and pray together – the traders of the islands were among the first to adopt Islam. Over time, Javanese princes abandoned their Sanskrit names and began to take the title of Sultan. By the start of the sixteenth century, virtually all of Java's rulers had converted; only Bali, directly to the east of Java, kept its Hindu courts and its caste system.

The people of the archipelago's various fiefdoms did not think of themselves as part of any larger whole. The constant to-ing and fro-ing of merchants did, however, create an easy openness and acceptance of difference among ordinary people that persists to this day. It translates into an almost voluptuous hospitality, and makes these islands a deeply seductive place to explore.

But the openness had a downside. It left Indonesia vulnerable to a European onslaught that changed the way that business was done.

When Constantinople fell to the Turks in the mid-fifteenth century, Christian businessmen could no longer easily buy from Muslim traders. By that time, spices were an essential ingredient in the larders of rich Europeans – spices preserved meat in an age before refrigeration, and they masked the taste when the flesh rotted. If Europeans wanted to maintain the supply of pepper, cloves and nutmeg, they would have to go directly to the islands where the spices were grown. That became possible in 1497, when the Portuguese adventurer Vasco da Gama sailed around the bottom of Africa and 'discovered' the sea route to the East. The Portuguese quickly found their way to Maluku, home to the most precious spices. They made first for Ternate, a volcano island cloaked in cloves. On its frilled skirt, a buzzing town now boasts relics of that time: two Portuguese forts and the Sultan's palace. These days, the bigger of the forts is part barracks, part government offices. Army wives drape laundry to dry over old cannons, while SUVs with the red number plates of officialdom ferry uniformed civil servants through a triumphal arch to their dilapidated offices. The Sultan's palace now sits not terribly palatially on a hump of land above the town football pitch, a jumped-up country cottage.

The palace used to be grander. The British sea captain Francis Drake described the Sultan of Ternate's court when he visited in 1579. Drake blew in to Ternate as one of his last stops on a voyage around the globe. Though this licensed pirate was no stranger to riches, he was duly impressed by the Sultan (the 'king') who, Drake said, was draped in gold cloth from the waist down. He wore red slippers, a huge gold chain, and rings on six fingers: two of diamond, two of turquoise, a ruby and an emerald.

> *As thus he sate in his chaire of state, at his right side there stood a page with a very costly fanne (richly embroidered and beset with Sapphires) breathing and gathering the aire to refresh the king, the place being very hot.* *

---

* Francis Drake, *The World Encompassed by Sir Francis Drake . . . Collected Out of the Notes of Master Francis Fletcher . . . and Compared with Divers Others* [sic] *Notes That Went in the Same Voyage*, ed. Francis Fletcher. London: Nicholas Bourne, 1652.

Even in Drake's day, the Sultan's chaire of state was no longer the comfortable place it had once been. Portuguese cannons had blown holes in the principle of free trade. They didn't want *some* of the spices, they wanted *all* of the spices. For them, trade was a zero sum game, though not, it turned out, one they were very good at.

According to Drake, 'The Portugals . . . seeking to settle a tyrannous government over this people . . . cruelly murthered the king himselfe.' Their plans backfired; the people of Ternate revolted and kicked the Portuguese out. Then other Europeans – Spaniards, British and Dutch – sailed in. As they competed to buy spices in Maluku and sell them in Europe, prices in Maluku rose and profits in Europe fell. The backers of these expensive expeditions were displeased. In 1602 the merchants of the Dutch republic decided to do something about it. They banded together to form the Dutch East India Company, the VOC.

The VOC was the world's first joint stock company, with 1,800 initial investors. The hype around the company's formation also gave rise to the world's first stock exchange; early investors were selling off their stake in the company at a premium before the first ship had even sailed. The company's directors, the 'Gentlemen 17', were under huge pressure to deliver value to their shareholders. The first step towards greater profits was to corner the market for spices, eliminating competition from other Europeans. Their strategies were bribery, co-option and brute force.

In the seventeenth century as now, many families in northern Maluku would spend harvest season knocking clusters of pink buds off their clove trees. Children spread the buds on flat, round trays woven out of palm leaves, and adults hiked them up onto the nipa-palm roof of the cottage to dry. After a few days being toasted by the sun and caressed by the breeze, the buds shrivel and blacken into the round-topped nails that we toss into mulled wine. If you are sailing downwind from one of the smaller islands of Maluku in the July clove-drying season, you can sometimes smell Christmas before you can even see land.

The VOC wanted to buy up every single clove, but they couldn't – almost every family in the northern Maluku islands owned trees, and they would rather sell them to Muslim traders than to these hairy white infidels. Then the Gentlemen 17 hit upon the idea of destroying the clove trees in all but one island, Ambon. They paid the local sultans handsomely to achieve this, beginning a tradition of bribing and co-opting local leaders that was to last for over three centuries.

The market for nutmeg should have been easier to corner, because at the time, it only grew in one place on earth: the tiny, isolated Banda islands which rise out of one of the deepest seas on the planet, barely visible on most maps. There, the Hollanders' co-option strategy failed. The islands have a strong tradition of village-level democracy and the Dutch found no sultan, no king, no central power to bribe or threaten. The people of Banda signed treaties with the Dutch, then sold nutmeg to the British. When VOC troops arrived to build a fort on the islands in 1609, the people of Banda ambushed them, murdering a Dutch admiral and thirty-three of his men. Twelve years later, the Dutch responded with brute force on an unprecedented scale.

Wandering around Banda on New Year's Day, 2012, I found the ghost of the VOC floating all around. The aisle of the church is paved with the gravestones of governors installed by the company. In a sandy side road of town, I came across an abandoned orchard behind a pair of heavy wrought-iron gates fashioned into the company logo. The insignia is carved into paving stones and walls, it is stamped on cannons, it graces the archways of several of the forts that dot these islands. The most imposing of these, Fort Belgica, glowers over the harbour as a warning to incoming ships: Don't mess with the Dutch. Walking around Banda Neira, one could be forgiven for thinking that the VOC was more a military than a commercial enterprise. It is a feeling reinforced by a painting which hangs in the museum in Banda Neira. In the centre is a fleshy Samurai mercenary, naked but for a loincloth, his legs a Jackson Pollock splatter of blood. He stands in a minefield of body parts; under one foot, an eyeball

pops out of a severed head. Gut-snakes writhe their way out of
chest cavities, disembodied hands reach from crimson pools. In
the background, a naked baby climbs into the lap of his wailing
mother. Dressed in historically unlikely Islamic clothing, she
begs for mercy as the stone-faced Samurai prepares to bring his
sword down on another Bandanese hero. A Dutchman waves his
rifle, encouraging the mercenary. Another Dutch soldier kicks
a prisoner. In the middle distance, the heads of five elders of
Banda look down sightless from the lances on which they are
impaled. Far beyond, in the bay, the warships of the VOC fly the
Dutch flag.

The painting is almost exultant in its brutality. But the events
it summarizes were brutal, too. The massacre of 1621 was led by
Jan Pieterszoon Coen, the ambitious new Governor-General of
the VOC, who had, as a young trader, witnessed the ambush and
murder of his boss by the rulers of Banda twelve years earlier. He
responded with genocide. His men killed anyone that they didn't
think would make a good slave, then exported the rest, reducing
the islands' population of 15,000 to a few hundred souls. The
Gentlemen 17 told Coen off for his excessive use of force. They
also paid him a bonus of 3,000 guilders.

The monopolies on cloves and nutmeg contributed dispro-
portionately to the income of the VOC for many decades, but
the cost of enforcing the monopolies was also high. The company got sucked into a series of expensive wars between squabbling Javanese princes, and was distracted, too, from its profitable
trade with China. The VOC began to lose money; in 1798 it
toppled into bankruptcy. By then, just four years short of its
200th anniversary, it employed 50,000 people and had a fleet
of close to 150 trading ships and dozens of warships. The VOC
was deemed Too Big To Fail; the Dutch crown took over the
company's 'possessions' and its debts. It was to rule the colony
of the Netherlands East Indies until the Japanese invaded 150
years later.

It was unclear, though, what exactly constituted the Netherlands East Indies. When the VOC crumbled, it had more or less

stamped its authority on Java and the spice-producing islands of Maluku, it controlled the buzzing port of Makassar in Sulawesi and it had an outpost or two in Sumatra. Over the following century and a half, the Dutch crown spread its tentacles across a much wider area, but only gradually. Like the VOC before them, the Dutch colonists were more interested in profit than people; they were driven always by the wealth of the land. They cut down jungles in Sumatra to plant rubber and cocoa, they cleared scrub in Java, Sulawesi and other islands for coffee, tea, sugar and tobacco. They opened the earth to dig out tin and gold, they sank wells for oil. If an island or a region could produce nothing of interest to Dutch businessmen, the colonizers allowed local princelings to carry on setting the rules until well into the 1880s.

Travelling in Indonesia, whether you are local or foreign, you'll hear one question before any other: '*Dari mana?*' 'Where are you from?' It's perhaps natural in this nation of traders, a way of calibrating what this stranger has to offer, what they might buy from you, how they are likely to behave. But it also provides an interesting insight into what Indonesians think of other countries. Including their former colonizers.

I used to struggle with the '*Dari mana?*' question. My mother is a Scot who grew up in England, but I didn't live in the UK until I was fourteen, and was only properly resident for five of the subsequent thirty-five years. My father is the grandson of Italian immigrants to New York. My parents met in an immigration queue when my father was hitchhiking around the world and my mother was hitchhiking around Europe. I was born in a city in the American Midwest whose name I consistently misspell, and grew up in Germany, France and Spain. I've actually lived in Indonesia for longer than any other single country in my life. But dozens of times a day, all of this gets boiled down to '*Dari Inggris*' – 'I'm from England.'

When I first lived in Indonesia and confessed to being '*dari Inggris*', the invariable response was: 'Wah! Inggris! Lady Di!'

In this age of near-universal access to televised football, it has become: 'Wah! Inggris! Manchester United!'* But then, with remarkable frequency, the initial reaction is followed with something else: 'I wish we'd been colonized by the English, not the Dutch.'

When I asked why, people invariably gave one or more of the following reasons. One: the Dutch only took things, they didn't give anything back, while the British built up the institutions of state. (What about all those great engineering works, I would ask? The irrigation systems, the ports? Those were only so that the Dutch could take things from us more efficiently, Indonesians would reply.) Two: the Dutch deliberately kept the local population stupid, while the Brits educated people. Three: the Dutch had a sliding scale of justice administered by political appointees which was always stacked against the little person, while the Brits had an independent judiciary and everyone was equal in the sight of the law.

These opinions came not from historians or academics but from people I met on boats and at coffee stalls, from truck drivers, farmers and midwives. I found it interesting that though Indonesians love to blame the Dutch for many things, they've done little over the last seven decades to change them. I suspect that's because all the Dutch did was to exploit patterns of behaviour that already existed in these islands when they first arrived.

The Europeans changed the rules of the trading game, it's true, and they made plantations and extractive industries more efficient. But the islands' many kings and sultans had been squeezing the peasantry for taxes and labour to finance their endless wars with one another long before the Europeans arrived. Education in pre-colonial times was essentially confined to itinerant scholars from India and the Middle East, and the gossamer-thin layer of courtiers they interacted with. And justice was dribbled out

---

* Manchester United's international marketing machine has captured Indonesian hearts and wallets. Local Bank Danamon issues Man U-branded credit cards 'for sports fans with a modern lifestyle', for example.

at the whim of the ruler. In the Javanese heartland, the new colony could consolidate power simply by buying off squabbling aristocrats and turning them into bureaucrats. Java's grandees were allowed, still, to strut their stuff in front of their people, to go out in great processions under twirling golden umbrellas, to stamp their feet, play boss and collect taxes as they had always done. But when they got back to their palaces they had to turn those taxes over to the King of Holland, taking a salary in return.

As the Dutch bosses got more demanding the grandees grew more oppressive. From the 1830s, farmers who had always grown whatever they wanted – mostly food for their families – now had to reserve part of their land to grow cash crops which the government bought at fixed prices. They also had to spend a certain number of days working on commercial plantations, pumping profits into the coffers of the motherland. At one stage, half of the Netherlands' national income was being siphoned in from Indonesia. At the beginning of the twentieth century, left-leaning politicians in the Netherlands forced through the 'Ethical Policy'. This recognized that the government of the Netherlands East Indies bore some responsibility for the welfare of the 34 million people who then lived nominally under Dutch rule. The colonists were obliged to start setting up schools for the children of the more privileged 'natives'. The new ethics did not, however, stop the government in the colony's capital Batavia (now Jakarta) from waging war on other natives.

In Java and some of the plantation areas of other islands there had been rebellions against the Dutch over time, while countless acts of civil disobedience poked holes in the hated system of compulsory labour. The colonists always replied with force. In the closing decades of the nineteenth century, they also became less tolerant of the quasi-autonomous fiefdoms that survived in other islands. Batavia launched campaigns to impose its will more completely across the whole island chain, and local rulers fought back. In Bali, just a canoe-paddle away from decidedly Dutch Java, local rulers resisted the yoke of Queen Wilhelmina until 1908. Aceh, at the western extremity of the island chain, fought off the Dutch until 1903. At the other extreme, in the jungles and swamps of 'Dutch West Papua', the colonial presence was even more notional. Papua was so far out of the fold that it was not even part of the nation that was handed over to Indonesian rule at independence. And in the eastern half of the island of Timor, the Dutch never set foot at all. The Portuguese had settled in East Timor after being ousted by the people of Ternate in the sixteenth century. It remained a Portuguese enclave until 1975, when Lisbon abandoned it following a socialist revolution at home. Indonesia quickly sent in troops and 'integrated' East Timor as the nation's twenty-seventh province.

Ironically, it was the well-meaning ethical policy that sowed the seeds of a true anti-colonial movement. For the first time, young 'natives' were allowed an education, and in a European language that gave them access to books and newspapers full of new ideas about sovereignty and social justice. For the first time, young men from across the archipelago came together in the major cities of Java, finding common cause against a common enemy. It was in the minds of these young men that the notion of Indonesia was conceived. It was made flesh in 1928, when a congress of youth groups from around the archipelago pledged, in the name of the 'sons and daughters of Indonesia', that they would fight for 'One Homeland: Indonesia. One Nation: Indonesia. One Language: Indonesian.'

It was to become the rallying cry for nationalists in their battle to throw over the Dutch. Those who shouted it too loudly were exiled by the Dutch to forgotten corners of the land where they could do no harm.

Banda, once so central to Dutch interests, was by the 1930s just such a backwater. Down a quiet side street I found a monument to the political troublemakers who had been exiled in Banda over the years. The two most prominent were both leading lights of Indonesian nationalism: Sutan Sjahrir, Indonesia's first Prime Minister and Mohammad Hatta, its first Vice President, who signed the declaration of independence alongside the nation's first President, Sukarno.

Every Indonesian has the date of that independence, 17 August 1945, engraved on their memory: 17 August is a national holiday. Villagers make triumphal archways out of bamboo and paint them with the anniversary: CONGRATULATIONS, INDONESIA AT 67! Even in Jakarta's slums people paint discarded plastic cups in red and white and string them along the side of the fetid canal; do-it-yourself 3D bunting.

In Banda, though, I stumbled over a monument that suggested a different creation myth: 'Raised by the people of Banda to commemorate the independence and sovereignty of the United Republic of Indonesia: 27/12/1949', it read.

Thinking I might learn more about this unorthodox view of Indonesian independence, I went to visit the house where Mohammad Hatta lived while in exile, which is now a museum. It is a typical Banda-style bungalow: three wooden doors with louvered shutters open out onto a long veranda. There was no one around, but the door was open so I wandered in. In one corner of the main room was an ornately carved love seat, the velvet upholstery of the genre replaced with cool wicker. It sat behind a wooden coffee table flanked by two other wicker chairs. On the table a wooden sign read: table and chair set. A couple of empty soft drink bottles blew around on the floor underneath. A glass corner cabinet housed a suit, a shirt, a pair of glasses, a pair of shoes. There was a desk with a typewriter on it. That was it. No information about why Hatta was exiled to Banda, let alone about the conflicting dates of independence.

The time lag between those two dates, the iconic 1945 and the rarely mentioned 1949, was in fact the time it took the Dutch to admit that they had lost their colony.

Throughout the 1930s, with the encouragement of leftist parties in Holland, the Indonesian nationalist movement had grown. But it had also diverged. One group thought that the hammers and sickles of workers and peasants would drive the colonists away. The other believed that the Koran was the strongest weapon with which to confront the Dutch. They probably would have gone on squabbling indefinitely had the Second World War not intervened.

It was the Japanese occupation that really catalysed Indonesian independence. By dispatching the Dutch so swiftly, the Japanese shattered the myth of European superiority. Espousing 'Asia for the Asians', they encouraged Sukarno and other nationalists to prepare for self-rule within an Asian commonwealth. And because they anticipated an Allied invasion, they set about militarizing the Indonesians, training many young men in the use of arms and guerrilla warfare.

Then came Hiroshima, the Japanese surrender and the hasty declaration of independence. The first item on Indonesia's long list of Etcs was simply to make sure that the former colonial power didn't settle back in. The Australian, British and American troops who moved in to reclaim Indonesia from the defeated Japanese were not enthusiastic about handing the territory back to the Dutch. But in the absence of any transfer of sovereignty, the Allies all still recognized the Netherlands as the legitimate authority in the archipelago. And the Dutch wanted their colony back.

The nationalists disagreed about how to stop that happening. Many leaders favoured negotiating their way to independence. But Sukarno, outstandingly the most charismatic of the young leaders, was for fighting. He set about trying to make the islands ungovernable through insurrection. There followed four years of intermittent warfare and bad-tempered diplomacy.

Very like the founding fathers of the United States in the late eighteenth century, Indonesia's young leaders disagreed about the best political format for the new country: should it be federal, or a unitary state with a strong central government? Hatta and Sjahrir, who were to become Vice President and Prime Minister respectively, were both from West Sumatra. They feared that in a centralized state, Javanese colonizers would simply replace the Dutch, imposing their will on other islands and cultures. Sukarno, later President, believed the nation's disparate elements could be held together only by a strong centre. He invoked a mythical past in which the Sriwijaya and Majapahit empires ruled the whole area coloured Dutch on the imperial map. In fact, the pre-colonial empires were much more limited than Sukarno claimed, their sphere of influence established largely through a loose system of tribute. But by retrofitting history, Sukarno was able to justify reclaiming the empire from the colonizers, recasting it as a republic, and ruling it from a central court in Java.

Sukarno did not immediately get his way; he was denied a place at the table at which the formal transfer of sovereignty from the Netherlands was negotiated because he was considered to have collaborated with the Japanese. When the Dutch offered self-rule for seven individual federated states within the United Republic of Indonesia, a commonwealth headed by the Dutch crown, Hatta and Sjahrir signed up. Within a year, however, support for a federation had imploded and Sukarno was firmly back on track towards a unitary state ruled from Jakarta.

Sukarno was a demagogue whose political recipe was one part populism and three parts theatre, seasoned with mischief and served with a large glass of charisma. He was also astute, and knew how fragile the idea of Indonesia was. Had he been in any doubt, rebellions in Maluku, West Sumatra, West Java and Sulawesi in the early 1950s underlined the fact that not all 'Indonesians' shared his centralized vision.

Sukarno came up with a political philosophy that was supposed to create room in his unitary state for everyone. It's known as Pancasila, the Five Principles, and it typifies the Indonesian talent for fuzzy philosophies that can be turned to any purpose. It encompasses:

1) 'Belief in the one and only God' – by not specifying which God, Sukarno intended this to enshrine the principle of freedom of religion. For Suharto, Sukarno's successor as President and his polar opposite politically, it was seen as a bulwark against communism.
2) 'Just and civilized humanity' – a vague concept coloured by the Javanese idea of the enlightened and

munificent ruler and espoused by many rulers who were neither.

3) 'The unity of Indonesia' – in Sukarno's reading, this guarded against federalism; in Suharto's, it justified weaving the military into every aspect of national life.

4) 'Democracy guided by the inner wisdom of unanimity arising out of deliberations among representatives' – intended by Sukarno as a safeguard against Western-style confrontational democracy, and used by Suharto to guard against any democracy at all.

5) 'Social justice for all Indonesian people' – for socialist Sukarno, this endorsed state intervention in the economy, while to capitalist Suharto, it suggested support for allowing free-market policies to trickle down to all people.

Every Indonesian can trot out the Pancasila in the way that even the most lapsed Christian can trot out the Lord's Prayer, but it has never unleashed great currents of nationalism. So Sukarno turned to gunboats and grandstanding. To entrench national unity, he needed a common enemy to replace the Dutch. He set about picking fights.

In fact, it was unfinished business with the Dutch that provided the first battleground. The Netherlands had retrospectively excluded mineral-rich West Papua from the territory it handed over to the nationalists. It's ours, said Sukarno, and went to the United Nations – a bold move for a newborn nation. Most countries at the UN sided with the flamboyant polyglot, though not enough to force UN action. That allowed Sukarno to keep up his nationalist belligerence. In 1961 he sent the paratroopers into Papua to begin the process of grabbing back what belonged, in the eyes of most Indonesians but few Papuans, to the republic.*

---

* In 1962 the Dutch agreed that West Papua could be transferred to Indonesian rule after an interim period of United Nations administration, on condition that the people of Papua were ultimately given the right to choose their future. Indonesia took over the administration in 1963 and staged an 'act of self-determination' in 1969. A handful of tribal elders, encouraged by a heavy

After that, Sukarno started thumping his chest in the direction of former British colonies to the north which were trying to band together into a new country, Malaysia. He used the UN again, this time withdrawing Indonesia from the world body in protest at Malaysia's seat on the Security Council.

Though they did carve Indonesian nationalism deeply into the world view of his generation, Sukarno's theatrics could not distract attention from the nation's collapsing economy and the frailty of its political structures. The republic was governed by fourteen different cabinets between the declaration of independence and the first legislative elections in 1955. Those elections put twenty-eight different parties into parliament. Sukarno's nationalist party only just pipped the big Islamic parties, which came second and third. Though the communists had, through a series of badly planned uprisings, made themselves unpopular with the infant republic's army, they did well at the polls, sweeping up one in six votes to come in fourth. The elections did little to increase stability; if anything, parliament became more raucous.

Finally the volatile Sukarno lost patience. He had never been a fan of confrontational parliamentary politics in any case. Much better, he said, to stick to Javanese village tradition, where people come to consensus in a discussion guided by a wise village elder – the fourth pillar in his Pancasila philosophy. In 1957 he declared that he would act as village elder to the nation. With the flair for euphemism which is characteristic of Java, he called his dictatorship 'guided democracy'.

Sukarno was a bold thinker and a true visionary, and he remains wildly popular to this day. But he guided politics as though he were Cecil B. de Mille. He wanted all Indonesians to become extras in a political pageant under his direction, and

---

Indonesian military presence, voted for integration and the territory became a province of Indonesia.

Papuans, racially and culturally different from the peoples of the islands to the east of them, have disputed the 'integration' ever since. The issue, which has grown more complex because of recent economic and political developments, continues to fester.

damn the cost. The script was anti-colonialism; because the Dutch had ruled in the interest of profit, being anti-colonial was synonymous with being anti-capitalist. The 1945 constitution is decidedly hostile to the private sector, specifying that the state must control all natural resources and all strategically important branches of production.

This was distressing to everyone of any economic standing in the Outer Islands; they lived and breathed trade. But it didn't serve Java well, either. As the economy languished and underemployment rose, the young people of Java increasingly joined in Sukarno's political pageant, staging rallies and marching in parades. When Muslim youth groups confronted young communists in the streets, Sukarno, who was determined that Indonesia should remain secular, encouraged the communists. By the mid-1960s the Partai Komunis Indonesia (PKI) claimed to have between two and three million members, making it the third largest in the world, after China and Russia.

The deeply conservative military, which lent a guiding hand to 'guided democracy', disliked both the communists and the political expression of Islam. The generals watched the mounting political chaos with dismay. On the night of 30 September 1965 the situation came to a head. The official version of events, publicly accepted for years, defies logic on virtually every level. It holds that a group of officers from the army worked in cahoots with the PKI to plan a coup against Sukarno. This seems unlikely; the army broadly loathed the PKI, while Sukarno was in fact a great supporter of the communists. The 'rebel' officers killed six generals and seized the national radio station. Suharto, then the commander of the Strategic Reserve, stepped in to save the day, ousting the traitors, restoring calm, and securing the safety of President Sukarno – so school children are taught. What they are not told is that Suharto later placed his predecessor under house arrest.

There are plenty of other theories, most of them published by foreigners: that Suharto planned the whole thing, or at least that he knew of it in advance; that it was an internal army squabble and

Suharto was simply in the right place at the right time and made the most of it, or that the attempted coup was plotted variously by the CIA, Britain's MI6 or some combination of the two.

Whatever the truth, the events of that night certainly unleashed a tsunami of anti-PKI propaganda, followed by revenge killings, begun by the army itself. Many ordinary Indonesians joined in with gusto. Different groups used the great orgy of violence to settle different scores. In East Java, Muslims got back at their long-time communist rivals. In Bali, as many as one person in twenty was killed – the highest rate in Indonesia. Though the rhetoric was all about protecting Hindus from the filthy atheists, the PKI were actually more of a threat to the privilege and landholdings of the island's upper-caste aristocrats than they ever were to its piety. In northern Sumatra, gangster organizations affiliated with business interests developed a special line in garrotting communists who had tried to organize plantation workers. The Dayak tribes of West Kalimantan used the supposed perfidy of the PKI to start pushing the ethnic Chinese off the land.

The carnage wiped out a whole generation of socially committed activists and pulled up the roots from which they might regrow. It crippled the development of political debate and made Indonesians citizens wary of political allegiance. And it served Suharto very well.

2

The Ties that Bind

The Four Seasons Hotel, Jakarta's poshest, rose like a Rajasthani water palace out of a temporary lake. In front of the uniformed doorman, on the water that washed across the valley between the edge of the highway and the raised entrance to the hotel, two giant blue laundry-bins were bobbing about. They were filled with guests, well groomed and slightly nervous-looking, who had clambered into them with the help of a ladder filched from the maintenance department. It was flood-time again in Jakarta, and enterprising hotel staff had set up an informal service to ferry guests to dry ground. The charge, not included in the US$250 a night room rate, was sometimes renegotiated midstream.

Jakarta is not an easy city to love. It is a vast, chaotic, selfish, stroppy monument to ambition and consumption, a city that seems to know no bounds. It is crowded, polluted and noisy, it is built on a swamp, and it floods ever year. Yet Jakarta's citizens have a remarkable talent for turning the city's vicissitudes into virtues. And its citizens are many. When the Dutch left, it was home to 600,000 people. But in the years that followed, Jakarta burst its banks and sprawled over 661 square kilometres, 40 per cent of it below sea level. By the time I started my trip in 2011, there were 17 times as many people living in Jakarta as there had been at independence, and the metropolis was gobbling up surrounding towns too. Greater Jakarta is now home to 28 million people – the second largest urban agglomeration in the

29

world after Greater Tokyo. Waterways and drainage channels have been built over with thrusting skyscrapers and marbled malls; the canals that remain are lined with squatters' shacks and clogged with garbage.

Unlike Tokyo, Jakarta has no mass transit system to speak of, so traffic jams are legendary. The super-rich rise above the problem; as a child, one acquaintance of mine used to be dropped at kindergarten every day in the family helicopter. But everyone else suffers to varying degrees. The lower-middle classes elbow their way onto sporadic, ageing trains and sordid buses or weave their way through the traffic chaos on motorbikes, dreaming of the day they will own a car. Each year, another 200,000 cars pour onto the streets. That means more traffic, and longer commutes. The chauffer-driven rich kit their cars out with mobile offices so that they can use the time they spend on gridlocked roads more productively. A few years ago, the city government decided it would cut congestion on the city's main arteries by insisting that in rush hour, each car must have at least three passengers. Again, Jakarta's infinitely creative residents made the most of the change. Within days, the pavements of the feeder roads were crowded with unemployed people hiring themselves out as 'jockeys', extra passengers for rich people's smooth, air-conditioned cars.

It's this sort of inventiveness that makes me love the city despite myself. When I first lived in Jakarta in the late 1980s, the capital already had a fair number of gleaming office blocks and traffic-clogged highways. But they huddled together for comfort, a few islands of self-conscious modernity in an ocean of tin roofs and off-kilter houses, of tangled backstreets and pungent markets. In the early post-Suharto years, when I worked at the Ministry of Health, the islands were growing larger and the sea was receding. But as I drove my motorbike through the rat runs of this low-rise city, taking shortcuts between one atoll of air-conditioned offices and the next, I would still catch glimpses into the heart and soul of the Jakarta I loved best. A schoolboy sat staring at a book, his hands clamped over his ears to block out the bickering of the three younger siblings who shared his room. A young father washed his toddler in a bucket on the street. Cycling past him was a tailor with an old Singer sewing machine welded to a workbench on the back of his bike. 'LEVIS' read the sign that hung from his handlebars.

Now, there's barely a ghost of that Jakarta left. I did see an itinerant tailor as I was fussing around in Jakarta in 2011 preparing for my travels. He was on what used to be one of my former rat runs, still with an old Singer sewing machine, still advertising Levi's. Yet the alleyways and the people who breathed life into them were gone. This man cycled slowly on the highway between the Stock Exchange and a forest of five-star hotels, abused on all sides by businessmen boxed up in their luxury SUVs who were impatient to get around the relic tailor and on to their next deal. It was a melancholy sight.

Nowadays, the capital of Indonesia is a city of malls, of condos, of fast-food restaurants and Indomarets – the ghastly over-cooled convenience stores that sit on every corner, wallowing in the miasma that wafts off gently warming chicken hot dogs. It is a city of expensive sushi joints and flashy nightclubs, of gleaming skyscrapers that stand erect and confident, beacons of the nation's prosperity. As McDonald's, Indomaret and gated communities have taken over from alleyway Jakarta, the city has grown almost feral. By late 2011, as I battled my way around town on a motorbike trying to track down ferry timetables and mosquito nets ahead of my trek around the rest of the nation, I was finding Jakarta increasingly unlovable. It seemed very different to the city I first got to know twenty-five years earlier. And all the changes in Jakarta stemmed from one fundamental change in Indonesia: Suharto was no longer in charge.

I had arrived in Jakarta to work for Reuters in 1988, when Suharto was in his twenty-first year in power, yet when I walked into the newsroom – a dreary, grey place inhabited by clunky screens winking green text against a black page – I had barely heard of the man. Suharto was remarkable among dictators precisely for being so outwardly unremarkable: a quiet, methodical person who lived modestly and put stability before all else. Where Sukarno had appeared at massive rallies in the guise of a visionary saviour of the people, Suharto appeared at family planning clinics in the guise of a concerned uncle. Where Sukarno had called together the leaders of the post-colonial world and kick-started the non-aligned movement, Suharto called together farmers and kick-started campaigns to keep rats out of rice fields. Sukarno's string of flirtations and four marriages, the last to a teenage hostess he met in a bar in Japan, had provided a permanent stream of gossip. There wasn't much to say about Suharto's fifty-year marriage to Ibu Tien.

There was nothing glamorous about Suharto. But the 'Old Man', as we called him, was a source of endless fascination, chewed over during a merry-go-round of diplomatic cocktail parties that filled the evenings of the city's foreign correspondents. I settled quickly into this rarefied life. In the leafy district of Menteng, I had rented a tiny Dutch-era villa set back off a narrow street used mainly by itinerant vendors wheeling kitchen carts, each with a signature sound advertising its wares. 'Ting-ting-ting' meant fried noodles were on offer, 'toc-toc-toc' signalled *bakso*, a meatball soup. Vocals came from the satay man or the vegetable cart: 'Te-EH, Te-EH. SAA-tay!', 'OOooo, OOooo, SAY-ur . . .!'

The roving restaurants provided the backing track for meals served under a candle-lit frangipani tree in my garden – a source of bemusement to my Javanese friends, who think frangipanis belong in graveyards. Around the table, journalists, diplomats and the braver Indonesian intellectuals put forward their theory about who was in, who was out, whether the absence of this minister from that cocktail party signalled that the Old Man was unhappy with a faction of the military or was a warning to a particular business conglomerate. Since nothing much was known, everything was plausible.

A young British diplomat named Jon Benjamin, whiplash smart and very grounded, frequently came down on the side of what he called the Fuckwit Factor. Behind all the smoke and mirrors, the most likely reason that this minister was not at that cocktail party was that his driver forgot to put petrol in the car. The cancellation of the joint military exercises with Singapore, the postponement of the trade mission to the US, the blackout at the radio station scheduled to broadcast a vice-presidential address: again and again Jon would advance the theory that someone, somewhere, just fucked up. As events unfolded, Jon was often proved right.

Sukarno had tried to pull 'Indonesia' together through sheer force of personality. Suharto used the steely threads of bureaucracy. The quiet general often paid lip service to the motto that appears on the national coat of arms: 'Unity in Diversity'. But he made it abundantly clear that he was more in favour of the tidy unity than of the troublesome diversity. His flunkies set about pressing the 'diversity' into acceptable forms: local costumes were redesigned for modesty, traditional dances were shorn of their flirtations.

The Suharto version of diversity was on display for me on the second day of my new job at Reuters. 'Come! We'll show you the country!' declared my Indonesian colleagues. They whisked me down a broad avenue lined with plate-glass office blocks, past several of the gargantuan socialist-realist statues erected by Sukarno to inspire the proletariat, and out to Mini Indonesia, a nationalist theme park designed by Suharto's wife Tien. Soon we were swinging in a cable car above a huge artificial lake dotted with the islands shaped like the major land masses of Indonesia. Then we trekked dutifully around a few of the pavilions built to represent the nation's hundreds of cultures. There was one pavilion per province, twenty-seven of them at the time, each an example of traditional architecture, each containing dioramas of people in traditional dress (though none of the mannequins topless as the women of Bali used to be, none of them wearing loincloths with severed-head motifs typical of the warriors of Sumba). There was one house of worship for each of Indonesia's approved faiths, too: churches Catholic and Protestant, a Hindu temple, a Buddhist stupa and, of course, a Mosque. There was no sign of the hundreds of folk religions that I later found bubbling alongside those sanctioned by Suharto. No ritual slaughter of buffalo here at Mini Indonesia, no midnight offerings of afterbirth on the night of a full moon.

While his wife scrubbed up the nation's more 'primitive' cultures for display in Mini Indonesia, Suharto himself imposed national symbols and institutions uniformly across the land. Though his rhetoric encompassed the nation, much of the symbolism was Javanese, and most was delivered through the state. Every Monday morning, schoolchildren sang the national anthem while the head boy and head girl solemnly raised the flag. There were other anthems of unity too, including a song that glorifies the union of the necklace of islands that runs between the towns of Sabang in the north-west and Merauke in the south-east. 'I used to be so proud, standing in my little red shorts singing "From Sabang to Merauke", before being forced to swallow everything about Java,' a Balinese friend told me.

Every Saturday throughout the Suharto years, civil servants from Arab-tinged Aceh to the Melanesians of Papua (5,000 kilometres and three time zones away) held their own version of the school flag-raising ceremony, all dressed in identical Javanese batik emblazoned with the national Pancasila Eagle motif. From the point of view of an outsider, there was something slightly comforting about these enforced displays of unity. In every unexplored town there were things you'd recognize. I knew there would be neat white signboards outside every official building, school and place of worship, giving its function and its address. At the entrance to each village, carefully hand-painted on strips of wood in many colours, would be the 'Ten core programmes of the Family Welfare Union' – a supposedly grass-roots women's organization that was in fact invented in Central Java and replicated throughout the land under the watchful eyes of the provincial governors' wives. These women – referred to as *Ibu-Ibu*, 'The Ladies' – represented a species of upper-middle-class wife found throughout Indonesia. Taking their lead from Suharto's Ibu Tien, they all wore their hair combed up and then lacquered into massive globes – rounder than a beehive, but puffier than the traditional *konde* bun. There was pancake make-up, much silk and brocade, and manicures that could strike terror into the hearts of small children. The look was Cruella de Vil meets *The Mikado*, but the '10 Programmes' they promoted were more domesticated, enshrining the duties of a good wife and mother. They ranged from the concrete – 'Health', 'Food' – to the more esoteric: 'Understanding and Practice of Pancasila'.

To try and iron out regional differences and modernize the bureaucracy, Suharto imposed an identikit framework of government across the whole country in the 1970s. Previously, local communities had organized themselves according to their various traditions – the Dayaks of Kalimantan gathered in longhouses under the supervision of a respected elder, for example, while in West Sumatra clans clustered around communally held land. By sweeping away these variations, Suharto undermined the very foundation of many of the nation's cultures. He hoped they would be rebuilt with a set of building blocks that were identical nationwide. There were five principal levels of government: nation, province, district, sub-district, and village.* They followed a fairly strict chain of command. Suharto stripped the provinces of any vestige of decision-making, appointing governors – many of them military men, several of them Javanese, all of them fiercely loyal – to do Jakarta's bidding. He backed them up with two uniformed armies, both also largely Javanese. The first was of soldiers, who were given licence under a doctrine known as 'dual function' to meddle in civilian life down to the village level. The second was of civil servants. The distinction between the two was not always clear.

When I travelled in eastern Indonesia during the Suharto years, it was rare to find a civil servant who spoke the local

---

* In urban areas a district is replaced by a city, and a village by a neighbourhood. The Indonesian terms are Nasional, Propinsi, Kabupaten/Kota, Kecamatan, Desa/Kelurahan.

language or had the dark skin and crinkly hair of the dry and neglected islands that nudge Australia. Most bureaucrats came from Java or other areas where accidents of colonial history had left a better-than-average educational system. The locals treated them like a separate species. During a trip to the tiny, arid island of Savu, just north of Australia, in 1991, I recorded the comment of a farmer I met: 'Here we eat once a day, for the rest we drink palm sugar. Except for civil servants, they eat three times a day.'

There was another species, too, that local populations regarded as quite separate from themselves. These were Javanese 'transmigrants' – poor peasants who were paid by the government to shift from the overcrowded rural heartland to roomier islands. The programme actually dates from Dutch times when it was called 'colonization'; it was judiciously renamed by Sukarno, who planned each year to send a million and a half Javanese, with their obedient, collectivist values, to other islands to homogenize the nation. Always better at vision than delivery, he managed to shift just one thousandth of his target number over fifteen years.

Suharto shared his predecessor's hope that government-sponsored transmigration might foster national unity. He ramped up the programme, sending around 300,000 people a year from Java and Bali to other islands. Halfway into Suharto's term, his minister of transmigration said: 'By way of transmigration we will try to . . . integrate all the ethnic groups into one nation, the Indonesian nation. The different ethnic groups will in the long run disappear because of integration and there will be one kind of man, Indonesian.'*

If the minister believed that transmigrants were happily flirting in coffee shops with the local population, settling in to make truly 'Indonesian' babies, he was mistaken. In fact, they clumped together like sticky-rice in villages named after their home towns. I visited a transmigration site in the north-eastern province of Aceh in the early 1990s; it was among the most

---

* Quoted in Brian A. Hoey, 'Nationalism in Indonesia: Building imagined and intentional communities through transmigration', *Ethnology* 42, no. 2 (Spring 2003): 112.

forlorn places I have ever been in Indonesia. Sidomulio, it was called – a Javanese name if ever I heard one. It was a tiny hamlet carved out of the jungle bordering a rubber plantation. There were a few creaky shops named after the great towns of Java – 'Solo Agricultural Products', 'Malang Barber'. They were all boarded up. Most of the houses had been stripped of their more valuable contents, padlocked and abandoned. Peeking in, I could see toys strewn across the floor, half-full glasses of tea left on tables. The only sign of life was a pack of hungry dogs.

An old man, Acehnese, appeared on a prehistoric motorcycle. I asked where all the villagers were. They had left because they were unwelcome, he replied. Acehnese rebels accused Jakarta of stealing its resources, and had launched a guerrilla war against the central government. But the people who bore the brunt of their ire were the unskilled landless peasants who had been sent here in a failed attempt to engineer national unity. The villagers of Sidomulio had left after their headman was stabbed to death in the middle of the night, presumably by guerrillas.

The victimization of transmigrants in Aceh was an extreme case of local dissatisfaction. But even where transmigrants rubbed along well enough with their neighbours, they carried on speaking their mother tongue, they cultivated the crops they grew back home, they set up the gamelan gong orchestras that mirrored those of Java or Bali. It was more transplantation than transmigration, hardly a homogenizing force.

Transmigration was a rare failure in Suharto's nation-building efforts. More successful, and perhaps more surprising for a man who was a peasant at heart, was his foray into television.

Suharto knew that if he were to replace the turmoil of the Sukarno years with more stolid progress, he was going to have to improve health, education and agricultural practices. And he needed a platform to tell Indonesians, *all* Indonesians, about their part in building this glorious nation. Telly was going to be that platform, he decided. In the mid-1970s Indonesia launched a satellite with a footprint that covered the whole country (and dusted most of South East Asia as well). It was a bold move – the US and Canada were the only countries in the world with domestic satellites at that stage – and it was a move Indonesia could ill afford. But it provided a megaphone through which Suharto could proclaim the gospel of development to all of his people. It also signalled to the world that a door had been firmly closed on Sukarno-style chaos, and a new door opened on to modernity.

Once the satellite was launched, the government began handing out 'public' TV sets, 50,000 of them a year. They usually sat in the home of the headman; the whole village crammed in of an evening to watch together. There was only one channel on offer, TVRI. The airwaves over the outer islands were suddenly crammed with images of national development. And with ads. Many in Jakarta worried about that. It was one thing to advertise consumer goods to the privileged few who could afford televisions in the largely urban areas covered by the terrestrial stations. But it was potentially dangerous to show the Have-Nots in the villages and on distant islands the cornucopia of consumer goods that was on offer to the Haves in Java. Satellite TV was supposed to turn the tribes of the land into Indonesians, not to turn them into an army of disgruntled Want-But-Never-Could-Haves.

In 1981 Suharto banned advertising on telly 'to avoid detrimental effects which do not promote the spirit of development'. That freed up more programming time for his own messages. More relentlessly than ever, TVRI's crashingly dull broadcasts promoted the spirit of family planning, dutiful citizenship and pride in the nation's glorious growth. Many an earnest researcher ran regression analyses showing that family planning messaging on television was especially successful, because the birth rate fell soon after a village got a public TV set. I was not the only person to suggest that watching television might simply provide something to do in the evenings other than make babies.

Then, in 1989, TVRI's monopoly was broken. Suharto handed out licences for private stations first to his son Bambang, then, in quick succession, to his cousin Sudwikatmono and his daughter Tutut. Suharto allowed his family to import soap operas from Latin America, to sprinkle them liberally with advertisements, to drop any pretence that TV might have a social purpose. At first these stations only reached an urban elite. Over time, though, they found their way onto the satellite and into the homes of people living on tuppence ha'penny a day in places that none of the Suharto children would ever visit. People very much like Suharto himself, in his younger days.

Suharto grew up as poor as the next villager, dropping out of junior high school and giving up a job in a bank because he fell off his bicycle and ripped his only set of presentable clothes. He joined the army, rose through the ranks, grabbed power. But he always cared deeply about improving life for the Javanese farmer, and once he was on the throne, he set about doing that with conviction. Though he put generals in charge of most aspects of Indonesian life, Suharto had the good sense to put the economy into the hands of a small clique of competent and cautious economists collectively known as the 'Berkeley mafia' because many of them had studied in California with sponsorship from the Ford Foundation. They first pushed through policies that got agriculture back on its feet. The country went from being the world's biggest importer of rice to being a net exporter.

Having watched South Korea and other countries grow rich by helping private companies make things other countries wanted to buy, the Berkeley mafia welcomed foreign investors and promoted manufacturing for export. The economy boomed. The proportion of kids in school doubled, access to basic health services rocketed. In his first two decades as President, Suharto kept the country on an even keel by delivering just enough to keep everyone on board, and to keep them obeying the captain's orders. It was a giant balancing act. If Catholics in the military were growing too strong for comfort, Suharto would throw a little meat to Muslim intellectuals. He allowed the army to keep its fingers in most of the huge state companies that were the legacy of Dutch times; in return, soldiers were obliged to keep workers in the embryonic manufacturing sector in their place. The President invited foreign companies to invest in Indonesia, then made them team up with one of the businessmen who bankrolled his own various political ventures.

This made for what World Bank economists called 'high transaction costs' and everyone else called corruption. And yet from the early 1980s foreigners *did* want to invest in Indonesia, precisely *because* of the stability that this web of compromise delivered. Many people saw the pay-offs to generals and cronies as a reasonable price for that stability. The investors turned a blind eye to the other price, the one paid by the communities whose objections to logging or mining were silenced with gunfire, by the workers who requested the minimum wage and wound up in hospital, by the journalists who were locked up for describing these things.

For many years, most Indonesians turned a blind eye too, because the stability that Suharto delivered worked well for them. On my very first day as a correspondent for Reuters in Jakarta, Suharto's autobiography was published in English. The reporter I was to take over from threw the volume across onto my empty desk. 'Give us a couple of pars on that,' he said. Seeing my panic, he added: 'The story's probably the extra-judicial killings.' And indeed in his autobiography, the serving president mentioned almost casually that he had, a couple of years earlier, ordered his defence minister to kill over 2,000 common criminals without trial. 'Shock therapy', Suharto called it. I went to a nearby restaurant in search of some 'vox pop' – Indonesians who might, in English, tell me what they thought of the President's admission. 'Before the killings, my daughter couldn't walk the streets at night,' shrugged one. 'Now, she can.' His daughter, and the sons and daughters of millions of other more modest Indonesians, could go to school, get decent primary health care, go to bed with a full stomach every night, and dream of what they would be when they grew up. Their parents' generation had not been able to take any of these things for granted.

Like most dictators, Suharto ruled past his sell-by date; the world remembers the ugly final years and it is thus unfashionable to concede that he ever did anything worthwhile. Yes, Suharto suppressed every form of political expression. Yes, he tried to press the country's magnificently diverse cultures into a single, Javanese mould. Yes, he turned over large chunks of the country's wealth first to his generals and business cronies, then to his increasingly rapacious children. But for the first two decades after his ugly confiscation of power, Suharto made life measurably better for tens of millions of Indonesians. He was genuinely popular.

It was about the time that I arrived in Indonesia in the late 1980s that things started to go badly wrong. They went wrong in part *because* life was getting so much better. With their basic needs met and a better education, people began to want more. They could see the economy booming, then saw all the growth go into a handful of pockets. Increasingly, they were the pockets of Suharto's children, who were growing up and getting greedy. Workers who heard ministers making speeches about the 'trickle down' economy felt that the profits from the Barbie dolls and Nike shoes that they were making weren't trickling down fast enough, and they started to say so. As generals watched joint ventures go to Suharto's children instead of to the armed forces, they did less to silence the workers' protests.

I don't want to suggest that Indonesia suddenly turned into a cauldron of dissent. To this day I keep a shirt of scratchy light-blue nylon, silk-screened over with numbers. It is made out of a banner which a group of workers from the nation's single government-approved union had strung up outside a footwear factory in the suburbs of Jakarta. On the banner was printed the article of the labour law that detailed the minimum wage. That was all; no call to arms, no commentary, just the amount companies ought by law to be paying their workers. It hung up there for just half a day before the army moved in and tore it down, leaving my friends in the union to cut it up and make it into shirts.

Indonesia was not South Korea, with its mass protests and street riots. It was not India, with its mouthy democratic opposition and million-strong sit-ins. But by the time I arrived in 1988, there was just enough stringing up and forcible taking down of banners, just enough outbursts of rage and looting of Japanese shops, just enough anti-Jakarta skirmishes in restive provinces to keep a journalist busy.

From my villa in Menteng, a former Dutch suburb and still the greenest part of Jakarta, I would leap on my motorbike and explore the less comfortable areas of town. I talked to the deckhands who congregated at the city's northern docks, waiting to sail glorious wooden cargo schooners to ports too small for container ships. I wandered the old Dutch city, a mini-Amsterdam of cobbled squares and elegant facades towering tall and thin over canals. It was neglected now, the canals clogged and fetid, the colonists' palaces of commerce taken over by petty traders and petty thieves. Under a colonnade that would once have sheltered pale wives from the tropical sun, a group of prostitutes and their clients now twirled to tinny music from a cheap cassette recorder.

I took up smoking in the service of my work. Nice girls didn't smoke in those days, but buying a single cigarette and borrowing a lighter was a good way to strike up a conversation with the street vendors who saw every change in traffic patterns around the presidential palace, who knew exactly which shopkeepers paid protection money to which branch of the police or military.

Quite often I was in the company of Enny Nuraheni, the Reuters photographer, my partner in all manner of crimes. Mostly we conspired to commit surreptitious acts of journalism, breaking through police lines around a church bombing, or charming our way into a refugee camp off-limits to the press. We must have been an odd sight, these two diminutive women, one white, one brown, trundling around on a rusty motorbike in unexpected parts of town. Sharp-eyed Enny would poke me in the ribs the minute she spotted something interesting. I'd skid to a halt without question, and she would swing her camera into the path of a monkey in a tutu dancing to an accordion, or a punch-up between men in suits outside the Stock Exchange. The punch-up was just part of the hysteria surrounding the growth of the Jakarta stock market. When I arrived in late 1988, there were only twenty-four shares listed on the Jakarta exchange, and foreigners were only allowed to buy eight of them. I bought a handful of shares in three listed companies on one day, just for the fun of it, and I accounted for nearly a quarter of the day's stock-market turnover. A year later, after technocrats pushed through deregulations that ate away at the anti-Western legacy of the Sukarno years, there were three times as many companies on offer and dozens more were queuing up for a listing. Banners up and down the thoroughfares of Jakarta screamed 'GO PUBLIC!' Men in suits fought to get their hands on newly minted shares; the application forms alone were trading for as much as US$170 each. And all the while, soldiers were tearing down banners reminding factory workers that they were entitled to earn 90 cents a day.

In a delightfully circular replay of colonial history, it was a clove monopoly that turned the public spotlight most firmly on to the rot at the heart of Suharto's state.

The biggest consumer of Indonesia's cloves nowadays are Indonesia's smokers, who like their cigarettes scented with the spice, not least because it doubles as an anaesthetic and smoothes the passage of toxins into the lungs. The country smokes 223 billion clove cigarettes, or *kreteks*, every year, thirteen times more than ordinary 'white' cigarettes. Many kreteks are still hand-rolled, some of them in small sheds cooled only by ceiling fans too lazy to send tobacco scraps flying, some in jarringly modern factories in which uniformed women work in air-conditioned spotlessness. Paid a bonus for productivity, they roll so quickly that viewing the factory floor from above feels like watching a speeded-up film.

Indonesia produces nearly 80 per cent of the world's cloves, and its cigarette industry translates most of them into the thick, languorous smoke that hangs over virtually every conversation about politics, family affairs or the price of rice or rubber in rural Indonesia. This did not escape the attention of the Suharto family. The President's youngest son Tommy decided to try a replay of the strategy that made the VOC rich three centuries earlier: a clove monopoly. Clove trees are moody as teenagers, coming out with smilingly generous crops one year, then sulking through periods of low productivity that last an agonizingly unpredictable length of time. Tommy claimed his enforced, fixed-price purchase of all the country's cloves was a way of stabilizing prices for farmers. Then he sold them on at three times what he paid for them.

Tommy doubtless thought he could get away with this because the cigarette firms were owned by a handful of toweringly rich ethnic Chinese families. The ethnic Chinese walk a knife-edge in modern Indonesia. They are assumed to be universally wealthy and are seen by many as leeches, but they provide the capital and business skills that keep the economy growing. Their wealth is tolerated as long as they stay out of politics, and they usually try to avoid controversy. This time, however, they refused to do as they were told. Many of the factories had huge stockpiles of cloves; they simply didn't buy from Tommy. In the end, at the President's command, Indonesian taxpayers bailed out Tommy Suharto.

The kretek affair uncorked resentment that had been brewing away, building pressure. Striking at kreteks in Indonesia is like messing with tea in Britain. Smoking is a social activity: every kretek smoked became an opportunity to have a little rant about the excesses of the First Family. That's over 600 million rants a day, nationwide. The normally silent Indonesian press began openly poking fun at Tommy's ham-fisted greed. Even the World Bank, which considered Indonesia one of its best clients and rarely breathed a word against Suharto, wrote a report pointing out the idiocy of the policy. It's hard to get a genie like that back in the bottle.

Suharto had little in common with the flat-nosed, curly-haired, plain-speaking men and women from the faraway eastern islands of Indonesia where cloves were grown, and he did little to defend their interests. Javanese farmers, on the other hand, were closer to the Old Man's heart. He rarely appeared happier than when he was among farmers in the rice paddies close to his birthplace, speaking in Javanese, using metaphors from the *wayang* shadow-plays which everyone in rural Java knew by heart. These were his people; when the greed of Suharto's own children threatened the welfare of Javanese farmers, he sided with the peasants.

I spent a day in 1990 wading around in rice paddies at one of the field schools Suharto's government had set up to help farmers grow more. When you first plop into a rice paddy off the bank, you feel like you'll be sucked in. The mud squishes up between your toes and covers your ankle; water sloshes up your calves but your foot continues to sink. Then, suddenly it hits bottom, not hard exactly, but bouncy-firm. You stop worrying about the quagmire, and start schlurping your foot up and squishing it down a little further on. The mud oozes between your toes again. It's slow going for a beginner, but fun. No one else at the Central Java field school was a beginner, of course. They had all grown up in the rice paddies and they had the squared-off feet of people who see shoes as an encumbrance. They were there to learn about bugs.

In 1986 Java's rice crop was destroyed by a tiny insect called a rice brown plant hopper. The plant hopper thrived on the back of another of Suharto's sons' businesses, which supplied all the state-subsidized pesticide in the country – US$150 million a year's worth. The pesticide killed the big bugs first, the spiders and water skimmers that used to eat the plant hoppers. But it didn't kill hopper eggs; with all the spiders dead, they hatched into fields deliciously free of predators. There they fed on the rice, and spread viruses. Farmers, naturally enough, reacted with even more pesticide. That meant more profits for Suharto's son but it didn't kill the viruses. In 1986, Indonesia lost its hard-won self-sufficiency in rice. That mattered more to Suharto than his family's income; he immediately wiped out subsidies, banned broad-spectrum pesticides, and set up thousands of field schools like the one I went to, to teach farmers to tell good bugs from bad bugs and so cut pesticide use.

Indonesia was the first country in the world to adopt eco-logically sound Integrated Pest Management as a national policy. But these moments of common-sense government became rarer as Suharto aged. As I write this now, two decades after the fact, I can't help being shocked at how much of Indonesia's economy was, in the 1990s, chopped up into neat lines on a mirror to be sniffed up by the small handful of guests still standing at the Suharto party. Goodness knows there's plenty of corruption around now, but at least most of it is on a fee-for-service basis. Someone takes a percentage because they helped get a new mining contract, they pushed through the approval of another province or district, they delivered a jail term of just three or four years instead of fifteen. It's still corrosive, but it seems somehow less contemptuous of the majority than the brazen plunder of the Suharto years, when money was taken from farmers and companies and given to the President's children just because.

Before I left Indonesia in mid-1991, I gave a big party in the mansion on the central square of the old Dutch city that had, during the time of the Netherlands East Indies, been Batavia's City Hall. It had become a museum, still filled with heavy Dutch furniture, gilded portraits and dusty chandeliers, and was run by a friend of mine. He let me use it on condition that neither he nor his staff had to do anything in the way of organizing or cleaning up. I spent the afternoon scrubbing out the loos and filling the marble fountain in the courtyard with blocks of ice to cool the booze. I had invited the street vendors who ting-tinged and toc-toced their way past my garden every evening to provide the catering; they rolled their carts up from the centre of town and set to frying noodles and grilling satay in the Governor General's courtyard.

I invited everyone I knew; cabinet ministers and generals, dissidents and activists, movie stars and designers, lawyers and economists. I spent the evening swanning around introducing colonel so-and-so to former political prisoner such-and-such, then watching them drink sangria and chat amiably with one another. I kept the guest book from that party. By the time I next set foot in Jakarta, some of the guests who had been in the cabinet at the time of the party were in jail, while some of the dissidents were in the cabinet.

After the clove monopoly got people talking about the previously unspeakable gluttony of the President's family, things had gone from bad to worse and quiet coffee-stall rants rose in volume. The fallout from the Asian financial crisis brought things to a crescendo. In the six months from July 1997 to January 1998, the rupiah collapsed from 2,500 to the dollar to almost 10,000. Imports disappeared and prices of everyday items shot up. Suharto's supporters tried to deflect the fury people felt about the excesses of his family by directing public anger against rich Chinese Indonesians. Glodok, Jakarta's Chinatown, went up in flames and hundreds of ethnic Chinese women were raped, but the fury raged on, eventually finding its true target: Suharto. Students filled the streets and occupied the national parliament building. Because the President had for some years allowed his family to eat into the pies that used to feed the generals, the military just stood by and let it happen.

In May 1998, after thirty-two years in power, Suharto resigned. A new Indonesia was born, but no one had the slightest idea who should raise it.

Three years after Suharto's resignation, a full decade after my farewell party in the former Batavia City Hall, I went back to Jakarta to work with the Ministry of Health. The weekend I arrived, a friend and I went for a walk around Glodok. Some of Chinatown's shops lay abandoned still, their plate-glass fronts smashed and gaping. Other buildings were stained gauzy grey by the flames that had licked over them during the riots. We wandered into a bookshop. I found myself looking at a whole table piled with books on the rise of Communist China and the history of socialism. I was open-mouthed; in Suharto's day such a display would have landed the bookseller in jail. I went to share my shock with my friend. He had drifted over to another table full of unimaginable books, and was flicking through one entitled *The Multiple-Orgasmed Woman*.

Other changes I noticed were the panoply of TV channels showing vapid game shows, the mouthy press, the willingness of all and sundry to voice political opinions, the relative absence of military uniforms in public gatherings and a huge increase in the proportion of women wearing *jilbabs* (the Indonesian name for hijab headscarves). I arrived just in time for one of the great tests of the era of *Reformasi* – 'The Reformation'. The Pope Suharto had been succeeded by his Vice President, B. J. Habibie. Though trained in engineering in Germany, Habibie was anything but Teutonic in style. He regularly allowed extravagant promises to escape his mouth before they had spent any time in his brain. Without so much as mentioning it to his foreign minister, for example, he made a public promise that the people of the fractious province of East Timor could hold a referendum on independence.

The Portuguese, who made the Dutch look like wonderful colonizers, had left East Timor in a pathetic state. When Indonesia invaded in 1975, it set about developing its twenty-seventh province with gusto. Jakarta sent in thousands of (mostly Javanese Muslim) civil servants to run the (entirely Catholic) state's affairs. In the eyes of Suharto and his supporters, they were doing the people of Timor a favour.

In my reporting days, I had frequently been called to army HQ for re-education about Timor. Widespread dissatisfaction among the Timorese? Where on earth did you get that from? A searing resentment of a military that was quick with a gun-butt and a steel-toecapped boot? Come now, Elizabeth! Individual soldiers may on rare occasions have been a little heavy-handed in their treatment of the locals, conceded Brigadier General Nurhadi, whose fate it was to set me straight. But the government had built roads and health centres, provided education and contraception. They brought to East Timor development, Suharto-style. In time 'tell them about the roads' became the press corps' shorthand for the denial that ran in the water supply of the Jakarta elite.

Habibie had drunk deeply of this source. He seemed genuinely surprised when, in August 1999, eight out of ten people in East Timor voted to boot Indonesia out and become independent. And he was unable to rein in the military when it unleashed a spiteful campaign of retribution that left much of the Indonesian-built infrastructure in East Timor in ruins. Though Habibie did initiate some quite radical reforms, he neither disassociated himself from his former boss nor secured the support of the military. In the last elections of the Suharto era, held in 1997 and contested only by three state-approved parties, the ruling Golkar party had won three-quarters of the vote. A year after Suharto stepped down, with forty-eight parties on the newly democratic slate, Golkar managed just over a fifth of the vote. Habibie was out.

He was succeeded by an ailing half-blind Muslim scholar named Abdurrahman Wahid, aka Gus Dur. Gus Dur was a brave but wildly eccentric man with no experience of government. He horse-traded himself into power after his party won just 13 per cent of the vote, striking fragile alliances with improbable partners. When I arrived in May 2001, a normally docile parliament had started proceedings to impeach him. On paper, this was because of a dodgy loan involving Gus Dur's masseur. In fact it was because the President, both blunt and stubborn, offended the very groups on whom he relied for support.

It was a very strange time for me. I had arrived back in a city that throbbed with political protests. And yet all around the demonstrators, my life went on as usual. If hanging out with transgender sex workers, rent boys and gay men half my age could be described as 'usual' – my job, at the time, centred around a survey of HIV and risk behaviour among these groups. I found it disorientating. Massage parlours where men sold sex to other men were a new feature of Jakarta's entertainment landscape, and there had been no gay bars when I last lived in the city. The transgenders, or *waria*, on the other hand, had been feature of Jakarta life for as long as I could remember.

Though the word is a mash-up of *wanita* – woman – and *pria* – man, waria live entirely as women, sometimes with a husband. Most still have all their male anatomy intact, though many take female hormones, and breast implants are increasingly common. Culturally, they play a very singular role. They are accepted in part because of a long heritage that stems from the Bissu priests who often sailed in the magnificent trading schooners built by the Bugis people of South Sulawesi. The Bissu are often described as 'intersex'; they are said still now to be able to channel the gods when in a trance. Though the Bugis ethnic group is fiercely Islamic, they have always accepted this duality. 'Well, of course God speaks through the Bissu,' the wife of a sub-district head in the Bissu's heartland told me: 'Because God has no gender. Allah is not a man and not a woman.' Minutes later – sitting in her doilied living room, wearing a pretty silk sarong – the senior Bissu in the area described how s/he cured white discharge from the penis with red onions, and asked my advice on what to do about genital ulcers.

While the Bissu still perform quasi-religious ceremonies, most run-of-the-mill waria are more likely to feature in cabarets. Their 'neither quite one thing, nor quite the other' status once afforded them a political role. Not unlike the fool in Shakespeare's plays, waria sometimes spoke truth to power when no one else was allowed to. Or at least to the wives of power. One of my abiding memories of the Suharto years was watching a cabaret in which a group of waria in a make-believe salon tended to their 'clients', puffing hair up into matronly helmets, pancaking on the make-up, and turning out perfect *Ibu-Ibu*: a replica of Tien Suharto's circle. The salon chat among the clients was of the minister's wife who was having an affair with the oligarch, of which foreign companies offered the best cuts for corrupt deals, of tips and tricks their husbands had developed for squeezing money out of Suharto's kids. These were things that no one else talked about openly at the time. The audience shrieked with laughter, they clapped perfectly manicured claws in delighted recognition. Almost everyone sitting watching the show was herself a real, dyed-in-the-silk *Ibu-Ibu*.

By the time I started planning the HIV survey, that special status had been eroded by the cacophony of free speech unleashed by the democratic reforms. The cabaret shows continued, but most waria made a living by working in a salon by day and/or selling sex on the streets after dark. So every night, I would go out with a team of interviewers, including three off-duty waria, and cruise the pavements, inviting people to participate in our survey. On the streets, waria specialize in blowing kisses and flashing body-parts, in shrieking and teasing prospective clients who cruise slowly past in cars or on motorbikes. They teased me, too, these biological men who wanted to be women, perhaps offended by my lack of femininity. Why couldn't I walk in high heels? Why didn't I ever have a decent manicure? 'Here, allow me ...' and they whip nail varnish out of their clutch bags, and I'd be sitting on a pavement after midnight having my nails painted by a transgender sex worker. The evenings were punctuated by high drama; one night, shortly before local elections when the mayor wanted to show how tough he was on immoral behaviour, there was a sweeping of sex workers and half the research team got arrested. There were cat-fights between waria who wanted to be in charge of study recruitment in their area, study staff ran off with clients mid-interview, and I once came close to losing all the blood samples we had collected because the cops at a road block saw used syringes, pegged me for a drug dealer and tried to confiscate all my kit.

They were busy nights, usually ending up with a delivery to the lab at 3 or 4 a.m. By eight in the morning I was back on my motorbike and on my way to the daytime part of my job. On the way, I was often accosted by a teenager in white robes and a chequered turban, a member of the Laskar Jihad fundamentalist group which was at the time openly waging war on Christians in the eastern islands of Maluku. He rattled his collection box and distributed pamphlets promising a Maluku cleansed of Christians. This was a lot more shocking than the blossoming of gay bars or bookshops offering socialism and multiple orgasms. Though it was easy to make fun of the vague assertions of Pancasila, I took it for granted that religious tolerance was central to Indonesia's continued existence. And yet in the jockeying for power that had been going on since the fall of Suharto, Indonesians killed one another in the name of religion, and the authorities did nothing.

After Gus Dur was impeached, Sukarno's daughter Megawati Sukarnoputri took over as president. She shared her father's strong belief in national unity, but not his charisma; she had the well-upholstered look common to *Ibu-Ibu* in the Suharto era, and was famously aloof. Though hers was a colourless presidency, she didn't needle the army in the same way as her predecessor had. Prodded into action by a bomb in a Bali nightclub that killed over 200 people in 2002, she began to take more serious action against Islamic extremism. The country gradually settled down.

In 2004 Indonesia held its first direct presidential election; until then, presidents had been chosen by the legislature. In over half a million polling stations nationwide, voters stuck a nail through a ballot paper to indicate their choice. One of the polling stations was directly outside my house in central Jakarta. From dawn when the volunteers, officials and ballot boxes arrived until the final tally in the early evening, the air was electric with excitement. The poll was as well organized as anything I've ever seen in Indonesia, and it made me rather emotional. Five years earlier, Jakarta was in flames and the economy was pulverized. Since then Indonesians had been traumatized by the loss of East Timor and the army-sponsored carnage that followed, they had watched civil war unfold in Maluku and witnessed bloody rebellions in Aceh and Papua, they had impeached and replaced a president, and they were still materially a lot worse off than they had been before 1997. But 140 million voters went peacefully off to the polls on a single day and, with barely an incident, elected a new president. It was quite an achievement.

Given a choice for the first time ever, Indonesians chose a Suharto-era general uniformly known as SBY, representing a party that had only existed for four years.

I left Jakarta for the second time a year later. When I came back in 2011 to begin the wanderings that make up most of this book, SBY had been re-elected for a second term. In my absence Jakarta had completed its transition from a collection of scruffy but friendly neighbourhoods into a grandiose-but-grumpy megalopolis. In the few remaining alleyways, the noodle men still ting-ting, the vegetable vendors still chant their wares. But they must compete with neon-lit Indomaret convenience stores and the just-add-water Indomie noodles of the New Indonesia. Indonesia is being homogenized by the same force that pulled these islands together into a map of a nation, drawn by the Dutch and appropriated by the Indonesians: commerce. Since SBY has been in power, the economy has grown by 5.7 per cent a year on average. That's close to five times more than the UK and nearly four times the US rate over the same period; it left Indonesians three times richer than they had been when I first lived in the country. The new wealth has created an army of new consumers armed with cell phones and satellite TV; it may have done more to blend Indonesia together than all of Suharto's flag-waving ceremonies and cookie-cutter bureaucracy.

I bought a massive map of Indonesia, folded it into my backpack together with the schedule for the national passenger ferries, left the cacophony and comforts of Jakarta behind, and set out to get to know my Bad Boyfriend better. 'You'll find an Indomaret on every corner,' teased my friend Gouri as I set off for Sumba, the little-known south-eastern island where I had taken tea with dead Granny all those years ago. 'You'll be bored to tears and come back in no time!'

Map A: Sumba Island, Nusa Tenggara Province (NTT)

SUMBAWA

KOMODO

FLORES

SAVU
SEA

To Flores

Waingapu

SUMBA

Anakalang
Tarung Village

Tambolaka

Waikabubak
Gaura
Wanokaka

From Jakarta

INDIAN
OCEAN

N

0km   15km   30km   45km

------- Elizabeth's Journey, 2011/2012

3

Sticky Culture

I had been in Sumba less than ten minutes when a young man thrust a cell phone at me. On the screen was a photo of a corpse lying in the marketplace. This one was definitely not receiving guests for tea. 'Look, there's his hand over there.' The young man zoomed in to give me a clearer view of the body part, hacked off in a frenzied machete attack in broad daylight just a couple of weeks earlier. 'It happens all the time.' He introduced himself as Fajar, a Javanese doctor posted here as part of a government programme that obliges newly qualified medics to serve in well-paid short-term posts in extremely remote areas.* 'Sumba's not like Java,' he said.

Sumba sits at about four o'clock in the squashed oval clockface of Indonesia, not far to the north of Australia. There are no steeply terraced rice fields, no volcanoes, no shadow-puppets or tiered temples. For a couple of hundred years, Sumba interested the outside world because it was covered in sandalwood. Once that had been clear-felled and sold, it turned into a landscape of rolling grassland, toasted brown for much of the year by the pitiless southern sun. In the dry season it's vaguely reminiscent of the Meseta Central in Spain, not least because it is good horse country and jousting is a favourite sport. It's not uncommon to see, silhouetted against the evening

---

* The government classifies postings according to their location: *biasa, terpencil* and *sangat terpencil*, ordinary, remote and extremely remote. Salaries in extremely remote areas are nearly four times higher than in ordinary posts.

sky, a man on a stocky pony holding a lance, for all the world like Don Quixote.

Arriving in today's Sumba from today's Jakarta, you feel like you have travelled through time as well as space. In Sumba a 'high-rise' is a two-storey building, and they exist only in the island's two largest towns. The landscape is dotted with megalithic tombs; they are scattered along the roadside, they sit in front of modern bungalows, they fringe the marketplaces. Most, even brand-new ones, are made of vast stone slabs arranged in a square and topped, mushroom-like, with an even vaster capstone dragged up from quarries by the sea. But there's now a modern version of the tombs, too, of cement covered with tile, that make Sumba look like it's oversupplied with public loos. There are none of Jakarta's business suits in Sumba; here a well-dressed man has always worn a head-tie and a large swathe of home-woven cloth wrapped around his waist and legs. The cloth (and many a commonplace pair of trousers too) is belted with a sling from which hangs a machete, a long, straight blade curling into a hooked handle of wood or buffalo horn, sheathed in a wooden scabbard. When I arrived at Tambolaka airport in the north-west of the island, the first thing I saw was a banner reading 'STOP VIOLENCE!' – the *Ghostbusters*-like stop sign drawn through a brace of machetes. Beneath it stood a large group of men with weapons hanging from their belts.

I had laughed at this. It was then that Fajar, who was sitting next to me in the share-taxi that would take us to the region's main town of Waikabubak, whipped out his cell phone and showed me the severed hand. 'Violence is just part of life here.'

He was not the first to make this observation. The one lonely administrator sent to establish a Dutch foothold on Sumba in the 1870s reported back to his bosses in the colonial capital of Batavia that 'there is no other rule than that of the strongest'. Headhunting and slave raids, he said, had 'reduced the value of a human life to a very low level, often well below that of a horse'. The Dutch didn't consolidate their hold on Sumba until 1913, after a bloody two-year fight against the famous headhunter

Wono Kaka. He had provoked the Dutch by decapitating soldiers and hanging their scalps with those of his other enemies on his clan's skull tree.

After the Dutch soldiers came Protestant missionaries. In the crowded islands of Java, Sumatra and Sulawesi, most Indonesians are Muslim. But out here in these eastern villages, I didn't see a single jilbab. The people of Sumba are nominally Christian, though on previous visits I had found that many still cleaved to the ancient Marapu religion, guided more by what they read in the entrails of a chicken than by what they read in the Bible.

I had chosen Sumba as my first stop after Jakarta in part because I remembered it from my first visit in 1991 as a forgotten corner of the country, bypassed by the changes of the Suharto era, about as far from Jakarta as one could get, even then. Now I was curious to see whether places like Sumba had changed at all or whether the gap with the increasingly brash Indonesia symbolized by Jakarta was simply growing. At first glance, Sumba was more modern now. People of all ages gossiped on cell phones in the marketplace, there were satellite dishes even on the grass roofs of traditional bamboo houses, and people who would until recently have walked everywhere were buzzing about on shiny new motorbikes. Would any of the arcane traditions that I had stumbled upon on previous visits have survived?

Twenty years after taking tea with a dead grandmother, I dumped my bags in a dispiriting hotel room, asked the staff to sweep away the dead cockroaches and set out to explore. Though Waikabubak is the biggest city in West Sumba, you can walk it end to end in about twenty minutes. The most imposing building in town is a church with a vaulted entrance that smacks of a miniature Sydney Opera House. There's a hospital that looks as though it dates from the 1930s, especially on the inside. Apart from that, Waikabubak is mostly boxy breeze-block shop-houses and small bungalows. I wandered along the main street, looking for a pair of shoes; Jakarta's vast marbled malls had overwhelmed me and I'd fled without buying any sensible footwear. The street was lined on both sides with small family-owned shops that could sell you virtually anything, so long as it was in one of 500 shades of grey. An enthusiastic contractor had dug up most of the high street and ripped out all of its pavements several months earlier, then ran out of money. Now, every passing minibus sent clouds of dust flying into the open-fronted shops to settle on bins of rice, stacks of plastic chairs, beach balls, coconut graters, sarongs, batteries, onions, soy sauce, salt crackers, dried fish, engine parts, sheet roofing, flip-flops, toothpaste, batteries, fishing lines, home-baked buns, kreteks, motorbike tyres and the myriad other things that villagers visiting this, the big city, might need. The owners of these Aladdin's Caves, ethnic Chinese to a man – and, frequently, to a woman – had an astonishing ability to poke a hand into a landslide of grey *stuff*, and bring it out clutching whatever the buyer asked for. Even during power cuts when the shades of grey thicken into a soupy dusk, the shopkeeper could put a hand into the pile and extract a flick knife, a length of ribbon, a notebook. I bought a pair of grey shoes. The first time they got rained on, they turned out to be green.

There were definitely no Indomarets in Waikabubak.

Raise your eyes from the undistinguished streets of Waikabubak and you'll see the other West Sumba. Much of this part of the island is made up of lumpy outcrops of rock, rising from flatter land. It is on these hills that the quarrelsome clans of Sumba built their citadels and it is there that the traditional villages sit to this day. Modern Waikabubak has seeped into the flat bits all around these outcrops; the villages stand proud above the concrete sprawl, in it but not of it.

The first village I spotted was Tarung. From the road, all I could see was a bit of thatch, a few pointy roofs teetering above a patch of jungle. As I scrambled up a rocky path towards the village, the scraps of thatch resolved themselves into a group of bamboo houses built on thick wooden stilts. Each one had two doors opening on to a wide bamboo veranda, and each was dwarfed by its roof, which started broad and low over the veranda, sloped gently up towards the centre of the house, then narrowed and shot high into the air. It made me think of a child wearing a dunce's cap jammed down over a thick fringe. I kept climbing, weaving past runaway chickens, piglets and children, and emerged suddenly into the centre of the village. A ring of houses decorated with the skulls of long-dead buffalo stood guard over a large oval clearing studded with megalithic tombs. On the carved top of one tomb, a fire raged. At its centre was some kind of animal.

As the flames subsided, I saw that it was a wild boar. The beast was on its back, four legs sticking rigid into the air, a smooth grey stone lolling in its mouth where its tongue should be. A village elder wearing a head-tie made of beaten bark leapt up onto the tomb, unsheathed his machete and cut a shutter in the boar's belly, then reached in and started dolloping innards onto a banana leaf. From a higher tombstone above him, a haughty, hook-nosed figure wearing an iridescent pink napkin on his head and a stunning woven *ikat* cloth around his waist in place of trousers directed the distribution of goods. An ear for this family, the tail for that. That gloopy yellow bit from near the liver to someone special.

Entirely by chance, I had happened upon the celebrations that mark the opening of Wulla Poddu, the 'month of bitterness'. In the Marapu religion, Sumba's particular brand of animism, the bitter month is the equivalent of Christian Lent or Muslim Ramadan. It's a month of restraint, a month when women are not allowed to pound rice after dark, and when there's no dressing up or playing loud music. Striking gongs, sacrificing animals and ritual celebrations are all forbidden. Except, of course, for the gongs, sacrifices and celebrations that go with the Poddu itself.

Of those there are many. That first night, I sat on one of the stone tombs in the centre of the village until well past midnight, lulled by the call-and-response between the priests and the young men of the village. The women all stayed in their houses during most of the action, but no one seemed to mind that I was there, or to take much notice of me. I didn't really know what was going on: I don't speak the local Loli language and (I learned later) much of the chanting is in any case in a sacred language that no one but the Marapu priests understand. But I listened to the beating of the sacred gong, an instrument brought out only during this month. I watched as, one by one, the village heads of household walked into the clearing between the tombs and laid down a bowl of rice as an offering to the ancestors.

It was quite hypnotic, the low light, the steady chanting, the slow, repetitive movements. Suddenly there was a blood-curdling yell; I snapped alert to find the young men of the village charging towards me in a pack, lances raised. Then the pack parted, flowed around the tombstone on which I was sitting and poured down to the back of the village. The young men hurled their spears into the thicket below, the village was symbolically purged of last year's sins, and the month of meditation could proceed.

I climbed back up to Tarung the following morning. An old lady with a wide, flat nose and a face made crinkly with smiling motioned me over to the veranda where she sat shelling beans. She was wearing an old cotton sarong printed with blue flowers, and a lacy top with a deep V-neck that looked like it was intended for someone fifty years her junior. As I took off my shoes and hiked myself up on to the waist-high veranda to sit with her, she disappeared without a word, then reappeared with a flowery tin tray that held a glass of tongue-numbingly sweet tea. In the other hand, half behind her back, was a little woven basket of trinkets: fake coral beads, golden earrings in the womb shape that confers fertility, strips of cloth woven with the word 'Sumba'. Not many tourists make it to West Sumba; she looked disappointed when I batted her offers away, explaining in my brash Jakarta accent that I wasn't really a proper tourist, that I lived in the capital, that I was at the start of a long journey and couldn't carry anything. Then I asked what she could tell me about last night's ceremony.

Mama LakaBobo clapped her hands with delight. She shoved the basket of trinkets out of sight and, in the lovely sing-song Indonesian of the eastern islands, embarked on the task of educating me about the culture of West Sumba. It is no easy task. *Everything* in Sumba's traditional villages has significance,

I was to learn: who gets to beat which gong in what location, who enters which house through what door. I learned that in the language of Tarung's Loli tribe there's one word for rice, for a machete, for a head-tie, when these things are in the village, but their names change when they are taken into the forest with parties of men hunting wild boar for ritual sacrifice. The sacred spear lives in this house, the sacred gong in that. Women are allowed to weave on this veranda but not on that one. To my endless 'Whys?' I always got the same answer. '*Ya, adat memang begitu*': 'That's our *adat*.'

Adat is one of those Indonesian words that defies translation; quite specific, but somehow hard to grasp, like a cloud. Crudely, adat is a cultural tradition, but in the days before Suharto and his wife tried to pare it down and scrub it up to display in the pavilions of Mini Indonesia, it was much, much more than that. Adat is rarely spoken of in big cities like Jakarta. But in many islands, the engines of communal life – birth and death, marriage and divorce, inheritance, conservation, education – are fuelled by the body of lore and transmitted wisdom that is adat. People in West Sumba say with pride that their tradition, their adat, is 'thick' or 'sticky', like condensed milk or treacle, though in truth it probably survived Suharto's efforts to reduce it to the graceful twirling of wrists and tinkling of anklets mostly because Sumba was so very marginal to the national economy. In this island, where adat is deeply entwined with the local Marapu religion, it takes on the cast of something sacred. But it can also be more sinister. In the post-Suharto years, adat has been reclaimed and sharpened up as a tool in electioneering and politics, and as a weapon in the battle for rights over resources and land.

In Tarung, adat is so sticky that it can't be rushed. Life passed slowly during the quiet month of Wulla Poddu. Whatever time of day I showed up, Mama Bobo would be sitting on the veranda, as if just waiting for a coffee and a gossip. Further up the village, too, verandas were scattered with people cycling through the tasks of life, methodical, unhurried. On one veranda, women were plaiting palms into pointy-hooded baskets that would hold the sacred rice at month-end. On another, an elder carved a drum. The haughty, hook-nosed man in the pink napkin, temporarily freed of his duties as High Priest, played a game of *congklak*, which involved moving dried-beans between hollows scooped from a squared-off log.

As the priest dismissed a group of young children who were lying to me about the rules of the dried-bean game, I remarked that the government's family planning programme didn't seem to have made much headway in these parts.

'Thank goodness,' he said. 'If you only have a few children, you're going to want to educate them. Then all of this – ' he waved his hand to indicate the witches-hat houses, the carved gravestones, the bloodstains that remain from the ceremonial slaughter the night before, the elder whittling at the drum – 'all this will be lost.'

The adat encompassed by that wave of the hand certainly keeps villagers busy. Never too busy, though, to share a cup of tea or coffee with me, to discuss the prospects of the various groups who were out hunting for wild boar, to explain why you should use buffalo-hide for a shield (tough) but horse-hide for a drum (sonorous).

It had been a few years since I'd spent any real time in rural Indonesia, but I found myself slipping quickly back into life as a curious but generally harmless outsider. I tried to help out with whatever task was at hand, if not shelling beans then sorting beads to make into trinkets, spreading corn kernels out to dry, bagging peanuts into penny packages to sell to hungry adolescents. On veranda after veranda, people would shuffle up to let me help with a task as long as they deemed it within my capabilities. If they didn't, they made no bones about it. It was less than five minutes before I was demoted from weaving baskets to chopping onions. In every household, we started out with the usual chit-chat in Indonesian. So that people could place me in the universe I told them about my imaginary husband, about my non-existent job, about my parents' village. Soon enough I just became part of the woodwork; people resumed conversations around me in Loli, I lapsed into companionable silence and all was well.

Mama Bobo had at first tried to treat me as a guest. I was invited into the house by the right-hand door, the men's side, stepping over a threshold made of the skull and spreading horns of a buffalo. There were many of these skulls nailed in tidy columns down the front of the house, the legacy of past funerals and sacrifices. The forest of remembered carnage is how a clan advertises its standing to strangers.

The men's side is the part of the house reserved for formal occasions, and, when the electricity supply allows, for watching television. Though the spirits that live in the towering roof hover equally above both halves of the house, the men's side seems lifeless. The action is over the chest-high partition in the women's side, where smoke billows from wood under the cooking cauldron and slops are pushed down through the cracks in the bamboo floor to the pigs and chickens that live below the house. Above this hearth hangs a huge wooden cage, crusty with soot. It's here that the sacred objects are kept. There are beautiful *ikat* cloths that eat up six months of a weaver's life and that will emerge only to be wrapped around a corpse and planted in the grave. There are heavy ivory bracelets, cracked with the passing of generations, without which no girl of good family can get married. There are drums and gongs which come out only for weddings and funerals. All growing gently smokier with every passing meal.

Mama Bobo was keen to show me all these things, but they could not be brought out without cause. 'You'll have to stay until someone dies,' she said.

Over much peeling of garlic and mending of clothes, I ceased to be a guest and our conversation changed. The intricacies of local adat were replaced by more universal topics. Mama Bobo would take me by the hand and draw me close. She always wore her hair in a bun, from which wisps of grey escaped to frame a kindly face. When she was upset, her twinkly eyes would grow cloudy. She was worried about her daughter-in-law, who wasn't getting pregnant. She was annoyed with her grandson, who wasn't pulling his weight in the rice fields. She wished the local government would stop promising things that they didn't deliver. She thought the many grandchildren who visited her veranda spent too much time playing with their cell phones and not enough time with their schoolbooks.

This diminutive woman was the steely core of a sprawling clan which snapped to attention whenever she chose to exercise her quiet authority. I started to do the same. 'There's a surprise tomorrow morning, be here at eight,' she'd tell me. And I would drag myself out of bed and up the hill at eight, to find that Mama Bobo had spent the night in another village and had not come back. Still, I had been commanded and I obeyed, sitting around doing whatever needed to be done until the matriarch reappeared, with a smile and no explanation, three hours later.

The quiet month closes with three days of partying, interrupted by mass murder. In the Marapu religion, the spirits speak through nature and their messages are interpreted by *rato* – priests, more or less. Once a year, the spirits write our fortunes into the entrails of a chicken. At the end of Wulla Poddu, every member of the clan brings a chicken to the clan house. One by one, their necks are wrung, one by one, their throats are slit, one by one they are impaled on a skewer over a fire to rid them of their feathers. A couple of lads are charged with parting their chests with a single blow of the machete to expose the entrails. Then the halved chickens are laid out in rows. Hard enough to distinguish from one another even when alive, they look almost identical once they've been skewered and singed naked. Yet no one loses track of their own bird. As the rato approaches a chicken, its owner sidles up, solemn, nervous. The rato takes his own machete, makes a careful slit in the gut, and exposes a line of fatty tissue. If it is thick and yellow, the owner has a marvellous year ahead. A fractured line, thin and whitish, and the owner leaves in tears.

These chickens tell our individual fortunes, but the sum of

all chickens tells the fortune of the clan. In traditional agrarian societies, the strength of the clan is in the number of workers it commands. In societies where tribal wars are common, more men mean stronger armies. In Sumba, where farming and warring have shared the billing in shaping society, wealth is a numbers game. I had increased the relative strength of Mama Bobo's clan by taking my chicken to her house for slaughter. By the end of the day, she had more than a hundred birds piled up in huge plastic bins. They would be stewed for the following day's feasting.

Initially, a couple of other families in the village were cross that I had chosen to take my bird to Mama Bobo's household, but it didn't last. The important thing, from everyone's point of view, was that I should 'belong' somewhere. One of the most important functions of these rituals is that they tie people into their place in the local cosmology, ensuring that everyone knows where they, and everyone else, fit.

I had picked out my own chicken in the market, choosing a cockerel with a cinnamon ruff streaked with black, and a cascade of glossy tail feathers. An auspicious fowl if ever I saw one. The seller looped its legs together and I went off with it swinging upside down from the handlebars of my bike, squawking crossly.

I stopped at the post office on the way up to Tarung, taking the bird in with me for safekeeping. In even the smallest town in Indonesia, the post office, dressed in orange livery, is a little island of efficiency. Its staff are well trained, friendly and almost embarrassingly helpful. They will keep the office open as you dash to the market to buy a rice-sack to wrap your parcel in, then help you sew the parcel up with thread that they dig out of their own handbags. They'll telephone to let you know that this week's boat has been cancelled so your parcel won't leave for another ten days. 'When Indonesian institutions have to line up at the gates of heaven, the post office will be let in first,' one old postmaster told me, and I agreed.

The chicken and I found the Waikabubak post office crowded. It was payment day for the families with poverty cards. The key to Indonesia's nascent social security system, these cards provide access to subsidized rice, free medical care and cash payments. They are highly prized, and because of a little payment here or a small favour there, do not always go to the poorest families. Still, today's queue was made up mostly of people who looked like they came from the traditional villages that were dotted on the hilltops around town. Since it was the end of Wulla Poddu, they were mostly dressed for the festivities to come, the women in woven sarongs, the men in waist-cloths and head-ties; none of them batted an eyelid at me and my squawking chicken.

Then in walked Fajar, the Javanese doctor whom I had met in the share-taxi from the airport; I'd since had supper with him once or twice, and I was pleased to see him. I greeted him enthusiastically. He looked me up and down. Like most of the other clients in the post office, I was dressed for the party in Tarung. I was wearing my best sarong. Slung from my shoulder was a palm-weave pouch containing *sirih pinang*, betel nut and limestone powder. This combination stains mouths into scarlet gashes, rots teeth into black stumps, and is the common currency of polite interaction in rural Sumba. You can't climb on to someone's veranda without being offered *sirih pinang*, and you shouldn't climb on to someone's veranda without having some to offer in return. In one hand, I held a parcel I wanted to send to Jakarta. In the other, I gripped a flapping chicken by its ankles. Fajar turned away, embarrassed.

It was as though I had joined the other side. It was not just that I was ridiculous, that I had so quickly 'gone native'. It was something worse. Along with all the other dangerous, ignorant peasants who were sitting quietly waiting for their social security payments, I was sullying the post office. We were bringing that distasteful old world of arcane traditions and primitive beliefs into the space inhabited by modern, functional Indonesia. I began to feel positively uncomfortable. The upside-down chicken somehow contrived to shit on the post office floor.

I'd get a similar reaction whenever I went into one of Waikabubak's many photo shops to get prints made for my new friends. I'd hand over my USB drive to a spiky-haired Chinese boy or to a teenager in a purple jilbab. They'd open up portraits of Mama Bobo and her family, photos of me with a group of *rato*, pictures of chickens or buffalo lying in pools of blood, and they'd look at me quizzically. 'These photos? Really, you want prints of these ones?' It was okay to take pictures of the quaint traditional houses and of the megalithic tombs that dot the villages and the landscapes of Sumba, but these people, these rituals . . . They are relics of a primitive past that we'd rather not think about. They are nothing to do with *our* Indonesia.

I thought back to my first encounter with Fajar, when I had laughed at all the men wearing their machetes under the banner reminding us of a ban on machetes. Since then, I'd seen machetes used to slaughter animals, to make drums, to hack open coconuts, to sharpen pencils.

I had also realized that the dismembered corpse in the photo Fajar had shown me was not an isolated case.

Violence seems to be woven into the fabric of this island, despite the best efforts of the soldiers, missionaries and bureaucrats who have trickled through since Dutch times. It's one of the reasons the people of Sumba still cling to their fortified hilltop villages; inconvenient for the women who have to spend three or four hours a day fetching water up from the valleys below, but more defendable than villages on the plains. To this day Loli can't stand Weyewa, Lamboya hates Ede, nobody likes Kodi. The smallest event can spark a conflict; in 1998 dozens were hacked to death and hundreds displaced when a complaint about favouritism in the civil service exams exploded into a full-blown clan war. Nowadays the outbursts are smaller but regular. As I headed up to Kodi on my motorbike one day, I got a text from Doctor Fajar: '5 corpses in Kodi. Because of elopement, apparently. Watch out for a war.'

I didn't see any corpses that day, but I didn't doubt they existed. In an attempt to reduce these fatal outbursts, the local government has banned machetes in town and at many traditional ceremonies too, with exceptions made for tribal elders. The banner at the airport reminded us that under Law 12 of 1951, carrying a sharp weapon without a licence could land you in jail for ten years. That law was made in Jakarta, by a parliament trying to put out fires lit during the five-year guerrilla war against the Dutch. It was a law for a modern, unified state, a state in which people no longer have to defend themselves against headhunting neighbours or wild animals.

Picturesque as the machetes are, arguing against restricting them is a bit like arguing against gun control in the United States. Yes, lethal weapons were a foundational part of the national culture in the US, when pioneers hunted wild animals and fought native tribes. But they are hardly necessary now that we hunt in the supermarket and expand our territory in courts of law. Machetes have far, far more uses than guns do, of course; most of Mama Bobo's sons and grandsons used their weapons daily without ever, to my knowledge or hers, hacking someone to pieces. But over time, modern life erodes even the legitimate uses that still make machetes indispensable in rural Sumba. In most of Indonesia, disembowelling animals after ritual sacrifice is not a common pastime. And even in Sumba's biggest city Waingapu and the modern part of Waikabubak, people have found other tools to do the job of the household machete. Pencil sharpeners, for example. Abattoirs.

Indonesia's diversity is not just geographic and cultural; different groups are essentially living at different points in human history, all at the same time. In the early twenty-first century, some parts of the country are hyper-modern. In other areas, people spend their days much as their ancestors would have done. Often, more-or-less ancient and relatively modern coexist in the same space; farmers get to their rice-field on a motorbike, villagers film a ritual sacrifice on their mobile phones.

In Waikabubak, where modernity has dragged its feet, the two extremes are only now beginning to bump up against one another. But the aspirations of young people in a modern economy have been clashing with the demands of family and traditions in other parts of the country for nearly a century. Indeed the first modern Indonesian novel, Marah Rusli's *Sitti Nurbaya*, deals with exactly this tension. It was published in 1922.

This presents the nation's leaders with a headache. If ancient and modern Indonesia coexist, which should they make laws for?

When I was preparing to go back to Indonesia in 2011, I came across photographs I had taken in Sumba during my first visit, two decades previously. I scanned them onto my iPad, and, in a moment of rainy idleness on a veranda near the south coast, I showed them to Lexi, the young man I was chatting with. Lexi was taken as much with the iPad as with the photos, swiping between images just for the fun of it. He swiped up a photo of a small boy in a primary school uniform and a warrior's head-dress, holding on to his pony and staring straight at the camera. The child exuded defiance. 'So small but so fierce,' I said. Lexi agreed. 'He's got that "don't mess with me" look, like our village head, Pak Pelipus.' He swiped on.

Then he swiped back.

'Wait, that *is* Pak Pelipus.' I laughed. It didn't seem possible. Apart from anything else, we were twenty-five kilometres away from Gaura, where the photo had been taken. In West Sumba that may as well be another planet: a different language, a different clan, a different set of loyalties. And the boy in the picture couldn't be older than thirty now, nowhere near old enough to occupy the venerable position of village head. But Lexi, whose wife, it turned out, was from Gaura, was insistent. 'It's him, I swear!' So we set out to find Pelipus.

In the one-size-fits-all government structure left by Suharto, village heads are supposed to keep office hours. I've never known one that does, but the office seemed as good a place as any to start looking for Pelipus. It was around 10.30 in the morning. A sleepy guard told us that Pelipus was off at an adat ceremony, he had no idea where.

Lexi and I bumped into one hamlet after another, hoping for news of Pelipus. Eventually, someone told us that he was in the next hamlet along, negotiating a bride-price. We teetered along a high ridge towards a clump of greenery, and parked the bike next to the village pigpen, which contained one sow and a large squeal of piglets.

Above us was a pointy-roofed house, its veranda creaking with the bride-to-be's family. They were waiting for emissaries from the groom's family, but they welcomed these other, unexpected guests. Grey-haired men rearranged head-ties and fished out pouches of betel nut to offer us. An ancient woman squatted quietly against the wall, rolling a golf ball of tobacco from side to side under her upper lip. There was the usual quota of teenaged boys, their hair carefully gelled for the solemnities. If an adult shifted and a small space appeared, it was immediately filled by a child. The kids were uncharacteristically tidy, scrubbed up in their impress-the-neighbours best. Negotiating the sale of a sister is a serious business.

In the middle of this press sat Pelipus. He was half the age of many of the men there, but he had clearly stamped his authority on the gathering. Though this was not his house, it was he who invited us onto the veranda, he who gave the nod to the women's quarters to get another round of coffee going. He was friendly enough, but decidedly haughty. There was no question about it: this was the defiant child that I had photographed more than two decades before.

Pelipus and the family elders were discussing their negotiation strategy. There would be a number of niceties to observe before they could get down to brass tacks. First, Pelipus told me, they would have to kill a dog chosen by the bride's family. A *rato* from each side would read the dog's heart, to see if the pair were well suited. The dog would become the first course in a pig-roast dinner, shared by all sides as a sign of good faith.

As he spoke, I noticed for the first time that there's a specific language for different types of carnage in Sumba: buffalo and pigs are 'slashed' (*potong*: their throats are cut). So are chickens, if they are for the pot, though if they killed for the omens they are 'parted' (*belah*: split down the middle to expose their entrails). Dogs, on the other hand, are 'beaten' (*pukul*: actually closer to bludgeon), whatever the purpose.

It's unlikely that the proposed marriage will be abandoned if the dog's heart tells a sorry tale, but it does affect the price the girl will fetch. A bad omen means a possible split, and no sensible groom wants to pay too much for a woman who might go crying back to her own family. That's a loss of property, theft almost; the groom's side will use a telltale dog's heart to beat the price of the girl right down.

Seizing on my interest, the men on the veranda launched into a role play of the impending battle of wills. In their make-believe negotiations, the dog's heart speaks generously, and Pelipus demands forty head of cattle (buffalo, cows and horses). The two older men playing the groom's side offer fifteen. Pelipus snorts in disgust. There's no point him even responding to that. A long silence. Okay, okay, twenty, says one of the elders. 'Right,' says Pelipus. 'Twenty now and the other twenty when?' The total offer goes up to twenty-five. Pelipus mimes shaking out some sleeping mats. He invites his opponents to sleep: we've had a good dinner, there's no point in discussing this any further. Let's take a rest. What then, I ask? 'By the morning they usually see sense.'

The guests had come and gone by the time I came back to the hamlet the next day. The sow and the piglets I has seen the previous day were still in the pen, but there were also fifteen buffalo, two cows and three horses. As per the script, a timetable had been agreed for the delivery of a further twenty beasts. Pelipus is a man to be reckoned with.

With the price of brides so high, you'd think that families would be happy to have a lot of daughters, but in fact that's not the case. For one thing, the transaction is not as one-sided as it first appears. In this case, besides providing the omen-dog, the bride's family had to come up with twenty women's sarongs and twenty men's waist-cloths ('proper hand-woven cloth, not that market junk'). There are further obligations: bracelets of silver (or, in the best families, of ivory) and kitchen implements, plus a horse that is broken in for riding.

I knew that riding-horses were a lot more valuable than ordinary horses, the ones that are used in ritual sacrifice and cooking, but the ones that were in the pen looked much of a muchness to me. I asked the bride's father which was the riding-horse. He pointed off to a spanking new motorbike parked near mine by the tree, all decked about in scarves and ribbons as though it were a champion steed in the ritual jousting matches that still take place every year. 'In this village, we're already modern,' he said.

So selling your daughter is not all profit. And there's something else at play too. When a woman gets married, she stops being part of her family and becomes part of her husband's. So, automatically, do all her children. This ownership doesn't end with her death. As I was soon to learn, corpses, funerals, burials and all the sacrifice that go with them contribute in perpetuity to the glory of a clan. The husband's clan, in the case of a woman.

I once made the mistake of asking one of Mama Bobo's sons if his mother would be buried in Tarung or in her native village, which is on another hill about three kilometres away. In a split second, three emotions swept over his face: confusion, then fury, then indulgence: What kind of question is that? How *dare* she? Oh, of course, she's not really from here. And he explained as simply as he could. 'It's like we bought her, right? She goes in our grave.'

In the general chit-chat about marriage negotiations in Gaura, I mentioned to Pak Pelipus and co. that I had visited the area two decades earlier to watch the *pasola*, a form of jousting that has become a ritualized substitute for human sacrifice.

I pulled out my iPad, a shining jewel in the dark shadows of the veranda, and found the photo of the young Pelipus. The crowd pressed in; faces popped out of the doorway, young heads craned over old. None of these people had seen a touch screen before but within seconds Pelipus was flicking back and forth through photos of the past, zooming in and out, coming back again and again to his own image, like Narcissus staring into a puddle.

I asked how he had morphed from bold-faced eleven-year-old to elected head of Gaura village in just twenty years. He told me that he dropped out of school at about thirteen, when his parents died. 'I turned bad. Cattle-rustling, thievery, you name it.' It wasn't until he got married and had a son that he began to hanker for the respectable life. 'I dared to stand for election as village head and the people put their trust in me'.

Several of the photos elicited clucks of recognition from the older viewers, those who were already adults when the photos were taken. Flick, flick, Oh look! There's so-and-so. Flick, flick, flick: Tsk Tsk, Hah! Remember him, he's from Kodi! Flick, flick: a sudden deathly hush.

The picture that silenced the crowd was of a warrior with wild, curly hair and a fearsome moustache, a young man that I remember as the hero of that pasola long past. Even the children went quiet at his image; Pelipus lost his sneer. For a long moment, the scene hung.

'Kurahaba!' pronounced Pelipus at last. 'He was the bravest of all.'

Kurahaba is no longer with us. He killed someone in a clan war in the mid-1990s, was jailed, and wasted away to his death. From their descriptions of the great warrior's last months, I suspect he died of TB. But many on the veranda think his enemies put a curse on him. Curses are just another part of Sumba's great network of exchange.

After Pelipus and his friends had explained how the marriage bargaining went in Gaura, it was my turn. What did the bride's side have to provide in my country, the old men wanted to know. Well, the bride's father has to pay for the party, I said. Yes, but for the dowry? I admitted that dowries were not really a feature of marriage in the West. 'Waaaaaaah! Did you hear that?' The current of surprise ran around the veranda and into the women's quarters.

I joked that I wished someone had read the dog's heart before my wedding; I might never have married at all. There's a sigh of relief: 'So you bludgeon dogs there too?'

And then, after much discussion: 'But if there's no dowry, why isn't *everyone* divorced?' Good question. On the one hand, these ritual exchanges create webs that tie people together and weave them much more closely into their communities than any of the sign-a-paper-and-give-a-party ceremonies of the 'modern' world. On the other hand the new wave of educated, urban Indonesians who make up the bulk of my pool of friends in Jakarta have a lot more freedom to choose their partners as they please, and leave them if they must. There are pros and cons to both systems, I think. It's where they rub up against one another that things become most difficult.

Squeezed uncomfortably between these two worlds was Delsi, who lived in a witch's house in a village perched on another outcrop that rose out of the sea of Waikabubak, this one just above the hospital. The first time I entered the village, two young boys were battling it out on the rough ground between the village graves. Their chosen weapons were turnip-shaped wooden spinning tops. The trick seemed to be in the launch: the boys both spread starfish wide, teetered back on one leg, then launched forward, only releasing the top when their arm was full-force straight. The idea is to knock the opponent's top off kilter, so that it wobbles and falls while yours still spins proudly upright.

Dewa, the youngest of Delsi's four siblings and the only boy, was the clear master of the tops. A charming child with a shy smile and a quiet curiosity, he coached me patiently for a while, but I am no spinner of tops. He was rescued from despair by Delsi, the eldest of his sisters. She invited me up onto the veranda for coffee, and launched into a discussion about Indonesia's place in the world and its prospects for the future. I was not surprised to find intelligent women in a traditional village, of course. Although it is men who do most of the chanting, posturing and even public negotiating in Sumba, women run complex family economies and are responsible for ensuring that everyone fits snugly into the local cosmos. Even so, I was surprised to find someone quite as worldly as Delsi.

She and Ira, the next sister down, were both in their early twenties, both high-school teachers. Delsi played the responsible eldest sibling, discussing politics and education policy in measured tones. Ira was the good-humoured rebel, impaling each new idiocy proposed by the government on her sharp wit. They had studied in the provincial capital Kupang, a two-day boat-ride away, and they still Facebooked college friends from other islands on their cell phones.

Delsi's family eventually provided me with a second adoptive home in West Sumba. Sometimes I'd go to the market 'down below' and stock up on unidentified vegetables. Then we'd squat together around the smoky cooking pot in the women's quarters of Delsi's house and the girls would teach me how to cook papaya flowers so that they were not too bitter. In the evenings we would sit talking of this and that while their widowed mother Mama Paulina knitted doilies and I sewed up my fraying clothes. Delsi gave me advice on the latest in Indonesian fiction – short stories, especially. Ira's thing was music. If we were feeling lazy, we'd sit out on the veranda watching DVDs on an ageing laptop.

All over Indonesia, strangers address one another using kinship terms. The most common for a woman is *Ibu*, 'mother', often shortened to *Bu* – it's also the most respectful. Regional variations are friendlier: *Mama* in the south-eastern islands, *Bunda* in the north-west. The male equivalent nationwide is *Bapak*, 'father', almost always shortened to *Pak*. These terms can be used alone, combined with people's names, or even combined with their occupation. It's fine to introduce the teacher simply as '*Ibu Guru*' – Mrs Teacher. It's very handy if, like me, you're bad with names. Even handier: many people (especially in Java) remind you of their names constantly, because they use them instead of personal pronouns. 'Elizabeth will come and visit Mama Bobo again tomorrow,' I might say to my friend.

Children speaking to adults will sometimes use the familiar

Tante and *Om*, Auntie and Uncle, a hangover from Dutch times. Adults who want to express friendship might use the terms for siblings: *Kakak* or *Adik*. These are gender-neutral — they can mean brother or sister — but they are age-specific. Kakak is elder, adik is younger; using them is freighted with judgements about the age of the person you're speaking to. It's slightly traumatizing at first to be called 'elder sister' by an old lady who looks like a shrivelled prune, but it is meant as a mark of both friendship and respect.

One evening, when Mama Paulina (who is, in fact, younger than me) called me her elder sister, I asked how much we would earn when we sold our girls. Paulina's second daughter, Ira, twinkled: 'A LOT!' Apparently, adat dictates that a daughter of good family must be worth at least as much as her mother was. 'And she — ' Ira nodded at her mother — 'fetched a hundred of these'. She stretched her arm out to full length and tapped her shoulder, indicating the length of those buffaloes' horns. A hundred long-horns per daughter, and four lovely daughters. A fortune. 'Wow, and then it will be just the two of us left in the kitchen and we'll be two very rich old ladies!' I said to Paulina.

We all laughed, but Delsi quickly came over all sensible. 'Actually, it's a real headache.' And she was right. Because really, who wants to pay one hundred long-horned buffalo for 'modern' girls, girls who have studied in Kupang, who read books, who think that slaughtering buffalo is a waste of capital? And yet if they don't pull in a bride-price, the girls will be betraying the clan which supported their expensive, modern education. That would bring shame on Mama Paulina herself.

Perhaps this is the central dilemma of modernization in collective societies: the all-encompassing security of a shared culture gets sold off in exchange for individual fulfilment.

I had grown accustomed to obeying Mama Bobo's quiet commands. She would look me over and make me change my Javanese sarong for a local one; she reminded me to leave a small banknote in the dish with my sacrificial chicken; she nudged me to go and sit on other verandas if she thought neighbours felt neglected. But when I had asked to see the sacred objects in the smoke-crusted cage above the fire, her response – 'you'll have to stay until someone dies' – seemed a command too far.

After I moved on through the islands, we kept in touch by text message, Mama Bobo's all the more urgent because THEY WERE ALWAYS ALL IN CAPITALS. After six months, she persuaded me to come back for jousting season.

When I reappeared in Waikabubak in April 2012, six months after my previous visit, the owner of the guest house brought me sugar-free coffee without even being reminded. The girl in the internet cafe cleared another customer out of my favourite desk as she saw me walk up the drive. The owner of a restaurant that I was fond of gave me a free plate of chicken to welcome me back. Climbing up to Tarung, I found Mama Bobo sitting on the veranda of her house, exactly where I left her. When she saw me she leapt up and jumped up and down with glee. I felt like a soldier come home from the wars.

Then Mama Bobo's pleasure left her, and she began to wail. She grabbed my hands, clasped them to her chest, shook her head, wailed some more. Her sister-in-law had died the night before. I made soothing noises, but she flapped my sympathy away. She wasn't upset about her sister-in-law. She was upset because she had urged me to come back for the jousting and I had come. But now, because she was in mourning, she wouldn't be able to come to the tournament with me. That meant she would break her side of the bargain. The delicate laws of reciprocity which hold everything in place in the Loli culture would be knocked off kilter.

I reminded Mama Bobo that this is just what she had hoped for. Now we could go to a funeral together. She seemed greatly cheered by this. I'd have to go and visit her dead sister-in-law first, of course, so that I could be properly introduced to her before the funeral. But there would be plenty of time; the corpse would be receiving guests every day for a week.

I suggested that we go the following day. Bobo shook her head and dropped her voice, something she often did when she considered that I had, out of forgivable ignorance, said something inappropriate. 'Not tomorrow. There are things still to arrange.' And I understood that even someone of Bobo's standing would take a bit of time to muster the gifts that they were obliged to take to the sister-in-law's clan, the family to which Mama Bobo had belonged until her marriage. The gift list would be dictated by a long history of exchange. Clan A gave us a pig when so-and-so died, family X brought a machete when Y was buried. I found another friend in Tarung at her loom that day: she was frantically weaving the ikat cloth that she would have to take as a mark of respect for Bobo's sister-in-law.

I hadn't been quite as aware of all the rituals of exchange when I had first taken tea with a corpse two decades earlier. I had gone back for the funeral that time too, but it had been a relatively simple affair; I remembered just one cow slaughtered. Now I scoured my iPad for photos of that earlier ritual, which I remembered as being in the general vicinity of the central town of Anakalang. I found the photos; the scenery around the grave site was undistinguished but there were other pictures, taken the same day, which showed a clutch of pixie-faced schoolgirls grinning at me from behind an elaborately carved tomb which would be easy to locate. I set out to see if I could find dead Granny's family. I parked my motorbike by the carved tomb, and showed the pictures to an old lady who was sitting on a veranda a few hundred yards away. She identified one of the funeral guests, and sent me to a village about a mile down the road.

The dirt road of my memories had been paved over by asphalt, but I did eventually find the house where I had first met Granny. Sitting on the veranda was Granny's niece Rambubera, a woman a few years younger than me who had posed proudly to be photographed with the corpse during my first visit. I proffered the photo, which I had printed out to give to the family. 'That's not me!' She was vehement, but her eyes were rheumy. I pulled out my iPad and zoomed in on her face. 'Not at all, not me!'

She rummaged around in her sarong, drew out a wallet, and produced an ID card, crispy with age. 'Look! There! That's me! That's what I look like'. She pointed to the tiny black and white photo.

I didn't want to upset her, and was about to leave when a man in denim shorts with smiley eyes came out of the gloom of the house to see what was going on. It was the boy who had invited me up onto this very veranda twenty years earlier. He remembered me, and called others out of the dark interior, where they were watching an Arsenal match on TV that seemed the only change to the place in two decades. They started looking at the pictures: 'Look, that's Uncle Timus!' 'Hey! There's me!' They teased Rambubera because she hadn't grasped that she would have looked different when she was younger. She sulked a bit, but couldn't resist the draw of the photos. Soon, she was recognizing and pointing and laughing with the rest. The man in denim shorts, still smiley but no longer young, offered me a cup of tea.

Two decades later, while waiting for my second chance to go to a dead lady's tea party, I enlisted my friend Jerome to come with me to the pasola jousting on the beautiful clifftops near Gaura, where the cattle-rustler-turned-village-head Pelipus lived. Jerome was a French researcher whom I knew from Jakarta; he studied criminality and urban gang culture. Looking for a bit of a break in a kinder, gentler Indonesia, he'd come to Sumba for a couple of weeks.

Tall, swarthy, heavy-lidded, Jerome was an instant hit with the younger ladies of Mama Bobo's clan. He was perfectly at ease sitting around on verandas for hours, washing in the river, eating dog-liver dinners. But he was, after all, on holiday; he still wanted to do some of those beachy things that ordinary people do when they are near the mile after mile of deserted white sands that Sumba provides. I did a deal with Jerome. If he would give me a lift to the jousting on the back of his bike, I'd promise to leave the ceremony early and go to the beach with him. He put his swimsuit in the well of the motorbike and off we went.

The pasola is a jousting match between groups of fierce young men wearing incongruous head-dresses: fascinations of feathers or a cone tied on with flowing scarves. They ride on ponies decked out in ribbons and pom-poms, in bells and coins. But there is nothing fey about the fighting.

The jousters of Sumba rub against one another in wheeling packs. The men of one village gallop around in a circle, clockwise. Their rivals race anti-clockwise in a second ring. In each circuit, every rider has a heart-stopping moment when they are charging towards their foe. With one hand, they hang on to the reins, steer the horse, and somehow also form a shield by twirling spare lances. With the other, they hurl a javelin into the fray, trying to score a hit in the split second before they wheel off into another loop. Often, they have to twirl, hurl and duck an incoming lance all at the same time. And all while riding bareback at thunderous speed. It's stirring stuff.

Getting to the pasola grounds was almost as stirring. Even Jerome's long legs had trouble steadying the bike up and down the steep, muddy hillsides to the jousting site. All around, motor-cyclists were going off-piste, upending themselves, dusting themselves off and getting back in the saddle. The jousters on their pom-pommed horses looked smug as they jangled past us up to the clifftop.

We did the rounds of the pasola field for a couple of hours, moving with the crowds, we cheered first for this team, then for that, we ate brown rice dumplings under the makeshift sun-shelter courtesy of the officials' wives, we checked in with village head Pelipus as he refereed the jousting. Finally, Jerome began to show signs of adat overload; he put on his Beach Face. It was obviously time to leave. We went back up to the bike.

No key.

Somewhere between the lady he bought water from (which was she?) and the tree he had sat under (this one, perhaps), between the wives with rice dumplings and the bush he had peed in, somewhere on a couple of hectares of long grass pounded down by horses ridden by warriors in Rolling Stones T-shirts and pointy head-dresses, by spectators jumping on one leg and ululating, Jerome had lost a solitary Honda key, without even a key ring.

I thought at first he was joking, but no. He looked almost hang-dog, as if expecting me to be cross. If we had been in London or Beijing I might have been. But here in Gaura I was overcome by a millpond calm. For all the frustrations and inefficiencies of Indonesia, it's almost impossible to get into difficulties that one can't get out of with a bit of humour and a lot of patience. *Semua bisa di atur* – everything can be arranged.

In the time we spent looking for the key, the pasola came to a sudden end and everyone started to leave in droves. Being stuck all alone five muddy, hilly kilometres from the nearest settlement with a locked bike would definitely stir up my millpond of calm. 'Arranging' everything became a little more urgent.

Jerome, too long in Jakarta's criminal underbelly, homed in on the loutiest guys he could find; he was looking for someone who could hotwire the bike so we could drive it back to town without a key. I, too long in the Jakarta bureaucracy, homed in on the person with the most authority. I settled for a cop with gold stars on his shoulders and a walkie-talkie in his hand.

I smiled a lot, explained what an idiot I felt, apologized repeatedly for the trouble and asked for his kind suggestion about how we might resolve the situation, all the while trying not to eye up his nice twin-cab flatbed truck too obviously.

He in turn called over someone with lots more gold on his shoulder. 'How awful for you. I'm so sorry,' said the senior cop, as though it was somehow his fault, not ours. He instructed Fewer Stars to get on the walkie-talkie, they called back the police transport truck that was already disappearing over the crest of the first hill, and we climbed on board.

When we came to where the motorbikes were parked, Jerome pointed out ours. Four well-built cops jumped out of the truck. While I shoved riot shields out of the way to make space, the boys wrestled the locked bike up in between the benches, and we were off.

It had all been so easy, getting the cops to steal our bike. Jerome, in a bit of a tizz just half an hour earlier, looked over at me from the opposite side of the truck. A wide, wicked smile split his face and he said in French: 'I should have pointed out a nicer bike!'

I went to be introduced to Mama Bobo's dead sister-in-law on the day before her funeral. The old lady was in a party dress, a big red bow fanned across her careful bun, a beautifully woven cloth pulled up around her knees. She sat on a chair of freshly cut bamboo. Her chin sank gently into her chest. It wasn't easy to tell the difference between her and a quietly sleeping version of any one of a number of wizened grannies who were crowded into the gloom around her. Surprisingly, given that it was the hot season and she had been sitting in a crowded room for the week since she died, she didn't smell. Mama Bobo prodded me, and I laid a huge bag of betel nut at my hostess's feet. Others, I noticed, put their offerings right in her lap, but that felt a little familiar for someone I had only just met.

The corpse was the second of Mama Bobo's brother's four wives. Her brother had died a couple of years before, the first wife a year later. 'They're pegging out in order,' said one of the attendant women, meaning the order in which they married their shared husband. She turned around to introduce me to wife number three, a tiny shrivelled slip of a thing, folded up in a corner behind the corpse. Her face had collapsed in on itself, its shape maintained only by the ball of tobacco under her lip.

Wife four needed no introduction; she was the one lording it over everyone else, at least a decade younger than wife three, gussied up in best brocade. Mama Bobo told me later that she never talked to her brother again after he married this woman, though she wouldn't say why. She just shook her head and repeated: 'It wasn't right. It was not right.' My friend made peace with her brother only after he died, with the offering of a huge buffalo.

The next day was the funeral proper. In Tarung, Mama Bobo's veranda was buzzing. People appeared with drums and gongs, and a great deal of energy went in to weaving a curtain of palm fronds. Around mid-morning, Mama Bobo's grandson Billy appeared, leading a magnificent white buffalo. Billy had bloodshot eyes, heavily lidded, and smooth skin, slashed across with a great scar; he was handsome. His charge, a precious albino buffalo, was fatted and newly bathed to its natural reddish pink, and they made a fine pair.

The men got to work. They wrapped yellow silk around the beast's horns and fashioned a rising sun over its brow. Then they fixed the palm-frond fringe to one silky horn-tip, draped it under the buffalo's throat, and swept it up to the other horn-tip, framing the animal's head. The effect was to emphasize the magnificent span of the buffalo's horns and thus the generosity of its donor. Billy got out the pig fat and massaged the buffalo until it shimmered in the noonday sun.

When they had got it looking in tip-top condition, the men of the clan lined up behind the buffalo. They were wrapped in ceremonial waist- and head-cloths, belted with their best swords. Each had a cigarette drooping from his mouth, each had a drum or a gong in hand. Their music advertised the Bobo clan's act of generosity as it paraded the three kilometres through town to the death-village. They could have taken a back route through the rice fields that lap around between the vast megalithic tombs on the outskirts of Waikabubak, but no, they drummed their way through the crowded market and along a main thoroughfare. In the streets, people gawped and scurried out of the way to let the procession pass. Wow! Look at that fine beast! That family is really something! Behind, minibuses and motorbikes were snarled up, resigned to the hurdles that adat ceremonies so often throw in their path.

Bobo had hired 'transport' for the women of the family. We all piled on to a flatbed truck and trundled through the rice fields to avoid the traffic jam, then waited for the men in the cool bamboo grove beneath Mama Bobo's birth village. One of the giant graves at the foot of the hill was surrounded by a sort of scaffold of newly cut saplings, arranged so that they could be used to winch up a carved capstone that must have weighed several tonnes. 'That's where she'll go,' whispered Mama Bobo. 'With my parents.' I was surprised; normally a wife would be buried with her husband, and rich husbands like Bobo's brother would have started a new vault for their own family. And indeed he did have a new vault, and the other three wives would be buried with him. Wife number two had chosen to spend eternity with her parents-in-law because she didn't want to be cooped up with hated Best Brocade. 'It was all decided a long time ago,' Bobo said. And she would say nothing more.

When the whole company arrived and the men had had a smoke break, we marched into the ceremony. Mama Bobo held my hand as we climbed the hill; she was electric with excitement. At the last minute she skipped up to head the procession along with handsome Billy and his fine buffalo. Our grand entrance was carefully timed for maximum impact; by the time we arrived every grave-top was crowded with people, every veranda weighed down with guests. Hundreds of people had a ringside view of Mama Bobo's munificence.

Bobo gave a little speech, then a representative of her birth clan gave a little speech, then our delegation all filed up to the headman to pay our respects, each in our turn. I was slotted in after Mama Bobo and the clan elders, but before some of Bobo's younger sons — a position of some honour. I watched everyone rub noses with the headman and did the same in my turn, wishing I wasn't sweating so much, suddenly aware of how much rice alcohol the men were consuming. My offering, a carton of cigarettes and a couple of kilos of coffee and sugar, was spirited away with the rest of the gifts, and it was back to the slaughter.

Already, a cream-coloured horse lay in the clearing, its

glassy-eyed head parted from its body with a wide gash to the neck. The horse had been the first to go, so that the old lady would have a smooth ride to the afterlife. One pink-horned buffalo was down, and another, this one garlanded in red, had just appeared in the ring. A young man leapt forward, whipped out his machete, and slashed at the beast's jugular. The man on the tombstone next to me let out a disgusted jet of betel juice that blended prettily into the horse blood below: his comment on a botched sacrifice. A furious buffalo now stamped and snorted, only partly held in place by a tug of war between a team holding ropes tied to one back leg and one front leg. After another few swipes, the buffalo dropped to its knees and the blood-bubbles at its throat sputtered to a halt. The young killer made himself scarce. His incompetence had brought shame on his clan; later he would have to pay a fine.

By mid-afternoon the space between the tombstones was a little crowded. In a lake of blood lay one horse, seven buffalo and a single Brahmin cow (slaughtered halal, for Muslim guests). Even in death, Mama Bobo's was the finest of them all. High above the pointy roofs of the village, birds of prey circled.

Now the butchering began. The men of the clan unzipped the animals' skins, then carefully unpeeled the beasts to reveal carcasses shiny and pink as giant worms. Bellies were slit open and organs scooped out. Steaming mounds of half-digested grass piled up on banana leaves.

As the sun sank, a Moulin Rouge of flayed buffalo legs kicked their hooves at the gravestones; a horse's head lay abandoned in the square like something off the set of *The Godfather*. On the flat tops of the tombs, a clutch of gongs, a horse-skin drum and a mound of glistening liver made for a macabre still life.

The meat was parcelled out at the direction of a clan elder who consulted an exercise book in which every gift and contribution had been carefully noted. I was rewarded not just for the gifts I myself had brought, but for my association with my clan's gifts: today's buffalo and the two pigs that went to feed guests during Granny's tea parties earlier in the week.

That meant I got a mass of meat hung about with a trail of coveted guts.

Outwardly, the gift of a buffalo is a mark of respect to the person who has died, and to his or her clan. Its splendid horns will be nailed to the front of the clan house, perhaps displacing some earlier, lesser sacrifice. To that extent, it's a gift that keeps giving; it visibly contributes to the honour of the clan for evermore. But in truth, Mama Bobo's trophy buffalo wasn't just about respect. It was about revenge.

Nothing, but nothing, in Sumba is really a gift: it's always an exchange. If I 'give' you a fatted buffalo, you are immediately in my debt for a beast with horns at least as long. It's a debt you absolutely must repay whenever it falls due, that unpredictable time when my granny dies, or my husband does, or I do. If you don't have a buffalo to spare, what then? You do whatever you have to. You can call in debts from other people, or deepen your web of obligation by borrowing. If payback means taking your kids out of school, selling your rice fields, or just stealing a buffalo in one of the cyclical cattle raids that dot the calendar of Sumba, so be it.

By 'giving' such a generous funeral gift, Mama Bobo was essentially storing up trouble for her late brother's brocaded fourth wife. As with the obligations surrounding marriage, this web of ritual exchange has an important cultural function. The warp and weft of these mutual obligations means that anyone can draw on the collective resources of the clan in times of need or trouble. It's a sort of elaborate insurance scheme in this parched corner of Indonesia, a place with no fertile volcanic soil, a place where the land can be unforgiving. And it seems to be a fairly effective way of ironing out inequalities in wealth over time. Daily life inside a one-skull house is not all that different from life inside a twenty-skull house.

Some people are clearly wary of getting tied into a web they can't escape. In cross-cultural experiments, psychologists have found that people who come from gift-giving cultures similar to Sumba's are most likely to reject generosity from strangers, because they fear the burden that will inevitably follow.* Mostly, the trouble comes when these ancient cultural obligations rub up against the demands of a modernizing world. In the closed communities of yesteryear, adat was a stepping stone to respect-ability and social prominence. But many younger Indonesians have much broader horizons than their parents did. Satellite TV, the internet, cheap airfares and scholarships sponsored by the local government have drawn back the curtains on a larger Indonesia and a wider world.

The main pathway to that wider world is education. And the High Priest in Tarung was probably right when he suggested, while celebrating the failure of family planning programmes, that education and adat are incompatible. I met many young people in Sumba who had to drop out of school because some adat obligation fell due. What agony, to have to lead a prize buffalo into a ceremony and slit its throat, knowing full well that you are watching your hopes for the future drain away with the blood that seeps into the dust between the graves. When I ask young people if this makes them angry, they shrug. 'Adat is adat. What can you do?'

The government believes that it would be easier to meet the aspirations of these young people if their elders stopped hacking up the family wealth every time someone dies. As long ago as 1987, the Suharto government in Jakarta tried to draw a line in the blood-soaked sand of Sumba: no more than five buffalos could be killed per ceremony. But the people of Sumba were a long way from Jakarta; the ruling never really took hold. More recent efforts by local politicians to restrict the slaughter have fared no better because they all cheat when it comes to their own family ceremonies and, indeed, campaign rallies.

When I was lost on a floodplain somewhere near the great sweep of Wanokaka beach on Sumba's south coast, I ran into Pak Petrus, a farmer who owned a substantial eleven hectares and who was one of the elders of his community. I needed directions,

* See Henrich et al., 'In Cross-Cultural Perspective: Behavioral Experiments in 15 Small-Scale Societies', *Behavioral and Brain Sciences* 28, no. 6 (2005): 795–815.

he needed a lift, one thing led to another and I ended up staying with him and his wife for a few days. One evening, we were sitting chatting with some of his friends. Pak Petrus wanted to know how much my salary was. I must be very rich indeed to be able to just go off and travel as I pleased! I laughed. 'Rich? With just one of the four buffalo you slaughtered at your last ceremony, I could travel for six months,' I said. 'And *I'm* the one who's rich?!'

Petrus and his friends were thunderstruck. He repeated this observation to everyone we subsequently met; each time, it led to much discussion and a great shaking of heads.

Later, after speaking to a West Sumba businessman, I began to guess at the source of Petrus's amazement. I had asked the businessman why almost every single shop in Waikabubak is owned by someone who is ethnically Chinese. 'It's the capital thing. In my clan, we count our capital in cattle, not cash. But however many hundred head of cattle you have, that won't buy you a single bag of cement.'

The assumption underlying the government's 'stop the slaughter' approach is that cattle and cement are interchangeable. Kill fewer buffalo, sell some of the survivors, buy a tractor or build a hotel. Make money. Buy another tractor. Get rich. In a word: capitalism.

But it doesn't yet work like that. In Sumba's sticky culture, there are two quite separate types of capital. Financial capital – money, cement, shops – can be turned into buffalo, tombstones and other forms of cultural capital. But it's a one-way street. Cultural capital is the property of the whole clan, living and dead. You contribute to it, and it assures your place in the world. You can't sell it off to pay for one child's education, a new generator for your workshop or an Indomaret franchise. When I implied that Pak Petrus could turn a buffalo into six months of travel, I might as well have suggested privatizing air and selling it to buy a gold-plated toilet.

It's not just in out-of-the-way Sumba that Indonesians choose to meet the expectations of adat before taking care of their personal needs and desires, before getting rich. Look at Bali, which has one of the most 'modern' economies in Indonesia, and one of its stickier cultures. Bali was the last bastion of the Hindu courts that once dotted Sumatra and Java, and it has inherited their traditions of pomp. Now hardly a day goes by without a miniaturized version of those court ceremonies. For every temple festival, every tooth filing, every torching of the funeral pyre, people knock off work, get dressed up, beat the gongs of adat. These festivals are a big part of Bali's attraction, bringing in three million foreign visitors in 2012. But they also make life difficult for people trying to run businesses in tourism. I heard the frustration from a foreign hotelier in Bali: 'Some Russian punter is happy to spend half a day snapping pictures of shapely brown girls with piles of fruit on their head, but if you tell him his laundry's not done because the staff had to go to the temple, he'll go ballistic.'

Bali does celebrate one ceremony-free day each year. That's Nyepi, the Day of Silence, when no one does any work at all.

Whiling away one rainy afternoon on the veranda of Mama Bobo's in Sumba, I had pulled out my giant map of Indonesia. It was a kid-magnet; within minutes a dozen small heads were craning over the map, and sticky fingers were grabbing, pointing, smearing. 'Where's Sumba?' I ask. Uhhhhhh . . . After some he-said she-said disagreement, one of the older kids pointed out where we were. And my home, in Jakarta? That one stumped them. They mixed up cities and islands, islands and provinces, provinces and countries. One child made Malaysia into a province of Indonesia: founding father Sukarno, who always looked at Malaysia with hungry eyes, would have been proud.

The children asked me where I was going next and I pointed to the tiny island of Savu, which interrupts the expanse of sea to the east between Sumba and Timor. Then I swept my hand vaguely across a string of microscopic specks representing the islands which run in an arc from the edge of Timor, along the top of Australia, and all the way up to the tip of Indonesian Papua. I named one or two of the specks, then dried up. I had never been to these places, and had never met anyone else who had been to them, either. The kids snatched the map, squinted at the specks, and began to test me. 'All right clever clogs, what island comes next to Kisar?'

We agreed to have a geography competition when I was next in Sumba, and that evening I walked around Waikabubak looking for a map to give them so that they could study. I could buy maps of the district of West Sumba, and even of NTT,★ the province in which Sumba sits. But in all of Waikabubak there was not a map of the nation to be had. I asked the stony-faced Chinese traders in the general stores, expecting hands to be inserted into the dusty mountains of goods and a map to emerge, but no. Nothing in the bookshop, or in the town's many stationery stores.

In Sumba, the nation didn't exist.

★ Pronounced 'En–tay–TAY', short for *Nusa Tenggara Timur*, East Nusa Tenggara. Islanders joke bitterly that it stands for *Nusa Tertinggal Terus*: the Perpetually Neglected Islands.

Map B: Eastern Flores and Surrounding Islands, East Nusa Tenggara Province (NTT)

N

FLORES SEA

ADONARA

LEMBATA

Lewoleba

Lamalera

SOLOR

Larantuka

Maumere

FLORES

Detusoko

Kelimutu Volcano

Ende

Boawae

From and to Sumba

SAVU SEA

0km   15km   30km   45km

4

Resident Aliens

In the smaller islands of eastern Indonesia, people have a very intimate relationship with boats. Kerosene, eggs, rice, sugar: all come in on big cargo boats, whose frequency determines how much things will cost in the market. Ferries provide an escape route to the wider world. There are slow, uncomfortable, flat-bottomed car ferries for inter-island hops of twenty-four hours or less. Large passenger ferries run by the state firm Pelni chug from end to end of the archipelago on routes first laid down by the Dutch 'steam-packets'. Islanders know each of these boats by name; in port towns, their timetables are engraved on the collective memory.

I planned to take the monthly Pelni ferry from Sumba's eastern port of Waingapu across to tiny Savu. As far away as Waikabubak, a four-hour drive across Sumba on a road first built by Japanese troops during the occupation, people knew when the ferry was due. My West Sumba friends booked me into a share-taxi, making sure I would get to the boat on time.

But when we arrived at the port, there was no sign of the ship. '*Lagi doking, Bu,*' the guard said amiably – it's in dry dock for its annual repairs. 'But it will be back in service next month.' Further down the pier, a snort of Sumba ponies were being herded onto a car ferry, headed for Flores to the north-east of Sumba. I joined them, squeezing myself between the wheels of two trucks of sour-smelling seaweed. Besides the ponies, my fellow passengers included a cluster of gamblers and a single

Brahmin cow with sad eyes, tethered near a big pile of grass. It was of accidents like this that my itinerary was made.

Animist Flores began turning Catholic when Portuguese missionaries settled here in the seventeenth century. Its coastal areas are dry compared with steamy Sumatra and lush Java, but the island's vertebrae – a dozen active volcanoes – keep the uplands fertile enough. Together with the long, lacy borders of white sand on the island's north-east coast, they provide some breathtaking scenery. In evenings the hills are shrouded with mist and life takes on a mystical air. On one such evening, walking into a valley near the tiny town of Detusoko, I stumbled on a group of women sitting in the river. A mother was holding her sarong over her chest for modesty's sake, while her daughter scrubbed Mum's back with a lathered stone. The women waved me over: 'Come and bathe!' 'I don't want to get cold,' I yelled back, and one of the teenagers laughed and splashed me. The river water was hot. I had not had a hot shower since the start of the trip. I waded into the river fully clothed, and let the warmth bubble up around me, one of earth's small luxuries.

I hadn't guessed that the river might be hot because there was no sign of its having been turned into an *obyek wisata*, a 'tourism object'. Though it sounds odd in English, 'tourism objects' lie at the core of Indonesian officialdom's concept of the travel industry. Spectacularly beautiful waterfalls are turned into obyek wisata with the construction of cement tables and stools fashioned to look like cut pine trees. Pristine beaches are walled off behind pink concrete, broken only by a welcoming archway that proclaims 'Welcome to Sunset Beach Tourism Object'! Hot springs get funnelled into slimy tiled baths hidden in rickety wooden sheds. Pathways through spectacular gorges are lined with vendors and littered with discarded drink cartons.

Central Flores seems miraculously to have escaped these horrors. About thirty kilometres from Detusoko is the Kelimutu volcano, one of Indonesia's better-known natural wonders. I remembered it from an earlier visit in 1989; three lakes, one white, one green and one blood-red, nestled in a single giant crater. 'The lakes have swapped colours now,' said a nun at the convent I stayed at in Detusolo. This I had to see.

As I waited on the main road to flag down a bus, a young man sitting at a coffee stall offered to take me by *ojek*. An ojek is a motorcycle taxi, usually a smallish Honda or Yamaha scooter and often, in the poorer provinces of Indonesia, somewhat decrepit. Fine for getting around town, but for a journey of thirty kilometres on mountain roads to a volcano? No thanks. 'Well, let me buy you a coffee then,' the lad suggested. So I did. I was still drinking it as the bus rumbled past. I took the ojek.

The road snaked along the top of a deep valley. Rice terraces, bathed now in the kindly light of early morning, tumbled down to the river below. As he negotiated the bends in the road, Anton, the ojek driver, told me that his real interest was animal husbandry. He was almost ashamed to be offering lifts for money. 'It's not that I'm stupid, Miss, or lazy. I graduated from high school. But look around. I can't afford to go to college, and what is there to do here except grow rice? It's not like over there, in Java . . .'

Java, that mythical Other Country whose values Suharto had tried to etch across the nation. I asked Anton if he had ever been there. 'What, to Java? Oh no . . .' His tone was of awed disbelief, as if I'd asked if he had ever been to St Peter's in Rome. Later, though, he mentioned that two of his brothers were working in Java. Couldn't he go and live with them, go to college, pay his way by driving an ojek over there, just like he's doing now? 'But things are different there, Miss. It's not like here.' He swerved to avoid a huge bite-mark taken out of the road by a landslide, then laughed. 'You see, you'd never have something like that in Java!' Anton was worried, too, that he wouldn't get into college 'over there', that he was too much of a hick. I gave him the standard 'you'll never know until you try / the worst that can happen is that you come back to doing what you are doing now' pep talk.

For several months, Anton continued to send me the occasional 'what's up' message, and I'd always reply. Then, nearly a year later, I got a surprise: 'Hello Miss, where are you now? I'm in Surabaya.' As it happened, the text came in as I was waiting for a flight to Surabaya, Java's second largest city. We met for a coffee the following evening. Anton was in college, studying to become a vet. 'I thought about what you said, and thought yes, she's right. I can't succeed unless I give it a go.' Java turned out not to be as impossibly alien as he had feared. He still felt like a bit of a country bumpkin, he said, but there were other students from Flores who were showing him the ropes. 'It's better than sitting waiting for passengers in Detusoko.'

When Anton dropped me at Kelimutu – even the name sings – it was one of those heart-bursting days of glittering morning air and infinite vistas. The birds serenaded, the butterflies flirted, and I was all alone in one of the most beautiful places on earth. Two of Kelimutu's lakes are divided by a single wall of jagged rock. One lake I remembered as being emerald green, the other a great pool of milk, The third, off at a distance, was sticky, oxidized blood. This time, though, the sibling lakes seemed to have bled into one another; they are now turquoise twins. As the clouds puffed in, smoky shadows flitted over their surface. I walked on up the dust-muffled path to the third lake, passing a solitary groundsman who was attacking the acres of scrub grass with a scythe the size of a Swiss Army knife. The blood lake, the one where locals believe old souls find their rest, had thickened almost to black. I wondered what had become of the souls of virgins and innocents now that the white lake where they used to seek refuge had morphed to blue. Geologists say these colour changes are the work of minerals burped up into the lakes from vents under the water. Though according to Kelimutu National Park's official website, locals believe they are the spirits' reaction to the election of a military candidate as president of Indonesia.

I sat for a while in a silence punctuated by birdsong and the occasional buzzing insect. It was mid-November, not high tourist season, but still, it seemed amazing that I could have this whole majestic scene entirely to myself. No busloads of rich kids from private schools in Java exploring the wonders of their nation. No groups of camera-clicking Japanese tourists with a niche interest in vulcanology. Not even any gap-year backpackers storing up exotic tales for fresher's week at university in Manchester, San Francisco or Berlin. I was thrilled by the solitude, of course. But I felt almost offended on behalf of Indonesia.

There's no doubt that Indonesia punches below its weight on the world stage. Just twenty-two athletes went from Indonesia to the Olympic Games in London in 2012 – not even one per ten million Indonesians. Though Indonesian soldiers were once popular as UN peacekeepers, very few Indonesians have made it to the top echelons of international organizations and none has ever headed one. No Indonesian has ever won a Nobel Prize.*

The country had a higher profile when Sukarno (who spoke nine languages) roamed the world denouncing imperialism and wagged his finger at interfering neighbours. But Suharto, ever the yin to Sukarno's yang, spoke little English and was uncomfortable in the international arena. He came out of his shell with his immediate neighbours; he was the driving force behind the establishment of ASEAN, the Association of South East Asian Nations, a sort of mutual support group for the not-very-democratic leaders of the region. But for three decades Suharto kept a low profile internationally, and Indonesians themselves did nothing to raise it.

Remarkably few Indonesians have chosen to settle in other countries. They do travel as contract labourers: in 2012, four million Indonesians trekked overseas to clean other people's loos, weed their plantations and build their hotels, mostly in Saudi Arabia and Malaysia. But almost all of these people are on 'package deal' schemes; they are sent out in batches by

---

* Unless you count the Dutchman Christiaan Eijkman, who won the Nobel Prize for Medicine in 1929 for his work on beriberi in the Netherlands East Indies, or the two East Timorese who were technically citizens of Indonesia when they were awarded the Peace Prize in 1996, largely for opposing Indonesia's rule. The next largest country in the world with no Nobel laureate is Ethiopia, at number fourteen in terms of population.

government-approved agents and will be brought home when their contracts are up. This is not the sort of migration of which a diaspora is made, and it is a diaspora that spreads a country's influence overseas.

I was mulling over the missing diaspora one night some years ago when I was out with my friend Luwi. Luwi is a well-educated upper-middle-class designer with a French grandfather, an international circle of friends and a well-stamped passport, exactly the sort of person who, if he were from Korea or Colombia, might have chosen to live in New York or Paris. It was four in the morning, and we were driving aimlessly around Jakarta in his blue Volkswagen beetle. I was rattling on about national identity. He looked over at me: 'Are you hungry?' As it happened, I was. 'Me too.' Within seconds we had pulled over at a pop-up street stall; a few minutes later we were sitting on a smooth palm-weave mat on the pavement with a freshly-made omelette and a glass of sweet ginger tea. I went back to my nationalist navel-gazing: why do so few Indonesians live overseas? One reason is that having studied or worked abroad carries great kudos in Indonesia; the social status and earning power it brings act as a magnet, pulling people home. But there's another reason too, suggested by Luwi as he dolloped shrimp chilli on his omelette and gave a contented wave at our impromptu midnight feast: 'How could you live without all this?'

Even Indonesians who are less contented with their lot, young men such as Anton the ojek driver, don't need to go overseas to look for a better life. Why bother, when there are plenty of places within your own country that provide opportunities almost as foreign? By drifting to another island, you can unlace the stays of place and clan, you can learn new dances and try new foods, without having to denude yourself completely in front of a foreign language, an unknown currency, an uncompromising police force.

✳

One thing that both unites and divides Indonesia is food. Every region has its own cuisine, but in the small towns in poor islands in which I spent the first months of my travels, the local fare was frustratingly difficult to sample. Only when I was invited into people's homes did I get to try papaya leaves with marsh weeds or sweetcorn and pumpkin mash. On the streets and in hole-in-the-wall restaurants, food is provided by a handful of itinerant tribes who have cooked their way across the nation. Most famously, the Minangkabau of West Sumatra who gave us nasi Padang, the cuisine named after their provincial capital.

The Minangkabau gave us the word most Indonesians use to describe migration: *merantau*. *Merantau* means to travel abroad to seek one's fortune. It's something Minangkabau men have always done. Until recently, several generations used to live together in large wooden houses whose walls slope outwards slightly, topped with a roof which sweeps up in a series of dramatic curves, like nested buffalo horns. These houses belong to women among the matrilineal Minangkabau. Young boys could live with their mother, but they had to move out when they grew up. After leaving mum's house, a young man had nowhere to go until he married and could move into his wife's house. The solution: to seek his fortune outside of West Sumatra.

The West Sumatrans conquered the nation one restaurant at a time, just as McDonald's conquered the United States, though without a corporation siphoning profits out of the pockets of hard-working family restaurateurs. Padang restaurants are signalled by a truncated version of the buffalo-horn roof, often sticking incongruously out from a row of flat-fronted shop-houses selling mobile phones or motorcycle parts. If there's no space for a curve of corrugated zinc, then they will at least have a Minang house logo painted on the window. The symbol is universally distributed across the nation, as recognizable as the Golden Arches to fast-food fans.

Padang restaurants have a subculture of their own. The cooking starts around dawn. By mid-morning, vats of food sit along the bottom shelf of the shop window. There will always be *rendang*, a stew of tough beef simmered for several hours with red chillies and coconut milk, until the liquid, spices and meat amalgamate into a stringy-tender whole. There will always be wilted cassava leaves or chunks of giant jackfruit swimming in a rich, coconutty sauce. But there will be dozens of other dishes too, many of them already portioned out onto small saucers which are stacked in pyramids on shelves above the vats. Shrimp cooked with the stink-beans which leave their pungent trace in later visits to the loo. Skinny aubergines in chilli paste. Lumpy brains floating in a thin grey sauce. Slabs of lung, fried to the texture of desiccated sponge. Boiled eggs, their peeled nakedness unevenly clothed in a gummy spice mix. Grilled fish, staring up through whited eyes. A whole dish of mulched green chillies. Not all of it is equally appetizing, but there will always be *something* that you like.

A lace curtain hangs behind the shelves to keep out hungry flies. In the bigger restaurants, a profusion of little dishes from behind the curtain simply appear on the table before you when you sit down, together with a coconut-shell-sized mound of rice. You pay for what you eat. In smaller places, customers just go up and choose for themselves. Takeaway is always possible: brown wax-paper cones of *nasi bungkus*, 'wrapped-up rice', are as common in Indonesia as sandwiches are in the West. And the food is safe for most Indonesians. The Minangkabau are strictly Islamic, so there's no question of anything that is not halal creeping into your nasi Padang, even if you are in a pig-slaughtering island like Sumba.

The Minang may have stamped their buffalo-horn iconography on hole-in-the-wall restaurants across Indonesia and pavement vendors from Java have the national franchise on fried tofu sewn up, but it is another itinerant tribe, the Sasak, that I always fall on with the greatest joy. The young Sasak men of Lombok, in the province of NTB (short for *Nusa Tenggara Barat* – West Nusa Tenggara), just east of Bali, have cornered the market in coconut juice across the whole sweep of Indonesia.

When you are hot, dehydrated and perhaps a little grumpy there is no sight more cheering that a pavement cart emblazoned, in letters cut from sticky neon-orange plastic, with 'ES KELAPA NTB', iced coconut water, NTB-style. The cart will be a bog-standard *kaki lima*: a wooden chest about two metres by one metre, usually painted in a lurid green or pink, topped with glass shelves that serve as a sort of shopfront, on which wobbly advertisements for the wares are stuck or painted. Es kelapa, fried tofu, barbecued satay, even nasi Padang, all can be found in this itinerant format. The whole structure is mounted on two large bicycle wheels. Sticking out of one end is a pair of handles by which it is pushed along the road, rather like a wheelbarrow. At the other end, a short wooden leg on which the cart is propped when it comes to rest. I like to think that the name of these carts – *kaki lima* or 'five feet' – comes from the two wheels, the wooden leg and the two legs of the itinerant trader who pushes his cart through the streets. Others, however, hold that the expression comes from a regulation that dates from Stamford Raffles' tenure as Lieutenant-Governor of Java during the brief British occupation of 1811–16, occasioned by the Napoleonic wars in Europe. Raffles decreed that all pavements had to be at least five feet wide. Because the carts sit on pavements, they absorbed the name.

These carts are ingeniously modified to suit most needs. Drawers, sliding shelves, built-in ice chests, on-board charcoal braziers or gas bottles, fold-out benches, pop-up umbrellas and pull-out awnings; each ambulant vendor has found his own way to minimize effort, maximize space and pull in the punters. Only the es kelapa boys have trouble, their wares too bulky to stow on board. So on the pavement next to them, or hidden behind a crumbling wall in an empty lot, sits a large mountain of green orbs, each waiting to be slashed open with a large machete, each eventually upended over a big beer-mug of ice, the jelly-flesh then scraped in fat white noodles into the glass, most often using a serrated bottle-cap nailed onto a stick of bamboo. A small ladle of reddish brown coconut sugar, a large dollop of condensed milk and the drink is complete.

The es kelapa boys are among the best-travelled Indonesians I know. They drift from island to island, from small town to small town. 'It never ceases to amaze me,' said one young Sasak man. 'There are coconuts all around, but the locals never think to sell them. Then one of us comes along, and we do a good business for two or three months. Finally, three or four locals decide that they can do it too, and then the market is saturated and we move on somewhere else.' Doesn't that mean that the window for itinerant sellers was getting smaller and smaller? 'Not at all. It's hard work, standing out here in the sun ten hours a day. The locals are too lazy to keep it going for long. They start selling only in the cool of the morning, or in the evening, but that's not when people are thirsty for es kelapa. So they start losing money, and they drop out. Then there's no es kelapa until another Sasak moves in.'

There are other tribal monopolies too. Barber shops across the nation are run by people from Madura, while women from Java have a lock on the sale of *jamu*, traditional medicine cooked up daily from roots and herbs. Boats are built by the Bugis of South Sulawesi; their schooners ruled the waves in both trading and piracy long before the Europeans arrived, and long afterwards too. Their close neighbours the Makassarese do well as traders, while the people of the once-proud sultanate of Buton, a hop across on the south-eastern limb of the truncated octopus that is Sulawesi, have always been traders of dried fish. The *merantau* tradition provides a sort of consistency across Indonesia. Anywhere I go, I will find nasi Padang and jamu Jawa, es kelapa NTB and a Maduran barber. Indeed, you could argue that the peculiarly predictable mix of these different ethnic specialities is the essence of Indonesia: 'Unity in Diversity' in action.

For 'Unity in Diversity' in the flesh, go no further than a Pelni passenger ferry. All life is here. Even the smallest ferries have a handful of cabins and a special dining room for the 'Class' passengers. On the economy decks – as many as five on them on the larger boats – plywood platforms are arranged in paired rows and divided down the middle by a few centimetres of metal above which teeters a luggage rack. On these platforms people spread their sarongs and sleeping mats, somehow respecting one another's territory in this so-public space.

The most common activity by far is sleeping, followed by just lolling around. People gossip, play cards, groom, massage one another. Children scream, everyone listens to tinny music on their cell phones and there's an awful lot of eating. The British naturalist Alfred Wallace, who spent twelve years shooting orang-utan and pinning down beetles in some of the most forlorn parts of the archipelago in the mid-nineteenth century, took one of the Dutch mail boats that were the precursors of today's Pelni. He described the food as follows:

> *At six A.M. a cup of tea or coffee is provided for those who like it. At seven to eight there is a light breakfast of tea, eggs, sardines, etc. At ten, Madeira, Gin and bitters are brought on deck as a whet for the substantial eleven o'clock breakfast, which differs from a dinner only in the absence of soup. Cups of tea and coffee are brought around at three P.M.; bitters, etc. again at five, a good dinner with beer and claret at half-past six, concluded by tea and coffee at eight. Between whiles, beer and sodawater are supplied when called for, so there is no lack of little gastronomical excitements to while away the tedium of a sea voyage.* *

These days, economy passengers can go to the pantry to collect their free meals three times a day – invariably a styrofoam box of gritty rice topped with overcooked cabbage leaves and the occasional lump of fish. Gin and bitters are sadly a thing of the past, but other 'little gastronomical excitements' are provided by ambulant stewards who tour the lower decks selling noodles, meatball soup and fluorescent sticky drinks in which swim

---

* Alfred Russel Wallace, *The Malay Archipelago: the land of the Orang-Utan, and the Bird of Paradise. A narrative of travel, with studies of man and nature.* London: Macmillan, 1869. Vol. 1, Chapter XIX.

green and pink worms of jelly. Even those are not enough; here a woman peels mangoes from her private store of food, there a family crunches through shrimp crackers or offers biscuits to their neighbours.

There is formal entertainment too. 'Ladies and gentlemen,' booms the inescapable tannoy, 'for your viewing pleasure, we're screening a romantic spy scandal starring the *beautiful* actress from Mandarin, Miss Beautiful Lingling Zhou. Please note, ladies and gentlemen, this *romantic* story of daring in the face of forbidden love is for *adults only*! Please join us in the mini-theatre, Deck 5, left-hand side. Just 10,000 rupiah.'* On the bigger boats, after the posh passengers have been fed, the First Class dining room is turned into a dance hall for the plebs. A band plays swing tunes behind a little square of parquet flooring, and passengers ('Couples only, please, dressed neatly and politely' enjoins the loudspeaker) can twirl around under the disco ball.

Strangers chat to one another with perfect ease. People swap stories of where they have been and where they are going, of exotic customs encountered in unfamiliar islands, of the foods and comforts of home, of incomprehensible pricing: in Bali they charge 30,000 for a kilo of sweet potatoes, imagine!

Almost every conversation starts off with the inevitable *dari mana*? – 'Where are you from?' Once tribal loyalties have been established, the teasing begins. 'I'd offer you some dried squid, but I know you Sundanese only eat leaves.' 'Oh, don't let him upset you. You know how Bataks are, always sooooooo rude . . .' 'Bugis, eh? Well, I'll watch out doing business with you, everyone knows how tricky you lot are!'

On Pelni ferries, most conversations are in Indonesian. They have to be, of course. A man from Maluku chats to a Timorese woman; there's an Acehnese talking to a West Sumatran; people

---

* For the duration of my trip, 2011–12, the rupiah hovered between 9,000 and 9,500 to the dollar, between 14,000 and 15,500 to the pound. While the book was being written, it crashed to 11,500 to the dollar, 18,000 to the pound. Conversions in this book are given for the time of travel.

from different parts of Papua are comparing notes on their time in Java. The national language is the only one these people have in common.

It's a funny one, Indonesian. Like many languages that evolved principally to ease negotiation in polyglot marketplaces, trading Malay/Indonesian is grammatically very simple. Instead of fussing with plurals, Indonesian just doubles up the noun. *Anak*: child; *anak anak* (often written *anak2*): children. There are no tenses; Indonesians just stick time words into the sentence to indicate past, present or future. 'I pay you yesterday,' or 'I pay you tomorrow.' It's also a very vague language, *besok* – 'tomorrow' – can mean the day after today, but it can also mean some unspecified time in the not-too-distant future.

The early nationalists chose Malay as the common language for the yet-to-be-created nation because it was easy to learn and already widely spoken, at least in the commercial realm. But there was also a more overtly political reason: it was not Javanese.

Most of the educated nationalists were Javanese speakers, and it would have been easy for them to adopt their mother tongue as the language for the new nation. It is a credit to them that they did not. Javanese is fiendishly complex; had it become the national language, Indonesians from other islands would have been at a permanent disadvantage. Javanese is also fiercely hierarchical; there are whole different vocabularies for talking to superiors and to inferiors. Sukarno and his cohort were at least rhetorically egalitarian; they did not want to entrench the feudalism which runs deeply through the culture of Java by spreading a class-conscious language nationwide. Sukarno delighted in being addressed as *Bung*, 'brother'. The paternalist Suharto, on the other hand, wanted to be called *Bapak*, 'father'.

Since independence, all schools have taught in Indonesian. Within a generation, almost all Indonesians spoke the national language; local languages persisted at home and crept into the marketplace, but I rarely heard them used in the public realm in either of my previous incarnations in Indonesia. That has changed, possibly because of a political decentralization which has reduced the number of outsiders in the civil service and puffed up local pride. In late 2011, on the verandas and in the coffee-stalls of NTT, in the market and the village head's office and even in some schoolyards, the chatter was in any one of the province's seventy-six local languages, not in Indonesian.

When I stepped onto a Pelni ship, a little floating Indonesia dependent on the national language, I could suddenly eavesdrop on almost every conversation. Most of them, I found, had a sub-text. Passengers were either off to seek their fortune, or on their way home after trying to make their mark in the wider world.

Those going 'home' had the swagger of success or spoke in muted tones that betrayed disappointment. If they were on their way to a new life, people fizzed with optimism and apprehension. Often, an uncle or an older sister had gone before; the newbie would be met off the boat, they would have somewhere to go. Still, it is a big step for people who have never lived outside the cocoon of the village, with its clear hierarchy, its well-known rules. When they stepped off the boat they would have to be more Indonesian than ever before. And they would probably be relieved to find that at their destination, too, they would be able to buy nasi Padang.

Off the eastern tip of Flores hang a number of small islands that rise dry and lumpy from the sea; life there depends largely on what people can fish out of the waters. On a smallish local ferry that makes the rounds of these islands, I met Mama Lina. She had the stolid, sago-fed build of the women of eastern Indonesia and she had tried to tame her frizzy hair straight with waffle irons; the look was matronly, but not unkind. She had been at a teacher training workshop in Flores and was returning home to the island of Adonara. 'Why don't you come home with me?' she had asked, and I had just said yes.

Mama Lina clapped her hands with excitement, but as the journey progressed, she became more and more flustered. What will this white woman eat? Where will she sleep? Don't white people use those odd toilets you can sit on? She started managing my expectations, perhaps even trying to put me off. There's no electricity in the village you know, there's no running water. But I had got on the round-robin ferry without even deciding which island I was headed for; I was thrilled to have a plan, and was not to be dissuaded.

Mama Lina's village is one of the most isolated in Adonara, sitting high on the slopes of the volcano. A concrete path leaps straight up the side of the volcano from the main road, the incline so steep that motorbike passengers have to press themselves up against the driver to avoid sliding off backwards. Since there was just one motorbike taxi hanging around at the bottom of the path, Mama Lina sent me on ahead. Where the concrete path came to an abrupt full stop and I was unceremoniously unloaded from the bike, a clutch of women sat gossiping. They stopped in mid-sentence and looked at me with wide eyes. I greeted them cheerily, commenting on the gathering rain clouds. It was as though a dog had just trotted up and started chatting about the weather. They continued to stare, unable to muster a response. Then Mama Lina arrived on another bike; she explained me with a curt 'My friend. She'll be staying for a while' and bustled her trophy guest off home with no further explanation, leaving them speechless still.

We scrambled as quickly as we could up a path that wound between wooden houses, but the clouds were ahead of us; the first, fat raindrops plopped down and we sought refuge with Lina's in-laws. Within minutes the rain was drumming down so hard that we had to forgo the niceties of introductions. Mama Lina's sister-in-law made coffee while Lina and I collected the rainwater that now gushed from the corrugated tin roof in determined rivulets. We'd position cooking pots under one or other of the individual streams, then reposition them as the wind blew the water out sideways. 'Look, that stream's bigger,' pointed out the sister-in-law, and we would shift one of the pots. 'Over here, over here.' More shifting. It seemed a haphazard way of collecting water in a mountainside village that had no well.

By the time it stopped raining it was getting dark. 'Sorry, no lights,' Mama Lina had repeated, and we slip-slid the rest of the way to her house through the mud by the light of my torch.

I was a little surprised, then, to see a satellite dish next to a papaya tree in the garden, and a TV in the inner sanctum of the house. The village, it turned out, had a communal generator. By common consent this was prodded into life every evening at an hour set by TV programming executives in Jakarta, a whole time zone away. As the lights came on and the television sprang to life, random neighbours would wander into Mama Lina's house, spread palm-weave *tikar* mats on the floor and flop down with the family for an act of collective worship at the altar of the *sinetron*.

The sinetron, or soap opera, has come a long way since Suharto first allowed his daughter to fill time on her newly minted TV station with imported Mexican telenovelas in the early 1990s. Dozens of locally made tales of intrigue, back-stabbing and redemption now compete for viewers and advertising dollars. The storylines are hackneyed but strangely compelling. Will Ricky's DNA test show that his love for Indra is incestuous, or is his mother not the beacon of probity he imagined? What about Siti's feckless husband – could he really prefer that simpering schoolgirl to his dutiful wife?

Stories of virtuous country cousins bewildered by the wicked ways of the city-slicker relatives invariably unfold in the upholstered sitting rooms of marbled houses. There's also a fair bit of slamming of car doors and storming off into the night, illuminated by the window-glitter of Jakarta's high rises. Curiously, the cars are never stuck in one of the three-hour traffic jams that eat up the lives of people who live in off-screen Jakarta. None of the characters lives in a hut cobbled together from plywood and old election banners on the banks of one of the city's stinking canals. No one ever pays a bribe to fix their residency papers, gets shaken down by a cop or a judge, or rushes a teenager to hospital because they've been wounded in one of the endless running wars between rival high schools.

Needless to say, the soaps are peppered with adverts. As I sat on the floor having eaten rice and dried fish for the sixth meal in a row, I wondered what Mama Lina and her friends made of these paeans to skin-whiteners and hair-enhancers, to ads for internet-ready tablets and quick breaks in Bangkok.

Some of the products advertised were, in fact, available in Adonara. Indomarets may not yet be universal across Indonesia, but the roadside kiosk certainly is, usually a slightly wobbly-looking wooden or bamboo shed with a small window carved out of the front. Hanging from a wire strung along the top of the window are strips of single-serving coffee powders in red and gold packaging, colourful sachets of hair gel, shampoo, washing powder, peanuts, almost anything else that can easily be divided into tiny portions. On the window sill there will be a little pile of betel nut and a pyramid of mangoes from the tree in the garden, perhaps, but also a tin of kreteks that you can buy by the stick. The Indonesian retail market has always been dominated by things sold in tiny quantities – a hangover from a time when a whole bottle of shampoo or jar of coffee would eat up more cash than people had handy.

Did Mama Lina and her friends think that a sachet of shampoo might smooth their crinkly hair into Sunsilky cascades? Did they aspire to become smiling mums turning Indomie noodles into sophisticated Western-looking dishes, served up to an adoring husband and two squeaky-clean kids who all eat together, using forks and 'sitting *at a table*!!!'?

This last note of astonishment came from a friend who knows what meals are like outside of Jakarta's middle-class bubble: the alpha male of the household is usually served first, most often sitting on the floor. Older children and teenagers grab food whenever they feel like it, carrying it off into a corner where they can play with their cell phones. Everyone eats with their hands except kids. It's a bit of an acquired skill, moulding together a little cone of rice between the thumb and the first three fingers of your right hand, then using that as a spoon to scoop up some sauce, a bit of chilli, a fragment of salt-fish. Once

I had acquired it, though, I began to agree with the contention of many Indonesians that food just tastes better eaten with the hands. The smaller kids are spoon-fed until they are five or six, usually by female relatives who follow them around the house or the yard, dolloping food into their mouths as best they can. Adult women scoop up the scraps left when everyone else has had their fill, often while watching the ads that sing of an 'Indonesia' that bears little resemblance to the one they themselves live in.

Even the actors come in a different flavour, not the *hitam manis* ('black with sugar') of dark-skinned Adonara, but *kopi susu*, 'milky coffee' – mixed-race Indonesian and European. These pale, rich people, ill-mannered and selfish, are what many people in other islands now think of as typical of urban Java. Suharto's satellite, his great project for national unity, is now delivering up images of the rich for the viewing pleasure of those who can only dream of riches. And those viewers are lapping it up, rather as a hungry urchin might stand on tiptoes in a snowy street to peek in at a family having a slap-up meal in front of a roaring fire. Then the daily fuel ration for the generator runs out and everyone troops off to bed by the light of a kerosene lamp.

On the one hand, the disconnect between *sinetron* Indonesia and village Indonesia might drive a wedge between city and country, between rich, Sunsilky pale and poor, crinkly dark. On the other hand, the *sinetron* expose tens of millions of people to hours of the national language every day. On top of that, the pap drama and game shows are interspersed with some news programmes that tell of goings-on in other islands. For all their sense of local identity, villagers now discover that they have much in common with Indonesians across the land; it's not just their own district head who is on trial for corruption, school rooms are collapsing in Sumatra as well as Papua, other farmers are also wondering how to spend the income from rising cocoa prices.

It wasn't all lounging around watching TV at Mama Lina's. Now that the rains had started, it was planting time. We each took a sharpened stick, stabbed it into the ground in the most easily accessible spots, tossed in a couple of dried maize kernels, kicked the earth over with our feet, moved on. It seemed impossible to me that the earth would reward our paltry effort with something edible, but Mama Lina texted me a couple of months later to report that she was cooking the maize I had planted.

My farming duties were not over. 'You're coming with me to the *kebun* get food for the pigs,' declared Lina's aunt Susannah, a graceful lady with white hair and smooth skin. She obviously used her Indonesian rarely: it came careful and correct from where her front teeth should be, and spoke of improbable things. She didn't know her exact age, but thought she was 'about 200'. She slung Lina's youngest on one hip; the hefty three-year-old wanted to come with us but was just too stubborn to walk. Then the old lady balanced an unsheathed machete on her head, and set off on a vertical course up the mountainside. '*Kebun*' is a vague word – it can mean anything from plantation to flower garden, from farm to back yard – so I wasn't sure what to expect. In this case it turned out to be a patch of tangled vegetation a couple of kilometres further up the slope, full of good things, though not obviously planted or tended.

Lina's two other children came too. The boy, bright, smiley and fond of geography, would climb a tree, pick a mango, throw it half-eaten to the ground because he needed his hands for catapulting. When he got peckish again, he would just climb another tree. The girl, with whom I had been sharing a bed, was in her monosyllabic post-pubescent phase; her purpose was to get high enough up the mountain to get a signal on her cell phone so that she could check Facebook.

Mama Susannah was absolutely tireless on the way to the *kebun*, but once we got to the family plot we did a lot of resting. We'd pick some cassava leaves, then sit down and eat a mango. Dig up a cassava root, then break for a bit of *jambu air* or rose-apple, a crunchy, bell-shaped fruit that hung in great clusters on the trees overhead. '*Istirahat dulu*,' she would say every few minutes. 'Take a rest first.' The cassava leaves were to feed to the pigs.

'Can't we have some too?' I asked. We had not eaten anything green in two days; indeed I'd barely had any fresh vegetables in weeks. Though plants seemed to spring out of the ground with no husbanding at all, many Indonesians, especially in the eastern islands, seem to feel that green vegetables are not real food. The result is that fertile Indonesia has astoundingly high levels of malnutrition. According to the Ministry of Health, more than a quarter of children under five in Indonesia are anaemic and 11.5 million Indonesian kids of that age – well over a third of the total nationwide – are significantly shorter than they should be for their age. Once I'd expressed an interest in eating pig food, however, Mama Susannah did show me how to pick the leaves tender enough for us; the ones whose stems had not yet toughened from green to red.

When we had finished working and resting, the 200-year-old balanced a cassava root about the size of a grown man's leg on her head, then heaved a sack of pig-leaves on top of that in preparation for the journey back down to the village. I carried a smaller sack of people-leaves and the stubborn three-year-old, and the three-year-old carried the unsheathed machete. Long before we finished the two-kilometre hike back to the village, I began to see that *istirahat dulu* was perhaps not such a bad way of maintaining your strength for the long haul.

Would we have had a better maize crop if we had been more methodical, chosen better seeds, spaced the plants more systematically, dug and refilled the holes more carefully? Probably. But if we could meet the family's maize needs with just fifteen minutes of stab, toss, kick, stab, toss, kick, what would be the point of doing more?

It's not that Mama Lina has no aspirations. She herself spent four years working as a housemaid in Malaysia; her cousin put in eight years. They got up at 4 a.m., worked until 10 a.m., rested until 3, then cooked and served supper. Room and board were given free, so the salary of US$90 a month went straight into their pockets. It is six times what Mama Lina now earns as a part-time teacher. But neither wants to go back. It's a question of what life-coaches would call 'work-life balance'. 'Here, there's no salary, but there's free food in the garden,' said the cousin. 'I can work when I feel like it, sleep when I don't. It's great.'

Ironically, the trek to drudgery in Malaysia has probably done more to foster pan-Indonesian nationalism than almost anything in the post-Suharto era.

The entrenched antagonism between giant Indonesia and its smallish northern neighbour is in part a hangover from President Sukarno's anti-Malaysia grandstanding of the early 1960s. And in part it's good, old-fashioned envy.

When Malaysia finally got shot of Britain in 1957, the country was on a par economically with Indonesia, which had by then been independent for over a decade. By 2011 Malaysia earned over three times more per person than Indonesia. And – here's where Malaysia's perceived superiority creeps into the consciousness of people even in the remotest parts of Indonesia – Malaysians are spending lots of that extra cash importing people like Mama Lina from deepest Adonara to sweep floors and tap rubber. Between 2006 and 2012 an annual average of 150,000 Indonesians travelled to Malaysia to work on official government-registered programmes, and many thousands more did so illegally. 'It's just embarrassing,' I would hear over and over, sometimes from people who were living on money sent back from relatives in Malaysia.

Nothing gets Indonesia's Facebook millions chattering more quickly than an attempt, real or imagined, to claim that batik, or spicy beef rendang, or even some obscure regional dance, originated with Malays that live on the right-hand side of the straights of Malacca (the bit that is now called Malaysia), rather than on the left (Sumatra, part of Indonesia). Their outrage is ironic, given that Sukarno laid notional claim to the whole of Malaysia based on the fact that the culture of the region was indivisible, but it is real nonetheless. Just in the months I was wandering the islands, young Indonesians felt the need to burn

Malaysia's flag, stone its embassy and/or send the #IhateMalaysia hashtag soaring up the Twitterboard at least three times because, they thought, those upstart Malaysians were laying claim to some of Indonesia's cultural icons.

On Monday morning, Mama Lina pulled on her beige teacher's uniform and we careened off down the volcano on the family motorbike; Lina's foot was slammed down on the brake the whole way, but gravity was the greater force. It was not yet six in the morning when she dumped me at the dock of a tiny fishing village, told me she'd text me when she needed money to replace the roof of her house, hugged me goodbye, and sped off.

Also waiting for the rickety wooden boat that crossed once a week to the neighbouring island of Lembata was a group of women wearing jilbabs. They sat surrounded by big woven baskets of dried fish and desiccated squid. The 'salt-fish ladies', Mama Lina had called them.

I'm not a morning person (inconvenient in a nation that tends to rise before dawn), so I kept my good mornings to a minimum and sat quietly, reading a book. The salt-fish ladies were definitely not quiet. They were not speaking Indonesian but they were clearly talking about me, and the discussion was growing heated. Finally, when one of them jabbed my nose, I was forced to engage. 'What is it, Mama?' I ask of the jabber. 'Ya, we're confused. We don't know if you are a Westerner or a Javanese.'

I couldn't help but laugh. I asked which side she came down on. '*I* think because of your long nose, you must be a Westerner. But they think that because of the way you talk and act, you must be from Java.'

These ladies were originally from Buton, the sultanate off the south-eastern tip of Sulawesi that produces a disproportionate number of the nation's fish traders. These Muslims had replanted themselves in the soil of Catholic Adonara; over several generations the Butonese have built villages and have invested their capital here. They are in Adonara but not really of it. 'They'll sell us food, but they'd never share a meal with us,' said Mama Lina, laughing. 'They're scared we'd feed them pork.'

These women speak Butonese at home, and when they sally forth in their jilbabs to sell salt-fish and cream biscuits to the people of Adonara, they use Indonesian. In lots of ways, they are emblematic of what it means to be Indonesian. And yet when they were speculating about my nose, they wondered if I was Western or Javanese. To these ladies who live not all that far from the geographical centre of the nation, Java-foreign was every bit as foreign as Western-foreign. The concept of 'Indonesian' was not even in play.

As I put-putted across to the island of Lembata with the salt-fish ladies and their dried squid, I began to wonder whether I was trying to write a book about a country that has ceased to exist.

Map C: EAST NUSA TENGGARA PROVINCE (NTT) AND THE SOUTHWEST OF MALUKU

5

The Emperor is Far Away

At Lembata's only bus station, I found the usual crop of Terminal Crocodiles, young men who have nothing to do but hang around transport centres, leaping on new arrivals and offering them motorcycle taxi rides, accommodation, anything that country folk might need when arriving in the Big City. In Lembata they are really only Crocodiles-in-Training, pale imitations of the boys in the provincial capital Kupang, who turn their bemo minibuses into rolling temples of rap and who set national standards for loutage. Still, this outpost offered a betel chewer in a 'Punks Not Dead' T-shirt, an anarchist, and a young man who wore his Liverpool jersey cut off below the pecs, showing a stretch of taut brown torso above low-slung cut-off jeans. Their fashion sense was imported on a roundabout route from the Bronx, the über-bling crosses on big-ass chains once so favoured in the 'hood here replaced with plastic rosary beads bought from the many Jesus shops that dot this predominantly Christian region.

Each had a variation on the all-important lout haircut. This is common to Terminal Crocodiles throughout Indonesia, a sort of elaborate mullet in which a spiky central column towers over close-cut sides (often with a pattern shaved into it), before squibbing into a wispy pig-tail at the nape. This look is particularly fetching in the sub-species *Crocodilus Timoriensis* because the young men of NTT, of Timor, Lembata and the like, are ethnically Melanesian and so have frizzy hair. Which means that no matter how much gel they use, the centre strip of the

117

mullet coagulates into a mass of curls that wobbles inelegantly over the sides, while the pig-tail twists in a satisfyingly pig-taily sort of way. As a bonus, attempts to dye the central reservation blond often stall at just that orangey-brown colour that is a symptom of malnutrition.

Eventually, a construction truck fitted with benches pulled up at the bus station and one of the louts nodded at it. It was the bus to Lamalera, already thudding out rap songs encouraging us to do unmentionable things to close relatives. I grabbed pole position, the place nearest the open back of the truck. It was furthest from the boom box and most likely to get some breeze and provide a view. We drove around town for an hour or two in search of passengers. The benches filled up and a bouquet of baggage flowered on the floor between us: potted plants, a piglet, a large stack of plastic chairs. On the chairs were enthroned two large trays of eggs; perilously close to the giant speakers, rattling menacingly with each throb of the bass line.

Eventually we left town and tarmac behind and lurched uphill, bamboo and long grass whipping our backs through the open sides of the truck. There were eleven people folded onto the bench opposite me and perhaps as many on my side, limbs pressed into odd angles against the baggage mountain. In the heavy air of noon, neither the discomfort nor the thudding music was enough to keep my fellow passengers from Indonesia's national pastime: sleep. Within minutes, every single one of them dozed, mouth open, head lolling. Each slumped domino-like onto the person downhill from them, piling finally on to the person right at the back. On my side, that was me.

After three or four hours, we crested a shrivelled brown hill and saw the village of Lamalera clinging to the shore below us, positively Mediterranean-looking. In a shrine on the hilltop, the Blessed Virgin Mary stood above a plaster whale. The village was festooned with drying flesh. Lamalera specializes in catching whales and dolphins – it was this that had brought me here. I had arrived two days after their biggest catch of the year: six sperm whales in one go, about thirty-six tonnes of meat. Every available clothes line, every bamboo rack, every metal pipe was garlanded with strips of whale meat. It hung between the remnants of other hunts: turtle shells pendulous on bamboo walls, dolphin jaws baring their razor teeth in casual piles beside a well. It looked as though the devil had got into the specimen cupboard of the Convention on International Trade in Endangered Species, multiplied its contents, and tossed them around the village.

From the fat yellow steaks of drying meat, oil dripped into corrugated zinc gutters and was channelled into sawn-off water bottles. On the beach, a gently rippling sea teased a giant spine back and forth. Lashed to a rock, a skull washed about, covered still with blackened flesh. Ribs reared higher than my head out of the dark sand. The whole town smelled of stale sex. And I was served whale meat for supper every day for four days.

I stayed with the widow of a local schoolmaster. On the wall was a whale map, like the posters that map the cuts of beef in a butcher's shop, showing who gets what when a beast is caught. This part goes to the eldest male in the clan of the person who harpooned the whale. That part goes to the clan of the boat owner. There are bits that go to descendants of the first clans in the village, other bits for the carpenter who maintains the boat, for the boat manager, and many others. All of these people will then divvy up their chunk; after a big hunt, virtually every family in the village gets something. The first person to spot a pod of whales shouts 'Baleo!' This cry is a hangover from the days in the sixteenth century when Portugal ruled these waves, spreading Catholicism, DNA and commercial mayhem in about equal measure. It sends virtually every able-bodied man in town rushing to the boats that while away the days under thatched roofs all along the beach.

The boats are between fifteen and twenty metres long, banged together out of heavy wooden planks. It's hard work just launching them down a sandy beach over rough-hewn bits of wood, especially if the able-bodied men have been frittering away their day in Lamalera's other male pastime: drinking palm wine straight from plastic jerrycans. Breathless adventure-travel rags give the impression that these men, eight or ten to a boat, power down on their quarry in a flash of paddles. My personal favourite, a *Daily Mail* feature from 2007 entitled 'The stone-age whale hunters who kill with their bare hands', informs us that they also use sails woven from gebang leaves and that 'each vessel is hand-made, with no nails or metal parts'. In fact, water wells energetically into the boats where nails have rusted away, and much of the whalers' time is spent fiddling with overused and underpowered outboard motors.

I happened to be on the beach when a group of hunters were heading out; they invited me along. Clouds frowned over an already angry sea. The boat was heavy, so heavy that the boys had to recruit some collateral drinkers to help launch it. We were ten people, six harpoons, and one rusty 25-horsepower engine.

The youngest of the whalers and I were on bailing duty more or less constantly, a task complicated by the fact that my half-jerrycan of a bailer had a large crack in it, so that as much water slopped back into the boat as slopped out each time I scooped. Along one side of the boat, raised on a couple of cleft sticks, were bamboo poles an ungainly four or five metres long. When the hunt was on, a vicious metal arrowhead shaped like a tight-angled number 7 would be attached to the end of the poles with a great length of rope. Until then the weapons lay coiled menacingly in the bottom of the boat. The Chief Harpoonist stood on a platform at the upturned bow. Most of the others stood not far behind, scanning the horizon for a whale's telltale spout. We saw no whales, but as we sighted the graceful arcs of a school of dolphin on the move everyone went completely silent. Elaborate hand signals took over from the teasing and gossiping of just seconds before. This despite the racket of a rusty outboard motor gasping to keep a heavy boatload of hunters moving through a rising sea.

The Chief Harpoonist took up his position, a perfect yoga Warrior Two, except that in this case what looked like an arm extended over his bent front leg was actually his harpoon, ready to be unleashed. But it's hard to spot a dolphin in a sea wine-darkened by the glowering sky. And the dolphins weren't helping. Though they could easily bolt away from us, they criss-crossed in front of the Warrior, flicking his attention first left, then right, then far right, then centre left, until he didn't know which way to look and he raised his harpoon straight up to the sky in defeat. I confess that I was not overly thrilled at the idea of having to bail diluted dolphin blood out of the boat as our catch was butchered at my feet. But as the hunt went on I grew less soppy. To get caught on a day like today, a dolphin would have to leap into a high arc directly in front of the Warrior and push the slow-motion button on itself as it breached the water to give the drunken harpoonist time to focus. Any dolphin that we took home that day had no place in the gene pool.

All this spotting, half-chasing, giving up was exhausting. The boys decided to take a break, just as the worst of the storm clouds rolled towards us. They switched off the engine, smoked tobacco folded into palm leaves and munched on bananas, unworried that we were drifting towards an obvious reef. At first I wasn't all that worried either: I had long ago put my camera in the 'dry bag', a bamboo tube with a tight-fitting cover of palm leaves. But as the whitecaps started to crash over my legs into the half-bailed boat bottom, I ventured a suggestion. 'Shall I put down the anchor to keep us off the reef?' 'Anchor? We don't have an anchor,' came the reply. We spent another few hours drifting, chasing dolphins, smoking, motoring around in apparently random circles, then went home, soaked and empty-handed.

Later, chatting with a couple of the whale hunters, I showed photos of the red plastic kayak that I like to paddle in the Atlantic, off the west coast of Ireland. I said that I often saw dolphins from my boat, and sometimes even a whale, but I wasn't allowed to hunt them. 'What, because you are a woman alone in a boat?' No, because it's forbidden.

'Oh right, it's that thing, those people – there's a word for it, isn't there? What's the word?' said the other bailer. '*Konservasi*,' prompted his friend. 'Yes, yes, that Conservation thing!'

For my part, I don't feel the maritime mammal population is too greatly threatened by a village full of people who get drunk and go out in leaky boats with no anchor and holes in their bailers and who don't throw a harpoon a single time in a six-hour trip through water roiling with dolphins because the effort of pulling the harpoon in again exceeds the likelihood of success. Perhaps they were less motivated than usual because of the vast catch of a few days previously. Because the fact is, they *do* catch whales, between eight and twelve a year on average. In the decade they've been using outboard motors they catch lots of dolphin too – my own band of drunks walked up the beach with dripping chunks of seven of those the very next day.

This makes some Western NGOs cross, and Western NGOs make emotive YouTube videos about the slaughter of dolphins and whales in places like Lembata. They demand that people stop eating tuna canned in Indonesia, because the country isn't dolphin friendly. This in turn makes the central government cross: in response to a video posted just a few months before I visited Lembata, the Ministry of Maritime Affairs and Fisheries in Jakarta called a press conference. They accused the dolphin-huggers of undercover protectionism, attempting to keep tuna canned in Indonesia out of European and American supermarkets.

'It is not true [that dolphins and whales are hunted in Indonesia]. How could that be? I have never heard of dolphins being hunted before,' the Director of Fish Resources told journalists. 'Local people consider them as man's best friends, so they would not go after them, let alone eat or use their meat as bait.'

These days, it's perfectly plausible that the Director of Fish Resources, sitting in Jakarta, had no idea at all what 'local people' do, especially in Lembata where you can only make a phone call by holding the trunk of a particularly tall cashew tree at the top of the village which seems to act as a natural antenna.

The chains of command so carefully wrought by Suharto – chains that passed the will of the capital's bureaucrats down to the villages and sucked resources and information back to the centre – have, during The Reformation, been shattered. And the shattering is deliberate. It was largely the idea of President Habibie, who stepped into Suharto's shoes when the Old Man threw in the towel in 1998. Decentralization was a reaction to Indonesia's loss of East Timor.

Blindsided by Jakarta's crushing defeat, Habibie was forced to wonder what implications East Timor's referendum on independence might have for the rest of the country. Lots of other regions felt they had been slighted by the Suharto oligarchy. In islands that were made of nickel and copper, that sat above pools of oil and gas, or that were once covered in precious hardwoods, the universal rhetoric was that Jakarta was sucking riches out from under local feet, and was using the treasure to develop Java. Yes, nearly 60 per cent of the population is squeezed into the single island of Java, but that still left a hundred million citizens in other islands. To add insult to injury, Jakarta had for years sent Javanese governors and Javanese troops to stamp on any sign of protest at this injustice.

Habibie, himself from the eastern island of Sulawesi, knew that Java could not continue to dominate the other 13,465 islands so completely if the nation was to survive in a more democratic form. That meant more power to the provinces.

But there was the dilemma: several provinces, including oil-rich Aceh in Indonesia's far west and mineral-rich Papua in its far east, were *so* cross that they might just try to follow East Timor's example and cut loose from Indonesia entirely. Better cut the provinces out of it and give power directly to the districts, Habibie reasoned. Then no single district would be strong enough to make a break for it.

Astoundingly, he made this decentralization happen. At a stroke, in the space of just eighteen months, the world's fourth most populous nation and one of its most centralized burst apart to become one of its most decentralized. The centre still takes care of defence, fiscal policy, foreign relations, religious affairs, justice and planning. But everything else – health, education, investment policy, fisheries and a whole lot more – was handed over to close to 300 district 'governments', whose only experience of governing had, until then, been to follow orders from Jakarta.

As regional Big Men began to realize what this meant, they lobbied for more districts. The result is like watching one of those glorious fireworks that blossom into a giant flower, and then burst again, right and left, into a series of smaller golden showers. In fact Indonesians even use the word 'blossoming', *pemekaran*, to describe the administrative shattering of the nation. Since Suharto resigned, the country has added another ten provinces; by the time I finished my wanderings in Indonesia in late 2012, the number of districts had increased by 70 per cent, blossoming to 509.

I had walked into the Ministry of Health in Jakarta just at the start of Indonesia's administrative fragmentation in 2001. At first, everyone in the ministry carried on as usual. We wrote guidelines and trained provincial staff, we talked to the planning ministry and lobbied parliament. Sitting happily in our air-conditioned offices in Jakarta, working with people in the provinces that my colleagues had known since before the firework display, we behaved as though decentralization didn't exist. And for a while, until districts began to assume the responsibilities that had been thrust upon them, decentralization didn't really make that much difference to the way the country was run.

The big change came after 2004, when citizens began to elect their district head or *bupati* directly.★ It was then that local politicians really began to flex their muscles, to introduce bold initiatives that may not line up with what Jakarta wanted, but that would go down well with the local electorate.

To this day, the central government ministries in Jakarta continue to behave as though they are in charge, but the disconnect between what comes out of the capital and what goes on in the districts is growing more pronounced.

★ A *bupati* is the head of a largely rural district, known as a *kabupaten*. Urban districts are known as *kota*, and are headed by a *walikota* or mayor. When I am speaking in general terms rather than about a specific individual, bupati can be assumed also to refer to walikota.

It was perfectly possible that the Director of Fish Resources was surprised to hear of dolphin slaughter in far-off islands. In response, Jakarta fired off a new injunction against killing the animals, underlining laws passed in 1975, 1990 and 1995. This they sent down through the ministerial hierarchy. Because Lamalera was named in the video, they must have made a special effort to get district officials in Lembata island to take note. But when officials in the district capital, Lewoleba, started muttering about national regulations, the people of the whaling village shut them up.

'They tried to do that conservation thing here a few months back,' said one of the hunters. 'But the whole village went to Lewoleba to demonstrate. The local government didn't have the balls to enforce [the new rules], so nothing came of it.'

Every day, before the sinetron, the national news now shows images of angry Indonesians massing in front of a government office, waving placards and venting. *Turun demo*, to go down to the streets and demonstrate, seems to be the Indonesian electorate's default mechanism for expressing its demands. But demos have become something of an industry, too. Brokers deliver up crowds to order, supplying readymade banners and briefing protestors on the gripe of the day. The demos sometimes run for days, often getting out of hand. Cars get overturned, buildings get burned down, sometimes the police are called in and people get beaten up, even shot.

'It's Democracy by way of Anarchy,' the retired director of a state company told me. But for most Indonesians, these raucous expressions of desire and dissent seem to beat the buttoned-down obedience to Jakarta of the Suharto years.

As I continued on my travels, I came to recognize the signs of a new district. From the boat, an island appears, fuzzy on the horizon. After a while, the cell-phone towers come into view, piercing the sky from the highest points. Then, as the boat steams towards land, a white smudge appears on a hill above the port. It looms into a palatial building, often with a princeling palace at its side. These are the Office of the Bupati and the District Parliament, respectively, often wildly out of whack with the size of the population. In one district in southern Maluku, for example, I calculated that the bupati's office had one front-facing sea-view window for every 441 residents of the district. This is not the office of the district government – each department has its own sizeable building – this is just for the elected head of the district.

I came to know that when I went up the hill to the bupati's office, I would find in front of it two lovely, smooth strips of asphalt, the only divided highway in town, sometimes the only smooth asphalt in town. Occasionally, there were added extras. In Anakalang, the capital of Central Sumba district, a spur of road smooth as a black billiard table branches off the dual carriageway and sweeps through a village of megalithic graves, pot-bellied children and pot-bellied pigs to stop, abruptly, right outside the door of the current Bupati's childhood home. 'A gift from the contractor,' said one of the uniformed adjutants who was washing the SUV parked outside the door of the house.

It takes a while for some previously raggedy market town to dress itself in the finery of a District Capital. Savu, the tiny island between Sumba and Timor that I visited after the whale hunt, was still in its Cinderella phase as a new district.

I was chatting with a group of civil servants outside the district hospital when a black SUV bowled through the gates. The beige uniforms leapt upright, stamping out cigarettes, pushing coffee cups out of sight. One of them tugged at my elbow to get me out of my chair and into the guard of honour. The car shuddered to a halt just inches from my nose and a good-looking young man in a snappy black uniform jumped out of the front passenger seat and sprang to open the back door. Slowly, as if he were the *capo dei capi* in a mafia movie, the Bupati of Savu stepped out. Our hastily assembled guard of honour clicked its heels, saluted and shouted something military-sounding. The Bupati, resplendent in a silk *ikat* shirt, golden badge of office glowing on his chest, clicked his own heels in acknowledgement. Through glasses that misted up as he left the air-conditioned bubble of his car, he spotted me. He shook my hand without a word, and swept into the air-conditioned bubble of his office.

Savu was crowned a district in 2008. According to a newspaper I picked up on a boat, it was the poorest district in Indonesia.* Two-thirds of households in Savu don't even make it to Prosperity Level I, the lowest of Indonesia's four wealth classifications; they are, in the government's delicious phrase, 'pre-prosperous'.

I remembered Savu from a visit many moons ago as a dry, desolate place where women wove beautiful *ikat* cloth and men chanted as they swayed in the tops of lontar palm trees collecting sap. *Ikat* is often translated as 'tie dye', but Indonesia's *ikat* fabrics have nothing in common with the ringworm T-shirts of the Woodstock generation. With *ikat* weaving, the pattern is died into the threads themselves, before the fabric is woven. A pattern which was visible only in the mind of a the woman who laid out threads, tied them in clusters, dyed them one colour, re-tied, re-dyed in another colour, emerges, as if by magic, when the threads are actually woven together on a back-strap loom. It can take several months to finish an especially elaborate piece.

In the hungry months before the corn harvest, the weavers were sustained by palm sap, boiled down into syrup. When last I visited, the syrup accounted for two out of three meals a day for many people in Savu. But now the main town, Seba, was a district capital. 'It's absolutely bustling these days,' a coffee-stall owner in Sumba had told me. He himself was from Savu but had left because business was too slow. He used to drive one of the six minibuses that constituted virtually all the motorized transport on the island last time I was there.

In 2011, three years after becoming a district, there were packs of brand-new motorbikes, a steady procession of the yellow

---

* In fact, several districts can lay claim to this title, depending on which measure of poverty is used. While Savu scores poorest on every one of these measures in the province of NTT, there are some pretty desolate pockets scattered among the mineral riches in Papua, as well as in Maluku.

lorries that speak of government-funded construction contracts, and a handful of flashy SUVs, almost all of them with the red number plates that signal government functionaries. There was a post office, still announcing its postcode as Kupang, the district from which Savu split. There were a handful of open-fronted shops along the two blocks that constitute downtown Seba. At the end of the road, the pier.

It was from here, two decades ago, that I had given up waiting for a 'scheduled' ferry that never came and persuaded the captain of a Bugis cargo schooner to take me across to Flores. I slept on the deck of this majestic wooden boat, regularly misted with spray like lettuce in a posh greengrocers, startled awake every now and then by the slap of a flying fish on deck, reassured by the crackling glow of the crew's kreteks. When we arrived, the captain said he had no landing permit. I jumped overboard, and kicked my way ashore, glad of the lifesaving classes that had taught me to swim while holding packages above the waterline. When I reached the beach, I hailed a passing minibus with seaweed still sticking to my clothes. Now, ferries came in to Seba almost every week. There was even a new ferry terminal with a blue-tiled roof, another ubiquitous sign of 'progress' in the outer islands.

But 'absolutely bustling'? Not yet.

I went back to the place I had stayed in 1991, the home of the local schoolmaster, now long retired. I remembered it because his wife had been unusually insistent that I register in her book, ruled into tidy columns: date, name, nationality, passport number, religion. She had hovered by my shoulder as I filled it in, tense, expectant. KATOLIK, I wrote in the last column and she gave an audible puff of relief. She would not need to scratch around for halal food to feed me with, then. Now, twenty years later, she was much more relaxed. She had a steady stream of Muslim guests from Java and elsewhere, sent by the central government to do the most basic tasks until Savu could find its own staff for its miniature replica of every government department.

Savu is in the process of a massive change. From virtually nothing just a few years ago, the local government now controls a budget of over US$30 million a year. Because it earned only US$29,000 in revenues and royalties on its own natural resources in 2012, 96 per cent of the funding comes straight from Jakarta's 'equalization funds'. There's a lot of equalizing to do. At the other end of the wealth spectrum from Savu stands the coal-rich district of Kutai Kartanegara in East Kalimantan, which made US$429 million, over 14,000 times more than Savu. As a consequence, less than 2 per cent of its income comes from Jakarta.

When I visited Savu, 4.1 million of those equalizing dollars were being used to build the statutory grandiose Bupati's office on the hill above town. While the construction went ahead, the Bupati, whose 'Vision/Mission' includes better health for all citizens, had requisitioned half of the only hospital in Savu. One of the hospital wards had been transformed into a debating chamber for the twenty MPs of the regional parliament. A posse of aides sat guard on the hospital porch; it was they I had been chatting to when the man himself pulled up. The civil servants on the porch were all 'from' Savu, but all of them had lived and worked most of their lives in Kupang or even Java. I asked the most talkative of them why he chose to come back. He looked at me witheringly. 'Chose? Your boss asks you to help with the development of the district. What can you do?'

I drove across Savu to discover what resources the Bupati might draw on to achieve his 'Vision/Mission': 'To make Sabu Raijua an innovative, advanced and dignified district.' There was not much to see.

At one point I turned off down a coral path and tipped out on to dunes which were covered in giant clam shells. There were hundreds of them, some more than a metre across, all grinning toothily up at the sky, each filled with grey water, slowly evaporating down to a crackly sand. Salt production, Savu-style. I stuck my finger into one of the shells, expecting the flaky sweetness of Maldon sea salt. The solution was viscous, almost oily, bitter on the tongue.

The beach swept around in a long, powdery arc. There was not a soul around, only vague reminders of human life. An outrigger canoe lay on its side in the brush. Beside a tumbledown shelter of palm fronds, a fallen tree trunk. The only sound was a tiny rippling of waves. It was a pleasure to be still in this shimmering place. I sat down on the tree trunk to read.

'I'm sorry, I'm going to have to chop that up.' I leapt up and found myself faced with a muscled torso, dark, shiny with sweat. Above it a thick beard, a mouth of blackened teeth, reddish eyes, wild curls crinkling slightly grey at the temples. The man was swinging an axe.

We stared at one another. Then he smiled. 'Come, meet my wife,' and he called her out of the tumbledown shelter next to which I sat.

The man was a fisherman, but during the west monsoon, when the sea was rough, he and his wife turned to cooking salt. He needed the tree I was sitting on to feed into the fire that smouldered under an oil-drum of seawater, boiling it down into pure white salt.

Without asking me a single question – not so much as a 'where are you from?' – the salt-cooker launched into a diatribe about the silk-shirted princelings who had taken over the hospital. 'Look, look around you, this is Savu, only this,' he swept his arm about over deserted beach, abandoned boats, the drum of bubbling seawater. 'But we think it is a good idea to have our own government, to build offices, to import posh cars for our very own crop of MPs.'

He described the Bupati and his various rivals as 'Savu Kupang' – meaning that though they were technically from Savu, they had been in the provincial capital across the water all of their adult lives. After the provinces lost power to the districts in the post-Suharto reforms, these bureaucratic migrants came back to whip up support for a new district, each in the hope that he might be crowned king.

'They went on and on at us, about how we could never realize our true potential as long as we were living on scraps from Kupang,' the salt-maker said. '[The Bupati and his clique] talk about dignity, but the new district was about *their* dignity. *They* want to be treated like kings. *They* want to be driven around, *they* want people to salute them, they want to go to Jakarta and be treated as Somebody.'

His wife, patiently skimming stray insects off the top of the salt-soup with a spoon shaped from a coconut shell, nodded quietly. 'Those were the people who wanted the new district. The ones ambitious to rule us,' she said. 'The funny thing is, before, they were proud to be big officials in Kupang. Now, suddenly, they are "one of us".'

It's hard labour, this dragging of dead palm trees down to the camp, the chopping of wood. But the market for fine-quality cooked salt is pretty good, the pair said. The previous week, they had sold a sack for 200,000 rupiah (US$22) to the hole-in-the-wall restaurant opposite the hospital. 'That's where all the officials get their lunch from,' said the salt-maker. 'Just think, maybe the Bupati has been eating my sweat.' His eyes twinkled.

People who want to hear heels clicked when they step out of their car sometimes lobby for years before parliamentarians in Jakarta finally agree to create a new district. Local worthies invite decision-makers from Jakarta to their area, organizing mass rallies that bear witness to the *aspirasi rakyat*, the 'Will of The People', all dying to be ruled by someone close to home. To those People, the worthies sell the idea of an end to neglect by far-off rulers and the dawn of a new era of prosperity.

In potentially rich areas, local power-mongers will try to have a new district carved around a natural resource, a big deposit of nickel or coal, for example. If we have our own district, they say to The People, we'll be able to keep more of our wealth. We won't have to kick the money up to the district capital in some other clan's land, to the province, to Jakarta.

In poor areas such as Savu, the local worthies argue instead that hand-outs from Jakarta will make The People richer because they won't go first through the capital of the old district, to be siphoned off by some other clan. The handouts from the centre will be used to kick-start the local economy, the princelings say, so that soon the infant district will be able to stand on its own.

In fact, these two contentions cannot both be true. If the central government wants to hand money out to more poorer districts, it has to take it from richer districts. In any case, Jakarta cannot legally spend more than 26 per cent of the nation's revenues on the equalization funds that provide handouts to the poorer districts such as Savu. Unless the creation of new districts leads to an increase in Indonesia's overall productivity, more districts inevitably means less money for each district.

I puttered further around the island, hoping to find some weavers. Only once, I saw a woman wearing a sarong in the classic flowered pattern that Savu was famed for when last I was here. I stopped to ask if she had woven it herself, but she was deaf. Her daughter wasn't interested: 'What, all that tying up cotton and dropping it into colours over and over and then eventually it comes out a flower or a bird?' she said, when I asked about *ikat* weaving. 'Who has the patience for that any more?'

I did come across a row of women perched on pyramids of grapefruit-sized rocks they had shuffled up in basketloads from the beach. Their task now was to sit under little palm-leaf shelters and use iron mallets to smash the rocks into chips for construction crews. The men, for their part, were still shinning twenty metres up the lontar palm trees to collect sap that could be boiled down into sugar or distilled into booze. A few people were farming seaweed; that involved tying empty water bottles at intervals along long ropes, attaching little bunches of seaweed palm-distance apart between them, then floating the whole necklace out in the water, wading-distance from shore until the little bunches of seaweed grew into big bunches of seaweed.

None of these things seemed destined to displace handouts from Jakarta as the source of 96 per cent of Savu's income, nor to make it 'an innovative, advanced and dignified district'.

The day after my encounter with the Bupati of Savu, I drove the coast road to the south of Savu, then ventured back to Seba across Savu's hump-backed spine, where lontar palms the height of a four-storey building sprang from the dry earth, and toasted hills swept down to azure sea. The view was beautiful, but the road was spiteful.

Driving on roads this bad is no fun at all. Your spine thuds down to half its natural length, then shoots back out at odd angles. Your right hand, locked around the handlebar, has turned to marble. Your left is buzzy-numbed by the accelerator. Your teeth rattle, and you can actually feel your eyes shaking around in their sockets as you flip your attention from the pothole coming up on the left to the loose scree a bit further ahead on the right. Your thighs are gripping the saddle of the bike and your calves are permanently tensed, the left one pumping your ankle back and forth over the gears, the right keeping a foot cocked attentively over the brake, both ready to stamp down into the dust or mud below at any moment to save yourself from going over. As my elegant Parisian friend Nathalie said when I slung her on the back of a motorbike and drove her across Sumba some years ago: '*C'est quand même un pays qui fait mal aux fesses*' – 'It's a country that's hard on the bum.'

By the time the sun notched down to evening cool, I was wishing I had not taken this 'short cut'. Then I crested a hill and saw before me a miraculous ribbon of black velvet unfolding down into the valley before me. Real, smooth tarmac. I quadrupled my speed, loosened my grip on the handlebars, relaxed my thighs and started to look around, to admire the majestic palm trees silhouetted against an oranging sky.

As I zoomed towards the top of the next hill, a solitary figure flagged me down. He was a well-dressed man younger than myself, shouting into a cell phone, an unexpected sight on this barren hilltop. I waited until he had finished yelling and offered him a lift. 'No, I've got a bike, thanks. I just wanted to warn you about the road.'

About five metres beyond the crest of the hill the road swerved sharply to the left, then disappeared, tumbling with no warning at all back into the river of rocks and ruts that I'd battled with for most of the journey.

This gentleman was, it turned out, the youngest MP in the local parliament, and a member of the public works committee. He had received the project completion report for this section of road from the public works department, and had come out to have a look. He found that the contractors had grown tired of digging the drainage ditch; it ran out a hundred metres before the tarmac did. The asphalt was neither bedded nor edged. This meant that the road would slide gracefully over the side of the hill at the first real rains. 'They may as well have just painted the dirt black,' he said, angry. He tried his phone again, but the contractor was no longer taking his calls.

I had seen on an information board in town that the twenty-five-kilometre road was being remade at a cost of 2.2 billion rupiah, so about US$10,000 per kilometre. Why not start from town and work progressively? Why was this little strip of tarmac airlifted into the middle of the wrecked road?

The MP explained that large contracts such as road-building, awarded by the public works department, are routinely split into several different *proyek*, each one awarded to a different contractor.

Proyek. It was a word I was to hear endlessly, part of the vast system of patronage that props up Indonesia's current 'Etc.'. What was interesting in this case was that a local MP was actually trying to provide some oversight for the 'project' doled out by the Bupati and his team. Few Indonesians expect local parliamentarians to make any real effort to call the executive to account. Their job, people often joke, is to perform the 'Four S's': Show up, Sit down, Shut up, Salary.★

I asked the MP how his committee decided on the technical specifications for the roads, and how much was allocated to maintenance. 'Honestly, I've no idea. We're new to this; no one really knows how to calculate a budget, so we just end up trusting the guys in the executive.' That was problematic in itself, he said, since the local public works department – the executive – had

---

★ In Indonesian, the 'Four D's': *Datang, Duduk, Diam, Duit.*

no trained engineers to speak of. 'It's the blind leading the blind.'

With each new flowering of the great firework of decentralization, Indonesia needs to find more people who can run a health department or who can plan infrastructural development, more people who can review budgets or plan a curriculum. Ideally, each district wants to identify that talent among its own local population. In dozens of the newly created districts in previously neglected provinces, that talent just doesn't exist.

'I'm not sure anyone in the department [of public works] can even read a spreadsheet,' the MP told me as he kicked a clump of loose tarmac from the newly laid road. 'And we can't go asking Kupang for help, because after all, we were the ones who wanted to split from them and have our own district.'

From Savu, I took the Pelni ferry to Kupang, in the west of Timor. I had wanted to hop another Pelni through one of Indonesia's newest districts, Southwest Maluku. Its forty-eight tiny islands dot the sea east of Timor, covering some 600 kilometres all the way up to Tanimbar in the west. But the monthly ferry had just left.

After much prodding, the harbour master at Kupang had told me that *perintis* boats made the journey up through Southwest Maluku every couple of weeks. He had looked me up and down dubiously. *Perintis* literally means pioneer; it's a polite way of describing services that go to places no other transport wants to go. 'You understand it's a cargo ship?' the harbour master had said, in a tone that suggested that I did not look like the right kind of cargo. 'We allow passengers as a service to the residents of the smaller islands, but . . .'

I asked about the route and declared that I would get on the boat at Wini, on the East Timor border. The harbour master at Kupang looked even more dubious, but he gave me a time and a date: 10 a.m. on the ninth. And so, at about 9.30 on the ninth, I cruised down Wini's only street and wound up at the pier. No boat at the pier, no boat anywhere on the horizon.

The small building that declared itself to be the office of the department of transport was deserted. There was no one else around. I texted the harbour master in Kupang. '*Sabar, Bu*', came the reply: 'Be patient'. So I sat under a tree and read a book. After about an hour, a young man rocked up. He obviously wasn't from Wini, so I asked if he was waiting for the boat. 'There's a boat? I haven't seen anything at this dock in the two weeks I've been here.'

He was an engineer from Surabaya, sent to oversee the extension of that very dock. Why extend it if it's never used? I asked. '*Proyek, kan?*' 'It's a "project", isn't it?'

Noon came and went, then one o'clock, then two. I was beginning to think about Plan B when I saw a puff on the horizon. The puff turned into cloud and within just over an hour a huge, flat barge covered in green and blue tarpaulin was sitting alongside the pier. No one got off and I was the only new passenger to clamber up the ridged plank that was thrown from deck to dock.

I looked around at my fellow passengers. I had expected a dozen hardy souls, but the deck was packed; there must have been close to 300 people on board. Every square inch of deck space was taken up. People were hunkered down in fortresses built of boxes of electronics, rice sacks, stacks of eggs in square cardboard trays. There was no eye contact; the whole scene bristled with hostility. I made for a mouse-hole of about two foot by three foot behind a sack of garlic, but was warned off by a growling neighbour. The only empty space seemed to be on top of a warm, humming freezer. There, I unrolled my sleeping mat. Immediately, a terrier of a woman bore down, menacing me with a giant wooden spoon. One of the crew directed me back to the mouse-hole, to the fury of the growling neighbour.

Saumlaki, where I was headed, was five days away.

To my horror, I found that the territorial wars were reignited almost every time the ship stopped. As the harbour master had said, Perintis ships are cargo ships, and cargo is carried under decks. That meant that in most ports we pulled in at, in the blazing sunshine of midday or the dead of night, the tarpaulin that covered us was rolled back, the box-fortresses were deconstructed and sleeping mats rolled up, the passengers clambered down a plank onto the pier, and the whole deck of the ship was lifted up so that it could disgorge its contents.

The unloading stops ranged in length from a couple of hours to a whole day. But the instant the first section of deck went back down, the battle for territory began. Passengers old and new swarmed on board to occupy prize spots, oblivious to the sections of deck still swinging from ropes at neck height. There was much shouting. The crew shouted at passengers who were in danger of decapitation. The people who had already been on the ship for two days shouted at newcomers to establish prior possession. The newcomers shouted back to signal firmness of purpose. Families shouted instructions at one another as they created pincer movements, one brigade unfurling mats while the other built box-castles.

Over time, I got better at choosing a homeland and establishing sovereignty. I wanted to be far away from the twenty-four-hour karaoke at one end, but not too near the smelly loo at the other. A spot close to a 'door' – a gap in the side tarpaulin – provided breeze and a view, which is nice, but also lashings of rain, which is not. Tears in the tarpaulin overhead could turn a cosy spot into a puddle, too, so I had to keep an eye on the roof. Large families generally made bad neighbours – Indonesian kids are poorly disciplined and given to screaming. But I definitely didn't want to be near the louts with the jerrycans of sopi palm wine, the boom boxes and the guitars.

A space along the side would allow me to move around relatively easily, but also meant that other people would be constantly trampling over my face. On day two I settled on a relatively quiet corner spot at the loo end, just next to the abyss leading to the cargo hold. It was in a dead end, so I was protected on two sides. I managed to hold on to it by making allies of an immobile old lady and her daughter.

They had come aboard at Liran island, where there was not

even a pier. A long, skinny fishing boat had pulled up alongside our cargo ship, bobbing about while the daughter had hiked the older woman up from below. A boat boy grabbed from the deck above and after a bit of heave-ho, the old lady flopped on board. Her daughter scrambled up after her and I pulled them both into my buffer zone. After that, I did my best to shame the vulturing passengers into showing some respect for the elderly. It worked well enough.

Life on the boat settled into a rhythm of sorts. The prow of the ship, up by the anchor, was open to the heavens, a pleasant place for dawn musings. By nine in the morning the pitiless sun forced everyone back into the fetid air under the tarpaulin, the fug barely stirred by the slow flapping of improvised cardboard fans. In the late afternoon the sun sank behind us. This was the nicest time of day.

The evening light touched the water with flame and the dolphins came out to play. Every day they appeared, arching out of the water beside us, leaping and plunging, sometimes shooting vertically up and doing little pirouettes high in the air, just for the hell of it. Even the toughest of the sopi-drinking louts was carried away by the magic of the spectacle, pointing out the mother and child pairs, laughing with delight when a dolphin materialized within arm's length of us. Then the light faded and the proper technicolor sunsets began, wispy pink surrounding soft greys in the clouds above, a cauldron of fire floating on the horizon below, the sea rippling glassy-dark to our bows. Inside, neon lights strung carelessly from the tarp-poles glared to life and the karaoke whined on, but here on the prow it was a calming time.

Five days is a long time to sit around on a boat, without even the lure of the beautiful actress from Mandarin, Miss Beautiful Lingling Zhou for distraction. I had planned to write dozens of letters, to read many worthy development reports, to Be Productive. But I found myself lulled into nothingness, a shameful amount of just staring into space, watching the light on the water, wondering idly whether to buy a plate of rice from the wooden-spoon-wielding terrier on board or wait for the next stop, at somewhere that may or may not be big enough to have a coffee stall.

The frequent stops gave me a chance to explore. In a seaside hamlet a retired soldier invited me in for strong coffee and a thick slab of home-made cake; he told me that things were getting better at the bottom of the armed forces but worse at the top. 'We used to have smart generals and stupid soldiers,' he said. 'Now it's the other way around; most of the troops have a decent education, but the cleverest graduates don't want to go into the army any more.'

Sometimes these tiny islands yield the most unexpected things. In Kisar, where we stopped for a whole day, a fellow passenger, Harry, offered to show me the sights. On his motorbike, we buzzed down to the end of the island and looked across at East Timor, now a nation in its own right. We slowed down as instructed in front of the military barracks. ('Nothing but trouble, those boys,' said Harry, contradicting what I had heard from the retired soldier.) We stopped to look at the airstrip. And we went to visit Pak Hermanus, an ancient, hook-nosed gentleman who speaks only Oirata, a minority language even on the island of Kisar, and is said to belong to one of the Lost Tribes of Israel. A busybody Christian from Jakarta had whisked Hermanus off to the Holy Land the year before in the hope of hastening the Second Coming of Christ. Outside his palm-leaf house, ten rocks now sit dolloped together with cement like a giant turd: a monument to the Ten Lost Tribes. It was one of those little Ionesco moments that make travelling in Indonesia such a delight. Better yet: the acting Bupati of Southwest Maluku district recently said he wanted to turn Kisar into a destination for spiritual tourism because the island, all 10x10 kilometres of it, reminded him of Israel. Both countries are dry and mountainous, the Bupati pointed out, and there are sheep and goats in both places.

Several times, people in the towns we stopped in called me in off the streets and offered me the use of their bathroom so that

I could scrub away the grime of the voyage. When I thanked people for the gifts of cake, companionship, cleanliness, they would wave me away. 'Nonsense, nonsense. You'd do exactly the same for me over there!' I knew it wasn't true, and it made me all the more grateful. I swam in a deserted cove and sat in the cool of an old stone church. I bought an octopus off a fisherman and had it grilled in the island's single dockside restaurant. Five days on a cargo boat wasn't all bad.

There was a lot of chatting on the boat, of course; at each stop there were new people with new questions, many of which were answered for me by fellow passengers who had already mastered my back story. I, for my part, learned why people were making this long journey.

A lot of people were on their way to or from Kisar, the temporary seat of the Maluku Barat Daya (MBD) district government, to hand in a project proposal. One man I met, the brother of a sub-district head, had just collected payment for an illuminated Christmas tree he had built out of used water bottles outside the bupati's office. Now he was submitting a proposal for Easter decorations. *Susun proposal*, to 'put together a proposal', was a phrase I had heard more frequently on this trip than in the previous two decades put together. I heard it from NGOs, of course, but also from priests, students, farmers, teachers, village women's groups, policemen and dozens more. These days, everybody in Indonesia seems to be proposing to squeeze small (and sometimes not so small) amounts of money out of the newly flush local governments.

The immobile old lady in my buffer zone was not putting together a proposal. She was going to hospital; her legs had swollen up and she couldn't walk properly. There was no hospital in Liran, nor should there be; the island has one village with a population of around 800 people. It does have a primary and a middle school, and a satellite health post staffed by a local lady with some training as a midwife, 'but all she has to offer are pills you can buy at the kiosk'. There was no hospital anywhere else in Southwest Maluku either, though the newly designated district capital was allocated a knock-down field hospital six months later.

In terms of transport time, the nearest hospital was in Kupang, the capital of NTT, a day and a half away. But this frail old lady couldn't go there, because Liran is in Maluku province, so her health card, which gives her cheaper treatment, wasn't valid in Kupang. So she sat stoically for three days and three nights to get to hospital in Saumlaki. Even there, she would have to pay a bribe to be seen. Now that Southwest Maluku has gone its own way as a district, the hospital in Saumlaki was no longer supposed to accept health cards from Liran.

If she were to do things by the book, this sick seventy-something-year-old would have to travel another three days to the provincial capital of Ambon. 'But if you know people from the old days, you can usually fix it,' the old lady said.

Map D: Banggai Islands, Central Sulawesi

Map E: Kei Islands, Maluku

6

Happy Families

It was coming up to Christmas 2011, and I was wandering up through the south-eastern islands of Maluku with only the Victorian beetle-collector Alfred Wallace for company. Wallace had spent the Christmas of 1857 on a ship close to where I now was, and he had been unhappy. 'The captain, though nominally a Protestant, seemed to have no idea of Christmas Day as a festival,' he complained. 'Our dinner was of rice and curry as usual, and an extra glass of wine was all I could do to celebrate it.'

It was an unusually morose note in an otherwise chirpy description of the bottom right-hand corner of the archipelago, the bits just next to the giant island of New Guinea. Wallace was especially taken by the Kei islanders, who streamed uninvited onto his ship to the dismay of his buttoned-up Javanese and Malay crew:

> These Ke men came up singing and shouting, dipping their paddles deep in the water and throwing up clouds of spray . . . They seemed intoxicated with joy and excitement . . . [The crew] reminded me of a party of demure and well-behaved children suddenly broken in upon by a lot of wild, romping, riotous boys, whose conduct seems most extraordinary and very naughty.*

---

* Wallace, *The Malay Archipelago*, Vol. 2, Chapter XXIX.

Wallace was certainly right that the people of Kei are abundantly welcoming. I had been in these waters before, in 2004. My boss in Jakarta had made a snap decision to close the office over Christmas and New Year and I had simply headed off into the wilderness. I ended up in Tual, the main city in the Kei islands. After just a few days my attention span for the spectacular beaches south of town was spent, and I had gone down to the port. A broad-beamed wooden passenger boat all loaded up with people was just about to raise the gangplank. I had jumped on board and settled down on a bench. The ticket collector came along and asked where I was going. 'What are the options?' I had replied.

The huge, shaven-headed man sitting next to me was immensely tickled by the idea that I had got on a boat without any idea of where it was going. 'She's coming with us,' he had declared. And that was that.

Pak Bram and his family were heading home to his native village of Ohoiwait in the thinly populated island of Kei Besar, just a couple of hours distant from Tual where they now lived. They were visiting his mother and a dizzying array of siblings and other relatives.

A battered jeep was waiting for us at the dock and the whole family poured into it, squirrelling homecoming gifts in every corner: sacks of rice and cement were lashed on the roof, cakes were pushed under seats, trays of eggs were held in laps. We climbed an unpaved road that wound along the spine of the island through forest and farmland scattered with undistinguished villages. Then the road dropped down to the far coast and came to an abrupt halt. We had reached Ohoiwait.

The upper part of the village tottered on top of a cliff. A wide avenue paved with polished coral blocks led from the church at the summit down to the edge of the cliff; simple wooden houses clung on either side. The houses were well kept, shutters and doors painted in contrasting colours, clean cotton curtains flapping in the salty breeze. Then, in a waterfall of 120 steep steps, the avenue tumbled down the cliff to the beachside. For some reason the flat lower village seemed to have let itself go, like a teenager who makes a point of drifting between unkempt and downright slovenly. Offshore, fish in a variety of technicolor costumes flitted around a beautiful coral reef referred to dismissively by the locals as 'coloured rocks'.

Bram, the youngest of thirteen children, had taken me straight to his mother, who was referred to by everyone, regardless of generation, as 'Oma', the Dutch term for grandmother. She welcomed me without question, and my place in the village was secured. Family members had already colonized most of the floor space in Oma's house with their sleeping mats, so I was stashed across the way at a cousin's house. The family made room for me at mealtimes, and wove me effortlessly into daily life in the village.

As Christmas loomed on my more recent journey, I thought with great fondness of that holiday seven years earlier. I had stayed in touch with Bram for a year or two after that visit in 2004; then he'd changed his phone number and I had no way of calling. Damn it, I thought, I'll go to Ohoiwait anyway.

In Tual I printed up several of the portraits I had taken on my first visit – Oma elegant in a white kebaya, Bram and his wife Maria and their kids in the wrap-around sunglasses that teenagers wear when they want to impress village cousins with their big-city cool, 'Mrs Dormitory' with whom I had stayed, 'Mrs Kitchen' in whose house the whole clan ate – and headed for Ohoiwait.

There were around 300 people squashed into 200 seats on the coffin-shaped speedboat across to Kei Besar. An old lady folded herself into half of my seat, fragile as a plucked quail. The boat lurched wildly; it reared up the face of one wave and slapped down on the next. The old lady squawked with each lurch. She grabbed my hand, pressed it until my knuckles went white, then threw up on my foot.

The road to Ohoiwait, still unmetalled, runs through forests edged with wild orchids. I sat on the back of a motorcycle taxi, thinking how odd it was that I should just turn up, two days before Christmas, at the home of a family I hadn't seen for seven years, people whose real names I couldn't even remember, and expect to be welcomed in.

My confidence in Indonesia's unstinting largesse was not misplaced. I had hardly got off the motorbike in Ohoiwait before I was scooped up by Bram's sister-in-law Ona and bustled off to Oma's house. The matriarch had died the year before, aged over ninety. Now Ona and Ince (pronounced Inchay – aka Mrs Kitchen) lived in the house with their husbands and one remaining small child.

Ona and I were looking at the photos I had brought when Mama Ince appeared. She spotted the photos. 'Those photos are from when Eliz was here!' she said. I nodded, waiting for a greeting. She, in turn, waited for me to explain how I had come by the pictures. Mama Ona looked at her feet, embarrassed. 'It's her,' she grunted. 'It's Elizabeth.' 'Wah! Bu Eliz!' Ince threw up her hands in delight. 'But you've grown so old!'

Within a couple of hours, Ona, Ince and I were squatting together in the kitchen peeling vegetables that we'd just picked from behind the house, as though they'd expected me all along, as though it hadn't been seven years since I had flitted in and out of their lives. 'You'll stay for Christmas,' Mama Ince declared, and I felt all sunny inside.

Ince reeled off all of my social obligations for the Christmas period, many of which were churchy. Ohoiwait is largely Protestant, though I noticed a mosque in the lower village that I did not remember from my previous visit. I saw too that a trickle of girls in jilbabs joined the groups of kids who went door to door over the Christmas period, singing, clapping, rattling maracas made of Coke cans and dried maize. They made up verses designed to shake sweets and coins out of adults. '*Ibu Eliz manise . . .*' they chanted: 'Sweet Ibu Eliz, Where are you hiding . . .?' It was impossible not to reach for the wallet and dole out 1,000 rupiah notes all round. When I commented to Mama Ince on the ecumenical mix of the Christmas trick-or-treaters, she said that some of the Muslims were visiting Christian cousins.

In clannish south Maluku, she told me, the ties of the extended family outweigh differences of faith.

First on my dance card was the Ladies and Gentlemen service, for which the adults of the village put on their traditional best, the women elegant in long kebayas and batik sarongs, the men in shirts of batik or more local woven *ikat* fabrics. Mama Ince and the other female church wardens were distinguished by black silk sashes, the men by white scarves. The benches had been rearranged so that we faced one another across the central aisle, women on the left, men on the right.

I was shooed into the front row, so I couldn't let my mind wander too obviously. For over an hour I prayed, sang and pretended to listen to an impassioned sermon from the female priest – there are now more women than men in the ministry of the traditional Calvinist church in Maluku. Then we reached the candle-lighting ritual. First up was the 'The Honourable Village Secretary, whose wisdom guides us all'. He walked slowly up the aisle, solemnly lit a candle, then trooped slowly back to his seat. Oh God, I thought, now we'd have the teacher and the midwife, and the head of the Family Welfare Union and everyone else with any kind of position, which in a village like this is almost everyone, and we'd still be here at midnight. My mind wandered off to consider local fashions in make-up: on dressed-up occasions such as this, dark-skinned village women puffed their faces with whitening rice powder, then smeared lipstick over mouths prestained with betel juice. The effect was vaguely menacing.

Suddenly, I felt Mama Ona dig me in the ribs. 'Now we call on Ibu Eliz,' intoned the celebrant, 'who through her visit reminds us what it is to love the country of Indonesia and the village of Ohoiwait.' And despite myself, I was moved. I walked slowly up the aisle and solemnly lit a candle, then trooped slowly back to my seat, just like everyone else. Such pageants do, after all, give everyone a sense of belonging. It is not a feeling one has very often in London or Jakarta, in the vast, anonymous spaces that shape the lives of an increasing proportion of human beings.

During the reading of the administrative notices, the church warden announced that there was a new *sasi*, a taboo, on collecting sea slugs, while the *sasi* on Pak Okto's mango tree was lifted. *Sasi* (or *pomali* further south in NTT) works as a traditional form of resource management. Most often, the taboo is declared by village elders to prevent overfishing in the breeding season or to husband communal resources.

Sometimes villagers who wanted their own crops protected from theft would slip the elders a small fee to declare a taboo. Pak Okto's mango tree hung heavy with fruit right over the coral thoroughfare that runs through the upper village; small boys passing up and down would certainly have stripped it of most of its mangoes had they not been cowed by the taboo. Now, with the *sasi* lifted, Pak Okto could go home from church and harvest what was rightfully his. That afternoon, his whole extended family gathered on the veranda, sticky with juice, gorging on the harvest.

In Timor a century and a half ago, Alfred Wallace noted that these bans carry a powerful charge:

> *The custom of 'tabu', called here 'pomali', is very general, fruits, trees, houses, crops and property of all kinds being protected from depredation by this ceremony, the reverence for which is very great. A palm branch stuck across an open door, showing that the house is tabooed, is a more effectual guard against robbery than any amount of locks and bars.**

Nowadays, taboos are even being used by politicians. Wanting to demonstrate who controlled the city during a squabble over local elections in Tual in 2003, one faction put a *sasi* on the only bridge over a wide rivermouth that bisects the city. Makeshift ferries popped up, charging extortionate prices. Kids had to get up an hour earlier if they happened to live across the river from school; government officials grew even less likely to make it to

---

* Wallace, *The Malay Archipelago*, Vol. 2, Chapter XL.

the office. For weeks, petrol, kerosene, rice, everything had to be unloaded on one side and ferried across on sampans to the other side. Prices skyrocketed. Though it made everyone's life a misery, no one dared violate the sasi; it required the intervention of the Governor of Maluku to get it dropped.

The weather over Christmas was foul. Every afternoon, and often in the mornings too, the wind whipped up off the sea, barrelled up the cliff and assaulted the little wooden houses of Ohoiwait. The tops of coconut palms danced histrionically, a Pina Bausch ballet in the air. Rain crashed in visible waves on to the corrugated-iron roofs, then blew in gusts through the open verandas. People closed their shutters, retreated inside, and waited out the storm by the light of kerosene lamps; the electricity had been blown out the day I arrived and was not restored by the time I left; only the church generator provided light.

No sinetron, no phones, no passage out by flooded road or angry sea: the village was cut off from the world. All we had was the radio. I remember the first time I was in Ohoiwait sitting with the village head listening to a special channel that passed on instructions from the central government down through its provincial and district networks to the villages. There were new restrictions on dynamite fishing; candidates were invited to apply for a village midwife programme. Every day the village head tuned in, took notes, went out to spread the news.

Now, every evening, Mama Ince turned on the radio to learn what was going on in the world immediately outside the village. There were endless Christmas greetings from various high officials. Then we learned of the shipping schedule. Pelni announces that the Ciremai ship will arrive in Tual on the 30th, two days late. Government offices will be closed on Monday January 2. After that, Family Radiograms: The Zain clan in Tual wishes to inform their Bugis relatives in Banda Eli that because of bad weather they will not be coming to visit. The Matutu clan in Tual asks Bapak Jafar in Waur to come to town immediately on important business.

Almost all the radiograms use the phrase *keluarga besar*, literally 'big family', a baggy phrase which I translate as clan. One rainy afternoon, I asked Mama Ona's husband Jopy who was really included in the concept of *keluarga besar*. He pulled out a piece of paper and started sketching just the clan that started with Oma, the elegant matriarch who had welcomed me into the family on my first visit.

There was Oma and her husband, their thirteen children, their forty-three grandchildren, twenty-eight great-grandchildren and the one brand-new fifth-generation baby. That's eighty-five direct descendants from a woman who had died only the previous year. It doesn't count the spouses, the in-laws, the cousins various times removed, just the bloodline. 'But if we really mean the whole clan, the wives or husbands, the relatives by marriage, and we go back to even my grandparents' generation, then it's hundreds and hundreds of people,' Jopy said. He pulled out another nice clean piece of paper so that I could draw my own family tree.

Starting with my paternal grandparents, we reached a grand total of three: my father, my brother and myself. Pak Jopy didn't know how to react to this absence of family; it was as though I had confessed to having been abandoned at birth and suckled by wolves.

The clan is a real, physical entity, tied to bloodlines that are meticulously remembered. It's especially important in this age of micro-democracy, where some 'big families' can produce enough votes for a seat in a district parliament. But the clan can also be metaphorical; networks of people bound together not by blood but by geography, by schooling, by gang membership, by occupation. In the Suharto years the papers were always full of the glorious social works carried out by the *Keluarga Besar* ABRI, for example, an organization of the armed forces and their families.

In both cases, the *keluarga besar*, the clan, is the circulatory system through which patronage flows. And patronage is the lifeblood of Indonesian politics and of the economy.

At the heart of the clan there is usually a Big Man (who is, occasionally, a woman). The clan pumps votes and (especially in the case of a metaphorical clan such as a youth organization) foot soldiers through the veins up to the Big Man. This allows him to maintain a position of power which gives him access to the oxygen of cash, of *proyek* and of jobs, which he pumps back into the clan.

At the district level, the Big Man might represent the Notabulen family over the Ingtatubun family, or the interests of Ohoiwait village over those of Elat. In national politics, they would be expected to deliver things for the whole district, maybe even the province. But everyone pulls out the stops for their real, descended-from-Oma bloodline clan.

One evening Pak Jopy and Mama Ona were telling me about their daughter. She had passed the civil service exams and snagged a coveted teaching job, fair and square. One morning, when Jopy was in Tual, he got wind of the fact that the letter assigning teaching posts was to be released later that day; his daughter was posted to Waur, a small Catholic town not too far from Ohoiwait.

This was not good; it's hard to build a career when one is stuck in a village in a relatively isolated island such as Kei Besar, far from the district office where the bosses who control promotion now sit. Jopy went straight to the department of education and complained, but the officer in charge shrugged: people knew the letter had been signed and that it would be made public in a couple of hours; it was too late for changes.

'Luckily, we have a relative who is an MP in Jakarta. I spoke to him, and he spoke to the guy in the district office, and it was fixed.' The announcement ceremony was rescheduled, the list was rewritten, and Jopy's daughter now teaches in a school in Tual. 'Cool, eh?' said the proud father.

A bit later in the conversation, I was telling a story about paying cops off to let me through a roadblock. 'I guess that makes me a corruptor,' I said. Ona and Jopy laughed. And then: 'It's a bit like the story of your daughter. In England, there are people who would think of that as corruption.'

There was a stunned silence; for a long moment, the air grew heavy. And then Mama Ona stood up and started clearing plates. 'Shall we go to church?' she said.

In retrospect, I'm sorry I made that comment. Not because I embarrassed my impeccably kind hosts, but because I was wrong. It may sound like sophistry, but I have come to make a distinction between patronage and corruption. Indonesians make the distinction all the time in their lives and their voting patterns, though not, interestingly, in their language.

Indonesians love to talk about corruption, which they usually abbreviate to KKN, for *Korupsi, Kolusi, Nepotism*. Once, I was sitting with a group of young lads watching soccer on TV. Arch-rivals Malaysia were beating Indonesia in a Southeast Asian Games match. When Malaysia scored again, one of the lads shook his head in disgust and said: 'I wish there were a World Cup for corruption. Then at least we'd be sure to win.'

But an awful lot of what people are talking about when they talk of KKN is the patronage that is made inevitable because of the way Indonesia organizes its democracy and its bureaucracy.

'Democracy', translated as the election of national and local leaders and the legislators that oversee them, is relatively new in Indonesia. But there's an awful lot of it. Indonesians directly elect their president, their national MPs, their provincial governor, their provincial MPs, their district head (the bupati or mayor), the district MPs and their village head. Participating in seven separate elections in any given five-year period, Indonesians have developed a keen understanding of the way their democracy works. And everyone agrees on one thing: the country's radical decentralization and democracy have made patronage/corruption both more necessary and more widespread.

It's expensive to become bupati. First, you have to pay a political party to back you. Then you have to pick up all the costs of campaigning; costs I heard about but didn't really believe until

I spent a few weeks in a campaign office a bit later in the trip. Unless you are massively wealthy, paying for all the electioneering will mean borrowing money. And that means payback. It's hideously difficult for the losers; admissions to mental hospitals are reported to rise after every election in Indonesia and several heavily indebted losers have killed themselves.

The winner, now the bupati, can't pay his debts out of his salary of US$600 a month (it almost always is a 'he' – at last count there were only eight women among Indonesia's 500-plus bupatis and mayors). Instead he repays with a permit to mine, an appointment to this post or that, a contract to build a new hospital or a blue-roofed passenger terminal. 'By the time they get elected they've got so many debts that they can't *not* be corrupt,' people would explain, over and over again.★

A lot of this payback is not actually illegal, any more than it is illegal for an American congressman to propose fracking-friendly policies after some oil giant has contributed liberally to the Political Action Committee that helped fund her campaign. Jobs go to cousins in the same way as internships in Britain's House of Commons go to that pretty daughter of a friend of Daddy's. But even legal patronage does often make for bad policies, bad appointments and bad roads.

During my rainy Christmas in Ohoiwait, I had come to feel almost sorry for Indonesia's Big Men. Once they've made it big, even without the direct support of their clan, they are expected to 'give back' indefinitely.

★ Sophisticated studies by Western academics seem to confirm this folk wisdom. One fascinating study of illegal logging uses satellite imagery to show that in the forested provinces of Sumatra, Kalimantan and Papua, the creation of a sub-district leads to an 8 per cent jump in tree felling, on average. This is true even in the areas where no new logging is allowed under national law. See Burgess et al., 2012. Meanwhile, spending on local roads doubled a year after budgets were handed to the districts, then doubled again in the year after the first direct elections for Bupati; government inspections show the quality of the roads fell despite a seven-fold increase in spending in the decade to 2010.

Pak Jacob, whom I heard about as soon as I arrived in Ohoiwait, had definitely made it big. He had been born in the tiny Maluku village on the clifftop, but had left to seek his fortune more than twenty years previously. Now Jacob heads the city parliament in Jayapura, where he has served several terms as MP. Jayapura is capital of Papua, physically the richest province in the country, one that provides unusual opportunities to its politicians.

Pak Jacob would be arriving in Ohoiwait the next day, I was told, his first visit home since leaving all those years ago. He would be honoured with a Hokhokwait ceremony, which welcomes a villager's bride when she firsts sets foot here. Jacob was actually on his fourth bride, but that didn't matter, she was the first to make it to this hilltop hamlet, and so it was she that would get the welcome. The village hummed with anticipation.

The following morning, I could see that the ladies of the village were putting on their best to welcome the Big Man. This threw me into a bit of a wardrobe tizz; I had to negotiate my whole social calendar of Christmas visits with only two decent sarongs which doubled as bed sheets. I smoothed out the one I had slept on the night before, put it on, and joined the trail of ladies down the steps to the lower village.

We made our way along the road to a riverside spot where the fertility spring wells up. The Big Man had sent provisions ahead; minibus louts unloaded slabs of Coke and Sprite, boxes of biscuits, trays of eggs: I noticed that the malnourished Mohican-to-pigtail fashion had reached even this far outpost of the realm. Then the minibus disappeared to pick up the Man himself. We waited. The ladies of the village hoiked up their pink and purple silks and squatted on flat stones in the river, scrubbing their betel-blackened teeth with sand. From the high banks opposite, naked boys bombed into the water.

When the blaring of horns announced the return of the bus, we all scrambled into position. The drummer started beating out a rhythm, the senior ladies hovered with a red silk cloth, and as the bus drew to a halt the whole company descended on the bride, a frightened-looking teenager who had clearly not been told what to expect. The red silk was pinned around her chin and pulled over her to hide the shabby beige housedress she was wearing. 'Tsk tsk,' clucked the ladies. 'Imagine letting your bride come to the village in a duster!' 'Duster', from the Dutch, is the word Indonesians use for a housecoat; something one might wear while slopping around at home or while doing the cleaning, not when visiting the in-laws for the first time.

The girl was led to the riverside for the fertility rituals; somewhat superfluous since she was eight months pregnant. Then the procession started: a pink umbrella was twirled above her head and we fell into formation behind her, shuffling, twirling our hands and chanting. Every hundred yards or so, some unknown female relative would accost this pale Javanese girl, thrusting at her sometimes small banknotes, sometimes pieces of fruit, but always the betel-nut and lime combination that signals honour but turns the stomach of those unaccustomed to it.

We danced through the lower village and started the steep hike up to the site at the centre of the upper village where the sacred stones and Dutch cannons sit. The sun came out for the first time in days. The teenage bride, waddling up the cliff followed by an excited crowd of people laughing, clapping and chanting in a language she didn't speak, looked like she wanted to cry. A village elder blessed her, then she waddled back down.

Her husband, more than two decades her senior and with a belly as big and round as hers, remained impassive through this whole ordeal. He did not seem the talkative type; indeed he and his wife did not address a single word to one another in any of their three public appearances in the village. I shook his hand in the reception line after the blessing, but we didn't chat.

After the trek up and down the hill, the pair sat uncomfortably on the floor of Jacob's mother's house, backs to the musty wall. The Big Man's mother threw herself into her son's lap, sobbing loudly. He sat motionless until she transferred her grief to her daughter-in-law, snivelling into the girl's long, straight hair, burrowing into her lap. The girl did some there-there back-patting and looked disconcerted. She smiled only once, to reassure two pale, Sunsilky-haired stepdaughters six or seven years younger than herself, the product of one of the earlier Javanese wives.

As abruptly as it had begun, the wailing stopped. The couple were forgotten and the party began. There were canned soft-drinks and prepackaged assortments of store-bought confections. These treats, rarely seen in the village, were taken as due now that there was a Big Man in town. Everyone grabbed for them with abandon, stashing them away to take home and fortifying themselves with more ordinary village fare: the cups of sticky tea and slabs of homemade cake that issued in waves from the back kitchen.

The dancing began, the women swaying and twirling in stately rows, changing direction with each ululation. Men kept time with drums, elders sang verses of traditional songs, and everyone had a joyous time. At a certain point it all got noticeably more joyous; the ululations trilling with energy and white envelopes being waved overhead. The Big Man had given the dancing ladies two and a half million rupiah between them, US$270, just because.

On Christmas Eve the stepdaughters turned up at church in matching electric pink. One wore a satinate flamenco dress, the other a lacy wedding affair. Both had pink-feathered fascinators on their heads, as if they were going to a society wedding; both wore miniature high heels. They came in late and flounced up the aisle to the front row with a 'look at me' imperative. The village girls flapped around them like moths around a flame. The father followed behind, still impassive.

His expression didn't flicker when the church warden read out the contributions the church had received from various members of the 'Big Family of Ohoiwait'. Pak Bram had sent a contribution from Tual. So had Pak Ayub, another member of Oma's clan who was now head of the Department of Social Affairs and Employment for Central Maluku. There were many others who had made Christmas donations to their home village: 150,000 here, 300,000 there. The visiting MP had outdonated them all by a factor of ten.

I wondered what it was like for him being back in this out-of-the-way place, a place with no air-conditioning, with no red-plated SUVs, with no fawning staff, hotel dinners, TV interviews. A place with no phone signal, even. He had come because his father had died recently; now he was technically head of the family. But he showed not a shred of pleasure at rediscovering the place where he grew up.

After the initial burst of excitement, which probably centred more on curiosity about the young Javanese wife than on respect for Jacob's position, the villagers were certainly not fawning. True, it brought honour to Ohoiwait when one of its sons made good. But villagers were displeased that Jacob had spent the last two decades taking care of a different clan – the smaller fish in his political party, the members of his congregation, everyone that made up his political machine over there in Jayapura, 1,000 kilometres away. 'As if we're not good enough for him,' sniffed one of the wedding dancers.

Even schoolchildren expect their Big Man to deliver. At an exhibition showcasing the writing skills of primary-school children in one small island group, I saw a letter which read:

LETTER for Pak BuPaTi, sangihe iSland DIstrict

HELLO HOW ARE YOU Pak Bupati? I'm happy to
meet you PAK BUPATI. BEcauSE I want to ASk for
something, but I MUST think first How so Pak Bipati
Will HeLp us. We want Electricity And we want a
football Field and we also want to Fix our motorboat
which is Broken, but How can it be FiXed? nobody
can make it work again, eVen the bosses can't fix it.
HopeFully you Pak Bupati can help us in Kalama Kola.
So these are our Requests for Pak BuPati, hopefully you
are in good health paK buPati oh yes happy birthday to
sangihe iSland diStrIct.

SWEET WISHES AdammI MENDOME

Each line of this slightly erratic letter-to-Santa was in a different colour. More sober in hue if not hope are the readers' letters (or rather text messages) that appear in every local newspaper in the land. 'Dear Bupati of South Buru,' wrote one reader. 'What's going on with payments for certified teachers from July to December. When will we be paid, Pak? Please share out the money, because that's our right as certified teachers. If possible, please pay us immediately. Don't keep putting it off. +628524934XXX'

These days, Indonesians have rather a low tolerance for real corruption, for pure, self-serving greed: the private mansion built to house the bupati's mistress, the official visits to Jakarta spent taking drugs with starlets in five-star hotels. That's corruption, and for that the voters of Indonesia will throw you out on your ear.

That other type of 'corruption' – the one that leads to bad appointments and bad roads – is complained about endlessly. And yet no one gets voted out of power for that kind of patronage.* That's because everyone continues to expect *their* Big Men to deliver to *their* clan. These days, there's so much democracy around that almost everyone has someone somewhere in the system delivering for them.

In Tual, main city in the Kei islands and just a couple of hours' travel from Ohoiwait, I met a young man who had done a degree in marketing and then worked for thirteen years as a broker at the now defunct Surabaya Stock Exchange. He got tired of working for other people, and came home to Kei to look for business opportunities. He started a shop selling perfume concentrates. He said it was a struggle. Not on the business side; that was fine. The difficulty was with his parents, who were adamant that he should get a government job. When he was out of sight in

---

* In the 2004 elections in South Sulawesi, eleven of the thirteen provincial parliamentarians who had previously been convicted of corruption were re-elected.

Java, the fact that he was in business wasn't so bad. But now he was home, his determination not to don the uniform of a civil servant and bathe his parents in its reflected prestige was almost shameful. 'People here educate their kids to be civil servants, not businessmen,' he said.

Poking fun at the bureaucracy is a national sport in Indonesia. Civil servants are lazy, self-serving blockheads out to fill their own pockets and throw obstacles in the way of upstanding citizens, everyone agrees. And yet everyone wants their child to become a civil servant, especially outside of Java, where there are relatively few opportunities in the private sector.

It's another hangover from Dutch times. At the turn of the twentieth century, a full century after the VOC trading company had been taken over by the Dutch state, there were just twenty-five 'natives' in secondary school. But the bureaucracy was growing; its appetite could no longer be satisfied by adventurers shipped out from the Netherlands. Over the next three decades the colonial government deigned to give 6,500 locals some secondary education. It then employed almost all of them. The perfume-seller's parents were just extrapolating something that had long been true: education leads to a uniform. But the reverse is definitely not true. Rather, an over-abundance of uniforms is undermining good education.

Given the geographical challenges of this scattered nation, it's something of a miracle that Indonesia actually manages to educate 55 million children a year. Nine out of ten children get through junior high school, and almost everyone aged between fifteen and twenty-four is functionally literate. More impressive still, Indonesia has the smallest number of pupils per teacher of any country in its income bracket. Indeed if you look at international league tables, class sizes in Indonesia are smaller than they are in the United States or Britain. And yet Indonesian kids consistently come close to the bottom in international tests of reading comprehension, science and maths. In the internationally standardized TIMSS tests in maths, just 0.4 per cent of Indonesian fifteen-year-olds reached the 'advanced' benchmark score indicating that they could organize information, analyse it and draw conclusions from it. More than half did not even make it to the 'low' benchmark, indicating that they 'have some knowledge of whole numbers and decimals, operations and basic graphs'. Of 65 countries included in the PISA international tests for fifteen-year-olds in 2012, Indonesia came 60th in reading and 64th in maths and science, a performance more dismal even than three years previously. Just 0.3 per cent of Indonesian students made it past the advanced benchmark in that maths test. Not one of the universities in the world's fourth most populous nation is rated as among the 100 best in Asia.

The dismal results are a result of dismal teaching, and that is in turn the result of patronage. A teaching job is the easiest way to squeeze into the coveted beige uniform of the civil servant; local politicians give jobs in schools to their political supporters all the time. That means the schools are rammed with people whose goal is to be a bureaucrat, not an educator. And they behave just like other bureaucrats in Indonesia: they see working hours as a movable feast and take time off more or less at will. It wasn't until a few months after my conversation with the stockbroker-turned-perfume-seller in Tual that I first saw the effects of this. By then I had reached the Banggai islands, which sit in the giant bay below the top arm of Sulawesi's distorted K. The landscape is watery even by Indonesian standards; until recently, Bajo fishing communities used to rise on stilts from the sea like a posse of daddy longlegs all huddled together in a web of raised boardwalks, far offshore. I had been invited to stay by Pak Zunaidi, a Bajo fisherman whom I had met in a guest house in Salakan, the brand-new capital of Banggai Islands district. He had delivered a petition for a new dock for his village, Popisi, and was on his way home.

In 2000 a tsunami swept away most of the Banggai Bajo's leggy off-shore communities, and the government had pressed the 'sea gypsies' to settle onshore. Zunaidi's house was still built on stilts over the water, Bajo-style, but it was joined to the land by a wide wooden boardwalk. Out the back of the house was a veranda which doubled as the kitchen. At the far end, behind some threadbare bamboo matting, was an oblong hole cut in the planks above the sea. This was the toilet; it afforded a stunning view of the aquamarine bay, criss-crossed by dugouts paddled by small children looking for shrimp and crabs.

As we sat on a bench in the veranda-kitchen staring out to sea, a young man in a well-worn dugout canoe paddled silently up to the offshore hut in front of us. He climbed the steps and began to dismantle the peripheral parts of the structure. I asked what he was up to. 'Moving house,' said Pak Zunaidi. Once the owner had stripped anything that might come loose, the hut would get lifted down from its stilts and floated off to its new location.

In the light of the setting sun I helped Zunaidi's wife, a schoolteacher, prepare supper. She motioned me first to the coconut-grater. The oblong stool was raised just a couple of inches off the floor. From one end, a metal arm curved upwards, swelling into a bulbous tip covered with steel bristles. My task was to squat astride the stool and, using the grater-blob rising from between my legs, to grind half a coconut around until its flesh lay shredded in a fragrant pile between my feet. Then, as Ibu Guru peeled onions and chopped garlic, I started squashing them together with chilli and lime into a *sambal* that would spice up our chunks of grilled fish. But I've never quite mastered the outward roll of the wrist that grinds the hooked pestles used by Indonesians evenly across the concave granite surface of the mortar. My sambal was forever a work in progress, lumpy, embarrassing. I offered to swap places with Ibu Guru and let her smooth things out, but she was aghast. Untold disasters will befall anyone who eats sambal started by one person and finished by someone else.

After supper, she showed me her teacher's union card. I realized, as intended, that she was a proper civil servant, not an 'honorer'. *Guru honorer* (or *honor*, as they are more commonly called) are locally appointed contract teachers, often unqualified. Though they make up around a third of the teaching force, they don't really count in the Indonesian world view because they are not civil servants, they have not been dignified with a job-for-life and a guaranteed pension. In this tiny town–on–stilts, the headmistress and four of the primary schoolteachers are civil servants; the other five are *honorer*. Ten teachers for a school with 120 children – about average for Indonesia.

At about 6.30 the following morning, Ibu Guru stood over a vat of hot oil frying up breakfast. Her youngest son came in wearing his school uniform and she told him not to be late; all over Indonesia, primary school starts at seven. Then a neighbour came in to chat. Ibu Guru put some more plantains in the oil, made another cup of coffee. By now it was ten to seven, and still she hadn't bathed or dressed. At about 7.15, I asked what time school started in Popisi. She looked sheepish, gestured at me, the neighbour, the fried plantains. 'It's okay. Everyone knows I've got guests.'

So it was my fault that she wasn't at work. I asked if I could come with her to school; perhaps I could help with the English classes? She looked hugely relieved; she bathed and washed in record time and by 7.30 we were at school.

It was mayhem. A hundred and twenty children were running around, screaming with joyous abandon. Half an hour after the start of the five-hour school day, there was not a teacher to be seen. Ibu Guru went and got a stick from the office and handed it to a child who, with great self-importance, struck a bell. Instantly, order was imposed and the kids fell into formation by class. One child stepped forward and barked. Everyone straightened up. Ibu Guru bid them good morning, and there was a polite chorus in reply. A girl led the school in singing the 'Merah Putih', a patriotic song about the national flag.

I took Classes 4 and 6 for English. Ibu Guru taught her own class, Class 1. Classes 2, 3 and 5 – aged seven, eight and ten respectively – were instructed to go into their classrooms and work through their textbooks 'until your teachers come'. The kids went into their classrooms. The teachers never came.

So there I was, faced with about thirty kids under the age of twelve, crammed into half a classroom (there aren't enough rooms in the school for all six classes so they use plywood dividers to make rooms). 'Good morning everyone!' A lusty response: 'Good morning, miss!' 'My name is Eliz; what is your name?' I addressed the question to one of the older boys who was sitting close to me. He had been learning English for three years. He was stunned to have been asked to answer something as an individual, rather than as part of a scripted chorus. Indeed he was speechless. The other kids quickly averted their eyes, lest I pick on them. I was grateful when one girl raised her hand. 'What is his name?' I asked her, pointing elaborately to the boy in the front row. 'My name is Fifi!' she declared, triumphant.

Pak Zunaidi's wife had called the headmistress to say that the school had a visitor. The head turned up at 9.30, and invited me into her cavernous office. High atop a bookshelf, well out of reach of curious children, stood three large globes, each carefully wrapped in plastic. There were anatomical models, too, one male and one female, both swathed in bubble-wrap, and a thicket of wall maps rolled around poles; they had never been opened. The headmistress explained that hers was not a teaching job; she was just supposed to keep the school going administratively. 'But sometimes I have to teach,' she sighed. 'We've got so few staff. What can you do?'

Some of the obsession with civil service jobs may be a hangover from the chaos and hyperinflation of the mid-1960s. Salaries were worthless across the board, but government jobs at least came with something useful: rations of rice, cooking oil and sugar. At a time when poor Indonesians wore sackcloth in the marketplace, there was fabric, too, for uniforms. Perhaps that contributed to the uniform-mania that persists to this day. Indonesians love uniforms of every type. Civil servants, even ministers and bupatis, wear uniforms every day. Most central government agencies allow formal batik shirts on Fridays, and some local governments require a weekly showing of the traditional textiles of the region. The national red thread: an engraved name-tag, white on black plastic, and a little gold badge of office.

The bigwigs can morph between uniforms, depending on the occasion. 'On the campaign trail, local politicians change clothes more often than Madonna during one of her concerts,' the political scientist Michael Buehler said when I noted the uniform-mania. 'The Governor of South Sulawesi is a bureaucrat in the morning, a boy scout at noon, a devout Muslim in the afternoon and a businessman in the evening.' He simply chooses the uniform of whichever group he's currently appealing to.

Civil service uniforms, mostly in dreary shades of beige, olive or blue, are splash-brightened by embroidered logos, one for the unit of government, another for the department. These have become such a feature of the Indonesian landscape that they have been copied by political parties, corporations, Vespa owners' clubs. Even listed terrorist groups have embroidered flash-badges that assert their identity. People from the same village going on pilgrimage to Mecca will dress the same. At weddings, the families will share a look, not just the bridesmaids, but the parents and siblings of both bride and groom, their various spouses and kids: the whole clan.

The 1960s turned the civil service into a welfare state for the well-connected; no one was paid much, but then they weren't really expected to do any work either. If they could use their position to squeeze a fee out of someone who did have some cash, all well and good. The ethos persists, though it's now easier to top up your earnings legally. 'My base salary is five million a month,' one bureaucrat told me – about five hundred dollars. The gentleman worked for the Ministry of Agriculture and was trying to encourage people in the eastern islands to reduce their dependence on rice and go back to eating root vegetables. He had arrived from the provincial capital on a Thursday afternoon for a supervisory visit. He had gone to the district office on Friday morning but found no one there, so he settled into our guest house to wait until Monday or Tuesday, when someone might show up for work. At least five days' travel money, for an hour-long meeting. 'After all the allowances, I never take home less than ten million a month, even before considering any "extras" I might like to take advantage of.' He made scare quotes with his fingers around the unspecified 'extras'. From my own observations in the Ministry of Health, they could have included anything from kickbacks on computers to payment for phantom training workshops.

All of the increments that bring a civil servant's salary up to a living wage are in the gift of that person's superior. In other words, every department of government is a giant clan, a pyramid of patronage that cascades from the Minister right down to the cleaners. The patriarchal structure is reflected in the language people use to talk about their underlings: *anak buahku*, which incorporates the word *anakku*, my child.

I was always surprised to see how carefully the middle managers that I worked with at the health ministry doled out the things that legally earned their staff extra cash: sitting on expert panels, overseas trips, stints at conference organizing. They tried hard to make sure that each of their 'children' got a fair crack at the extras. On the one hand, this meant that training courses were full of people who were there because it was their turn, not because the subject matter was in any way relevant to their jobs. On the other, it was admirably equitable, a modern example of the sort of distribution you see at adat ceremonies – a slab of liver for this person, a snout for that one. Since the boss decides who gets what, they never get rumbled by their staff if they fill their own pockets a little too full.

A small fraction of jobs in the bureaucracy are awarded based on competitive exams. But most of the jobs that are not given out to political supporters get sold. The most expensive jobs are in the 'wet' ministries, the ones awash in money for *proyek* or services: Public Works, for example, and the Ministry of Religion which has a monopoly on organizing the annual Hajj pilgrimage to Mecca. But even relatively 'dry' ministries such as health can charge two years' base salary under the table for an entry-level job. The result is a lot of incompetent bureaucrats. The minister in charge of the 'state apparatus' recently said that 95 per cent of

Indonesia's 4.7 million civil servants didn't have the skills they needed to do their jobs.★

Indonesians complain about this system all the time. Yet, in the newer districts of Indonesia at any rate, they do nothing about it because it delivers to so many people. I can't think of a single family I stayed with anywhere in Indonesia who was separated from the bureaucracy by more than two degrees of kinship. Not the rice farmers in West Sumatra who invited me to stay because I helped them rattle tin cans to scare birds off their crops. Not the nursing-home orderly in Java who worked a nine-hour day and came home to cook for her in-laws. Not Pak Zunaidi in his stilt-house. Certainly not Pak Jopy and his family in Ohoiwait.

Ohoiwait had been a delightful place to spend Christmas: familiar and almost absurdly welcoming, the warmth spreading through the village like hot honey poured into porridge. But it was also quite hard work, all the church services and ceremonies, the being permanently on display, this strange beast from another world. I decided to take a bit of a holiday, and spend New Year in the Banda islands. Forts, cannons, a volcano rising majestically from the sea and stunning coral reefs: these things had combined to make Banda into a micro tourist destination. I would meet other foreigners, chat in English about familiar things. I would stay in a guest house; my host would not call other villagers in at six o'clock in the morning to watch me drinking 'empty coffee', coffee without sugar.

The Pelni ferry north from Tual arrived eighteen hours late, took many hours longer than the scheduled forty-four to reach Banda, and left me within walking distance of a guest house with a lovely wooden deck right opposite the volcano, Gunung Api. The first evening, I had the place to myself. I sat simply admiring the volcano as it loomed out of the water, its tree-clad slopes stroked to honey-green by the evening light. A breath of

★ This excludes the 465,000 members of the armed forces and 412,000 cops.

mist hung idly in front of the mountain; a fisherman in a canoe hollowed out of a kenari tree drifted silently by. His passage sent tiny ripples across the volcano, which was mirrored upside down in the mercury-still water. It was a moment of utter calm, smoothing away thoughts of the devastation that this very mountain had wrought through the ages.

The most recent eruption of any consequence was in 1988. I visited Banda a year later, and remember the seawater growing hotter and hotter as I swam into a cove at the base of the volcano. The gas bubbling up from underwater vents had turned the sea into a salty hot-tub. The British naturalist Alfred Wallace, writing 150 years ago, described a much angrier mountain, one whose tantrums caused earthquakes and tsunamis as well as lava flows. 'Almost every year there is an earthquake here,' he wrote, 'and at intervals of a few years, very severe ones which throw down houses and carry ships out of the harbour bodily into the streets.'*

The guest house was shouting distance from the town pier, from which small wooden water-buses left for the surrounding islands. I wanted to cross over to Lonthor, where the bigger nutmeg plantations were found. 'Is there a schedule for the boat to Lonthor?' I yelled across to the boatmen. 'Of course!' they yelled back. 'When do you leave?' I bellowed. 'When the boat is full!' came the reply.

A couple of hours later, I was padding around a forest of huge kenari trees, their buttress roots flying high above my head. Beneath these skyscrapers was another layer of more modest trees, droopy with a fruit that looked like a small yellow peach, hard as a billiard ball. A few of these fruits were split open in a scarlet grin, the dark nutmeg-shell barely showing through a web of crimson mace: a two-for-one spicefest. The mace, waxy and pliable when fresh, crisps up as it dries to a browny-orange, great for flavouring soups, curries and Christmas cookies. It is wrapped lacy around a brittle inner shell. Rattling around inside that is the

---

* Wallace, *The Malay Archipelago*, Vol. 1, Ch. XIX.

nutmeg itself, a puckered oval whose principal use these days is as an ingredient in Coca-Cola's magic formula. Between the trees people padded barefoot; they stabbed at fallen kenari nuts with cleft sticks, hefting them into woven rattan baskets on their backs. It was peaceful, but for the whining of mosquitoes that dive-bombed my ankles. So I escaped to a clearing, emerging into the platinum sunshine of midday in front of an old stone well.

'Drink!' The command came from a little gnome of a man with a quick smile who had been bouncing along a narrow path through the plantation; two giant baskets of nutmeg swung off a bamboo pole over his shoulder. 'Is the water good?' I asked. 'Of course it's good. It's a sacred well! It's only bad when it runs dry.' Today the sacred well was full of clear, cool water. I drank.

We were standing halfway up the mountainside; opposite us loomed the volcano which sits at the centre of this group of tiny islands, once so improbably the beating heart of globalization. I mentioned to the gnome that I had last visited the Bandas just after the eruption of twenty-three years earlier. 'Yes, 1988. That's when the sacred well last ran dry.' He explained that the water disappears to warn of impending disaster. Then, after a pause: 'Actually, it went dry in 1998 too, just before the conflict.' 'The conflict' in this part of Indonesia was a proxy religious war in which thousands died. I was mildly surprised that the sacred well would warn of political as well as natural disasters. But it made sense in its way: nature and politics had always been inseparable in this part of the world.

He invited me to see his *kebun* – that vague garden-to-farm word again. In this case, it referred to an area about the size of a football pitch which the farmer had fenced off inside the forest. There was a nursery of nutmeg seedlings, several adult trees groaning with fruit and one, its trunk serially slashed, that had almost no nutmegs. 'That's the male tree,' said the farmer. 'It's not very productive, but it encourages the female trees to work harder.' He cracked his gnomish grin. 'Just like humans,' he said. Then he hacked his machete into the trunk of the male tree. It oozed scarlet liquid. 'Just like humans,' he repeated.

By the time I got back to the guest house that evening, my prime location on the deck was occupied by a white man reading a book. Next to him sat a cold beer. I was nervous. There had been occasions in the last few months – peeing in the sand, wiping my nose with the back of my hand, eating chunks of mango off the point of my pen-knife, all the while scheming about how to keep my spot on the ferry after the next stop – when I'd realized that I had become a little feral. I approached my fellow guest. 'What are you reading?' I asked, by way of opening.

He turned the book to show me the cover. *The Wisdom of Whores*, it was called. I must have looked shocked. 'It's not what you think,' he said. Long pause. 'Are you enjoying it?' I asked. 'It's actually very good.' Phew. I confessed to having written it. He stared at me, looked at the author photo, looked at me again. It was hard to say which of us was the more surprised.

The guest house formed an odd little colony; John, who was reading my book, was an English teacher in a Korean school in Jakarta. Besides him there were a couple of prematurely retired Canadians who were keen divers and a Swede who believed that colonialism was a natural part of the human condition. There was a pair of bog-standard Finnish backpackers who talked a lot about money, a delightful young Dutch couple who were surprised by how much the historical narrative they found in Banda differed from the narrative in their childhood schoolbooks, and a German who became bellowingly confessional after his fourth beer. All this was topped off on New Year's Eve by a dippy trust-fund blonde with a posh English accent and a beefcake boyfriend. The dippy blonde was dressed for a beach disco in Ibiza, a spaghetti-strap white jersey number cut very high on the thigh and very low on the cleavage. The look worked well early in the evening when she was draped over the beefcake on the guest-house deck, less well after midnight and many drinks, when she was draped over the local policeman at the village street party.

On the second of January the whole company went into a bit

of a panic. It was rumoured, then confirmed, that all flights off the islands had been cancelled. They would have to wait for the next Pelni ferry back to Ambon, the provincial capital, a ten-hour journey to the north.

In fact, the flights hadn't exactly been cancelled. They had just lapsed. Flights to Banda are subsidized, chartered by a provincial government which hopes to curry favour with voters by providing cheap transport between districts. The government renews the tender for these charter flights every six months; it doesn't invite new applications until the previous contract has run its course. So twice a year, there's a period of several weeks where there are no flights. One of those gaps always falls in late December and early January: peak tourist season.

Inevitably, some islanders believe this is a plot by Ambon to undermine tourism in Banda. 'The government in Ambon is jealous of us,' said a woman who owns a guest house and has her finger in several other tourism-related pies. 'They hate that tourists just stay in Ambon for a day before heading to Banda for a week.'

When I asked the airline agent whether he thought the interruptions in service were deliberate, he laughed at the idea. 'That would be too complicated,' he said. So why don't they start the tender process six weeks earlier? I asked. 'That's the bureaucracy in this beloved country of ours. It's just how it is.' *Begitulah.*

Map F: Southern Sulawesi, Showing Buton Island   Map G: Halmahera, North Maluku

7

Spoils of the Earth

Daylight comes quickly to the tropics. Arriving before dawn in Ternate, the capital of North Maluku, I sat at a street stall waiting for it to get light. One minute I could see no further than my flowered glass of grainy coffee, the next, I was looking at the grey velvet outline of Mount Gamalama, the volcano which makes up most of Ternate. A few moments more and velvet solidified into hard-edged green. The platinum disc of the sun soared up from behind the mountain and the city, which patterns the south-eastern skirt of the volcano, sprang to life.

Gamalama is both the source of Ternate's wealth – its clove crop – and of its repeated destruction. Just over a month before I arrived in January 2012, the volcano had started coughing out great clouds of ash. A few weeks later heavy rains turned the thick blanket of ash on the upper slopes of Gamalama into a river of black mud. The cold lava oozed down the mountain, gathering force and boulders, some of them four metres across. By the time it was on the lower slopes, it bulldozed everything in its path. 'Everything' included around eighty houses and three lives.

I went to have a look at the area that had been worst hit. I found a man shovelling gravelly mud out of a house that had lost its windows, but appeared otherwise intact. His wife invited me in, apologizing because she couldn't offer me a cup of tea. The lava may have entered politely enough through doors and windows, but it had been less gentlemanly as it left, gashing through the peach-plastered back wall, leaving a three-sided room a bit like an architect's model, but muddier.

This area has always been designated high risk, and construction of houses is forbidden. But flattish land is at a premium in Ternate, so people build anyway. The woman hoped that the government would now resettle her family somewhere safer.

While waiting for a new plot, this family was living down in the local technical training centre. When the mud-flows started there were 4,000 refugees crushed into the centre; as the threat of more lava receded and the army bulldozed the mud out of the surviving houses, most drifted home. By the time I visited, around 300 people were still scattered around the training centre. They had divvied up the assembly hall, marked out territory with towers of cardboard boxes, children's bicycles, raffia strings of school uniforms, the forlorn remnants of a life before the all-embracing mud. People seemed remarkably resigned to their temporary fates, however, and for the kids, who had access to the swings and seesaws of the neighbouring kindergarten playground, it was an adventure.

It sounded as though there was a bit of a party going on out the back. I followed the sound of the music and found an olive canvas *M*A*S*H* tent: the communal kitchen. A volunteer trained in disaster preparedness used a stainless-steel garden shovel to dole rice from a waist-high cooking drum into family rice-bowls. Other volunteers plopped a few pieces of fried fish from a plastic laundry tub and a spoonful from a vat of soupy greens on top of the rice.

When the feeding was over, the music was cranked up and the kitchen turned into a temporary disco. People, mostly men, started dancing that bent-kneed, bum-jutting, twirly wristed dance that goes so well with *dangdut* music. Dangdut is an Indonesian pop music which combines vaguely Indian melodies with the dang-*dut* dang-*dut* beat of conical *gendang* drums, a sort of Bollywood–House Music mash-up.

Someone arrived with a clutch of durian. The dance floor cleared as everyone fell on the fruit, splitting open the spiky oversized hand grenades to reveal the pale yellow smush inside. You're not allowed to carry durian on planes in Indonesia, or take them into posh hotels, because their methane smell oozes through the air-conditioning system into every corner. It's an acquired taste that I've never acquired, less because of the stick-to-the-back-of-your-throat taste than because of the stick-to-the-roof-of-your-mouth texture: creamy, oily and sticky all at the same time. But now people were competing to offer me the most luscious gobs of this aphrodisiac: 'Here, here. Eat mine! Mine's sweeter than his!' There's always a lot of *double-entendre* in durian-speak.

There was a palpable sense of good-natured camaraderie among the volunteers. But when the supervisor was giving me a lift home, he looked up at the thunderclouds that had closed ranks around the top of the volcano and shook his head grimly: 'That's a big storm up there,' he said. 'Tomorrow, we cook for more refugees.'

Yes, the volcanoes destroy things. But the ash they cough out also makes these islands some of the most fertile on the planet. Indonesia strings together 127 active volcanoes; down one side of Sumatra, the giant island that guards Indonesia's western flank, and along the whole spine of neighbouring Java, volcanoes spur rice fields to extraordinary bounty. Many farmers manage three rice crops a year, against just one in less fertile regions, and they produce an abundance of fruit and vegetables too. The fire-mountains bypass Borneo, taking the southern route and sweeping up in a great arc through the hundreds of small islands that make up Maluku, and pimpling the northern tip of Sulawesi as well. It is in these eastern regions, and especially in the smaller islands such as the Bandas and Ternate where sea breezes waft constantly over the volcanoes' slopes, that the ash gives life to spices.

The vulcanology services can afford to monitor around half of the mountains that are currently active. Occasionally a big eruption wakes up some of the dozens that are sleeping. Mount Sinabung in Sumatra, which has been snoozing since at least 1881, for example, suddenly came back to life in 2010. This

Sleeping Beauty effect was probably a slow reaction to the kiss of an under-sea eruption six years earlier. That eruption led to the tsunami on Boxing Day, 2004, that killed 170,000 Indonesians, mostly in Aceh, and that marks lives and behaviour to this day.

I was in the highlands of Aceh in April 2012 when my phone started beeping madly, the messages coming in from Jakarta, Sumba, even more distant Papua. 'Where are you?' 'Are you OK?' I was in a minibus, clipping along over bumpy mountain roads on the way to Takengon, wondering why everyone was standing out in the street. 'Massive earthquake in Aceh. Tsunami predicted in 20 minutes.' That message was from Singapore.

In twenty minutes I was in the lobby of a quasi-posh hotel in Takengon where guests, staff and people like me who had come in off the street were all glued to the TV. The live coverage spoke of an earthquake measuring 8.6 on the Richter scale. In Banda Aceh, the coastal capital of Aceh that had only recently rebuilt itself from the devastation of 2004, people were screaming and running, getting on their bikes, in their cars, making for higher ground. As we watched the panic down on the coast, the kitsch chandelier in the mirrored ceiling above us started to tremble, then really shake. Everyone went deathly silent for a long moment; we looked at one another, as if waiting for leadership. Then someone said 'Here we go again!' and we all quick-stepped out into the rain.

That second quake was even bigger than the one of half an hour earlier. My teeth rattled along with the windows of the hotel, and the pit of my stomach began to thrum. The hotel receptionist had seized on to me. She gripped my arm until my hand went numb. By the time the chandelier stopped its tinkling, we were soaked through. The vibrations in my belly continued for quite a while, and there was no let-up on my arm. The receptionist was utterly undone by the quake; all the blood had drained from her face and her knees were weak, but she wouldn't sit down because then she'd feel the shaking all the more. She didn't want to go back inside and get out of the cold mountain rain. 'Trauma,' she kept whispering. Just that one word: 'Trauma.' Later, she told me that her mother, a brother and two sisters had been swept away in 2004. She had moved to the highlands to climb away from her memory, to silence the idea that buzzed like a mosquito in a darkened bedroom: it could happen again, it could happen to you.

People who have moved to a city, who live under a watertight roof, who control their body temperature with air-conditioning, can easily zone out the threatening downside of the nation's geography, which can wipe out your present and change your future in a few minutes. But many millions of Indonesians still pass each day in the knowledge that they are at the mercy of this unstable land.

Mother Indonesia can be menacing, certainly, but she is also extraordinarily bountiful. 'The people of Maluku got spoiled because spice trees made us rich with very little effort, there's lots of land, the sea is full of fish,' Edith, a maths professor in Ambon, the capital of Maluku, had told me.

I'm never sure whether Indonesians know how unfashionable they are being when they trace human behaviours to climate and the wealth of the land and sea, particularly if those behaviours are laziness, profligacy, a failure to plan ahead. But they do it all the time. Maybe it is only unfashionable in the world of 'development', where (mostly white, cold-climate) people earn good salaries trying to atone for the sins their forefathers have visited on (mostly brown, warm-climate) people. The 'generous earth makes people lazy' argument seems to tar people in warm latitudes with a single, undesirable brush simply because of where they were born; akin to racism, almost. But from Indonesian mouths, '*Kami di manja bumi*', 'Mother Earth has spoiled us', is something I heard over and over.

The staple food in Maluku and Papua is sago, which is scraped out of the centre of a palm tree and made into a flour which can then be baked into dry pancakes or used to make a gluey paste which provides ballast to a good fish-head curry.

The pancakes taste to me like so much dried cardboard, and the English adventurer Sir Francis Drake, visiting these islands in 1579, described wet sago as 'tasting in the mouth like sour curds', but it provides a lot of calories with a minimum of work. It takes a family about four days of cutting, scraping, washing and drying to harvest enough sago to feed themselves all year. 'People around here never had to think ahead,' said Edith. 'We got lazy.'

It's not just Maluku. In terms of land mass, Indonesia is the fifteenth biggest country in the world. But it is among the world's top three producers of palm oil, rubber, rice, coffee, cocoa, coconuts, cassava, green beans and papayas, as well as cinnamon, cloves, nutmeg, pepper and vanilla. It's also in the world's top ten for tea, tobacco, maize and groundnuts, together with avocados, bananas, cabbages, cashews, chilli, cucumbers, ginger, pineapples, mangoes, sweet potatoes and the humble pumpkin. It's a top-ten producer of forestry products, and pulls more fish out of its seas and waterways than any country except China.

And there's another layer of bounty, under the crust. Indonesia sits above huge chambers of natural gas. The Grasberg mine in Papua has more known gold reserves than anywhere else on the planet, and it's not even a gold mine; its day job is to produce copper. Indonesia is the world's second largest producer of tin and coal, after China, and it's by far the biggest exporter of both minerals. It produces bauxite (for aluminium) and lots of nickel – again, it's already the world's number-two producer (after Russia, this time) and number-one exporter. It even digs out of the ground things that I had always thought were manufactured. Asphalt, for example.

When I was with the Bajo fisherman Pak Zunaidi in Sulawesi's Banggai islands, I met a lobster farmer who told me that his brother Dauda managed an asphalt mine in Buton, which hangs off the bottom stroke of Sulawesi's K. Huh? I had always thought that asphalt was a by-product of petroleum. 'No, no. You dig it out of the ground. My brother will show you the mines.' So when I got to Buton, I called Dauda. It turns out that Indonesia is one of the world's largest producers of natural asphalt (though asphalt can also be manufactured as a by-product of petroleum, as it happens). And Buton is the biggest producer in Indonesia. On its website Buton Asphalt Indonesia proudly posted photos of highways as smooth as Formula One tracks. The highways were in China, admittedly, but still, they looked impressive. I inspected the map; the village where Dauda's mine was said to be wasn't marked, but it was in an area that seemed to be about seventy-five kilometres from town, a fair distance for a day-trip on the girly, automatic transmission motorbike I had hired in Bau-Bau, but doable.

Dauda was having none of it. 'You can't come by bike. The road is terrible!' In Java I used to wave such objections away: I'm not scared of a bit of mud. But in recent months I had learned that in the eastern islands 'the road is terrible' means something between impassable and non-existent. I went down to the bus station and asked about transport to Nambo, but everyone shook their head. 'No one wants to do that route any more. The road's terrible.' For the only time in that year of travel, I hired a car and driver.

With a punky twenty-two-year-old at the wheel, I could just enjoy the view. We drove through a pretty valley of tidy rice-paddies, incongruously dotted with Hindu temples. The punk described the village as 'pure Bali', a transmigration site that had been here since the 1960s. The temples were breeze-block imitations of the red-brick originals of Bali. While the houses in the surrounding villages were colourful wooden affairs built up on stilts, here concrete homes squatted on the ground. Along the roadside in front of them, election posters showed candidates for bupati of the fiercely Islamic district of Buton posed next to Photoshopped pictures of Balinese maidens with towers of fruit piled on their heads.

Ten kilometres out of Bau-Bau, the tarmac burst apart into a spine-jolting mass of lumps. Further on, it joined forces with a stream. As we hydroplaned our way through a dark forest, the punk reached for a kretek, looked at me, put it back in the pack, looked at me again. After months on public buses, it hadn't occurred to me that someone might have qualms about lighting up. I invited him to smoke. He grabbed a cigarette and lit up urgently. I laughed: wow, you really needed that! 'It's not that, Miss. The thing is, this is where the bad spirits are. The smoke keeps them away.' When a wild boar ran out into the road-stream in front of us, the punk nearly drove into the jungle.

Eventually, the stream dried up, but the mud didn't. As the lumps of tarmac became less frequent, we skidded around. We were laughing, but I held on to the dashboard and the punk's knuckles were white on the steering wheel. And then suddenly, close to our destination, the road smoothed out. It wasn't tarmac, exactly, but it wasn't mud either. I got out to have a look and found the road spongy under my feet, like that rubber stuff they put under the swings in children's playgrounds so that no one gets hurt too badly if they fall. We were driving on natural asphalt, just sitting there on the earth's surface, compacted into something that looked like a road by the weight of the trucks from the mines.

Mine manager Dauda had a degree in political communication from an Islamic university in Luwuk, in Central Sulawesi. He had no luck getting the dreamed-of civil service post; rather than do nothing, he took a job at an asphalt mine in his mother's village. We walked together to one of the 'mines'. It was nothing more than a giant bite taken out of the hillside. From a distance the ground looked like broken granite, but it had the same spongy feel as the road. I picked up a grey lump and broke it open; it was black, gooey, it oozed treacle and smelled of roadworks on a summer's day. I had just mined asphalt with my bare hands.

When I think of mining I think of shafts and props, of smelters and railheads, I think of thousands of grubby figures streaming in and out of the bowels of the earth like ants in and out of an anthill, an L. S. Lowry painting. The asphalt mines of Buton could not have been more different. Here, three guys were sitting smoking under a blue tarpaulin set up to shelter them from the sun and rain. Two yellow diggers sat idly on a carpet of asphalt; all the lads had to do was activate them, position the claw over the ground, scoop up the asphalt and dump it into a truck. They weren't doing even that.

'*Istirahat dulu?*' I teased. Taking a rest? No, they had run out of diesel for the diggers. I had spent the previous day at a petrol station for fishermen, and had heard chapter and verse about inefficiencies in the fuel delivery system, so I sympathized. But this wasn't about late delivery. 'They just forget to order it. Now they have to wait ten days,' Dauda laughed. 'It happens all the time. We're not very good at forward planning in Indonesia.'

The failure to order fuel actually didn't matter much, as it happened. Asphalt mining in Buton had more or less ground to a halt when I visited because the government had, maybe, banned exports of unprocessed ore and minerals. By law, the ban was not supposed to come into effect until January 2014. Then the Ministry of Mines and Energy in Jakarta changed its mind. In February 2012 it suddenly announced that mining companies had just three months to submit full plans for processing the minerals and ores they mined. If they didn't put in plans by the deadline, they wouldn't get any more export permits.

I visited the mines in Buton the week after the deadline. No one had any idea whether they were allowed to export or not. Does the regulation cover asphalt? No one knew. What constitutes processing? Dauda's company smashes up the lumps it digs out of the ground and sticks the smaller lumps in sacks. 'That's semi-processed, we think, so we should be okay.' But they were uncertain, and it was hard to check; the ministry had put the new regulation on its website, then taken it down the same day. The 'build a processor' measure was supposed to add value to exports and create jobs for Indonesians. But for now, Dauda had laid off all the day labourers at the mine. The few regular staff had shifted over to sewing sacks. 'But there's only so long we'll be able to go on paying them, so we really need to know what's going on.'

The export ban was struck down by the Supreme Court six months after it supposedly came into effect. A month after that, the Constitutional Court had its say. This time, the court handed back to the districts certain powers that the ministry had tried to swipe for the national government. That was just two days after another major confusion, about a regulation that required foreign mining firms to sell over half of the equity in their Indonesian ventures to Indonesian companies.

When that rule was announced, some of Indonesia's largest foreign investors made their displeasure known in no uncertain terms. The two ministries involved clarified the situation. We've decided to postpone the rule, said the Minister for Energy and Mineral Resources. No, we haven't, said the Chief Economic Minister, the same day.

Asphalt brings in plenty of taxes and royalties, and the potential for future earnings is huge: Buton's reserves are estimated at 3.6 billion tonnes; at current prices that's a 'street value' of US$360 billion. Judging from the road we'd arrived on, not much of it seemed to be going into local infrastructure.

Dauda and I wandered down to the shore, where a long, low mountain of raw asphalt sat waiting to be shipped out – 50,000 tonnes of the stuff. Behind it, a dozen or so young men in cut-off jeans and torn T-shirts were filling little wooden cribs full of river-rocks, then scrambling around to pack them in between rusting steel rods and shaky wooden planks. This was the skeleton of a new pier that is being built to promote exports.

In front of the mountain, a billboard featuring a photograph of the pine-studded shores of Canada's Lake Banff welcomed visitors to the asphalt mine and gave a cell-phone number, all in Chinese characters a foot high. Ban or no ban, a ship was scheduled to come in that night to cart the asphalt off to China. 'They had the export permit before the ban came in,' explained a young man who was squatting on the mountain. 'They've just been a bit slow to ship it out because of other administrative matters.' He rubbed his thumb and forefinger together. 'And they were hoping that the pier might be finished.'

It seemed quixotic, the idea that a functional port might blossom in this abandoned corner of Indonesia. But I had seen things just as unlikely on my travels. In North Maluku's Halmahera, for example.

❋

The promiscuous sharing of cell-phone numbers with fellow passengers on Indonesian ferries often leads to later encounters in port. In Ternate I had been invited to supper by an engineer I'd met on the boat. Sitting next to us as we feasted on great slabs of grilled fish down by the waterfront was a bird-like man with the broad, high-cheeked face of one of Halmahera's indigenous minorities. In the way of small-town people when they come to the big city, slightly distrustful, slightly awkward, he kept his rucksack strapped to his back as he attacked a plate of fried chicken. But when he overheard us chatting about the relative merits of different nearby islands, he barged straight in with tales of Halmahera, his home village Lelilef, and the nearby town of Weda.

The sum total of the information I had about Weda was the comment of a website dedicated to travel in the extremities of Maluku: 'a scruffy village with muddy roads'. But Pak Piter painted a different picture. The town was now the capital of Central Halmahera: 'absolutely booming'. It was an especially good time to visit, he said, because the Bupati was marrying off his twin daughters. 'Everyone who is anyone will be there,' he said.

Halmahera sits right next to tiny Ternate. Geographically the island, shaped like a squashed spider, dominates North Maluku. Politically, though, it has always been overshadowed by its little neighbour, and much neglected. When I first visited Halmahera in 1989, it was one of the least developed parts of Indonesia. I had hitched a lift through the jungle by night in an army jeep – there seemed to be no other transport except bullock carts. In the middle of the velvety jungle, a single tree was fairy-lit with the greenish white of hundreds of fireflies. It was a magical sight. Over four hundred years earlier it had impressed even Queen Elizabeth I's favourite adventurer Francis Drake, who described it thus:

Among these trees by night, did shewe themselves an infinite swarme of fierie-seeming-wormes, flieing in the aire, whose bodies (no bigger than an ordinarie flie) did make a shewe, and give such light as if every twigge on every tree had beene a lighted candle, or as if that place had been the starry spheare.*

I had marvelled at the starry sphere but when daylight came, the sight was less magical: the beautiful beaches of Halmahera were littered with rusting Second World War tanks. The Japanese had a large garrison here, which they kicked into action in late 1944 after the American General MacArthur decided to use neighbouring Morotai as a base for his Pacific adventures.

Fireflies, tanks and bullock carts are all I remember about the island from that visit in the late 1980s. Twenty-three years later, Halmahera had split into several districts, discovered nickel and generally come up in the world. Pak Piter described the transformation of his own village, Lelilef. Once a grubby hamlet of sago-palm houses and middle-school drop-outs, it had blossomed thanks to the presence of Weda Bay Nickel, a giant, foreign-owned mining company. Now, Piter said, it was a town of two-storey houses, there were cars on the roads, youngsters went to college in Java. Large foreign mining company as the hero of a development story – that was something you don't often hear. I resolved to go to the Weda weddings, then visit the mine.

I arrived back at the same harbour as I had on that first visit. There was not a bullock cart to be seen. The sole army jeep of yesteryear had been replaced by nose-to-bumper SUVs. It was as if the car park of an expensive organic supermarket in a posh suburb of London or Melbourne had been air-dropped into Halmahera. They were mostly share-taxis, waiting to speed passengers to the extremities of the island's stumpy spider-legs. I would never have imagined such a transformation.

I chose a car that was headed for Weda. We barrelled over newly tarmacked roads laid through hilly forests, we forded rivers around unfinished bridges, and eventually we cruised into

---

* Drake, *The World Encompassed by Sir Francis Drake*, p. 96.

a town that showed all the symptoms of being a new district capital. There was the divided highway, and the bupati's office towering over the town from the hill above. There was the gleaming new plate-glass hotel, which would doubtless soon moulder into a funk of dank carpets and mildewed walls like the other members of the species across Indonesia. There were a few rows of Legoland houses, and electricity even in the daytime.

I had missed the weddings by a day. Behind the plate-glass hotel, the wreckage of the feasts was still in evidence. Under a white silky-nylon awning, on red carpeting covering the area of a couple of football pitches, catering staff from the provincial capital of Ternate fussed about, stacking up hundreds of chaffing dishes, wondering what to do with industrial-sized waste-bins of leftover rice.

Party Central was fenced off from the surrounding fields and building sites by hoardings displaying larger-than-life-sized Photoshop fantasies: one of the twins as a child in front of an antebellum mansion in the American South, the other twin, dreamy in satin robe overlooking generic modern cityscape. Interspersed among them were pictures of the Bupati and his wife in exotic foreign locations (not Photoshopped) and, in particularly strategic positions, massive portraits of the Bupati in uniform, with a checklist of achievements during his first term.

First on the list: 'Building the infrastructure of government at all levels'. Another of his achievements: 'Freeing up the protected forest of Gebe island for use by the mining sector.'

'Ah, you should have got here yesterday, you could have come,' said Vera, the owner of the guest house I stayed at. 'It was a blast; we danced all night. I can't imagine what it cost!'

In fact, a fair part of the cost, some 35,000 dollars' worth, had been paid for out of the public purse. The Bupati was unapologetic about this. The loving couples had paraded across a series of trays filled with rice, symbolizing a long marriage without hunger. It was part of the local adat custom which neither Vera nor anyone else I spoke to remembered, and that was exactly the Bupati's point. His administration was trying to promote local wedding traditions, he told reporters. It was only natural that the culture and tourism department's budget for this programme should help support the biggest wedding of the year, one which was rescuing local adat from oblivion.

This revival of wedding adat burnished the Bupati's credentials as a guardian of local culture with his guests. Among the 7,000 people he had invited were the provincial governor, the provincial chief of police, the military commander, three neighbouring bupatis and some of the bigger bosses from the nickel mine across the bay.

The Bupati tacked on some more parties, the better to entertain all these Big Men. The third day of frolics was dedicated to celebrating the birthday of the PDIP, the political party which was backing the Bupati in elections later in the year. The PDIP's buffalo logo graced red-silk flags that flirted with the sea breeze in front of the hotel, outside every government building, outside the offices of other political parties. On the back of a flatbed truck, the local transgender or *waria* contingent gyrated to dangdut music, with the Bupati's face stretched over their silicone breast implants. Though they had sexed up their T-shirts with punky slashes and safety pins, they were careful not to deface the Bupati's image. Waria are simply part of the landscape in Indonesia's larger cities, widely accepted as long as they don't stray too far from the niches the community has carved out for itself: beauty salons, entertainment and sex work. On my travels to some of Indonesia's more remote areas, I now discovered that waria are also to be found in every district town. They are often imported into smaller villages to do the make-up for weddings or to dance at election rallies. Back in the tiny whale-fishing village of Lamalera I had run into two waria who had crossed the island from the main town to help decorate a new church for its inaugural mass.

The one hundred or so young people in the marching band that led the parade in Weda had upmarket polo shirts on which the Big Man's portrait was fringed by the slogan: 'My Bupati, Your Bupati: Keep Going!' The guest-house owner Vera drove past wearing a red T-shirt proclaiming 'I'm a Big Fan of Aba Acim' – the Bupati's nickname. She pointed at me and tugged at her shirt, mouthing: 'Where's yours?' I'd missed the hand-out.

Bustled along by a cheering crowd – 'Five more years!' – I marched past the Big Man himself. He stood outside his house flanked by loyal retainers, not a Big Man at all, it turned out, but a little round man with a squashed bald head, his metronome arm serially slapping high-fives into the passing crowd, his chubby face bisected by a grin of proper delight. The high-fivers in the crowd were equally delighted, as if they had just slapped hands with the Queen. In this town, at least, the Bupati seemed genuinely popular. Central Halmahera had been a district for eighteen years before Aba Acim, a Weda boy himself, became bupati in 2007. He promptly shifted the district capital to his home town; it was he that brought blue roofs and a posh hotel to this 'scruffy village with muddy roads'.

The following day was the birthday of the district, as well as the fourth anniversary of the capital's move to Weda. The 8 a.m. ceremony was compulsory for almost everyone in town, the civil servants, the schoolkids, the Family Welfare Union, the scouts and the cops, each colour-coded in the uniform of their tribe. All gathered around the town square, the cast, stage-crew and audience in the Bupati's theatre of state. A rickety ferris wheel loomed incongruous above the serried ranks, a reminder of the carnival which would come to life after the solemnities of the day.

There was a marked hierarchy among the guests. The school children and lesser civil servants stood on the far side of the square, with no shelter from the rain that threatened. I sat on red-plush stacking chairs with the Family Welfare women, under an awning just outside the community centre, which was the beating heart of the celebration. Inside, on chairs draped in white satin, were the women of the Dharma Wanita, the organization of civil service wives. The schoolkids got nothing, we got a box of sticky cakes, the Dharma Wanita got a fried chicken lunch. The front row of armchairs was reserved for the biggest bigwigs;

they got tins of Coke and Fanta to our plastic glasses of water.

There was an attempt at military precision. The 'Commander in Chief' of the ceremony kept barking orders over the tannoy system: 'High-school students, two steps to the right. Arms up! Ready: *one! two!*' And the high-school students measured off the distance between themselves and their neighbours with one arm stretched forward, the other to the right, and goose-stepped into place. 'Trendy sunglasses: *off!*' Sunglasses disappeared into pockets. 'Cell phones: *off!*' No visible activity. After another five or ten minutes of waiting, the newly serried ranks puddled back into disarray and there was more barking.

At about 9.15 the inner sanctum began to fill with buzzing walkie-talkies and the military commands became more urgent. The Bupati's twin daughters arrived in long satin gowns, baby blue with fuchsia sequinned tops, similar but non-identical, like the girls themselves. Their new husbands wore matching blue shirts with shiny fuchsia ties. There was a hum of anticipation, an ululation, and then a stream of dancers, culminating in a parade of white-clad figures in tall, cylindrical masks with vicious jutting noses, topped in the folded-napkin headgear of Halmahera. The effect was more than a little menacing. I asked Vera what they symbolized but she couldn't say. '*Adat baru, kali,*' she said, laughing. 'Some new tradition, I imagine.'

Behind the ghosts came a large, bottomless plywood 'boat' carried by policemen dressed as local warriors – they couldn't use the real kora-kora war canoes demanded by tradition because the new parade grounds were far from the beach. Inside the boat, curtained by palm fronds, shuffled the Bupati and his wife. Once the Bupati was installed on his throne in the community centre, the ceremony proper could begin. There was a little history of the district, a lot of gratitude for enlightened leadership, then a dizzying show of interwoven marching, drumming and snapping about of rainbow flags, all led by three towering majorettes in flowing gold lamé cloaks who marked time by stamping their sequinned maxi boots.

In their quest to justify new districts or to consolidate their power, local Big Men across Indonesia have been bathing themselves in ceremonies that they once shunned as the stuff of backward peasants. They scrabble in the attic for long-forgotten traditions, and if they can't find them, they conjure up new ones. Sub-districts grind to a halt as local leaders disappear to the district capital for heritage celebrations that last a whole week. At each of these, vast fairgrounds mushroom with elaborate stalls representing every branch of government. 'There's no opting out,' complained a nurse who was manning a health department stall in Aceh Singkil. 'We're overworked in the hospital as it is, but for a whole week we have to come here and put up bunting, give out leaflets, try and get more people to sign our visitors' book than theirs' – she jutted her chin towards the Family Planning Bureau stall opposite. Every sub-district has a stall as well, pimping the delights specific to their own tiny republic. Here I was offered a plastic cup of iced seaweed soup, there I was allowed to try spinning silk from local cocoons ('Our moths are famous all around the world').

These fairs are an orgy of competitive identity-creation. And yet, observed Ed Aspinall, an Australian researcher of Indonesian politics, in response to my musing on the reinvention of local traditions, these ceremonies follow the same pattern nationwide. 'To me it's the local cultural stuff that seems cheap and ersatz,' he said. 'It's the bureaucratic impulse and template that seem deep and authentic. It's *very* Indonesian.'

The giant nickel mine about which Pak Piter had been so enthusiastic was less than two hours by speedboat from the town of Weda. The project, covering nearly 550 square kilometres in Halmahera, was authorized by Suharto just before he resigned. Then the fireworks of decentralization began. No one knew if licences signed at the national level would be honoured by provinces or districts; indeed it wasn't even clear which province or district this particular mine was in: Maluku when the deal was done, notionally North Maluku a year later, though the new province had no functioning offices, competent staff or clear district boundaries. As if that weren't enough, the whole region was being shredded by a war between Christians and Muslims. It was hardly an ideal time for foreigners to sink billions of dollars into an unmovable industry.

The project was revived in 2006 when French mining giant Eramet bought a stake.* Then a group of Jakarta-based NGOs, run mostly by well-educated middle-class activists and with strong support from international lobbyists, protested because a large part of the area slated for open mining was also zoned as protected forest. They fretted that if there were rare bats in unmapped underground caves, they would be disturbed by the mining, and that indigenous tribes who live in the area covered by the mine might suffer. And they worried about the company's plans to dump waste from the mines in the bay, an area rich with corals and fish. The NGOs said they were speaking on behalf of local people who were too scared of reprisals to give their names. When the NGOs organized demos, some locals then staged counter-demos in support of the mine.

When I went down to get the speedboat to Lelilef, the lads on the dock grabbed my bag and loaded it on to the Weda Bay Nickel company speedboat. Odd how, without changing a thing myself, I was pressed into different shapes in different parts of Indonesia, moulded according to the die cast by the foreigners who have gone before me. I clearly wasn't a tourist: I was too old, I had too little exposed flesh, and I didn't want to go to the beach. And I was alone, whereas tourists travel in pairs. 'Don't you have any friends?' I was often asked.

The possibilities for a short-haired white woman with a face battered by months of boat travel, dressed in long-sleeved cottons, sensible shoes and a black photographer's waistcoat, a woman who spoke with a Jakarta accent and was always scribbling in a notebook were: in Sumba, a researcher on a malaria study; in Tanimbar and Kei, an anthropologist. In Flores, a nun (!) When

---

* It shared the deal with the Japanese firm Mitsubishi; a bone of 10 per cent of shares was thrown to the Indonesian state mining company.

I got over to post-tsunami, pre-ballot Aceh, I was either an aid worker or an election monitor. In Kalimantan, I must be from an environmental NGO. In the smaller regional cities of Indonesia, an English teacher. Here in Weda they assumed I was an engineer.

I retrieved my bag from the company boat and sat in the public boat with Tesi, who was on her way home to Lelilef after the Bupati's twin weddings. I had been handed into Tesi's care by her cousin Vera, the owner of the guest house I had stayed at in Weda. 'That's what family is for!' insisted Vera. Tesi didn't say a word; she just made room for me in the boat.

In less than two hours, the speedboat deposited us on a squonky wooden dock and we made for land. We piled all of Tesi's city purchases into a flatbed truck, and drove past a one-room infirmary. Then a market, which consisted of two wooden kiosks, closed, and three ladies sitting on the ground behind little pyramids of sago and cassava. I saw two churches and a mosque. There were several new houses with multi-coloured porticoes, but not much else. Either the short drive from the dock to Tesi's place did not take us through town, or Pak Piter, who had painted pictures of a boom town in my mind, led a rich fantasy life.

Tesi's house was much bigger than I'd expected. The front entrance, with obligatory portico, led into a sitting room dominated by a sofa set – one big leatherette sofa, two matching armchairs and a smoked-glass and aluminium coffee table; the sort of room you have to have for negotiating dowries and entertaining census enumerators but that is otherwise never used. In a cavernous central room with a cool, tiled floor sat a giant flat-screen TV, a big karaoke machine, and nothing else. Off that were a couple of bedrooms. I was assigned one furnished with a foam mattress on the floor and a Hello Kitty poster on the wall.

By the side entrance there was another sofa set; this is where friends are received, palm wine is poured and many cigarettes are smoked. Unusually, there was a room with a big dining table and a fridge, the latter used as a cupboard because the generator only runs in the evenings. The kitchen was a concrete cavern out the back. In every room, snakes of wires writhed down walls and across the floor, slithered over doorjambs and under sofas and chairs. This whole house had been built, just in the last few years, without any internal wiring.

Along all four roads that make up this town, wooden and palm-leaf huts are being elbowed aside by concrete and tile confections. Some have glazed windows and many have creative paint-jobs: fake marbling on the columns, variegated panelling on shutters and doors. Though it was not the boom town I had imagined, it was all very *gengsi*. Gengsi is showing off, keeping up with the Joneses – a habit that most Indonesians say they despise, and many engage in with great enthusiasm.

I wandered the town looking for something to eat, and stopped to chat with a woman washing vegetables on a boardwalk that tottered over the bay. At the sound of my Jakarta accent, two young men appeared. They were from Ternate, had been in Lelilef for two months, and were taut with boredom and frustration. Hired to train staff at Weda Bay Nickel in English and computer skills, they had given their first lesson only that day. 'I took this job because I didn't want to deal with all the bureaucracy that you get in government,' said the English teacher. 'But this is worse. The Japanese guy doesn't want to do it the French way, and the French guy won't talk to the Australian, and no one will talk to the Batak. If this work unit wants it, that sub-division will try to block it. It's mind-blowing.'

In 2007 Indonesia became the first country to pass a law obliging companies extracting natural resources to invest in the local community, but the habit is not yet entrenched. Over the next day or two, I heard all sorts of tales of well-intentioned Corporate Social Responsibility programmes gone horribly wrong. Early on, the community liaison officers had encouraged locals to grow vegetables for the workforce. The cabbages appeared, the workers didn't – construction had been delayed for the umpteenth time. The company let the vegetables, and their own reputation, rot in the hands of the farmers.

Once the workers did start to arrive and the canteen opened, the CSR officers asked the locals to raise chickens. When the birds were squawking around ready for the pot, the international catering franchise which ran the mine's canteen refused to buy them, saying they didn't meet the standards set by bosses in Geneva or Turin. A private-sector version of the Fuckwit Factor, I imagine, though locals saw something more sinister in the company's incompetence. 'It has to be deliberate, they couldn't be that stupid,' smarted the chicken-farmer who told me of the fiasco.

My quest for a plate of rice was thwarted: neither of Lelilef's food stalls opened after noon. I found a plastic bin of freshly baked buns on the side of the road. I took all twelve buns, left 12,000 rupiah in the bin, and wolfed one down on the way back to Tesi's. There was no one at home; I put the buns on a plate and set them on the table for when Tesi and her husband Frilax came back. Then I went to have a shower, scooping cool water over myself out of the big concrete tank, trying to wash the dust of progress out of my hair.

I emerged to see an empty plate. A crowd of small boys had swooped on the bun-mountain and demolished it; they raced around squealing until Tesi's daughter, with all the authority of an eleven-year-old, charged in the door and chased them off. She and her friend went to cook supper. There was rice and cassava, and because the family had just got back from Weda, there were some eggs too.

They had barely finished cooking when the next swarm of locusts descended, these ones in their late teens, pie-eyed with drink. They took turns in the bathroom; in Indonesia even the louts are impeccably clean. Then they attacked the kitchen, taking hostage all the food the girls had just produced. Who are these guys, who just storm in, use the bathroom, clean out the larder, with not a please or thank you between them? 'Saudara,' shrugs Tesi's daughter: 'Relatives'. Tesi's younger brother was to be married the following day, it turned out, and the clan had turned up from villages all around.

When I went into my designated room that evening I found the daughter and her friend already bedded down on the one mattress. I pushed them over and made room for myself, wondering whether I wouldn't be better off just laying my sleeping mat on the floor of the big, empty central room. I was glad I hadn't. When I emerged the next morning, I found seven or eight of the louts strewn across the floor, felled by alcohol and exhaustion while still fully dressed.

As they downed their supper, these boys had vented about the mining project. In an earlier age a nod from Jakarta was enough to guarantee that a large mining company could just get on with its business, whatever boys like this thought. Most villagers would not have conceived of protesting; any that did would find themselves quickly under an army boot. Now, however, locals are encouraged to express their frustrations by a domestic and international protest industry with access to a free press and the Twittersphere. These activists hope that more local engagement will put pressure on mining companies to do less harm to the environment, pay fairer prices for land and labour, and invest more in communities around mine sites.

The boys at the dinner table were certainly engaged. The drunkest of the bunch, a lad with a weaselly face and leering eyes, complained that only the grunt work went to locals, all the good jobs, ejining, architing (he broke down on the multisyllabic words of the engineering professions) were going to outsiders. 'That's why I was right in there with the demos, burning the speedboats and that. We got to show them who's boss.' I asked what skills he had. 'Getting drunk!' replied another of the louts. A third young man, a softly spoken lad who had been to school in Java, looked embarrassed. 'You want good jobs and you burn speedboats. It's just a way of shooting yourself in the foot.'

Proud though he was of his demo record, Weasel-face was happy enough to roar off after dinner on a brand-new motorbike bought with money that Weda Bay Nickel had paid his family for land. Later that night he drove the bike into the sea. It was found at low tide the following morning, marooned in the sand and lapped by the waves. There was no sign of the key.

Over breakfast, I tried to hatch a plan that would get me past the security post and into the mine. A good-looking young man from western Indonesia came into the coffee shop where I sat mulling. He was wearing a smart, dark-blue uniform that I couldn't immediately identify. 'You're from Jakarta,' he observed, and we started to chat. Amir was a policeman from Java, stationed in Weda and currently on loan to the Weda Bay Nickel security team. He was bright, he was bored and he was friends with the doctor at the mine. Minutes later I was on the back of his motorbike, driving out past the company airstrip, through the pit of orange earth where the port and the smelter will be, and up to the mine site. There was a bit of walkie-talking back and forth at the security post, and then I was through the gate.

It was like stepping into a different world.

The medical centre was in temporary housing, basically a series of converted containers, yet it was the cleanest and best-equipped health facility I'd seen in rural Indonesia.

Amir's friend, a doctor who works for the private contractor SOS Medika which runs the mine clinic, invited me to lunch. She put on her steel-capped boots, and we both put on hard hats, then we walked across fifty metres of open courtyard to the canteen. There was not a piece of construction equipment for miles around, but hard hats are part of the protocol. In a country where one regularly sees people hanging off electricity pylons splicing wires together with their bare hands, that alone was astonishing.

The canteen, air-conditioned to within an inch of its life, looked much like any other canteen I've eaten in: the one at the World Health Organization in Geneva, or the World Bank in Washington, or the BBC in London. It doesn't have the decent wine selection of the International Monetary Fund or the competitive array of national olive oils of the European Commission, but there's a salad bar, a soup station, and fresh cold-climate fruits. A cheese selection, even. Cheese! I wished we hadn't come in just as they were starting to clear up.

Everyone else in the canteen was either white or had the straight-haired, light-skinned look that signals Java and the western islands. They lived in a hermetically sealed environment for several weeks at a time, then got flown out on company planes for R&R in Java, Bali or some other 'civilized' part of the country. Soon, their environment would be even better sealed; as Amir and I drove back to town we passed workmen putting up the skeleton of a cavernous building, several times larger than anything in Lelilef. It was the new security post. Giant security posts rising from the jungle, soldiers and police where they've never been seen before; these surely add to the tension between mining conglomerates and the locals who live off the land in mineral-rich areas. And yet I found myself sympathizing slightly with Weda Bay Nickel. They have invested a lot in trying to figure out how to get maximum ore with minimum damage to the environment. They are at least *trying* to fund local doctors, install village generators and improve education and training opportunities for locals. It may be largely tokenistic, hamstrung by the profit-seeking habits embedded in the DNA of mining companies, but it is a start.

The same can't be said for the other two nickel miners in the area, both Chinese owned. They dumped tailings upriver so that five villages lost their drinking water and the turquoise corals of Weda Bay were threatened with brown sludge. While Franco-Japanese Weda Bay Nickel invested billions in a nickel processing plant which will create hundreds of jobs locally and allow Indonesia to get more for its minerals, Chinese cargo ships sat in the bay coughing out toxic fumes for just long enough to load up and ship off. Their goal was to get as much nickel ore out of Indonesia as they could before the ban on raw metal exports came into force. The locals refer to them as 'scratch and runs'.

People complained about Tekindo, the largest of the Chinese miners, all the time. They are skinflints, they break promises, they treat the locals like dirt. And yet no one burned *their* speedboats, no one demonstrated against *them*. I asked why not. 'What's the point?' said Tesi's husband Frilax. 'Chinese companies, they're all shits.'

✳

When I got back to Lelilef from the mine, I was swept into the preparations for yet another wedding. Tesi's brother was getting married and the dirt-floor and sago-palm-walled kitchen of their mother's house had been turned into an industrial bakery. Little tin box ovens were heating over wood fires or gas rings. From these boxes appeared loaves of chocolate-swirl bread and pound cakes in ring moulds, flavoured and tinted green with pandan leaves. In the yard a woman used a wooden oar to stir sticky rice, brown palm sugar and coconut milk together in a giant wok suspended over an open fire. When it was done, she paddled it into flowery enamelled trays to set.

There was quite a bit of sartorial *gengsi*, of showing off, at the wedding. Tesi's mother and I were the only two women wearing the traditional sarong kebaya – a long, fitted tunic over a sheet of batik, carefully pleated into an ankle-length skirt and held in place with an elasticated corset. All the other women were trussed up in 'modern' kit. The bride wore a tiara and a Western-style wedding gown in white satin with a silver lace overlay. There were long gowns in apricot chiffon, polkadot dresses with puffy bolero jackets, a lot of leatherette handbags. One wizened granny who had long since lost her teeth wore a sequinned Spandex top over a tulle skirt that fluttered well above the knee. She twirled alongside the *cakalele* war dance, led by the more important men of the village who used palm fronds in place of swords, until trickles of sweat traced brown pathways through her rice-flour face powder.

Later, after the wedding, I sat on the floor of Tesi's living room, chatting with her for the first time. 'What's your name?' she asked. I had shared a mattress with this woman's daughter for two nights now. I had washed clothes at her well, grilled fish with her husband, worked in her mother's kitchen and been to her brother's wedding. And she didn't even know my name. It somehow made her hospitality all the more gracious.

Tesi was a middle-school teacher. She seemed ambivalent

about education in general: her nine-year-old son had not been to school for over a week simply because he didn't want to. She had tried to put his maroon school shorts on him one morning but he had thrown a tantrum and run off. She immediately gave up, saying only: 'Boys. What can you do?' There was no question of her giving up her civil service position, but she complained that her job was boring as well as poorly paid. Almost all Indonesian teachers complain, with very good reason, about how little they are paid. Most do other jobs on the side – take in laundry for example, or run a coffee shop. I asked Tesi if she had thought about setting up a business. Like what? she asked. Well, I said, within a year or two there would be at least 6,500 workers at Weda Bay Nickel. And there were only two food stalls in town, both closed in the evenings. She finished teaching at noon each day. How about opening an evening food stall?

She considered this for a while, then shook her head. '*Nanti capek*': too tiring.

Tesi's verdict made me think back to Mama Lina up the volcano in Adonara, and the casual expectation of bounty implied by her stab, toss, kick, stab, toss, kick approach to planting maize. The deeply rooted village populations of Indonesia have always lived fairly close to subsistence and millions remain contented with that life.

Those with more ambition have tended to move to the city or to another island to seek their fortune. These people, including the salt-fish ladies of Buton, the nasi Padang cooks of West Sumatra, and aspiring professionals like my friend Anton the *ojek* driver from Flores, are collectively known in their new homes as *pendatang*. *Pendatang* translates literally as 'a person who has arrived', though Indonesian friends offer alternative translations that range from 'guest' to 'invader'. These are the savers and planners, the people who work hard and invest thoughtfully in education or a little business, in things that will improve the prospects for their family and their kids. The millions of

Indonesians who embody middle-class values, in other words.

Now, suddenly, the wealth that lies under Indonesia's skin and that sprouts from its fertile soil is catapulting villagers in places like Lelilef into the ranks of the middle classes, at least according to the World Bank, which rules a line through an income level of US$2 a day and labels everyone above it 'middle class'. Villagers in some very out-of-the-way parts of Indonesia have, in the commodities boom of recent years, earned well over two dollars a day for palm oil, rubber, copra, cocoa, nutmeg, cloves and other plantation crops. Others have sold their land to mining companies. But their new wealth does not always come with save-and-invest values.

'Look! Look at her!' sniffed my neighbour on the cake production line as we prepared for Tesi's brother's wedding. She was a hefty woman with just two teeth, one blackened by betel, the other gold. She jutted her chin towards a younger woman who had casually stretched her arms forward so that everyone could see the new-model cell phone she was playing with. 'See that? They sell all their land to the company and get a chunk of cash all at once. They build a flash house, fine. But then they buy five motorbikes on credit. One family. Not just any motorbikes mind you, smart ones that cost twenty million. Then three cell phones each. And in two years' time they will have nothing to eat and no land to grow anything on and debts still to pay. Then what?'

At the time of my trip, the Indonesian government was behaving not unlike the villagers of Lelilef; raking in money from commodities, living easy and spending large, though not on anything that contributed much to economic growth. Then what? It seemed like a question that pinstriped researchers at banks in Hong Kong, committees of think-tank worthies, or foreign journalists might be asking. But they were, at the time, busy heaping Indonesia's economy with praise.

The economic pundits waxed lyrical about Indonesia's 'demographic dividend' – the bulge in the young working-age population, which looks great on a computer screen in Hong Kong or Jakarta. In theory, young households save up and banks lend those savings out to new businesses. More young workers means more people making things, ergo more wealth. In practice, though, a third of young Indonesians are producing nothing at all, four out of five adults don't have a bank account, and banks are lending to help people buy things, not to set up new businesses.*

One of the think-tanks, McKinsey Global Institute, was so excited by Indonesia's prospects that it bypassed the middle class and its save-and-invest values entirely, suggesting that the country would get rich through shopping. 'Around 50 percent of all Indonesians could be members of the consuming class by 2030, compared with 20 percent today,' the management consultants said in a report that was immediately trumpeted across the newspapers. That would add 85 million New Consumers – people with net incomes of more than US$300 a month – to today's 55 million.

McKinsey consulted 'many experts in academia, government and industry' for its report: nine Indonesian cabinet ministers, a couple of ambassadors and another seventy-five economists and captains of industry. I wondered how many of them had ever seen what the demographic dividend was delivering in villages like Lelilef.

---

* 2012 figures indicate that three in ten Indonesians aged between fifteen and twenty-four are neither in education nor working, even informally. Over 6 million Indonesian high-school graduates are currently unemployed; many companies find them unemployable. Companies say that close to half of the 'skilled' workers they do hire don't have the critical thinking, computing or English language skills they need to do their jobs well.

Map H: THE SANGIHE AND TALUD ISLANDS, North Sulawesi

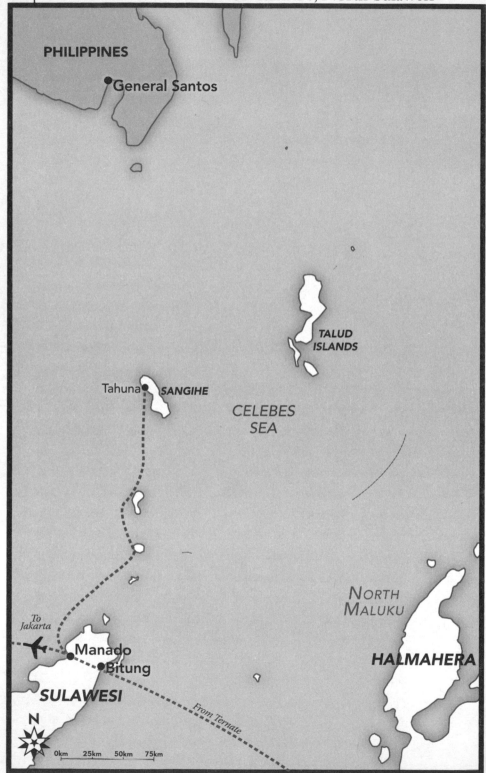

8

Profits on Ice

I love frontier towns. There's always something slightly shifty about them, as if nothing is permanent, as if everyone is wheeling and dealing. Tahuna is such a place. It sits on the island of Sangihe, one of the lumps that arc upwards from the north-eastern limb of Sulawesi, and of all Indonesia's towns it is among the closest to the Philippines. It's been infiltrated with things from its brash northern neighbour: motorcycle rickshaws fitted with huge boom-boxes and blinged-up stickers of buxom blondes, Coca-Cola in giant glass bottles, pop-tarts with fluorescent fillings. There's less of the torpor that one often finds on small islands.

I unfolded myself after a cramped ferry ride and set out for a stroll along Tahuna's sea wall in the golden light of evening, admiring the fishing boats that dot the harbour, each painted in its own distinctive strip, pale blues, bright oranges, sea greens, lots of white. The boats, big and small, have V-shaped hulls, long and narrow, flourishing into an elegant curl at both prow and stern. On either side are bamboo outriggers, hanging off lanky struts that straddle the hull. On land, these give the boats the look of long-limbed grasshoppers; at sea they are more colourful versions of those water-skimming insects that flit over the surface of ponds on still summer evenings. I thought it might be fun to go out in one for a day.

I kicked a football about with a couple of kids, chatted for a while to a priest who was full of ill-focused indignation and alcohol, and wondered idly about the bank of grey thunderheads that had appeared out of nowhere and was massing in the sky like a rugby team getting ready for a scrum.

Minutes later, with the now-you-see-it-now-you-don't suddenness of tropical downpours, the heavens opened. I dashed into a kiosk above the esplanade, but I was already soaked. Spray pounded up the bank, blustered through the opening in the bamboo weave of the kiosk wall, misted everything in salty dampness. The kiosk owner, another Elizabeth as it turned out, motioned me to a dryish corner and slapped down a steaming glass of tea – 'Here, this will warm you up' – and a dish of Christmas cookies, left over from the celebrations of a few weeks earlier. They were little lumpy crescents of crumbly pastry and nuts, flecked with orange peel and dusted with icing sugar, absolutely identical to the Christmas cookies my grandmother made every year until her death in 2004. A wave of nostalgia swept me close to tears.

Ibu Elizabeth and I chatted for a while about this and that – her dead husband, the price of oranges, the dangers of overdoing the spices in Christmas cookies. She thought that maybe she and my grandmother, born a century ago and 15,000 kilometres away, shared recipes because they shared a religion. Then her son wandered in. Jongky was probably in his early thirties. He stood bare-chested in front of the gap in the wall that passed for a window, silhouetted against the storm, his spiky hedgehog hair ruffled back and forth by the wind. While he chatted, he wrapped strong, clear fishing twine around a smooth wooden donut the size of a hubcap. On the end was a hook not much bigger than a crooked earring.

I asked what people around here fished for. Tuna, said Jongky, in a 'what else is there?' sort of way. What, with that thing? I had thought tuna fishermen were either Hemingway wannabes in speedboats with strapped-in rods, or the crew of vast long-line factory-boats, carelessly hauling in strings of dolphins as collateral damage. But Jongky and his friends fished off two-man outriggers, sheltered from merciless sun and driving rain by nothing more than a small tarpaulin. The front of the boat is a covered coffin into which, with luck, the fishermen will load the tuna they catch – yellow-fin mostly, or big-eye. Though the outriggers look like balsa-wood models, there's space for three fish, each up to one and a half times my weight.

Jongky showed me how the fishing is done. He stood legs apart, as though on a wobbly deck, put his left forearm through the donut, which he held with his left hand, then wound the twine several times round his right hand. The trick, he said, is to pull the fish in quickly, so that it doesn't wear itself out. A titanic fight is bad for the meat quality and it tires you out, too. But if you bring it in too quickly, the fish has a better chance of snapping the line and getting away. He jerked up his right hand, demonstrating the struggle, and I saw that it was badly scarred. Why didn't he use gloves? He sometimes did, he said, but it reduces your sensitivity, your ability to tell if the line is so taut that it might snap.

Jongky's techniques, and his equipment, are probably not that different from those used by the first tuna fishermen, who Australian scientists say were at work south of here, near the island of Timor, some 42,000 years ago. Other than small inboard engines, there's not all that much about the boats that couldn't have been around for thousands of years either. But the market is very different indeed.

Jongky does not cut up his tuna to feed to his mother Elizabeth, to his teenage sister and to the posse of children from even smaller islands who board with them here in Tahuna so that they can go to secondary school. He does not hang it out on a washing line to dry, like the whale fishermen of Lamalera, to be stored up and parcelled out through the months when the fishing is lean. Jongky hopes that the fish that his hand hauls in on Thursday will be served over a sushi bar in Tokyo at the weekend. Sometimes it makes it, sometimes not. It's a question of infrastructure.

Tahuna's electricity, shaky at the best of times according to Elizabeth, had cut out during the storm. By the time the rain stopped it was dark; the potholed road outside the kiosk was a necklace of mud-traps. Jongky insisted on walking me back to my guest house, and Elizabeth gave me a little parcel of cookies to take with me 'in case you get hungry in the night'.

As we walked through the soggy darkness, Jongky told me that he had worked for eight years in an office in Jakarta. His elder brother was still there, working for a well-known interior decoration and lifestyle magazine. When their father died, Jongky drew the short straw and came back to Sangihe to support Elizabeth. 'I didn't want to be a civil servant, and fishing is really the only other game in town,' he said.

I liked this quiet, naturally courteous man who did not complain about the cards that fate had dealt him, who seemed pleased that I was curious about the profession he had wound up in. I asked if I could come out fishing with him the next day.

Long silence.

'You're that interested?' Yes. Another long pause. 'But we only eat rice.' No problem. 'The sun's very strong.' I've got a hat. 'And it's the rainy season.' I've got a rain poncho, too. 'Well, come if you want. But eating only rice gets boring after four days.'

Four days? On an outrigger with one small piece of tarpaulin for shelter in a season of flashing thunderstorms? I had imagined a nice, out-at-midnight, back-by-sunset expedition. I decided the 'just say yes rule' didn't necessarily apply to things that I had invited myself to.

Jongky could see what I was thinking. 'Let's talk about it again tomorrow,' he said. Then, with impeccable tact, he never mentioned it again.

The following day, I watched a pair of fishermen load up their outrigger. The donut-lines were thrown over a pole at the back of the craft; an Indonesian flag fluttered above them. There were a couple of large jerrycans of petrol for the engine, some of water for the fishermen, a sack of ice-bricks to put the catch on, a sack of rice, a bucket of bait and a large wooden crate of smooth, round rocks that looked like stone grapefruit.

The rocks are tied on to the line when it is first dropped, so that it takes the bait quickly past layers of hungry but uninteresting smaller fish to the depths where tuna hang out. A bit of wiggling and the rock drops off, leaving the bait free to tempt the prey. I asked the guys how long they expected to be out. '*Tergantung rezeki*,' answered one: it depends on our good fortunes. *Rezeki* is a word one hears a lot in fishing communities: it implies a livelihood that is in the lap of the gods. 'As long as the ice lasts,' said the other.

In fact, the trips last until:

1) the fish–coffin is full
2) the rocks run out
3) the ice threatens to melt before getting the catch back
4) the petrol or water look like they might last just long enough to get home.

The price the fishermen will get paid for their catch melts away along with the ice. Block ice is a common sight all over Indonesia, especially in the early mornings: flatbed trishaws delivering huge oblong blocks of ice from the local ice factory to the women and men laying out their goods on market stalls. And yet here even the bigger outriggers, the ones with eight-man crews that can load up to thirty tuna, use ice-bricks that the people of Tahuna make in plastic bags in their freezers. The fishermen call it 'thousand-a-piece' because they buy the little bricks at 1,000 rupiah each, about eleven cents. There's no ice factory in Tahuna.

I set off to explore the island, stopping in at the tourism department's office in search of a map. Behind a wall of large, faded photographs of 'Tourism Objects' pinned behind crispy yellow cellophane, was a large, open-plan office. Eight people wearing smart batik uniforms, each neatly labelled with their name like pots of stock in the freezer, sat behind eight tidy wooden desks. More than tidy: not one of the desks had anything on it. Not a single sheet of paper, not a pencil or a calculator, not even a phone. The liveliest thing in the room was the television, which was blaring out a sinetron.

I bid everyone a cheery good day, and asked if they might have a map I could look at. They turned their heads, panic-stricken. A map! A MAP! There's a guest, and she wants a *MAP*! Eight worker bees scattered in eight directions. Cupboards were opened, drawers were rummaged in. Someone produced a brochure about underwater volcanoes. There were blobs showing me where they were in relation to the larger blob of Sangihe, but no information about how I might visit them. 'There's a German guy in Manado with a boat, I heard,' ventured one of the staff. Manado is the capital of North Sulawesi. It's an overnight ferry ride away.

We made general small talk about tourism in Sangihe (pronounced Sangur by the locals). Did they get lots of tourists? Hmmm. Hard to know exactly. Lots of them come from Manado, you see. But yes, probably lots. At least 200 every year. And how did they know what to visit? 'Well, if they come here, we give them a brochure,' said one of the ladies.

I rented a motorbike from a kindly Bugis trader in the market who gave me a little bag of salted bananas chips to stave off hunger, and headed off down the coast. The road hugged the lumpy side of the island, snaking above a series of beautiful curved bays, winding through villages of tidy bungalows standing in flower gardens. Painted shutters were flung open to reveal matching curtains; graduation portraits and crucifixes graced the walls.

After about thirty kilometres, the road dropped down to the coast and a triumphal arch announced the Dagoh special fishing port. I drove past a largish clump of buildings that looked abandoned; a commemorative plaque told me they dated from the 1970s and had been inaugurated by President Suharto himself. There was no sign of life.

Then I spotted a sizeable boat getting ready to cast off from a pier behind the buildings, a boat with a proper cabin, with bunks, with a kitchen. It had eight numbered hatches on its deck, each one a fish-coffin that could hold between ten and twenty tuna. The boat-owner was on shore saying goodbye to his wife and young son: he was bound for Manado, some 240 kilometres away, with a cargo of one hundred tuna that he had bought from the small traders in Tahuna.

What did he do for ice? I asked. 'I get it from the factory,' and he nodded his head towards the derelict building behind us. How come the fishermen in Tahuna all complain there's no ice factory, then? Only one of the three ice machines is still working, the boat-owner said, just enough for the bigger wholesalers. There's not enough electricity in the grid to run the other machines, and no money for a generator. He said he and other private businessmen would be happy to make the investment, but the local government wouldn't let them. They said the factory is a state asset, that it can't be privatized.

He excused himself, nodded at his wife, hugged his son, gathered his crew around him, and prayed for safe passage to Manado. It would take eighteen hours.

As they chugged out of the harbour, a tiny, two-man outrigger rounded the bay. There was much whistling and yelling, the engines of the bigger boat went still, there was some elaborate swinging about of ropes, and three more tuna were loaded on board. 'The fisherman will be happy,' observed one of the boat-owner's staff, who had stayed onshore. 'They get a better price if they cut out the middleman.' I thought the boat-owner *was* the middleman, I said. 'I mean the smaller middleman,' he laughed. 'You know how it is in Indonesia. The middle is very crowded.'

A couple of days later, Jongky called to say that some of his co-workers, Filipinos, had just come in and were about to take the catch down to the wholesalers. Did I want to go with them? What a sweetheart: having tactfully sidestepped the issue of the four-day trip, he was offering me 'tuna industry lite'. I went down to Elizabeth's kiosk, scrambled down the sandbank, and waded out to the outrigger.

One of the fishermen, a man in his late forties, was immensely smiley but spoke little Indonesian. The younger one was chattier; his Indonesian polite but idiosyncratic. Good trip? I asked. Okay, he said, they had been out three days and had caught one big tuna, two smaller ones. We puttered down the coast and tied up in the blinding sunshine below the sea wall near the centre of town. Up on the esplanade was a makeshift weighing station. There was a metal receiving table, a pile of Styrofoam cool-boxes, two big sacks of ice-bricks – the same 'thousand-a-piece' ones that the fishermen used – and a flatbed scale. A couple of chickens scratched around in the dust and a dog licked at yesterday's blood. There was no sign of the wholesaler. We waited.

The older fisherman stretched out for a snooze on the bamboo platform that jutted at right angles from the side of the boat. 'Bedroom,' said the younger man. When it's not raining and the waves are not crashing over it. He himself squatted on the other side of the boat, scrubbing at a plywood box that was balanced over the water on two sticks. 'Kitchen.' It was badly charred: 'Yesterday, a fire,' he said with a laugh. I read my book. We waited.

Another boat pulled up next to us and the lone fisherman started to tear open plastic bags of melted ice, throwing them one after another into the sea. 'Dirty', pronounced the younger of the Filipinos. Then he leant close to me. 'People here get price, drink it all up,' he said. 'Make God angry.'

By the time the wholesaler showed up three hours later, the younger fisherman had given the older one a haircut he didn't need and washed a big tub of plastic dishes from the trip, and we were all very hot.

The boys opened up the fish–coffin; I expected a rush of cold air but the ice was long gone; three eyes gleamed up from a soup of blood and droopy plastic bags, three magnificent fish were hoisted onto the shoulders of the wholesaler's helpers and got pitter-pattered along the sea wall and up the steps to the 'checking table'.

A teenage boy stuck a long skewer into each fish, just in front of the dorsal fin, then solemnly plopped three fat pink worms of flesh into the wholesaler's outstretched hand. This was the moment of truth that decided the price: she poked and prodded each one, then pronounced, 'One A, two C.' The fishermen showed no emotion.

Luckily, the biggest fish was the A-grade, good enough to be shipped to Japan for sashimi; they would be paid 25,000 rupiah a kilo for that, about US$2.70. C-grade sells for 20,000 rupiah; below that is the dreaded 'lokal' – good enough only to go to the local market at half the export price.

When a dog began to sniff around the biggest fish, still sitting on the scales, the ethnic Chinese buyer yelled at her staff: 'Come on, get that on ice or it will be C-grade before it gets to Manado.' The boys lifted it off the scales, slipped it into a Styrofoam box, and dumped some thousand-a-piece ice bricks around it. The fish would wait for the night ferry to Manado. From there it would be flown to Bali or Jakarta, because that's where the companies with the export permits are – a product of a customs and excise system that gives big firms close to the central government the right to ship things out of Indonesia. The fish would change hands again, and eventually be loaded onto a cargo flight to Tokyo, this time properly chilled. A fish that Jongky catches will spend a minimum of three or four days surrounded by melting ice-sacks and losing value, and another two days at least in cold store before it gets to market.

Unless he opts to break the law, and make a run to the Philippines.

Sometimes, he does exactly that. So do most other fishermen in Sangihe. Later that evening, I walked northwards along the coast, past dozens of grasshopper outriggers big and small, all pulled up above the waterline. I met a fisherman who had just come in and was lashing his boat to a coconut tree. 'Good trip?' I asked. He beamed: 'Seven tuna'. I asked if I could have a look at them but he said I was too late. 'I sold them over there,' he said, and jutted his chin out to the open sea.

'Over there' is General Santos – GenSan to the locals – a major port city in the southern Philippines. 'Over there', fishermen get paid three times as much as they do in Sangihe. The fisherman showed me the Philippine flag that he keeps for his illegal runs. Then he took me through the maths: seven fish, around forty-five kilos each. It cost him an extra million rupiah's worth of petrol, an extra sixteen or seventeen hours of open sea journey each way. By selling in the Philippines, he made an extra US$1,600 on the trip. 'I'd be stupid not to sell over there,' the fisherman said. 'But it's a shame for Indonesia. The country is losing so much income by not paying fishermen higher prices.'

Even before the headache of export permits, there's local paperwork to do. 'In the Philippines, you go and get the guy out of bed and he comes in his shorts and types three lines and you've got what you need,' said one wholesaler. 'Here, we have to wait until Monday morning, then sit in the office from eight o'clock until the guy shows up, in his uniform of course, at around eleven, and all the time the value of the fish is falling.' Even more important, he said, was infrastructure. In the Philippines there is a dedicated tuna-export processing port, built with the help of the Japanese taxpayer. Private companies have built docks and their own cold storage plants as well. Exporters charter cargo flights from GenSan, the wholesaler said. 'You pull up at the dock, they put the fish straight in to cold store, they do the paperwork and it's on its way to Tokyo.'

There's no doubt that Indonesia's infrastructure is in a parlous state. It's the largest country in the world to consist entirely of islands, yet the World Economic Forum ranked it 104 out of 139 countries for its port infrastructure; even landlocked countries such as Zimbabwe, Switzerland and Botswana reported better access to ports. It did nearly as badly on roads, air transport and electricity.*

---

* A 2011 study of nearly 12,400 businesses in nineteen provinces showed that businesses in Eastern Indonesia had to deal with electricity cuts on average four times a week and water cuts twice a week. In Western Indonesia, shortages were still reported universally, though only half as frequently. See Asia Foundation, 2011.

It's hamstrung in part by decentralization, which has created a war of egos. Individual districts can't afford huge investments in things like ports or railways, so they need to club together. But no bupati wants to put his own district's money on the table for a port which provides jobs and bragging rights for some other district, and provincial governors can't bribe them to, because they've got so little cash of their own to bring to the table.

In its airily vague economic Master Plan, the central government dreams that half of the money Indonesia needs to pour into infrastructure over the next decade – some 90 billion dollars' worth – will come from private investors, despite a dodgy legal system, capricious export rules and price-limits that bring in votes for politicians but make it nearly impossible for companies to turn a profit. Over the course of my travels in Indonesia, I spent hundreds of hours burning up fuel in intercity minibuses, not getting from A to B, but just driving around town for an hour or two before departure, looking for extra passengers. With subsidized petrol then at just 4,500 rupiah a litre, bus drivers didn't have to worry too much that they'd burn up more in fuel than they'd make in extra fares.*

Households pay less for their electricity than it costs to generate it. In places with twenty-four-hour electricity, Indonesians seem to leave the TV on permanently and the lights on all night, if not in the bedroom itself, then certainly in the sitting room and on the veranda. The fear of ghosts outweighs the price of electricity.

Power is subsidized for domestic consumers, not for industry, so the money the government shells out does little to create jobs or stimulate the economy. Through energy subsidies, the government is channelling a fifth of its total spending into the pockets of middle-class people with cars, air-conditioners and microwaves. Every mention of a price hike brings people out

---

* Fuel prices were raised to 6,500 rupiah a litre in June 2013, around 65 cents at the time, saving the government about $1.3 billion a year. At the time, the World Bank estimated the government would still have to pay $18 billion a year in fuel subsidies. The rupiah has fallen dramatically since then, sending the bill for subsidized fuel even higher.

onto the streets and revives the ghosts of 1998, when a demo about rising fuel prices spiralled into the nationwide protests that brought down Suharto. What private company would step into that market?

Private companies are right to be wary. At least since the days of the Dutch VOC traders, the political Powers That Be have stuck their oar into every aspect of production and trade in these islands. The colonial government let private companies run the plantations but they essentially dictated what crops would be grown, and often what price would be paid. Sukarno tried to use the constitution to write the private sector out of the economy.★ And Suharto was paternalistic to his fingertips. It happens that he chose to turn the economy over to a group of people who tried to cut through red tape rather than to impose it. Culturally, however, Indonesia's bureaucrats still feel they have a right to meddle in the market at will.

In early 2013, nationalists in the government hoped to make themselves popular with farmers by banning the import of a long list of fruit and vegetables including garlic.

If the people who had slapped the list together had spoken to any farmers, or indeed to any importers, they might have discovered that Indonesia grows just 13,000 of the 400,000 tonnes of garlic it eats each year. But they didn't do this basic homework. The price of garlic tripled in the fortnight after the ban. The result: a handful of happy farmers, and tens of millions of furious housewives.

Some business people chide their colleagues for whining too much about bureaucratic meddling and red tape. Take Ade, for example, a Chinese Indonesian born in Lombok whom I had met in Waikabubak, in West Sumba. He was a locksmith; the

---

★ This provision is still taken quite seriously. In 2004, for example, the Constitutional Court struck down a law that would have allowed for the privatization of electricity plants, arguing that the state must retain control and manage the power sector for the benefit of all Indonesians.

police had dropped me, Jerome and our still-locked motorbike at his shop after they had rescued us from the jousting fields. Ade has lived round and about Indonesia: Surabaya, Bali, even Biak in faraway Papua, he's traded vanilla with Madagascar and cloves around the world. 'Indonesia's a really easy place to do business,' he said. 'If you've got an idea, you can just get on and make it happen.'

What about all the red tape, all the permits, all the fees? 'Those come later,' Ade said. If he gets asked to show his permit early on he simply explains that he's just trying out the business, he doesn't yet know if it will succeed. If it flies, he tells the authorities, then he'll get all the permits he needs. 'Everyone's fine with that.' A friend of mine who runs a dive resort agreed. I ran into her by chance at an airport in early 2012, when she was on her way to sort out building permits for the resort. Were they expanding? I asked. No, these were the permits for the existing bungalows, the ones built six years previously.

Ade was the only locksmith in western Sumba. Mostly, he said, the cops come to him when there's been a robbery, to ask if anyone had had keys cut recently. Ade imports cloves when the local market is short. He also repairs refrigerators and radios and is the only person in the west of Sumba licensed to sell guns and ammunition; there's a rifle stuck up on the wall of his general store, between the fishing nets, the slabs of Fanta and the piles of disposable nappies.

'All you have to do to make money in Indonesia is to figure out what no one else is doing,' Ade said. It made me think of how often I had noticed copy-cat businesses in smaller Indonesian towns. I was caught out by it early on. In Waikabubak, for example, every third shop prints photos. Even the little tailor opposite the market has a sideline in photo printing. This made me lazy; having promised to print photos and send them to people before I left Waikabubak, I thought: I'll do it in the next town I go to. But the next town is all pharmacies – there's not a single photo printer. Here it's wall-to-wall perfume sellers, there it's all hair salons. When I commented that I thought his approach unusual in small-town Indonesia, Ade agreed. 'People see a business doing well, and they just copy it,' said Ade. 'The concept of market saturation is not well understood.'

Elizabeth, baker of Christmas cookies and mother of Jongky the tuna fisherman, wanted to go to Jakarta to visit her grandson. But like many Indonesians, she was horrified at the idea of travelling alone. 'We'll go to Jakarta together,' she declared one evening as I sat drinking tea at her stall.

I hadn't really been thinking of going to Jakarta, but Elizabeth was not to be dissuaded. 'You're from there, and I want to go there, and we have the same name, and your grandmother bakes the same cookies, and now we'll go to Jakarta together.' And next thing I knew, Jongky was fussing around booking ferries and flights.

We took an overnight ferry from Sangihe to Manado, the nearest town with an airport. The *Holly Mary* (*sic*) had an upper deck of comfortable-looking cabins and a lower deck of tightly packed bunks. Out the back, stacks of tuna in styrofoam cold-chests dripped blood, blocking the passage to the communal loos.

Elizabeth and I lay side by side on our bunks and gossiped. She told me how much she was looking forward to seeing her grandson. 'He's my son, really.'

Very little about Indonesia's fluid and complex family arrangements surprises me. I've attended the funeral of a friend's mother, only to be introduced to her mother again weeks later, very much alive. When I raised an eyebrow, my friend quickly explained: 'My other mother.' People seem to move around between 'families' almost at will. But still, I was a bit shocked to find out that Elizabeth's grandson was also her son.

'No, I mean he's not really,' she said hurriedly, seeing my face, 'but he feels like he is.' Elizabeth had gone to Jakarta for the birth. 'But his parents both work. I felt sorry for the kid. So I took him.' The child was five weeks old. He lived with Elizabeth in Sangihe until he was eight.

At Manado airport I turned to talk to Elizabeth and realized she wasn't with me. I saw her standing, forlorn, at the bottom of the automatic escalator; she couldn't bring herself to step onto it. It's not as though Elizabeth had never been out of the village before. She had been on planes, she had stayed with her sons in Jakarta. Logically, her discomfort at just about everything in Manado's bright, modern airport made no sense. But I found myself able to sympathize. I have seen plenty of bright, modern airports, but after just five months in the slow lane of small-town Indonesia, I felt as though I had stepped backwards in time. The return to Jakarta was a jolt.

Map I: Aceh

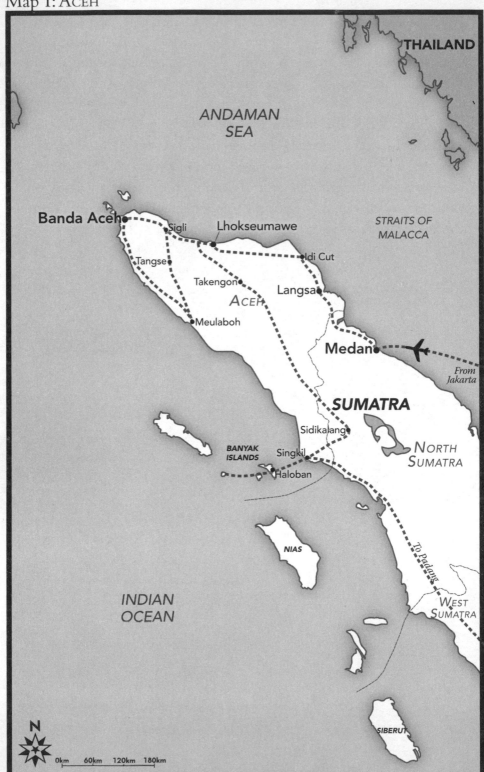

THAILAND

ANDAMAN
SEA

Banda Aceh

Sigli

Lhokseumawe

STRAITS OF
MALACCA

Tangse

Idi Cut

Takengon

Langsa

ACEH

Meulaboh

Medan

From
Jakarta

SUMATRA

Sidikalang

NORTH
SUMATRA

BANYAK
ISLANDS

Singkil

Haloban

NIAS

INDIAN
OCEAN

To Padang

WEST
SUMATRA

SIBERUT

N

0km   60km   120km   180km

9

Historical Fictions

My first day back in Jakarta, I went to the opening of an exhibition by Renjani Arifin, an artist friend who was showing her new sculptures. The gallery was in a cool, marbled mall, a place where I once used to spend as much on a set of underwear as I now spent on a month of travel. In the gallery, seven-year-olds were playing with hot-off-the-press iPads, and the bohemian glitterati of Jakarta wandered about with glasses of wine, air-kissing one another and cooing at ambiguous stone statues of naked girl-women holding teddy bears and gazing wistfully at an untouchable universe. One beautifully curated woman complained that it had taken her nearly an hour to come from Pondok Indah, an eruption of McMansions just a kilometre or two away. And you?

'Sangihe,' I said. The woman looked blank. Like many Indonesians of her class she had been to Paris and New York, to Melbourne and Bangkok, but in Indonesia itself, she had never ventured out of Java and Bali, never heard of the Sangihe islands. I began to describe the life of a fisherman on a two-person outrigger, then saw her eyes glaze. I realized with a heavy soul that I had become one of those slightly earnest foreigners who has gone native. I shut up.

The sculptor's brother Luwi extracted me and bundled me off downstairs to inspect a cup-cake stall run by another friend, Nungky. He bought three cupcakes for 45,000 rupiah. Everywhere in rural Indonesia, a cake costs 1,000. None of them is piled up with pink and purple swirls of buttery icing like these ones; none is sprinkled with little silver sugar-stars. But still, if he were in the States and paid the same amount compared to average wages, Luwi would have just shelled out US$400 for three cupcakes.

Nungky, an architect who owned the cake stall as a side venture, happened along. She had a fantastic new hairdo, a two-tone look dyed half white, half black, shaved up one side of her head, angled radically down on the other side. With her was Dotti, a documentary producer, dressed principally in electric-blue Lycra leggings. Over the leggings ballooned a batik top, perhaps a bit long to be called a jacket, but certainly too short to qualify as a dress. One arm was crooked outwards to provide a perch for a puff-ball handbag, white leather petals flapping in all directions off a central globe.

I tried to imagine what the salt-fish ladies of Adonara would make of Nungky and Dotti. But of course they would never see the Lycra leggings. If Dotti went to make a documentary about Butonese fishing communities in eastern Indonesia, she'd doubtless morph into a NGO/researcher/anthropologist lookalike complete with khaki trousers and black backpack.

If I felt out of place in Jakarta, it was because I hadn't morphed quickly enough back into nice underwear and air-kissing mode. It seemed like a huge mental effort to switch back to someone more recognizably 'me' just for a thirty-six-hour interlude between a dormitory ferry in northern Sulawesi and a fourteen-hour bus journey in northern Sumatra.

After the Jakarta interlude, I headed for Aceh, the province that sits on the northern tip of Sumatra, the giant island on Indonesia's western flank. It was election season in Aceh — the governor's job was up for grabs, and there were also polls for most of the province's bupatis and mayors. An acquaintance of mine, a human rights lawyer who had studied in the US named Nazaruddin Ibraham, was running for Mayor of Lhokseumawe, halfway up the east coast. He invited me to witness his campaign.

I bought a couple of silk scarves that I could use to cover my head with: jilbabs are compulsory for Muslim women in fiercely religious Aceh and though non-Muslims didn't technically have to wear them, it seemed polite to make an effort to fit in. Then I flew to Medan, the biggest city in Sumatra, and took a bus up through the tidy and well-established towns of the north-east coast. In eastern Indonesia I'd become accustomed to seeing banners congratulating a district on its fourth or fifth birthday, perhaps it's tenth. But northern Sumatra was plantation country; the Dutch had stamped their presence on this region centuries ago. As I drove past the colonial-era villas and well-maintained Chinese shop-houses of Langkat, I noticed that the district was celebrating its 262nd birthday. The border with Aceh was marked by a change in billboards; those advertising fertilizer and pesticides were displaced by a thicket of posters promoting pairings of hopefuls for the posts of bupati and vice bupati. Most showed two gentlemen wearing the elaborate gold tea-cosy hats that signify Acehnese aristocracy, the preferred headgear of local candidates. One aspirant who had been unable to rally a running-mate left a blank cut-out where his partner's photo should be. There was a fair bit of orange, the party colour of the incumbent governor of Aceh, Irwandi Yusuf, who was running for re-election. But the dominant colours by far were the red and black of Partai Aceh, Indonesia's first legal regional party. Partai Aceh was the political offshoot of *Gerakan Aceh Merdeka*, the Free Aceh Movement or GAM. This was hard for me to take in; the previous time I had visited Aceh, in 1991, GAM leaders were sitting in exile in Sweden, prodding along what they said was a fight to the death against the Indonesian state. Now these same men wanted to be elected officials of that state.

Free Aceh was a separatist movement begun (under a series of different names) by an Acehnese businessman called Hasan di Tiro, who had been based in the US for many years. In 1976 he returned to Indonesia and declared himself head of an independent Aceh. He appointed a full cabinet of ministers, including many of his friends and relatives. In his memoirs he describes reading Nietzsche, listening to classical music and writing patriotic plays in the jungles of Aceh for just over two years before Suharto's army weeded him out. He ran off to exile in Sweden in 1979, and the rebellion sputtered to a halt. It was kick-started again a decade later, after Hasan di Tiro managed to organize guerrilla training in Libya for a group of young rebels-in-waiting. At the time, though, it wasn't really clear that separatists were behind the new wave of violence.

From where I sat in the Reuters newsroom in Jakarta, the first signs of trouble were reports in the national news agency, Antara, of small raids on police and army posts in rural Aceh. I ambushed military spokesman General Nurhadi outside his office and asked him about the attacks. Were the raiders separatist rebels hoping to split from the state? 'Rebels? Nonsense! They are common criminals!' he declared. Though the way he referred to them as *Gerakan Pengacau Keamanan* – 'Security Disturbing Movement', or GPK for short – suggested they were more organized than most common criminals.★ He had trouble explaining, just a few weeks later, why the government had rounded up a clutch of these common criminals and put them on trial for subversion and separatism. Or why our minders at the Department of Information wouldn't let journalists visit Aceh.

In July of 1990 I waltzed up to Defence Minister Benny Moerdani at a cocktail party – I was twenty-five and didn't know any better – and asked him with a smile if I was being denied access to Aceh because the military was killing civilians in the province. When I think about that now, it makes me queasy. Moerdani was the person who had overseen the extra-judicial killing of criminals that Suharto confessed to in his autobiography; he was not a man to be crossed lightly. But the general smiled back at me. 'Not at all, my dear, you can go any time you like. We have

---

★ Even this has been rewritten over time. More recent papers about Aceh render GPK as *Gerombolan Pengacau Keamanan*, the 'Security Disturbing Gang'. It is as though the 'freedom fighters' take pleasure in making the army's epithet more dismissive than it actually was.

nothing to hide.' With BBC correspondent Claire Bolderson, I visited Aceh several times over the following two years, trying to make sense of a very messy situation.

At the time, it was impossible to tell who was behind the attacks. Only once, we saw a letter addressed to Indonesian newspaper editors, claiming responsibility for this wave of raids. Written entirely in lower-case, the letter was an eccentrically spelled mish-mash of anti-Javanese invective, childish threats, wounded pride and separatist rhetoric. In a one-page communication, the name of the organization was variously given as: the national liberation front acheh sumatra (that one in English), neugara islam atjeh sumatra, atjeh meurdekha sumatra and atjeh merdeka.

But in the coffee shops of Aceh, the site of endless political plotting over the centuries, none of these names was ever used. People called the troublemakers the GPK, just as the government did, and they had many theories about who they were. Most involved some combination of the following: disgruntled former soldiers who had been fired in a short-lived campaign against corruption in the military; thugs who wanted a bigger share of the marijuana trade (*saus ganja* was once a common ingredient in the cuisine of the region, and Aceh remained a centre of production for the crop); hot-blooded separatists back from training in Libya. It seemed wildly improbable to me that an organization that didn't have a shift key on its typewriter and couldn't spell its own name would be linked to international terror training networks; it was only years later that I found that some of the fighters were indeed graduates from Middle Eastern training camps, though all the other theories also proved to be true.

What I did find at the time was plenty of brutality on all sides. Convoys of army trucks barrelled down the main highway along Aceh's east coast, lights flashing, horns blaring. In the back of one truck, we saw soldiers in black balaclavas waving their semi-automatics over the heads of a small posse of bedraggled captives. A helicopter whumped overhead. Every few kilometres there was a checkpoint, manned by blustering Javanese soldiers in their late teens. Who are they looking for? I asked one bus driver, himself a former soldier. He laughed. 'Headaches. They are looking for headaches.' The checkpoint soldiers beat people up for no reason. People whose ID cards were out of date were made to swallow the laminated plastic. 'They're putting revenge in a savings account,' said the squaddie-turned-driver.

Schoolchildren told us that they would no longer take the short cut through the plantation to class in the mornings because they so often found dead bodies dumped there by soldiers. The 'rebels' were no less vicious. An NGO worker in a remote mountain village said she had recently seen a soldier's corpse left on the roadside by the rebels, stripped naked 'for the flies to feast on', his penis hanging out of his mouth. 'The GPK [rebels] come to your door and ask for rice,' she said. 'You don't give it to them, they shoot you. You do give it to them, the army will come tomorrow and shoot you. If you're lucky, they'll leave the body in the village, where your family can bury it. If you're not, it will end up in a ditch miles away where no one will dare touch it except the flies and the dogs.' Denying people a decent Islamic funeral was one of the greatest black marks levelled at both sides.

The conflict was fuelled by a reinvention of Aceh's complex past by rebel leader Hasan di Tiro. From his Swedish exile, he proclaimed a simple version of history, one that could only mean war.

Aceh has always been rich. For centuries it sold pepper, camphor, gold, silk and other goods to Arab traders. Passing along the coast of Sumatra in 1290, Marco Polo describes the kingdom of Ferelech (thought to be near present-day Lhokseumawe on the east coast) as a place of 'Saracen merchants, who come with their vessels and have converted the people to the laws of Mohammad'. It is the first record of an Islamic state in South East Asia, though the Italian explorer did note that the converts didn't extend beyond the city (in the hills beyond were cannibals who worshipped the first thing they saw when they rose in the morning). The 'Saracens' and those who followed have left their mark on the population; many Acehnese are tall and well built, with smooth, caramel skin, aquiline features and fiery eyes. They call their homeland the Veranda of Mecca.

The riches of Aceh attracted the attention of European traders once they reached these waters, but they resolved not to fight over the territory; the Anglo–Dutch treaty of 1824 recognized the Sultanate of Aceh as a sovereign, free-trading state. When the Europeans changed their minds and the Netherlands East Indies moved in to take over, the Acehnese fought them off. Over the last three decades of the nineteenth century, the Acehnese killed 15,000 Dutch troops and crippled another 10,000 in a war that was cast as a conflict of Muslims against the *kafir* infidels. The colonists finally got the upper hand in 1903 and the Dutch ruled Aceh until the Japanese invaded thirty-nine years later. These details were passed over in rebel leader Hasan di Tiro's version of history. He claimed that Aceh was always an undefeated sovereign state, and that it could not therefore become part of the Indonesian nation when the Dutch handed over sovereignty. He ignored other inconvenient facts too: that Aceh had invited the republican government to set up shop in the province when Indonesia was fighting the Dutch, that wealthy Acehnese merchants pooled their gold to buy the fledgling country its first planes, breaking the Dutch blockade. The way di Tiro and his GAM rebels saw it, Aceh's future grew inevitably out of its glorious, independent and undefeated past, and it would fight for it to the last. As the exiled rebel said in his autobiography, *The Price of Freedom*: 'Either we live free or we die free.'★

As I travelled the province in the early 1990s, I recorded plenty of death, on both sides. My reports on the shadowy rebellion in Aceh and on the Indonesian army's brutal response to it drew angry responses from di Tiro as well as from the Indonesians. After one series of reports on Aceh, I was called in and ticked off by the military spokesman General Nurhadi, who accused me of giving the rebels undue importance. When I got back to the office, there was a fax from Stockholm, from Hasan di Tiro himself, berating me for the same stories but for the opposite reason. On the Reuters wire I had described the

★ Hasan di Tiro, *The Price of Feedom: The Unfinished Diary of Tengku Hasan Di Tiro*. Norsborg, Sweden: National Liberation Front of Acheh Sumatra, 1984, 321.

anti-government fighters as 'an apparent mix of vengeful soldiers sacked by the army, separatists and discontented Acehnese . . . [Though] savagery has exploded in the year-long conflict . . . it is still unclear what the rebel goals are.' In his fax the separatist-in-exile took exception to this: 'Achehnese political prisoners . . . are being misrepresented by the Javanese as "rebels without a cause" and you, ladies and gentlemen of the Reuter, should be ashamed for disseminating Javanese propaganda!'

Now, less than twenty-five years later, all that earlier confusion had evaporated. A decade and a half of carnage has been rewritten as a chapter in a thirty-year struggle for justice. In the coffee shops of Aceh, the issue of Acehnese sovereignty was rarely mentioned and the self-proclaimed former rebels who were now fighting on the hustings for positions of power within the Indonesian state never spoke of it at all. In a Medan newspaper I read as I travelled to Aceh for the first time in over two decades, I saw a photo of the Javanese general Soenarko – one of the Indonesian army commanders who had done most to crush the rebels in Aceh – embracing Muzakir Manaf, the former guerrilla commander of GAM. Muzakir was now running for vice governor of Aceh, alongside another former rebel. Soenarko was supporting their ticket. That really did my head in; it's like a senior Israeli general becoming campaign manager for Hezbollah. As the former rebel welcomed his old enemy into his party's campaign team, he declared that they also shared a single aim, vision and goal: *Negara Kesatuan Republik Indonesia* – 'The Republic of Indonesia, Indivisible!'

My bus trundled on past more campaign posters, and several huge green billboards reading '*NKRI Harga Mati!*' *Harga mati* literally means 'dead price'. It's what you don't want to hear if you're bargaining in the market: the bottom line, non-negotiable. These 'Indonesia, Indivisible: Non-negotiable!' signs had a non-identical twin, also in green, which read: *Damai itu Indah!* – 'Peace is Beautiful!' I don't remember either of these slogans from earlier times. But as I travelled around Indonesia in 2011/2012, I realized they were a sure sign that I was in a trouble zone. There are no *Damai itu Indah!* signs in Jakarta. You don't see *NKRI Harga Mati!* in the buzzing Central Java port of Semarang or around the beach resorts of Bali. I didn't see the signs in Sumba or up through NTT. They began to appear in the small islands opposite East Timor, which voted to leave Indonesia in 1999 and which was set alight by militias backed by the Indonesian army in revenge. There were plenty of green signs in Maluku and Central Sulawesi and I later saw them in West Kalimantan. They were spread thickly across Papua. And here they were in Aceh. Though the signs tend to be paired, there's more Beautiful Peace in places where the population make a habit of taking to one another with machetes – Maluku, Central Sulawesi, West Kalimantan – and more Non-negotiable Unity in the parts of Indonesia that have most openly expressed a desire to break away from the motherland – Papua, around East Timor, Aceh.

The threat of separatism has hung like a thundercloud over the nation since the earliest days of the republic, when Sukarno prevailed over fellow nationalists who sought either a federal or an Islamic state. Several parts of the new nation revolted in the 1950s. Rebels wanting an Islamic government fought Jakarta in West Java, South Sulawesi and West Sumatra as well as in Aceh, while at the other end of the country, Maluku tried to hive off a Christian state. The republican army squashed all of those rebellions; their grip on the nation tightened even further when Suharto came to power. But his rule fertilized another type of resentment. Jakarta is stealing the riches of our land and using it to build highways in Java, complained people in Riau, Sulawesi and Kalimantan as well as in Aceh and Papua. Meanwhile, we have to host thousands of transmigrants, the detritus of Suharto's overcrowded homeland. Our adat is being scrubbed up for tourist brochures, and we're force-fed national ideals based on a foppish and compliant Javanese culture that has nothing to do with us. By the late 1980s, several parts of Indonesia were disgruntled. But there were active rebel movements in only three of those areas

– East Timor, Papua (at that time called Irian Jaya) and Aceh.

Neither East Timor nor Papua was part of the nation at the time of independence. Both felt they had been swallowed up by the Indonesian behemoth against their will. Papuans feel that they were tricked into becoming part of Indonesia in 1969, when Jakarta manipulated a UN-backed referendum by allowing only carefully groomed community elders to vote. The East Timorese never had any choice at all about 'integration' with Indonesia. When Portuguese colonists abandoned the territory practically overnight in 1975, Suharto simply marched his troops in. Given their history, it was no surprise that these provinces had produced guerrilla movements. But Aceh had been an integral part of Indonesia at independence (Hasan di Tiro's protestations to the contrary notwithstanding). Its later rebellions were no more or less serious than those in other regions. In fact in many respects, Aceh actually had less to complain about than other provinces on the geographic periphery of Indonesia. The governor, several bupatis and many in the upper echelons of the army and police in the province were Acehnese, whereas in many other provinces they were Javanese. Aceh wheedled more development funds out of Jakarta in 1990 than any other province.

These facts did not deter the young men who had learned from Hasan di Tiro that Aceh has always been sovereign, could only be sovereign, from reigniting their quest for independence. The guerrilla warfare continued in fits and starts for another fifteen years, directed largely by exiles in Sweden, financed by exiles in Malaysia. The Indonesian military's response came in waves too, exceedingly aggressive in the early 1990s when I was reporting from Aceh, then more brutal still under the nationalist presidency of Sukarno's daughter Megawati from 2001 to 2004.

It wasn't until the tsunami of 2004 swept away 170,000 Acehnese lives that the unelected leaders of the movement, most of whom had not set foot in Aceh throughout the decade and a half of fighting, conceded that it may be time for the killing to stop. Virtually everyone I spoke to in Aceh in 2012 pointed to iconic images of mosques standing unscathed in a landscape otherwise flattened by the tsunami as signs of God's anger at the senseless war. To me, depending on the age of the building, they were signs that the mosque was built by Dutch engineers, or signs that contractors are less likely to cut corners or use substandard materials when they build a mosque than when they build a school or a housing complex. But it is certainly true that the unimaginable tragedy of the tsunami allowed both Jakarta and the rebel leaders to climb out of the trenches they had dug for themselves and to talk peace. The torrent of support from ordinary Indonesians helped too; the rebels could no longer argue that Indonesians wanted only to take from Aceh, not to give.

The tsunami provided an opportunity to start again. And it brought in US$7 billion in aid, and lots and lots of construction work. This meant contracts for former rebel leaders and jobs for the boys; it helped reintegrate the fighters into society, a condition of a peace agreement signed in 2005 between Jakarta and the Stockholm-based separatists. The agreement gave Aceh a bigger cut of mining, logging and fishing revenue than other provinces got. On top of that, there's around US$1.2 billion a year in no-strings-attached cash transfers from Jakarta to Aceh's districts, and another US$700 million a year in 'special autonomy funds'. Most importantly, the agreement allowed former guerrilla leaders to form local political parties in Aceh, though these remain forbidden everywhere else in Indonesia. That meant that men who led the charge for Acehnese freedom in their youth could now, in their greying years, run for office without being seen to join the Indonesian establishment. That in turn meant that the former rebels could get their hands on all the money that flowed from their sworn enemies. Jakarta had found their price, and bought them off.

A similar process of co-option is underway in Papua, a term I use to refer to the western half of the island of New Guinea, formerly Irian Jaya and at the time of my visit in 2012 technically split into two provinces, Papua and West Papua. It's one of Indonesia's richest regions, made of gold and copper, covered with precious hardwoods and surrounded with valuable fish. In Suharto's day, Jakarta didn't even pretend to do anything for the Papuans. They were lesser beings (they don't even eat rice, imagine!), capable of working the mines and the plantations but not of governing themselves. Jakarta sent in managers and bureaucrats, and they worked with foreigners to extract the riches and send them back to the motherland. It was a replica of the way the Dutch had treated the Javanese for a couple of hundred years.

Papuans had been fighting a low-level guerrilla war against Jakarta since their land was first 'integrated' into Indonesia. When Indonesia decentralized after the Suharto era, Papua was extremely ill-disposed to remain shoehorned into the republic. Losing tiny, unproductive East Timor during the transition to civilian rule in Indonesia had been a blow to the nation's pride. But losing what many Papuans sourly refer to as *Dapur Java*, 'Java's Kitchen' – that would be a huge blow to the nation's income. And so the co-option began. Jakarta still sucks in taxes from Papua, but a special autonomy bill similar to Aceh's now feeds most of the royalties from mining, logging and other resource extraction straight to the new Papuan elite.

This makes some other parts of Indonesia resentful. 'We try to be good citizens and we get nothing,' the head of a local government department in Maluku had told me. 'It turns out it's only if you run around killing soldiers that you get everything you ask for.' But the integration-by-bribery makes a lot of Papuans resentful too. In the same way that a small handful of Dutch-educated Indonesians had a lock on power at independence, so a small handful of Java-educated Papuans now control most of the area's resources. 'There's been a straight switch. Papua's wealth used to be stolen by Jakarta. Now it's stolen by the Papuan elite,' a preacher in the Papuan capital Jayapura told me. In his view, they got away with it for two reasons. 'One: most Papuans are so used to blaming the Javanese for everything that they don't even look at what is really happening. Two: the elite has been very clever at co-opting anyone who might object.'

The unrest in Papua continues. But in Aceh, around the time

of the elections in 2012, it seemed as though Jakarta's co-option
was succeeding.

I got off the bus in Langsa. Along one side of the main square
in town was a vast banner, perhaps twenty metres long:
'DECLARATION OF PEACEFUL ELECTIONS, 2012',
it read. It declared the intention of the populace to ensure an
election free of violence and shooting, and urged the security
forces to refrain from those vices also. It was signed by everyone
from the current Mayor to the head of the Langsa Scooter Club.
Across the square was a giant poster of a fat man in a suit, drooling
at the mouth and rushing for the Mayor's seat. From his pockets
fly red 100,000 rupiah notes; an empty trouser pocket is marked
'5–20 billion', indicating that in this part of the country it costs
between 5 and 20 billion rupiah to get elected: up to US$2
million. 'Right, like he's not going to be corrupt to pay that back,'
observes a character in the poster, which was erected by the city
electoral commission. 'Stop MONEY POLITIC . . . !' runs the
headline, the last two words in slightly erratic English. From this
I deduced that politics in Aceh was not so different from politics
anywhere else in Indonesia, local parties or no local parties.

   A woman I met in Medan had given me the phone number
of her son as well as her former husband, the acting head of
the local parliament in Langsa (the real head was in detention).
'Let's have breakfast on Sunday,' the ex-husband suggested when
I called. 'Meet me at the central square at 6.30.' I peeled myself
out of bed, covered my head with a silk scarf and went bleary-
eyed to the square. Music was thudding out of giant speakers; up
on the raised bandstand, a woman was barking orders: 'One and
two and *pump* your arms, and three and four and *spin* around.'
The municipal aerobics was led by a clutch of lithe women in
tracksuits and jilbabs up on the stage. In the square beneath, a
motley collection of townsfolk, including a surprising number of
portly middle-aged men, struggled to keep up. I looked around
for anyone who might answer to the description of Deputy

Speaker of Parliament, then gave up and joined in the pumping and spinning.

As the aerobics wound down, one of the middle-aged men grabbed the microphone. With the air of someone who was looking for votes, he thanked us all for committing to the healthy lifestyles that would power Langsa to a glorious future. I guessed this was my man. I introduced myself and he invited me to join his posse for breakfast. I had been hoping for a quiet chat about local politics, but it seemed there would be ten of us for breakfast – the politician, his wife, seven flunkies and myself. I asked one of the flunkies if he went diligently to aerobics every Sunday morning. He pulled a face. 'There's nothing diligent about it, Bu. It's compulsory,' and he nodded at the Deputy Speaker.

I tried to engage the politician but it was difficult; he was busy with his phone, then there was a discussion with his wife about the price of a pink laptop. But I did learn that he believed that Partai Aceh sporadically instigated violence in order to wring concessions out of Jakarta. 'Basically, whatever Aceh wants, Aceh gets, as long as we don't ask for independence. Anything but that, we get given right away,' he said. This was not, in his view, a good thing. It perpetuated dependence on support from the centre, and made for a very fragile democracy. The threat of violence had become a negotiating tool, one that may become hard to control.

Langsa is a relaxed town that feels more like Medan than Aceh. Young people zip around on fixie bikes and the coffee shops play jazz rather than dangdut music. Feeling the need for a bit of youth culture, I called the Deputy Speaker's son Reza on the number his mother had given me. He came to pick me up in a jeep. He was in his late twenties, bright as a button, and not at all concerned that I had dashed out of the hotel to meet him without remembering to cover my head. We were cruising around the large central square when Reza suddenly barked at me. 'Head down! Head down!' It sounded urgent. I put my head between my knees. After a bit, Reza said, 'All clear!' and I popped back up. In the wing mirror I could see a phalanx of olive uniforms – the women in jilbabs and long skirts – pulling people over. They were the religious police, state employees whose only job is to enforce sharia regulations, and they were checking to see that all Muslim women were wearing jilbabs. Technically, I was exempt from the regulation. 'But there's no sense looking for trouble,' Reza said.

Later, I carried on up the coast to Lhokseumawe and latched on to my friend Nazaruddin's campaign team. The city is engraved on my memory from a reporting visit in 1990, when I was investigating tales of a rebel attack on a gas plant that was selling seven million dollars' worth of gas to Japan and Korea every day. Most of the proceeds were split between US petrogiant Mobil, which ran the plant, and Suharto's government in Jakarta. This made rebels cross and reports of an attack plausible, though it turned out that the alleged 'attack' was actually an industrial accident that the company did not want publicized. When I got back to my hotel room after slipping past security and visiting the gas plant, the phone rang. 'Is that Miss Elizabeth?' Ya, Pak. 'This is Intel,' said the disembodied voice of Indonesia's military intelligence service. 'We seem to have misplaced our skeleton key, we might have left it in your room. Could you have a look around for it?' Of course, Pak. 'I'm so sorry for the inconvenience,' he said.

To this day, I've never been sure whether they were trying to intimidate me, or whether they really had lost their skeleton key. Both seemed equally possible.

Since then, Lhokseumawe had sucked dry its reserves of natural gas and gone into a bit of a slump. Nazaruddin wanted to pull it back up by its bootstraps. He dreamed of building up a major industrial port complex, drawing in commodities from around fertile Aceh, processing them and exporting them across South East Asia and beyond. His campaign office was easy to find; it was right behind a gargantuan poster showing Nazar and his running-mate in front of a futuristic mosque-scape. 'BRIDGE TO METROPOLIS CITY' read the slogan, in English. He was running as an independent; I noticed that he and his running-mate were the only candidates to appear bare-headed on their campaign posters. Candidates from local Acehnese parties all wore gold tea-cosies; everyone else, including other independents, wore the black velvet *pecis* of a good Muslim.

The campaign office was open-fronted. On the wall inside was a giant red palm-print, a reminder to voters to choose Nazar's number, five, on election day. Under it sat an assortment of men: campaign workers mostly, but also hangers-on. In the middle of them was the candidate himself, a good-looking man of around forty-five with a million-watt smile. He leapt up when I arrived, and whisked me into an air-conditioned back room, closed off from the main office. 'What a relief to have an excuse to get away from those crocodiles,' he said. I became familiar with them over the next couple of weeks, the 'campaign crocodiles' who hovered around the office talking about how many votes they had locked down in different parts of town. They flattered, they wheedled, and they invented many excuses to shake hands with the candidates and their senior staff, each time hoping that a banknote would be pressed into their palm.

'You can't turn them away completely, because they might go off and run a "black" campaign against you,' explained Nazar's running-mate, Zoelbahry Abubakar. 'So you give them sometimes 50,000, sometimes 20,000, sometimes just posters and stickers to give out. It gets to the point where it is worth it just to get rid of them.' Once paid their two-to-five dollars, the crocodiles moved off to another campaign office and repeated the procedure.

They were not the only ones who were promiscuous. One day a poet came into the office; he had penned verse in a classical Acehnese format in praise of Nazar; it would be read out at a 'community meeting' which would also feature rap music and comedians – 'We want to appeal to younger voters, too,' said the candidate. The poet began to read his verse – five pages of close type – interrupting himself every now and then to explain a particularly complex allegory. He had forgotten to insert the name of his new patron, however, and thus sung the praises of the Partai Aceh candidate to whom he had already sold the verse. Nazar pressed two red 100,000-rupiah notes into the bard's hand nonetheless, then answered a clearly fake phone call, using that as an excuse to shoo the man out of the office.

Nazar invited me to a fundraising dinner with a couple of Chinese businessmen, in a restaurant owned by one of the target contributors. The restaurant staff brought out dishes piled with grilled prawns in chilli sauce, with barbecued fish, with garlic-fried squid. While I tucked into this feast with the rest of Nazar's entourage, our Chinese hosts picked at prawn crackers. The candidate launched into his pitch. He said that the private sector was the engine of the economy, that as mayor, his first priority would be to cut red tape, to facilitate job creation and stimulate growth. The entirely chinless restaurant owner, whose expression had so far hovered between resigned and fed up, actually cracked a smile when Nazar diverged from the 'you give me money, I give you projects' script that he expected from those aspiring to win an election. But he also knew that the politician would have to get elected before he could realize those neo-liberal dreams. The prospects for any independent candidate were slim. 'Of course, you understand that we can't support everyone,' grunted the second restaurateur. They urged us to enjoy the feast they had laid on, then excused themselves politely and moved off to another table. There, the Partai Aceh candidate and his courtiers were devouring chilli prawns, waiting for their turn with the purveyors of slush funding.

I once asked a Chinese businesswoman which party she supported. 'With my vote, only one,' she replied coyly. 'But with my facilities, well, pretty much all of them. This one needs to borrow a car, that one needs some posters printed, why not?' She was not interested in the contracts that might flow from this relationship so much as the access that it gave her to (sometimes compromising) information. 'You want to know about local politicians? Ask a businessperson,' she said. 'We're the ones who really know.'

In Lhokseumawe, all candidates are allotted time in one of the city's big public spaces so that they can hold a campaign rally. Nazar wouldn't be using his slot; with no political party picking up the tab, it was just too expensive. There was the cost of providing entertainment: several thousand dollars for any singer good enough to bring in the crowds. You need to buy T-shirts and jilbabs in party colours, then pay people to put them on and show up to the rally – around three dollars per person. A minibus driver told me that he got paid three times for each rally, once to hang election banners on his bus for the day (US$25), a second time to ship in the participants (at double the regular fare) and a third time to hang around near the rally grounds causing a traffic jam (price negotiable). 'They want it to look like it's really busy; all you have to do is park somewhere inconvenient, and spend the afternoon smoking,' he chuckled. 'I just *love* election time.' On top of that, rally participants expect to be fed and watered. It is an expensive business.

Instead of holding a rally, Nazar went to the market to meet voters. He walked about shaking hands and flashing his brilliant white smile at all and sundry. The rest of the *Tim Sukses*, the success team – candidate for vice-mayor, campaign manager, various flunkies and several well-heeled wives – bustled behind handing out cards. 'Vote number five, vote number five.' This was the extent of the policy discussion. One team member videoed the proceedings, another took photographs. Later, he would submit the pictures with text to a local paper, who would print the 'news story' in accordance with their agreed 'package'. Two thousand dollars buys a photo and a three-column spread every day during the two-week campaign period. On the corner, always a few steps ahead of the candidate and his trailing 'journalists', was a huge, bald-headed man wearing wrap-around sunglasses and an unmissable shirt in fluorescent pink. He stood with legs wide and his arms folded across his chest, impassive. Everyone in the market could see that Nazar was important enough to need a bodyguard.

Later in the day, when the afternoon cooled and people were sitting on their verandas ahead of evening prayers, we did the rounds of a fishing community on the outskirts of the city. Like the Queen, Nazar did not carry money. But he instructed one of his entourage to buy shucked oysters from the ladies at a street stall on the corner, another to help a supplicant with a small donation 'for my sick child'. Again, the handing out of cards, the 'vote number five'. 'We're easy to remember, the ones with no hats,' said the candidate for deputy mayor. The voters looked expectant, then, when no envelopes or T-shirts were proffered, disappointed. 'Skinflints,' I heard more than once as I trailed behind the cortege. No one asked about policies.

The next day I went to a Partai Aceh rally on the vast square in front of the skeleton of the new mosque in Lhokseumawe. The red party flag fluttered from almost every lamp post in town. It streamed out, too, behind the convoys of flatbed trucks and motorbikes that raced around town, horns blaring, ratcheting up the excitement. The streets close to the rally grounds were choked with SUVs covered with hologram portraits of the Partai Aceh candidates. A few were decorated with a black and white photo of a feeble, elderly gentleman in owlish glasses, above the English headline: 'MY KING OF HEROES'. It was Hasan di Tiro, who had come back from Sweden to live in Aceh in 2009, just eight months before his death.

Yes, there were women in standard-issue jilbabs. Yes, their children were gorging on free candyfloss. But this rally, which looked like a funfair set up in an army barracks, was electric with genuine enthusiasm, almost fervour. Men wearing red, white and black military fatigues and red berets stomped about in solid lace-up boots, barking into walkie-talkies. This was the party's own militia. They moved with aggressive self-importance through the crowds, young boys tiptoeing reverentially in their wake. Many people listened rapt to the speeches of the heroes of the revolution.

The stage was set up as for a triple wedding, three love-seats in a row, each with its canopy of silk and brocade, each with its awkward-looking bridal couple, the candidates for governor of Aceh, bupati of East Aceh and mayor of Lhokseumawe with their respective running-mates. The governor/vice governor pairing seemed the most unlikely match. The aspiring governor was a portly, avuncular medical doctor with spectacles and a neatly trimmed moustache who had lived much of his adult life in Stockholm – he was Hasan di Tiro's cousin, in fact. His political sweetheart was a central-casting guerrilla fighter with three-day stubble, a study in rugged chic. This was Muzakir Manaf, the man who had recently embraced the general who once tried to annihilate him, the man who was now so adamant about an indivisible Indonesia.

I had climbed up the building-site mosque to get a good vantage point and was writing notes when I was accosted by a Partai Aceh activist. He had seen my bookmark, one of Nazar's election cards. He stuck out his hand, demanding to see it. When I handed it to him he scrunched it up and threw it to the floor. In Asia this constitutes a frontal assault but he was unapologetic. He gave me an emphatic lecture on the treachery of independents, how they were contravening the peace agreement, how anyone who didn't vote for Partai Aceh was a traitor who was just asking for trouble. Then he invited me home to meet his parents. I said yes. (Later, after giving me a long lecture on Islam as the guardian of virtue, he invited himself to accompany me up to the hill town of Takengon – 'So romantic, Bu!' I said no.)

At his home, smallish, neat, sitting alongside disused railway tracks, he introduced me to his parents and to the local 'district commander' of Partai Aceh in his neighbourhood, another carefully stubbled man with a slim, straight nose and sleepy lids over disconcertingly fiery eyes. The Commander treated me to his version of history, which he said he learned 'in the school of the jungle'. Aceh hosted the republican government in the 1940s, yes, and the merchants of Aceh contributed gold to Indonesia's nationalist cause, certainly. But this was not in any way because the sovereign state of Aceh wished to be part of the emerging nation. 'That's always been a misunderstanding,' the Commander said firmly. 'These were simply gifts of solidarity to a brother Islamic nation, to keep, sorry Bu, but to keep the *kafirs* at bay.'

Aceh has never been defeated in war, Aceh has never been successfully colonized. Ergo, we must be an independent nation.

I was slightly nonplussed to hear Hasan di Tiro's version of history fall unedited from the mouth of a man under thirty who had never left Aceh, particularly since he represented a political party now busily campaigning for elections within the Indonesian national system. Obviously the script hadn't been rewritten as completely as the current leadership of Partai Aceh, which is doing very nicely indeed out of integration with Indonesia, might like.

On the night before the election, I went out for supper with Nazar. Usually, he texted me from the car when he was outside my hotel, then waited for me to emerge. This time, though, he came bounding in, taut with nervous energy. 'There's something I have to ask you, Eliz,' he said. I raised an eyebrow. 'The thing is, I need thirty million rupiah before tomorrow morning.' Thirty million rupiah. That's three thousand dollars – more than three months' budget for me. I stared at him. 'I mean, of course, I'd give it back next month, and it doesn't all have to come from you . . .' Then, somehow we were at the cash machine, and I was looking at the balance on my private savings account, the one I keep for friends in need, occasional indulgences, emergencies. It contained 12 million rupiah. I took out half of my savings, stuck the money into a brown envelope, and gave it to Nazar. He nodded, put it in his pocket, and that was that. I guessed, correctly as it turned out, that I would never see the money again. He didn't even tell me what it was for, and I didn't ask, though I later found out it was to pay students to monitor the polling stations.

Later, I wondered what had got into me. I always gave 'kitchen contributions' to families I stayed with, and they were always graciously received. But I was wary of giving people money for other things. In Indonesia's what's-yours-is-mine culture, where forward planning is the exception and people feel they have an absolute right to draw on the resources of the clan, a single act of generosity can establish me as a member of the extended family; that leads inevitably to an endless stream of wheedling text messages: 'You are so good . . . we little people . . . since the car accident . . .' Like Nazar's Chinese restaurateurs, I can't support everybody, so I end up refusing all but the greatest needs. And yet here I was giving a US-educated lawyer running an expensive no-hope political campaign six hundred dollars to pay his election monitors. It would have been a life-changing amount for some of the people I had met on this trip. And it made me realize, though only in retrospect, how easy it is to get carried away by the excitement of a campaign.

The following morning, Nazar and his retinue went off to the polls. 'Vote with heart. No intervention!!!!' read the election officials' polo shirts, in English. And it did indeed seem that people were doing exactly that, waiting in orderly queues to get their documents checked and take their turn behind the plywood screen that shielded their hole-punching from public view, then pushing the folded ballot paper into locked tin boxes and dipping their fingers in purple ink to indicate that they had done their bit for democracy. My phone rang; it was the activist who had accosted me at the Partai Aceh rally – 'your PA boyfriend', as Nazar laughingly called him. He too was full of adrenalin. I complained that I felt left out, not being able to vote. 'I'll take you to one of *our* polling stations,' he said. 'Then we can fix a vote for you.'

We met in a coffee shop, and buzzed off on his motorbike to a polling station in the grounds of a mosque in the east of town. It was overrun by the thuggish short-haired men with sharp jaws and mirrored sunglasses that I had come to recognize as the Partai Aceh faithful; there was much slapping of backs and shaking of hands. 'My friend needs a vote,' said my PA boyfriend, and one of the thugs nodded and started looking down a list. Though I quickly made it clear that I had been joking, I'm pretty sure they would have arranged a ballot for me if I had wanted. Three times in the half-hour that I was there, sharp-jawed men came in carrying stacks of invitation letters with ID cards stapled to them.

They distributed these among their friends, who trooped in to vote. The election official checked that the name on the letter matched the name on the ID card, but didn't check that the ID card matched the person who carried it. A nod, and the ballot was cast. The monitors who were being paid by other candidates to check for fraud sat in a corner playing with their cell phones. When I asked one of these re-voters if he was 'inked', he held up his pinkie for me to see. Purple ink sat in droplets on a coating of wax on his fingertip.

I witnessed the vote count at the polling station directly outside Nazar's office. Of the 274 cast there, my friend got 10. Overall, Nazar came fifth of eleven candidates. 'The highest of those who didn't play money politics,' his campaign manager said encouragingly. As expected, the Partai Aceh candidates won in Lhokseumawe, as they did in well over half of the districts in Aceh. In elections for governor of Aceh, the doctor from Stockholm (who once had the title of 'foreign minister' in the mythical cabinet of Aceh's government-in-exile) and his stubbled running-mate won hands down.

I was interested by the rewriting of Aceh's recent as well as its more distant history. The hiatus in guerrilla activity from 1978 to 1989, the mish-mash of interests that threw separatists together with former soldiers and drug dealers in the early 1990s, the brutality of the rebels during that period and their later habit of burning schools, killing teachers, terrorizing migrants, executing supposed collaborators and squeezing all and sundry for money to support the cause – all these things seemed to have disappeared from the story of the conflict that I now heard in the coffee shops of Aceh.★

★ The brutality of the early 1990s I witnessed myself. For accounts of later periods, I'm indebted to Ed Aspinall, Elizabeth Drexler and Kirsten Schulze. Schulze reports that in Lhokseumawe, the rebels routinely demanded US$4,000 from every city ward, a 5 per cent cut on all business deals won by international contractors and 20 per cent from local contractors.

I thought back to two people who I remembered particularly from my reporting trips two decades earlier – a student and an NGO worker – and decided to try and find them again, to see whether their accounts of those times had changed at all.

I met the student, Hanafiah, during a reporting trip to Aceh in November 1990 with Claire, from the BBC. It was close to curfew, and we had stopped in the tiny coastal village of Idi Cut and knocked on the door of the only guest house in town, which was barred shut. An eye peeked from behind a curtain, there was a lot of uncertain murmuring and some more peeking eyes. Eventually the door opened and we walked into what looked like a birthday party for a skinny, balding young man with an odd head-dressing, half turban, half bandage. This was Hanafiah. Claire and I left our bags and went straight off to the market for a quick, pre-curfew supper. One of the young man's sisters, a teacher, tagged along. I left a copy of *Tempo*, an Indonesian news weekly, lying casually on the table of the restaurant. On the front cover was a smoking gun and the word 'Aceh'; inside, a report questioned the veracity of stories I had written about rebellion, brutality and mass graves in Aceh. Critiquing the Reuters reports was *Tempo*'s way of backing into what would otherwise be forbidden territory for the Indonesian press. It landed me in hot water with the military but it was worth it, because it kick-started a lot of conversations in Aceh.

As Claire and I ate thick chunks of fish stewed in turmeric and coconut milk, the teacher devoured our copy of *Tempo*. She gave it back in silence, and would not be drawn into conversation. But as we wandered home, she chatted away in a low voice. 'It's hard these days in the teaching profession; the government doesn't pay well but at least it's secure. My brother was imprisoned by them for a month and just came back yesterday. And of course in Aceh most of the private schools are Islamic schools and it's hard for a woman to get a job there. That's why he looks so terrible; they beat him and didn't feed him. But in the private sector the salaries are higher . . .'

Later, behind locked doors, in the dark and in whispers, we

heard Hanafiah's story. His sister did most of the talking; Hanafiah himself sat looking numb. He was still at college, and had been working in a photocopy shop to pay his fees. A fellow student came in for copies and he chatted to her, friendly. A soldier who fancied the girl took offence at Hanafiah's familiarity, and smashed him in the head twice with the butt of his semi-automatic, knocking him unconscious. The next thing he knew he was in a cell four metres by five metres with seventy other men. As his sister told us this, the boy suddenly squatted down on the floor. 'There was no space,' he whispered. 'We lived like this,' and he pulled his skin-and-bone limbs in like an insect trying to make itself inconspicuous in front of a predator. Then he held out a cupped hand. 'To eat, just this much rice every day.' He lapsed back into silence.

The boy was questioned, poked and prodded for three days, then – perhaps because there were so many witnesses to his unprovoked beating – he was pronounced innocent. Still, they kept him in the suffocating cell for a full month, with no treatment for a festering head wound. Then they released him back to his family. It seemed like a strategy guaranteed to escalate rebellion. My notes from the time observed that a history of detention, even wrongful detention, would 'put the boy out of the running for almost any job or respectable marriage, probably for ever'.

Now, twenty-two years later, I went back to the guest house in Idi Cut to look for the teacher and the skinny boy with the head wound. I knocked. A woman answered the door. Before I could explain who I was, she grabbed me by the hand: 'You're the one who came just after Hanafiah got out of jail!' She dragged me over to an inside wall. There was a photo of Hanafiah, all dressed up in his wedding finery. Properly fed, he turned into a good-looking man, strapping, almost, with narrow eyes, high cheekbones and a generous moustache. 'He's a Big Man now, in the Department of Public Works.' Next to that photo was a framed portrait of his sister, the school teacher. 'She was taken to Java. She's dead now.'

The woman, another sister, gave me Hanafiah's phone number. I called, and launched in to an awkward 'you-won't-remember-me-but . . .' introduction. He remembered me perfectly, this man whom I had not seen or spoken to for over two decades. He spoke almost as though I were a friend who was just back from a couple of months away in the capital. When we met, a warm smile spread over his face and he took my hand in both of his and held it for a long moment. He bore no resemblance at all to the raggedy skeleton with the bandaged head wound that I remembered from 1990, and yet there was a familiarity which went far beyond the ID check that I got from having seen his wedding photo. Sharing or even just witnessing someone's adversity, however glancingly, seems to create a visceral sort of bond. Hanafiah was more talkative these days, but he still spoke in a near whisper, as though he didn't really trust the peace, as though he thought anything he said might still, some day, be used against him. Sometimes, he would just let sentences trail off . . .

He said that he never went back to college, and for two or three years after the soldier bludgeoned him he could do no real work. 'I was no use to anyone, I used to faint all the time,' and he flopped his body sideways in his chair, letting his head roll and his tongue loll. Despite constant harassment, Hanafiah's family kept up the pressure on the military. Hanafiah said that the soldier who had attacked him was eventually court-martialled and dismissed from the army.

After the way the army treated him, I thought that Hanafiah might have joined the rebels. GAM fighters were given a lot of plum posts after the peace agreement, so that might also explain Hanafiah's job in the Department of Public Works, the 'wettest' of all the government agencies. But when I asked if he had joined GAM, he looked horrified. 'Why would I do that?' he asked. 'The rebels were no better than the army!'

In 2000, when a civilian president was trying to bring the military to heel, the government offered jobs to people who had been on the wrong end of army violence in Aceh. Hanafiah was one of them. Some of these people had no more than a primary school education; all had been brutalized by the very government they were going to work for. I asked Hanafiah if that hadn't been strange for him. 'I try not to bear grudges,' he smiled, spreading his hands as if to say: what's the point?

The second person I remembered very clearly was Asya, a slim young woman with long, wavy hair about the same age as me who worked at a Save the Children-sponsored safe motherhood project. The office was in the tiny village of Tangse, in the hills of north-eastern Aceh, which was said to be a rebel stronghold. When Claire and I arrived, we found Tangse swarming with soldiers. A clutch of them were lounging around at a coffee stall, drinking tea or coffee and smoking kreteks in various states of undress, shirts undone or stripped off, legs splayed, booted feet hoisted onto empty benches. The village children circled in cautious fascination around weapons dumped carelessly on the table or slung over the back of a chair. The soldiers were Javanese boys in their early twenties, but if they were at all frightened to be in the thick of guerrilla warfare, they didn't show it. One of them started hamming it up in our honour, stroking the barrel of his gun, billing and cooing at it. 'She's my wife,' he explained. 'I kiss her, I sleep with her and she kills for me.'

Tangse huddles on the edge of a fertile valley in the eastern foothills of the Bukit Barisan mountains. Wooden houses are hoisted on stilts like elevated Swiss cottages, their gables elaborately carved and painted with flowers, vines, the crescent moons and stars of piety; they are raised to keep them out of the flash floods that sometimes sweep down the river. At dawn, a pink mist hangs over the rice paddies and fuzzes up the tops of coconut trees that seem somehow out of place in this mountain landscape. I was leaning out of the window of the wooden NGO mess where we had stayed the night, contemplating this picture of tranquillity, when the silence was shattered by the crunch of boots on stone. The youngsters from the coffee stall, now strapped up in full combat kit, jogged past in formation. When they caught sight of me, a couple of them waved their weapons overhead. 'Now we'll get them!' they yelled. 'Now we'll kill them!'*

Asya, Tangse born and bred, came and stood next to me. She rolled her eyes, then turned away. In daylight, she would not say a thing. 'The only way to survive is with your mouth shut.' But after dark, she and her colleague had bolted the door of the mess and whispered of life in the hills. They were absolutely disgusted with the way the soldiers behaved, and just as horrified by the nameless rebels. 'They're brutes, the pack of them!' It was Asya's colleague who had told me of the soldier left stripped naked by the roadside with his penis in his mouth.

I went back to Tangse in 2012 and found Asya still living there. She had filled out over the years; when I knocked at her door and disturbed her at her prayers, her dumpling form was accentuated by her puffy white prayer robes. She welcomed me in. 'We couldn't say much back in those days, could we?' Now, she had the slow, elliptical speech of a woman who spends too much time on her own. Her husband disappeared in 2000 and had never been heard of since. She had no idea who was responsible. 'It was so messy,' she said, raising her questioning palms to the heavens. 'I could blame this one or that one but really, it could have been either side and if you try to blame you end up hating them all.' Save the Children shut down because it seemed too dangerous to continue work after the conflict intensified, even though the project had successfully reduced deaths among mothers and babies. 'Such a shame,' Asya said, shaking her head.

There's nothing about Asya of the 'that would be tiring' that I had heard in the languid villages of eastern Indonesia. She does whatever she can to make ends meet: she takes in washing, cleans houses, plants rice for other farmers, dries rice crops out after harvest, does the occasional evaluation for a village development

---

* I later learned from people who had fought on the rebel side in this area that the regular troops, those who had been stationed in the area for a while and who worshipped at the same mosques or belonged to the same martial arts groups as men who were rebels, would sometimes radio ahead to warn the fighters of an upcoming raid.

project. With this, she is putting her one child through college. 'What I pray for is peace. I pray that my child does not have to live as we did, always afraid, always confused, never trusting anyone.'

Now that I look back through my notes, I realize that I heard comments like this with fair frequency, but never in a coffee shop. In the women's territory of the kitchen, squatting around a tub of vegetables that needed peeling or standing over a wok of slowly roasting coffee beans, I would hear less triumphalism, fewer stories of glorious battles fought in the name of justice, a more nuanced view of history. The coffee shop is the place where men gather to sharpen their resentments and hone their grudges, the pastimes of a wealthy trading nation that has always been able to afford leisure and war. It is here that you get the braggart's view, and it is that view, expressed in the public realm, that most often makes it into history.

Of all the cities I revisited on my recent travels, the one that has changed most is the capital of this troubled province, Banda Aceh. Previously a pretty but dusty sprawl of low-rise villas, it was rebuilt almost from scratch after been flattened by the pitiless tsunami of Boxing Day, 2004. Banda Aceh is now a real city, with multi-lane roads, orderly traffic roundabouts and gleaming government offices. There are new hospitals and university buildings, huge supermarkets, and a lot less public transport than there used to be. In Indonesia, that's taken as a sign of progress: everyone's rich enough to have at least a motorbike. The city has also become markedly more religious. Restaurants and shops bar their doors against customers during Friday prayers, though I did discover that Tower, the city's slickest internet coffee shop, operates a lock-in policy rather like an Irish pub. As long as you're inside at closing time, they'll lock the doors on you and allow you to keep drinking.

The west coast of Aceh, too, has become suddenly more modern. When I was there in early 2012, steamrollers were flattening down the very last stretches of a splendid highway that now runs the length of the coast. For a while, it hugs the mountainside. Below, a ribbon of white lace marks the place where an innocent sea kisses a peaceful shore, but it's a spooky drive; it's impossible not to think of what that sea can do when it's enraged, the utter devastation it can wreak. As the road flattens down to the coast, more reminders. I passed whole plantations of what look like telegraph poles standing in waterlogged soil. These were once coconut trees, now dead and leafless, utterly forlorn. I was woken at dawn by the call to prayer from a mosque which consisted of nothing but a loudspeaker rigged up a high wooden pole. And all down the coast, I saw thousands upon thousands of prefab houses, standing in tight clusters, almost all on the inland side of the road, facing the hills. Indonesians have never shared the Western obsession with a sea view; all around the country beachfront houses have their bathrooms and kitchens where a picture window would be in the West. But on the west coast of Aceh people have especially good reason not to want to while away their evenings contemplating the sea.

All the houses in any given cluster are identical, though the models vary between groupings. There were one or two complexes of wooden houses tottering on stilts in traditional Acehnese style, but most were grounded breeze block and cement, in this village painted hospital-ward green, in that village the pinky beige of a school-lunch caramel pudding. Each cluster was funded by a particular donor. Logos have become addresses. 'Ibu Amna? She lives in Oxfam, by the football field.' Over time, the dwellings have been modified by their residents, the backs of houses are swollen with lean-tos, satellite dishes sprout from roofs. But very few have been repainted. The uniformity acts as a reminder that we are all equal before the wrath of God.

In the centre of the new Banda Aceh stands the tsunami museum. It commemorates something that is etched on the mind of everyone who was in Indonesia at the time. For days, maybe weeks, after the deluge, every TV station played funeral music and ran rolling images of the disaster: rows and rows of dead children, their corpses laid out like dolls in a toyshop; walls of black water powering towards hastily climbing cameras; buses, houses, trees all uprooted and carried relentlessly inland. The mosque in Banda Aceh rising majestic from the ruins, the ship tottering on top of a roof, the wailing survivors, the grim rescue workers, the unimaginable scenes that follow when the vengeful ocean rises thirty metres out of its bed and crashes down on a civilization going about its business.

The tsunami museum is an impressive building, a great, rounded sweep of latticework raised on vast pillars that from one angle looks like a cresting wave, from another like a ship. Walking in, you squeeze down a long, dark passage hemmed in on either side by black walls of water. I felt both awed and slightly panicky.

When I emerged on the other side I found holes in the walls, patches of mould, wiring hanging out of the ceiling, all in a monument that cost US$7 million and was built less than three years previously. The library was locked, the bathrooms too. On dozens of lecterns showing the identical slide show on a continuous loop, in the photos pasted higgledy-piggledy onto panels interspersed with drawings of the museum itself, in the bright 1970s-style dioramas hectic with mannequins and plastic coconut trees, even in the nine-minute film that I watched in the company of children not even born when the wave struck, there is virtually nothing that recreates that muffled-thudding, sludgy-sick feeling that we all felt when we first saw the rows of shrouds on TV. In fact, in this vast museum dedicated to an event that killed 170,000 people in Aceh, there was almost no death. I saw just one photo which included, peripherally, a single orange body bag.

I commented on this to the staff member who was shepherding the schoolkids around with a loudhailer. He shrugged. 'Maybe they wanted to avoid rousing emotions.' A monument to something you don't really want to help people remember. A museum of amnesia, a selective rewriting of history. On reflection, it seemed oddly appropriate to Aceh.

Map J: SUMATRA

10

Misfits

Aceh, indeed all of Sumatra, proved quite different from the parts of eastern Indonesia that I had been drifting around in the previous months. Sumatra is vast, so vast that if you smushed all 4,100 islands of NTT, Maluku, North Maluku and the Sangihe chains together, they'd only take up a quarter of the area of that single western Indonesian island. A forested mountain range wells up in Aceh in the northern tip of the island, then runs for 1,600 kilometres down the west coast. On the eastern side of the range, the rainforest tumbles down onto flatter land, then peters out, leaving a huge marshy plain criss-crossed with rivers; that's what makes is such good plantation country.

It's culturally diverse too. The Acehnese, sitting on the 'Veranda of Mecca', pride themselves on being more Islamic than anyone else in Indonesia. Just to the south of Aceh, around the huge upland Lake Toba, Christian Bataks are as clannish as any ethnic group in Indonesia; their enthusiasm for funerals and other sacrificial festivals rivals that of Sumba. The Minangkabau of West Sumatra are proud Muslims and energetic intellectuals as well as purveyors of the nasi Padang dishes that unify the nation. On the east coast, the traders of Palembang, also staunchly Islamic, take plain speaking to levels unknown in mealy-mouthed Java. And that's just four of Sumatra's dozens of tribes.

The bus journeys from Medan and around Aceh had surprised me not just because they passed through thickets of posters proposing former rebels for governor. On the first trip, from

Medan up to Langsa, I had bought a numbered ticket for a bus that was scheduled to leave at a fixed time. It seemed an odd concept – in eastern Indonesia the scheduled departure time was 'whenever the bus is full enough'. But from Medan we had left at the appointed time, with me comfortably ensconced in my appointed seat.

Not a kilometre out of the bus station, the driver screeched to a halt to pick up someone who was standing on the road-side, flapping their hand. Then another, and another. At each impromptu stop the driver's assistant would scoop the new passenger into the back door and a friend would pass up sacks of rice and baskets of chickens. One early addition to the passenger list smiled at me. 'Excuse me, you don't mind if I . . .' I quickly averted my eyes but it was too late. Now there were three of us in two seats. Another few kilometres, another few dozen stops, more smiling and I'm so sorries, and we were three and a half, the newcomer balanced between the seat edge and a pile of cement bags.

For a nation that is so much on the move, Indonesians are rotten travellers. On boats they get seasick (*mabuk* – 'drunk') before I can even tell that we've left the dock. And on buses, every second passenger seems to clutch a little bottle of *balsem* under their nose. *Balsem*, a cure-all that smells like a mint julep infused with Vicks VapoRub, is supposed to settle the stomach. It is a sure sign that vomiting will ensue. The woman who had squeezed herself into my numbered seat early on that first fourteen-hour bus journey from Medan duly began sniffing balsem, then retching quietly into a plastic bag. The sound was drowned out by the dangdut music that pounded from the speakers positioned every two metres along the length of the bus.

The alternative to the long-distance buses is to take a series of short-hop minibuses (in northern Sumatra they're called 'L300s' after the Mitsubishi model that most drivers use). These stop even more frequently for flapping hands, and take long detours to drop someone at home or to pick up a package from Auntie's house. Designed for eleven passengers, they often squeeze in as many as eighteen. That makes it a good idea to wheedle a seat up in front, with the driver. Sitting up front has lots of advantages beyond actually being able to see anything other than the back of someone's diamanté-studded jilbab. Because drivers like to protect their own space, they rarely put more than two other people in the passenger seat. Drivers know their area well, and are often chatty and informative, providing recommendations and sometimes door-to-door delivery to a friendly guest house. Being up front puts you in reach of the stereo system; I became adept at turning down the volume with my elbows while pretending to rummage in my bag. Sometimes, the driver would let me plug in my USB stick and play my own music for a while; from passenger feedback I soon learned that I could get away with Lyle Lovett and k.d. lang but not with flamenco or anything classical.

Watching the drivers was fun, too. I started giving out mental prizes for multitasking. On a one-lane road that snaked from blind corner to hairpin bend, I watched one driver light a cigarette. Then, with it hanging from his mouth, he peeled a *salak*. A salak is a teardrop-shaped fruit, white and waxy inside, covered in crispy brown snakeskin, fiddly to peel. He steered us around the hairpins with his forearms as he attacked this task, chatting all the while, steering just with his right elbow when he needed his left hand to change gear, flick the ash from his cigarette or answer his phone.

I was flapping my hand on the roadside just north of Lhokseumawe on the east coast of Aceh one afternoon, when an L300 screeched to a halt. I asked the driver – a handsome man in his mid-fifties with a clipped moustache – whether he could drop me in Sigli. He waved me into the front seat, and introduced himself as Teungku Haji. That confused me: Teungku is an Acehnese honorific accorded to people who are considered to have a lot of Islamic learning, while Haji is an honorific used for a person who has made the pilgrimage to Mecca. It was like calling yourself Sir Reverend. Over his short-back-and-sides haircut, Teungku Haji wore a white Islamic cap, embroidered in gold. He chatted cheerfully about the usual things, the incompetence of the government, the elections, the prospect of higher fuel prices. He fed me salted fried banana crisps. 'You're too skinny.' Eventually, he asked what business I had in the uninspiring coastal town of Sigli.

Actually, I said, I just wanted to change buses there, to head inland to the tiny mountain village of Tangse – this was when I was hoping to reconnect with Asya, the NGO worker I had met two decades before. 'It is the will of God that we met!' declared Teungku Haji. Of the hundreds of daily buses that pass where I had flagged him down, his was one of only two that go to Tangse. As we turned off the main road and headed west through rice fields, the clouds that hung over the mountains of central Aceh flamed orange and the evening call to prayer echoed from mosques up and down the valley. By the time we drove into Tangse, the mountains had turned to dusty purple and one or two stars embroidered the sky. Teungku Haji asked where I planned to stay. I asked which guest house he'd recommend. 'Guest house? There are no guest houses in Tangse.'

Pause.

'Why don't you come home with me?'

Pause.

I didn't want to be rude. But 'just say yes' doesn't necessarily extend to accepting invitations issued at dusk to stay overnight with a bus driver in an isolated village, Islamic prayer cap or not.

I tried to extricate myself. 'That's such a kind offer. Really. But I think it's not necessary. Please drop me at the NGO mess.' I was sure I'd recognize the Save the Children house where I had stayed all those years before. But the driver had no idea what I was talking about. 'There's no NGO in Tangse.'

And then again: 'Come home with me.'

He looked over at me, and I quickly averted my eyes. Then Teungku Haji burst out laughing and slapped the steering wheel with glee. 'Aduh! I don't mean like *that*, Ibu.' He explained that he was an outsider in Tangse, from Bireuen on the coast, but that his wife was Tangse born and bred. 'You come home with me, she'll know what to do.'

Ibu Hamidah knew exactly what to do. She unrolled two carpets on the living room floor and spread my sleeping mat on top of them. 'There. Your bed.' The carpets had been on loan to the local mosque for a visit by the current Governor of Aceh, Irwandi Yusuf, and had just come back from the cleaners that day. 'You see,' said Ibu Hamidah. 'It is the will of God that you should stay with us.'

That's how I made friends with Yufrida. Yufrida is Hamidah's daughter (and Teungku Haji's stepdaughter; it's the second marriage for both of them). When we arrived, she was sitting in the front room in a red wheelchair. I was introduced to Hamidah, and to Hamidah's parents – her father a tall, dignified man with vaguely Arab features, her mother's pudding face slashed by a betel-stained mouth and narrow, distrustful eyes. But I wasn't introduced to Yufrida.

I said hello to her myself, and she greeted me in response, slurred, but comprehensible enough. Yufrida has extraordinarily twinkly eyes and a light-up, buck-toothed smile.

'Don't bother with her,' said Pudding Faced Grandma. 'She's a cripple. Go on, give us some money.' Just like that.

Yufrida sat in her wheelchair, her feet corkscrewed in towards each other, her right arm held rigid in front of her body, her left hand bent upwards in a hook at her side. She said nothing. Now Hamidah introduced her properly. 'This is Yufrida,' and she ruffled her hair affectionately. Hamidah treated her daughter with great kindness. But still she complained, in front of Yufrida, how exhausting it was to care for a thirty-year-old daughter who had been disabled since childhood, to spoon-feed her, to bathe her, to heave her on and off the toilet.

I rather ignored Yufrida for the rest of the evening. Most of the time, she sat quietly in her chair. When she did speak, I could make little sense of it, and from the way everyone but her mother ignored her, I assumed she was talking nonsense, though I realized later she was speaking Acehnese.

The following day, I went to plant cocoa seedlings with Ibu Hamidah and her father. At the age of eighty-three, with a fifty-kilo sack of fertilizer hefted onto his shoulders, he strode across the fields so fast that it was hard to keep up. When we came back, Yufrida greeted us joyously. When her cousins from further up the village dropped in to say hello, she engaged with them as much as their awkwardness with her allowed. I realized that Yufrida's mind was in perfect working order. I just hadn't made much effort to understand her.

In the evening, I said I thought I'd wander along and visit the cousins, and invited Yufrida to come with me. She was thrilled, but Granny was horrified. 'You mustn't!' she waved her hands at me, as if to make me disappear in a puff of witchcraft. 'She never goes out. It would be too shameful.' I asked Yufrida if she would be ashamed to come for a walk with me. She shook her head vigorously. '*Tidak!*' No! Clear, emphatic. Hamidah smiled: 'Well if you're going visiting, you'll want to look your best.' And she helped her daughter into clean clothes, brushed her hair, and dabbed on face powder and lipstick, until I felt quite dowdy by comparison.

We must have made an odd pair, this unknown Caucasian woman, leathery with travel, a badly tied jilbab slipping off every few minutes to reveal shorn hair, swearing and apologizing as she pushed the wheelchair over the lumpy stone road. In the chair the younger Acehnese woman with alabaster skin, not just uncomplaining but grinning as she was lurched from bump to bump. Later, her mother took me aside and explained that I needed to tilt the chair back on its rear wheels when coming up to a difficult patch. 'Yufrida asked me to explain. She thought she might hurt your feelings if she told you herself.'

People stared at us as we passed, but when we yelled out our good evenings, me in Indonesian, Yufrida in Acehnese, they responded. By our third evening walk, the villagers were greeting us as soon as we lurched into sight.

The next day, Ibu Hamidah and I set off on her motorbike; we drove the forty kilometres or so up the river valley to

Geumpang. In theory we were trying to find informal gold miners – I'd heard there were many of them panning in this area – but as much as anything we were just going for a girls' day out. It was a glorious day, clear and slightly blustery. As we climbed beyond the rice fields that lined the river plain around Tangse the valley closed in on itself. An energetic river churned over grey boulders on the valley floor, carving a gorge between the road and a cliff of rock on one side and a steep wall dressed in tumbling green vines on the other. We passed a collapsed suspension bridge that now consisted of two wires strung high above the gorge. Balanced mid-air on the bottom wire and clinging to the top one for safety were a middle-school girl with a knapsack of books on her back, a boy in the maroon and white uniform of primary school, and two young mothers with babies strapped to their backs.

In a restaurant built out over the gorge, we stopped for a coffee. We gossiped and laughed about this and that. Like her daughter, Hamidah had a beautiful, open smile; her eyes twinkled with fun behind little oval glasses. She was confident and assertive, without being bossy. 'Are you sure you want to go out without your jilbab?' she'd ask, if I made for the door having forgotten to cover my head. 'Just saying . . .'

Now, sitting quietly away from home and family, she told me her story and I began to understand just how strong she was. She had Yufrida and two other children with her first husband, whom she described as a good-for-nothing. 'He used to steal cars from the military. Then he'd sell them and gamble away the money so that when they caught him, he couldn't pay them back.' She shook her head as if wanting to disbelieve. At one point he disappeared for two years, leaving her with the three children. It wasn't until she was introduced to another batch of children that she discovered he had long ago taken another wife. He was, of course, no help with Yufrida. Hamidah learned to be self-reliant. She was living in Banda Aceh at the time of the tsunami. She grabbed the immobile Yufrida and climbed out of reach of the waters, but their home was destroyed. 'The good thing about the tsunami was that we finally got a wheelchair, from one of those help-the-victims NGOs.'

That was the only assistance Hamidah has ever had in caring for her daughter, despite petitioning the department of social welfare for help for years. I asked about schooling, about physical therapy, about speech therapy. None. Yufrida is clearly a sociable person, and bright. I suggested to her mother that with a little bit of support, she could probably live a much more independent, engaged and fun life. 'After all,' I said, 'she's not mentally handicapped.'

Hamidah, usually so quick-witted in response, said nothing. She looked at me for a long time, then looked away, then looked at me again. At last she said quietly, 'That's right. She's not mentally handicapped.'

The next day, a group of ladies were teaching me to make Acehnese cakes. Yufrida watched me trying ham-fistedly to copy their rolling and squeezing of dough, and laughed. I asked her what I was doing wrong. 'Too thin,' she said of my scrawny attempts.

A neighbour with a face like a horse wrinkled up her long nose and spoke over Yufrida. 'She's handicapped,' she said, as though this might have escaped me. 'She has to be spoon-fed, and you think she knows how to make cakes!'

I opened my mouth to respond, but Ibu Hamidah cut in, low voiced, icy: 'She's not mentally handicapped.'

Horse Face looked shocked, as though the distinction between physical and metal disability was something entirely new to her. She made her excuses and left. 'She's not mentally handicapped,' Hamidah repeated, as her neighbour walked out the door.

Later in the trip, in Kalimantan, I met a young Dutch volunteer who was providing free physical therapy for the disabled. She felt that religion was the first hurdle many Indonesian parents faced when considering how to care for disabled children. 'This child was sent by God to test me. I must bear the burden with equanimity.' The second, perhaps related, was a sense of shame. I have an imperfect child (perhaps a punishment for some misdeed of mine?). Better not to let anyone know. The third was a fear of the costs that would be involved in treatment. Finally, many parents simply didn't have any idea that treatment was possible.

All of these things are partly true, I'm sure, though perhaps not of Hamidah, who had at least tried to get some help for Yufrida. But the biggest challenge for Yufrida and hundreds of thousands of other disabled Indonesians is surely the attitudes of people like Horse Face and indeed her own grandmother, upstanding members of a society that simply does not deal well with misfits.

My own efforts to fit in as best I could with the people among whom I was travelling came a cropper in a group of microscopic islands off the coast of Sumatra. Pulau Banyak ('Many Islands') is technically part of Aceh province, but the local population speaks Malay and the police chief in the main town referred to himself as 'not from here at all: I'm an outsider, from Aceh'.

The police chief railed for a while about the short-sightedness of the local fishermen. Breathing air pumped down a tube from a primitive compressor on a canoe above, the divers sink to great depths, then squirt potassium cyanide on lobster, grouper and other expensive fish, a technique illegal since 2004 but still widely employed. The toxin stuns the animals and allows them to be captured alive and sold to seafood restaurants for their aquaria. But the poison also gets caught in the sea currents, killing swathes of the very coral on which the fish and other valuable species such as lobsters and sea-slugs depend. 'I don't even know how to begin to explain to them how stupid that is.' The policeman shook his head.

While they were busy wiping out their own future earnings, the divers often got the bends; several had been paralysed and a couple had died. I remarked that there were many ways to die around here; just that morning I had heard that a woman in neighbouring Haloban had been eaten by a crocodile. 'Only her bones were left,' the person who told me had said, with some relish.

The police chief nodded. 'But it's okay, they're hiring a shaman to catch it,' he said. He explained how it worked. The Crocodile Whisperer goes to the shore where the person was eaten, and drives a sacred spear into the ground. That calls together the fraternity of crocodiles. Then the good crocodiles, the ones who haven't done anything wrong, point out the naughty, woman-eating croc. The shaman catches the murderer, and the other crocs go back to eating fish and minding their own business.

It seemed unlikely that a police chief who railed against idiotic short-termism among local divers could simultaneously believe that a man with special powers could convoke a conclave of crocodiles. Does it work? I asked. 'Oh yes,' said the police chief. 'Unless, of course, the shaman is a fraud.'

I resolved to go to Haloban to talk to the Crocodile Whisperer, hitching a lift on a boat with a couple of curiously laconic Dutch volunteers who were passing that way en route from a turtle monitoring station I had visited. The weather was filthy, but it didn't deter the boat boys. They emptied the water out of a small boat through a hole in the gunwales, then plugged the hole with a bit of old flip-flop. We launched out through the crashing surf.

My yellow rain cape proved helpless in the face of water which sloshed and sprayed all around. The volunteers looked miserable. 'In Ireland, we call this kind of weather "lumpy",' I shouted across the roar of engine and waves, fake-cheerfully. The young Dutchman nodded silently. Then he spoke for the first time. 'In Holland,' he said, 'we call it "shit".'

It took nearly two hours to get to Haloban, plenty of time to wonder idly how many weeks it would be before anyone noticed if I drowned out here. By the time I arrived I was cold to my bones and my hands were almost too numb to hold my bag. I clamped my sodden jilbab firmly over my hair and dragged my bag along the muddy street past Haloban's only coffee shop. The coffee drinkers eyed me silently. Not one *Dari mana?* – 'Where are you from?', not one 'Hello Mister', just a wall of stares.

Haloban has one guest house, run by a woman from the island of Nias. She was elaborately kind, but treated me as though I were a bit simple. She spoke Slooooowly and Cleeeaaarly, and scattered in the odd word of English every now and then, just to make me feel at home. '*You* mandi dulu, habis itu *you* lapor diri, baru kita *eat rice*,' and she mimed scooping food into her mouth. After I'd washed, I could go and report to the police, she said. Then we'd eat.

After I'd washed and dug dryish clothes out of the middle of my damp bag, I went and sat under an awning in the street in front of the guest house. Lying on a bench under the awning was the village cop. In the Suharto years, foreigners were supposed to report to the police when staying in rural areas, and in Aceh the habit persisted throughout the conflict that ended in 2005. I sometimes still report in very remote areas when I am staying with villagers just to spare them any suspicion. Besides, the cops are often a good source of local gossip. But the policeman lying on the bench obviously did not have the slightest desire to register me. He had hiked up his T-shirt and was scratching his belly with one hand, his other hand was busy texting. I said good evening but he studiously ignored me. Somehow, I was glad to be relieved of the need to launch into the polite chit-chat which would bring me to the burning topics of the day: Crocodile Whisperers and the theft of turtle eggs.

In truth, after seven months on the road, I was feeling a little fragile about the whole just-say-yes, of-course-I'll-get-into-a-leaky-boat-in-a-lashing-rainstorm travel experience. I started playing with my own phone, reaching into my other world for the first time in three days. I texted a writer friend in Jakarta: 'How will I ever make sense of this country?' I wailed. 'That's what editors are for,' he replied.

I scrolled through my e-mails. There were a few requiring grown-up policy recommendations for HIV treatment services in Papua – a reminder of a day job that seemed very far away. One from the editor of a magazine in London wanting an Indonesia think piece, a cheery hello from my mother, and a message from Sara, my editor in London, the one who had commissioned this book in the first place.

She was quitting her job.

My book would be orphaned. I'd have to wrestle this impossible jelly all by myself. The sky was falling. For the first time since I'd been on the road, I burst into tears.

The cop, his belly still flapping in the wind, continued to ignore me. I can't sit in the street in this unfriendly town sobbing, I thought. I made a dash for the dark cubicle that served as my room, through the front hall where the whole family, including grandparents and assorted teenagers, was sitting on the floor watching sinetron. I closed my door and suddenly seven months of staying in damp, windowless flea-pits, of being woken at four by the mosque, five by the chickens and six by the schoolkids, seven months of defending my childlessness, being asked why I didn't have any friends, being told I must have been pretty when I was young, seven months in a world without loo paper, alcohol or English conversation, seven months of wearing the same six pairs of knickers, of endlessly packing and repacking bags, seven months of getting over foot rot only to come out in a mystery rash, seven months of trying to make sense of things that made no sense, above all, seven months of trying to fit into a world that was, quite simply, not my world: it all came crashing down on me. I started really sobbing: hiccupy, snotty sort of sobbing.

The mosque bellowed out the evening call to prayer from just next door. (Great!) Then an announcement: there would be special prayers to implore Allah to support the work of the Crocodile Whisperer, who had already been camped out at the Beach of Death for three days with no success. '*Aduh!*' I thought. 'I've got to stop sobbing so that I can go to the prayer meeting for the Crocodile Whisperer.' And then I was laughing at myself and sobbing at the same time, and thinking how postmodern it all was. Ibu knocked at the door. 'Dinner.'

I blew my nose and dried my tears as best I could, and emerged to explain that I was just going to the mosque for the crocodile prayers, that I'd eat after that. Ibu was having none of it. She took me by the hand, led me to the table, sat me down, and put a plate

of rice in front of me. Then she sat down and put her face close
to mine. 'Eat!'

I ate. She watched each forkful disappear into my mouth, as if
I were a wayward toddler. After a bit, satisfied that I wasn't going
to wriggle down from the table before finishing my dinner, she
sat back. 'You're sad,' she said. Mmmmmm. 'Why?'

How am I going to explain to this kind, solicitous lady that
I've got swollen eyes and a snot-trailed face because my editor
has quit? I chose the easy option. 'My friend died,' I said.

'Oh,' she said. 'Well . . .' She hinged a forearm at the elbow, and
snapped her hand smartly down on the table-top. '. . . At least she
wasn't eaten by a crocodile.'

Eventually, I made friends with some of the silent, staring
fishermen at Haloban's coffee stall. None of them would tell
me where the woman had been eaten; the Crocodile Whisperer
couldn't be disturbed until he'd made his catch, they said. After
a couple of days, they began muttering about the shaman. He
had been brought in all the way from Simeulue island, eighty
kilometres to the north of Haloban, and had been paid three
million rupiah, twice the average monthly income in Aceh.
But after five or six days: still nothing. Maybe he wasn't a real
whisperer, this one, maybe he was a fraud.

I decided that I couldn't wait around in Haloban for a shaman
who might be a charlatan to catch a croc. The next day I packed
up and walked down to the pier. I was negotiating passage out
with some fishermen when 'Crocodile, crocodile!' the shout
went up. Up and down the creek where the fishermen kept
their long, thin canoes, men ran to boats, piled in, puttered off
to the Beach of Death. 'What are you waiting for?' one of my
coffee companions motioned me over to his boat and we joined
the convoy. There was some texting back and forth: 'They say it's
seven metres long!'

The woman had been eaten while searching for clams in the
muddy mouth of a small creek. Now, dozens of boats were trying

to get into the creek, bumping and jostling for prime real estate. Our boat was towards the back of the crowd; my companions motioned me to get out and wade to shore. I wondered how well secured the seven-metre crocodile was.

I pushed through the thigh-high water towards a little shack with a palm-frond roof. On the ground was a sleeping mat, a little cooking pot, a harpoon and a bag of rice. This was the Whisperer's lair. Looking around, I realized that although plenty of women had been flapping around excitedly in town, not one other woman had come to witness the capture. The men, on the other hand, nudged and pointed, keen to explain the process to me, all wanting to be heroes by proxy. The crocodile had shown himself on the other side of the creek, some said, though no one had actually seen him. The shaman was apparently trying to coax him into a rattan noose, see, over there.

It started to rain. I put on my yellow poncho. Two men tried snuggling under it for shelter; I shooed them out; laughing at their cheek. It was all very good-natured. Then, from the other side of the creek, there was an angry shouting and a flapping of arms. It semaphored itself across the water. The men on my side turned towards me and started shouting and flapping too. I realized that I was the object of this sudden collective wrath.

'No women allowed! It takes the shaman's power away!'

I retreated to the edge of the wood; the men who had been so friendly just moments ago all turned their backs on me. The air went icy.

After another few minutes of faffing around, it was clear that no one would be trapping a crocodile today. No one but the Whisperer himself had actually seen the croc. Now, he was claiming that it had got away because the Foreign Woman had polluted the scene. The men who had swept me so enthusiastically into their boat on the way here would no longer look at me. The men who had laughingly muscled in under my poncho – all became silent and hostile. One younger man with spiky hair and bit of urban slang took some pity on me; I could walk back to town with him, he said. But in the hour and a half that it took to stumble back to town through the sandal-sucking, toe-nipping mangroves, he didn't speak to me at all.

I'm still not quite sure what went wrong, but my guess is that the men knew that women weren't really allowed in the hallow-ed world of crocodile capture. Because I was such a strange beast, though, I stood outside their whole cosmos; as a woman I didn't really count. Then, when the Whisperer failed to produce his croc, he seized on me as an opportunistic excuse. It was fright-ening how quickly I had turned from an irrelevant curiosity into a pariah.

Close to the middle of Sumatra, in Jambi province, sits the Bukit Duabelas National Park, which takes up 600 square kilometres on the map. It is home to a tribe of hunter gatherers somewhere between 1,500 and 5,000 strong, known to some as *Orang Rimba* – the Forest People – and to others as *Kubu*, which translates roughly as Savages.

Until the early 1990s the Rimba People had virtually no contact with the world that they call *Terang*, 'The Light'. It was around then that the chainsaws of loggers, plantation companies and plain old land-grabbers began to let the light into the thick primary rainforests of the area they inhabit. Realizing that the Rimba could neither defend their way of life against the intruders nor choose any workable alternative unless they could engage at least minimally with the outside world, an acquaintance of mine, Butet Manurung, had started an informal school for children of the tribe. I had been fascinated by her book about the experience, *The Jungle School*; now Butet put me in touch with some of her former students, firing off texts to Mijak and Gentar. Both men were among Butet's earliest students, both studied despite fierce opposition from their families, and both became teachers in the school. They are friends and co-conspirators in trying to shape the future of their tribe. But they could not be more different.

I had arranged to meet Mijak in Bangko, a largish provincial town where he and a group of young friends had organized themselves into an NGO that focused on conservation and tribal rights.

The night before we were to meet, a young woman named Ira, who ran a coffee stall near the hospital, invited me home. There I met her sister and two unidentified relatives. One was a red-eyed man with a thick moustache who spoke only in Malay except when insisting that no respectable woman would travel without her husband. The other seemed more bohemian. His look – long, blunt-cut hair, squared-off glasses, manicured hands – was more Jakarta art gallery than provincial artisan. Not so his attitude.

I mentioned that I was planning to spend a few days in the forest with the Rimba. He looked questioningly at Ira's sister. 'The savages,' she prompted quietly. Immediately, he said I shouldn't go. First of all, he said, they had powerful magic. 'Make sure you don't spit. If you spit, they'll collect it up and put a curse on you and you'll never come back.' Secondly, the savages were dirty and stupid. The proof of this was that when they came to town, they washed their hair with shampoo, but used water from the gutters for the washing. To me, that seemed a logical enough thing to do if you've grown up in a jungle where every water source is clean, but to the bohemian, it was so stupid that he repeated the story three times.

Ira's sister's advice was more sympathetic. 'Try not to wrinkle your nose when you meet them, and don't tell them they stink. They don't like that,' she said. Some Rimba were trying hard to become civilized, she said. 'Lots have converted to Islam. So there's been some progress.'

The next day, Mijak came to pick me up on his motorbike. This 'savage' had just got back from a trip to Jakarta and was wearing a brand-new pair of Converse sneakers, trendy Levi's cut-offs and a long-sleeved button-down, ironed, over a clean polo shirt. As we left town and the road got dustier, he pulled on gloves, to protect his hands from the sun, and a surgical mask.

We drove through a string of 'trans' – small towns inhabited mainly by transmigrants from Java, full of mobile bank vans and women selling *jamu*, herbal medicine. All over Indonesia one finds these jamu ladies, very often dressed in a traditional Javanese sarong kebaya even when they had drifted to parts of the country where women wear all-obscuring full-length dusters or to cities where T-shirts and tight jeans are the norm.

Every morning before dawn, the jamu ladies cook up their various potions – this one of ginger, that one of seaweed, perhaps a bit of goat bile here and a handful of jasmine flowers there. They pour them into glass bottles that once held Coca-Cola, cheap whiskey or even Dutch-era gin, and stop the bottles with little cones of banana leaf. Then they load the bottles into a big wicker basket, sling it onto their back with a sarong, and set off on their rounds.

I generally choose a mixture of viscous yellow turmeric (anti-ageing) and 'bitter', the latter a thin, brown punishment cooked up from sambiloto leaves, an excellent stimulant for the immune system, they say. The jamu lady lays down her load, picks a small glass out of a bucket of water, and doles out this healing cup. Then she waits, expectant, with another bottle at the ready; a large splash of a galangal-and-honey cordial rinses the remainder of the medicine out of the glass, and the bitter taste out of the mouth. Jamu ladies are a well-distributed tribe; I must have drunk my morning jamu on at least a third of the days I was on the road.

Soon the towns grew fewer and the plantations larger. We passed a house that looked like a cross between Versailles and a prison, a caramel confection with engraved glass windows over-looked by three watch-towers. 'Rubber money,' nodded Mijak.

After a couple of hours, we stopped in front of a chained gate. A woman appeared, collected 5,000 rupiah from us, and allowed us into a rubber plantation. The toll gave us the right to buck and plunge on a ribbon of cleared mud that was at times axle-deep. On the worst stretches of this private 'road', I got off the bike and walked, angling up the banks and holding on to roots and branches to get around the deepest mud-pools.

Just once, I slipped. My foot disappeared, then my shin. I was gradually doing the splits, one leg sucked deeper and deeper into the morass, the other wedged behind a root on the bank. I pulled, wiggled, levered, until the mud ejected my leg with a great *schluuuurp!*

No shoe.

Mijak, who had driven safely through the quagmire, was busy wiping mud from his Converse sneakers, trying not to watch me. Until now he had been rather formal with me; his guru Butet had charged him with my care and he took the task seriously. But the sight of my one bare foot, coated to the knee in milk-chocolate mud, was too much for him. He dissolved into giggles.

I could imagine how ridiculous I looked, but I couldn't sacrifice half of my only pair of sandals. I slipped back into the mud, now submerging my forearm and elbow as well as my leg. Nothing. I slithered my hand around in the mud soup for a while, weak-kneed with laughter. Finally I felt something solid. Another great *schluuuurp!* and out popped my sandal, scooped high with mud. I waded to more solid ground and rinsed it in a puddle. It was missing its ankle strap, and I was damned if I was going back to the mud-hole to look for it. I improvised a strap out of a piece of purple ribbon cut off the top of my mosquito net. It remained in service until the end of the trip, six months later.

Whenever we met another Rimba on the road, the drivers would pull bikes up nose to nose, turn off the engine, and then just sit there for a long time, looking one another up and down in silence, like ants meeting on a trail to and from the anthill. Eventually, one would ask a question, there would be a short exchange of information, another longish silence, a curt nod, and then both would move off.

Our longest stop was for Mijak's *temenggung*, the democratically chosen head of the small group of unrelated families which is the basic social unit for the nomadic Rimba. He was an impressively built man who wore nothing but a small beard and a loincloth. Across his shoulders he carried a rifle which looked like it might date from Dutch times. He walked with an odd, pigeon-toed gait that I saw in many Rimba as they tripped along in single file through the forest. Two hunting dogs trotted at his feet. Mijak showed him the greatest respect. 'We chose him because he's the toughest of anyone,' he told me later.

At a certain point even the plantation mud-ribbon tailed off; we parked the bike and walked. As we plodded through the rubber trees, we passed halved oil drums filled with latex. It smelled toxic, like a garbage-strewn back-alley in New York on a hot summer's day. Every now and then we'd come across a couple of Javanese workers quietly tapping trees, and they would call out polite greetings – '*Monggo, monggo*'.

I asked Mijak who owned these plantations. Mostly Rimba, he said. So why the Javanese? 'The Rimba hire them to do the work; two-thirds goes to the tapper, a third to the owner.' It's these sorts of 'one-third/two-thirds' relationships, the ones that began as the Rimba brushed against the cash economy, that made schooling, and with it a knowledge of basic mathematics, important. Rimba don't do their own tapping for two reasons, says Mijak. 'First, Rimba are lazy. Second, they don't know how to do it right. The Javanese work hard and don't kill the trees. Everyone's happy.'★

In 2005, when Butet started teaching at the site where the jungle school now stands, it was a two-day walk through thick jungle from the nearest road. But as the rubber trees spread, so the road lengthened. Just about twenty minutes after we parked the motorbike, we arrived at the clearing where the school stands. There stood a teenaged girl combing her hair, ankle deep in litter – Indomie wrappers, snack packets, sheets torn from exercise books, plastic bags. Around her hips she wore a flowered sarong, around her neck a pink plastic necklace. Nothing else. It was like a dystopian Gauguin, a honey-coloured bare-breasted

---

★ This is a good example of the misunderstandings that may arise because of the vagaries of Indonesian, which often dispenses with the subject of a verb. Mijak actually said: 'Second, don't know how.' I have inferred the 'they', but he could equally have meant 'we'. He used both in talking of his own tribe, depending on the circumstance.

nymph grooming herself in a sea of garbage. Behind her, two tiny boys with miniature bent-wood bows fired arrows at small furry things up a tree.

Above the clearing stood the stilted schoolroom, wooden, thatched, open-sided, home-built. The school aims to work around the rhythms of forest life, equipping anyone who wants to learn with the basic skills they need to interact with people in the 'trans', perhaps even to interact with the other forces that are shaping their world: the authorities that deal with national parks or that try to enforce land rights, the opportunistic cowboys who threaten those rights.

I slept on the schoolroom floor with Mijak and two other Rimba boys who were now teaching at the school. In the morning, one of the boys stood and shouted: School-time! '*Sekolah!*' No one appeared. When I went down to the river to bathe, I found a gaggle of small boys splashing and giggling. What about school? I asked. Maybe after hunting, they replied.

Later that day, Mijak and I went off to find Gentar. He was in a different part of the forest, about two hours away by bike. The plan was to meet him in the 'trans' – the Javanese transmigration village – nearest to his home patch, then go into the forest to stay with his family grouping. When we found him, he announced a change of plan. A child was sick with an 'outside disease', one their own shamans couldn't fix, and the group had moved out of the forest to be close to a Javanese shaman. Plan B was to stay in Gentar's house in the trans, and make a day trip into the wild the next day.

I was disappointed. I had been looking forward to a bit of forest living, a change from the breeze-block bungalows that people had kindly invited me to stay in so often already, tidy houses with cement floors, pink satinate curtains hanging where doors would normally be, and bare lightbulbs that were left burning all night.

But Gentar's house was not a bungalow with pink curtains. It was two square metres of black plastic tarpaulin under an oil palm, in a plantation. The tarp was strung over a central pole and held up by a stick at each corner. The floor was made of the spines of palm leaves. The kitchen was a cleft stick wedged over an open fire under the front corner of the tarp. In this space sat Gentar's wife, a beautiful, bare-breasted girl who looked as though she was still in her teens, and their three naked children.

Gentar brought offerings from town: parcels of cooked rice and catfish, instant noodles, cheezy potato chips. His wife and children fell on the latter, systematically munching through the junk food, then throwing the shiny rainbow packaging on the ground of their otherwise largely biodegradable home.

'Where's your tarp?' asked Gentar. Mijak and I looked at one another. I had a sleeping mat, a mosquito net and a couple of sarongs, but no tarp. I produced a rain poncho, but Gentar was unimpressed. He sent us back up to the trans to get supplies.

When we got back, Gentar had changed his shorts for a scarlet and gold bathroom towel, and was playing with his kids. The youngest, a pudgy girl of about two with a runny nose, was strung about with amulets to protect her from evil spirits. Gentar handed a large machete to his middle girl, a five-year-old, and asked her to give it to the house-builder. As if born to carry sharp weapons more than half her height, the child carried it over and handed it to Mijak. He looked panicked.

He shuffled from one brand-new Converse to another and wrung his hands, still encased in the gloves he wore to protect himself from the sun on the bike. Since we would only be here a couple of nights it hardly seemed worth building a shelter, he said. I looked at the rain clouds massing overhead, then looked back at Mijak. He turned away. I suddenly guessed that although Mijak had grown up hunting and gathering in this forest with the rest of his tribe, the aspiring lawyer had no more jungle survival skills than I had. I wondered if you could will incompetence in certain tasks onto yourself, a sort of psychosomatic response to worlds you don't really feel you belong to. Mijak's true place, one couldn't help feeling, was sitting drinking cappuccinos with a bunch of young student activists in a trendy cafe in Jakarta.

We both looked hopefully at Gentar. '*Aduh!* City slickers!' shrieked Gentar.

Gentar had thick, curly hair and a broad nose which seemed to take up a lot of the real estate on his face. Though his eyebrows were painted in a severe line across his face and his eyes drooped under them, he was the twinkliest Indonesian I have ever met. Each grin revealed a meagre collection of teeth, and the grins were many; Gentar was a born tease, and seemed to enjoy nothing more than a good-natured prodding of his friend Mijak's pretentions to urban modernity. Mijak reciprocated in good spirit. The two had recently been to Jakarta on a trip organized by their former teacher Butet. On the way into town from the airport, Mijak had to stop Gentar from getting out to see what was wrong with the car, which wasn't moving. 'An everyday Jakarta traffic jam, and this jungle bunny thought we had broken down!' Mijak teased. But he was happy enough to let Gentar build a shelter for us.

Over the next few hours, people drifted across from the shelters they were staying in, a few oil palms distant in this direction or that, until quite a crowd had gathered. Men in loincloths or shorts, bare-breasted women, an infinity of children wearing tiny sarongs, outsized shorts, amulets or nothing at all. They all squatted a safe distance from me, and there was a bit of speculation about my gender. '*Jantan atau betina?*' they asked one another: Is it a boar or a sow?

One man, who had obviously had more contact with The Light than most, declared solemnly that I was a '*banci*', a transgender. He was one of the more beautiful people I've seen; his smooth caramel skin stretched across high cheekbones between perfect almond eyes and a full, symmetrical mouth. He had a hint of a moustache and a goatee and long, wavy hair. He had wrapped a woman's sarong into a loincloth that revealed perfectly formed buttocks. Out of the corner of my eye, I considered his flowing locks and the flowery design of his lilac-coloured sarong and thought: *I'm* the tranny?

For most of the time I was in and around the camp, this

permanent gallery simply stared at me, utterly expressionless. If I smiled and waved, I got no reaction at all. When I told Gentar's family the story of the lost shoe with much pantomime and schlurping sound effects I could hear the spectators howling with laughter, but when I turned to look at them they went rigid again, as if we were playing that game where people try to sneak up on the leader, but get disqualified if the leader turns around and catches them moving.

After dark, Gentar and his wife went down to the river to hunt frogs. I wasn't entirely clear about the process – the only equipment they had was a torch, a small cooking pot and a large machete – but I went along anyway. Within seconds: *Thwack!* Gentar had leapt down the riverbank into the water, stunned a largish fish with the handle of his machete, and popped it into the cooking pot. The same method seemed to work for frogs and for fish as small as my little finger, though the latter could also be grabbed with bare hands. By the time we went home to our tarps the cooking pot contained one big fish, half a dozen small ones, and a single frog. Though I had waded thigh high in the water lunging at everything that moved, my contribution to the catch was nil. The next morning, the eldest girl came over and presented me with a steaming basin of rice. Sticking out of it was a twig on which was impaled freshly barbecued fish and a frog's leg. It was one of the better breakfasts of the trip.

After breakfast, Gentar, Mijak and I set off to 'go inside', to penetrate the forest that is the Rimba's true home. We drove through miles and miles of oil-palm plantation, interspersed with occasional bits of scrub. In one scrubby bit, we found tracks of the sun-bear. This black animal with a deep yellow V on its chest is the smallest of all the bears, though adult males still weigh more than me. It has a very long tongue, adapted for winkling wild honey out of nests hidden in tree trunks. I had never seen one in the wild – they are classified as 'vulnerable' by the International Union for the Conservation of Nature. Do you see bears a lot? I asked Gentar. 'See them a lot?' he twinkled. 'We eat them a lot!'

Cresting a hill under a threatening sky, we were faced with a scene of devastation. Felled branches, charred tree stumps, upended rootballs being washed gradually skeletal by the rains. There are few landscapes as dispiriting as a recently-but-not-all-that-recently cleared patch of rainforest. The new growth – weeds, vines, grasses, nothing beautiful or even useful – sprawls over dead tree stumps like gang members invading rival territory. Far away, a wall of green marks the place where the chainsaws stopped. It's a reminder of the forest that stood on this spot for thousands of years, before the whirring and creaking, the shouting and thudding reduced it in a matter of days to this post-apocalyptic wasteland.

Gentar, who had been chatting cheerfully all the way, went quiet. I asked him if the area that we had been driving through for the last hour and a half was all forest when he was a kid. He stopped the bike, turned and looked at me, and said: 'It was all forest in 2006.'

That was the year that 'Bapak Seribu' – Mr One Thousand – came to these parts. The boys could tell me nothing about him except that he was from Medan. They said this man provided the capital and equipment to cut down thousands of hectares of primary forest, then parcelled the land up into lots, and sold it to villagers for a million rupiah per hectare. By what right? I asked.

'Right? Right! Hah!' Gentar exploded. 'No permits, no rights. What he had was balls, that's all!'

Later, when Mijak and I had left Rimba territory and were back on a state road, a posse of men roared past us in a cloud of petrol fumes and fresh testosterone. They were helmetless, heavily tattooed; strapped like weapons of mass destruction to the back of their outsized trail bikes were huge chainsaws. Mijak's whole body tensed up. '*Preman buka hutan,*' he said: Forest Terminators.

The forest that once stood where Gentar had stopped his bike had always been used by the peripatetic Rimba, but they had put up no fight when Bapak Seribu sent in the Terminators. Partly, the boys said, because Rimba are culturally averse to conflict. But also because the very concept of 'rights', let alone of Indonesian national law, is something that only began to exist for the Rimba once Gentar (Butet's very first Rimba student) learned to read, write and speak Indonesian, once he began to teach Mijak and his friends, once they began to interact with activists and NGOs.

Now, Mijak was trying to act as a translator between the world of his birth and the modern world of his dreams. Through their little NGO, the young Rimba have hooked up with AMAN, an umbrella organization that claims to represent 1,992 indigenous groups across Indonesia, and that provides a forum through which they can lobby at the national level. AMAN helps identify which laws Mijak needs to read up on, but the battles the Rimba have to fight are mostly fiercely local. The NGO records and reports violations to the police, it paints banners and organizes protests in front of the office of the Governor of Jambi. All, so far, to no avail.

It's not an easy task they have set themselves. Indonesia has fifty-two national laws, treaties and decrees governing the environment. Many contradict one another. To make matters worse, the two government departments responsible for trees – the Ministry of the Environment and the Ministry of Forestry – use different maps. In 2010 the President launched a project to create a single map, but it stalled. While everyone agreed that there should be one land-use map for Indonesia, no one could agree whose data it should be based on. Some 40 million hectares of primary forest appear on one of the two maps but not the other. In other words, government departments have between them 'lost' an area of primary rain forest larger than all of Japan. That's just at the centre. District maps, as well as district laws on land use, are different again.

In practice, it hardly matters, because no one seems to take much notice of the regulations or the maps in any case. After driving another few kilometres over cleared land patchworked through with newly planted oil palms, Gentar stopped again, leapt off the bike and started kicking around in the undergrowth, first curiously, then increasingly aggressively. He was looking for a boundary stone for the national park that used to sit here, marking the point beyond which no forest may be cleared.

There was no sign of the marker. There was no sign of the forest.

As the ground got hillier, oil palms gave way to rubber. After about half an hour, I spotted something that looked like real forest in front of us. As we approached it, we fell on another scene of carnage. This time, there were no weeds or washed-out rootballs. Magnificent ex-trees lay prostrate where they had crashed, probably the day before. The tree trunks were still surrounded by sawdust, splinters stuck up jagged as a newly snapped toothpick.

Finally, more than two hours after leaving a place that was still jungle in 2006, we made it to the cool shelter of the forest. I was longing to get off the bike and walk, to swap the roar of the engine for the magical thrum of the jungle. I wanted to crane my neck and not be able to see the tops of the trees, I wanted to feel the decomposing crunch-mulch underfoot, to savour what was left of this majestic but impotent kingdom. But to young men who grew up as forest nomads, there's no sense in walking any further than is strictly necessary. We stayed on the bikes as long as the path was passable.

Less than a kilometre into the forest, the sombre canopy was pierced again by sunshine and bright, weedy green. Young rubber trees were planted at careful intervals; cassava and other food plants grew around the edge of the clearings. These plantations belonged to Gentar and the other families in his grouping. Close by stood a small bamboo house raised on a platform, shoulder height. 'My real house,' Gentar smiled his toothless grin.

Once a year, Rimba families spend one day clearing land in the forest. They hack trees down with an axe, burn off the remaining scrub to fertilize the soil and plant cassava, sweet-potatoes and other staples. Much of the rest of the diet comes from hunting (frogs, fish, bears and many other animals besides). When we were ordering food at a nasi Padang place in the trans town, I suggested chicken. Gentar stuck out his tongue in disgust: no real Rimba will eat an animal that has been raised by man, he said. The Rimba gather plants and roots to eat, as well as honey, rattan and wild rubber to sell. As transmigrants and plantation workers began to seep into the lands that were once Rimba territory, the market for these products grew and the Rimba began to 'know money', a period Mijak dates from the mid-1990s.

Cash from wild rubber meant that people could buy chainsaws, and that made nonsense of the rules through which the Rimba had always restricted deforestation: overnight, the amount of land a family could clear in a day increased by over tenfold. More cleared land also meant the Rimba could plant rubber trees and generate more cash. And when it's planted with rubber, the cleared forest does not revert to jungle as it used to when families used small plots for rice and vegetables for just a year or two before moving on.

Rubber equals cash equals chainsaws equals more rubber and more cash, equals a motorbike to get between market and new plantation more easily, equals more time in town, thus rice, sugar and cheezy potato snacks in rainbow packages as well as petrol and rubber seedlings, so more need for cash, so more trees cut and rubber planted, and so it goes around.

Gentar filched a cooking pot from the abandoned camp and we wandered on through the forest a bit until we hit a river. With astounding efficiency, he snapped a few twigs into a perfect campfire – Mijak sat tidily on a plastic bag and watched – and soon we were lunching on instant noodles, brought in from the trans town.

After that, it was time for a siesta. We climbed up into someone's 'house'. The open bamboo platform stood at about chest height. Beneath it hung a chainsaw. At one end of the platform sat a big cardboard carton that until recently held a television set. Bits of broken styrofoam were strewn on the forest floor around the hut. I pointed to the carton and raised my eyebrow, questioning. 'It's a TV', Gentar said flatly. Watched with what electricity? 'A generator'.

Gentar's wife told me later that when Gentar was away in Jakarta, leaving her bikeless, she and the three kids had spent six hours walking from their forest camp down to the plantation where I met them. 'Like the old days,' she said. Now that nearly everyone had motorbikes, she said, things were much easier. But if motorbikes are followed by television sets and generators, it seems to me that moving about will soon be more difficult than ever. If the rubber prices stay high, consumerism might put an end to the nomadic life even before deforestation does.

On the long drive home through the plantation, I spotted one tree standing majestically high above the dreary spikes of the oil palms. Small wooden pegs stuck out at intervals up its trunk. 'Our honey tree,' said Gentar. For generations, bees have congregated in particular trees, yielding small-celled forest honeycomb which the Rimba collect in a quasi-religious ritual. The community had protected the tree when the chainsaws came. But: 'The bees don't want to go there any more. There's nothing for them around here.'

After dark, Mijak and I lolled around in our little shelter, talking of the future. Mijak said his goal was to achieve secure land rights, 'so that the Rimba can continue to live in the forest according to their adat'. I asked if that's what he really wanted, to live in the forest. 'That's different,' he shot back. 'I'm Muslim now. My private hopes are something separate.'

Gentar padded over to join us as Mijak unfolded his private dreams. First, he would go to an organic-farming school run by a friend of Butet's in Java. He'd buy a couple of hectares of land, not too far from Gentar's, and put them under rubber as security for his children. Then he would go to college and study law. In his second year, he would get married 'but not to a Rimba girl. Firstly, we'd have different religions, and secondly, I already know how the world works and she wouldn't know anything . . .' Gentar and I were already pulling faces, but Mijak was not done with his plans. 'Then we'll have two children, first a boy, then a girl, and then . . .'

Gentar shrieked with laughter. 'Wah, first a boy, then a girl.

Why did you need to go and get a religion? You've already become God . . .!'

Gentar had promised his own parents that he would never leave the forest or the Rimba way of life. And so it has been. He married the girl from the tree next door, hunts frogs at night, and is one of the most infectiously happy people I have ever met. Not in an unthinking, Noble Savage sort of way. More in a considered, what–more–do–I–need? way.

He is acutely aware of the threat to his lifestyle posed both by the annihilation of the forest on the one hand and the excessive zeal of what he calls the 'tree-loving NGOs' on the other. But for now he can still play with his children, tease his friends and sell his rubber. 'I saw those people in Jakarta just sitting in their cars all day,' he said. 'How is that better than sitting under a tree?'

As we left the forest, Mijak asked me what month it was. In speech, many Indonesians just refer to the months by their numbers. Month five, I said. Right, he said. Then: 'Does that mean June?' No, it's May. 'Ah.' Pause. 'So what comes after May?' This young man who can quote Conservation Law 5/1990 and Spatial Planning Law 26/2007 but who was raised in a world where time is marked off as durian season or honey season, could not list the months in order.

In theory, the NGO that Mijak and his friends have set up to defend the rights of his fellow Rimba should allow him to plant one clean-sneakered foot in the world of cappuccinos, land titles and 'civilized' religion, while keeping the other, muddier foot in the world of frog-hunting and bear dinners. But it does not seem likely that the world of Bapak Seribu and his Forest Terminators can coexist for long with that of the Rimba and their honey trees. Mijak can only defend the Rimba's traditional way of life if he fights his battles by rules determined out in The Light. To do that successfully, he has to fit into that world himself, he must blend into modern Indonesia, where there's no longer any room for the Rimba cosmology.

When we met his headman in the forest, Mijak had shown him every respect. Afterwards, though, he had grown despondent.

'The elders talk on and on about adat,' said Mijak. 'But they don't realize that Rimba adat is worthless out there in The Light.'

I sympathized with Mijak as he tried to coexist in very different worlds. My atheist, divorced, unemployed, itinerant reality presented no problem when I was in Jakarta. But in other parts of the country, I had to smooth those things away if I wanted to be accepted into people's homes and lives. For months now, I had been lying about myself dozens of times a day. I was on long leave from the Ministry of Health. I lived in Jakarta with an Indonesian husband who worked in the private sector, a Muslim. I was a practising Catholic; my husband and I respected one another's faiths, and it didn't pose too many problems because we had no kids.

My childlessness was the only thing about the made-up me that was entirely true. I knew it would cause comment, but I hadn't guessed how much. From the fat woman in the jilbab I'd get: 'What do you mean, no kids? You mean not yet.' Then, after a look at the wisps of white at my temples. 'How old are you?' Then someone with a pock-marked face would butt in: 'Where have you been for treatment? You should go to Singapore, they can do anything in Singapore!' An elbow to pockmark's ribs: 'No, wait, she should meet my cousin, he has a special medicine. Three women in the village got pregnant after he gave them the special treatment.'

From the men: 'What do you mean, no kids? Why don't you go out and get one?' Some thin, wolfish man would narrow his eyes. 'I suppose your husband has left you, has he? How many children does he have with his younger wife?'

I can't tell people that I've never wanted kids. That would *definitely* not be acceptable. So I respond by looking self-pitying, pious and mystified all at the same time. I point heavenwards, indicate that they should ask the Good Lord why I have not been graced with offspring, and shrug to show that I am resigned to my fate. Still, it gets wearing, having your ovaries interrogated by strangers day after day. About a week after emerging from the Rimba's devastated forests, I was having breakfast in Tanjung Pandan, the main town in Belitung, a tin-producing island off the east coast of Sumatra. It's a prosperous town of Chinese shop-houses and colonial-era bungalows. From the photo on the wall, I judged that the coffee shop I was in had not changed since it was established in the 1940s.

The owner, dressed in nylon shorts, a string vest, plastic sandals – the uniform of Chinese traders when they are just minding the shop – was counting grubby 1,000 rupiah notes into the drawer of a teak desk. He welcomed me to sit with him and his friends, and we ran through the script. 'Dari mana?': Where are you from? 'Wah, Inggris, Manchester United! But your Indonesian is so good. Where is your husband from? . . .' When we got to the 'How many kids?' it just popped out of my mouth: 'Two. They're already grown up,' and the conversation moved on. I kicked myself for not having invented children months earlier.

After his friends left, the coffee shop owner introduced himself as Ishak Holidi, a member of the local parliament. The coffee shop is a family business and a good place to keep in touch with what people are thinking and talking about, he said. We talked for a couple of hours about local government, investment in education, political accountability, policies to reduce dependence on mining. The next morning, when I went in for breakfast, Pak Ishak was dressed for work. He waved me over. 'We're celebrities now,' he laughed. He handed me the local newspaper. There we were, he and I, grinning stupidly at someone's camera phone, over a headline that read 'FOREIGN VISITOR PRONOUNCES BELITUNG CAKES DELICIOUS'. And in the story: 'Elizabeth, mother of two . . .'

My non-existent children caused me other headaches too. With men, they put a full stop to the fertility question quite quickly. But women expected my children to have names, genders, ages, occupations, whole back stories of their own. It proved to be a lot of effort and I soon went back to being childless.

Map K: Kalimantan (Borneo)

PHILIPPINES

SULU SEA

SOUTH CHINA SEA

SABAH

BRUNEI

MALAYSIA

CELEBES SEA

SARAWAK

EAST KALIMANTAN

Singkawang

Putussibau

WEST KALIMANTAN

BORNEO

Equator

Pontianak

Sintang

From Jakarta

CENTRAL KALIMANTAN

MAKASSAR STRAIT

SULAWESI

SOUTH KALIMANTAN

JAVA SEA

WEST JAVA

Semarang

MADURA

BALI SEA

JAVA

CENTRAL JAVA

EAST JAVA

Yogyakarta

BALI

LOMBOK

FLORES

SUMBAWA

SUMBA

INDIAN OCEAN

N

0km   80km   160km   240km

11

Indigenous Arts

Miss Equator stood ramrod straight in the blazing midday sun, sweat trailing in rivulets down her powdered face. Balanced precariously on her head was a large silver globe shot through with an arrow. It was a styrofoam-and-tinfoil replica of the monument that towered above her.

After another brief pit-stop in Jakarta, I had flown to Pontianak, the largest city in West Kalimantan and the only city in the world that sits exactly on the equator, and it was the day of the autumn equinox, the day when, as the sun reaches its zenith, people's shadows disappear. At the equator monument, built by the Dutch in 1908 and massively expanded by a proud local government only recently, gaggles of visitors to the equinox festival jostled forward to have their photos taken with the shadowless beauty queen.

The Mayor of Pontianak attended the festivities wearing a pearl-grey silk outfit, his waistcloth positively stiff with gold thread; his wife's sarong was embroidered to match. They were protected from the sun by a giant umbrella twirled overhead by a batik-clad flunky, and looked for all the world like a pre-colonial era Sultan and his wife.

Kalimantan is the Indonesian part of the giant island of Borneo, which dominates the map of island South East Asia. The four provinces that made up Kalimantan at the time of my trip occupy the southern three-quarters of the island. To the north, over the mountains swathed in jungle that cover the centre of

Borneo, are the Malaysian states of Sabah and Sarawak, and the tiny independent sultanate of Brunei.

Though it's relatively empty – there are only twenty-five people in each square kilometre of Kalimantan, compared with 1,055 in Java – Kalimantan manages to be racially complex. The Mayor of Pontianak's grey silks were the traditional dress of the Malay Muslims who originated in Sumatra and the Malay peninsula and who settled on Kalimantan's coasts and drifted up its rivers long before Europeans reached these shores. The forests of the interior have always been home to the many tribes that now crowd under the umbrella term 'Dayak'. They generally lived in communal longhouses close to a river, paddling or trudging into the nearby forest to clear land for temporary plantations. And as early as the eighteenth century, a large Chinese community established an independent state in the west of the island. Much more recently, migrants from Java, Madura and other over-crowded parts of Indonesia filtered in, some on government-backed transmigration programmes, others drawn by work in the oilfields and coal mines that have made southern and eastern Kalimantan among the richest parts of the nation. Nearly one in five people in Kalimantan was born elsewhere.

Behind the monument, thirteen school groups were showing off their equator-themed science projects for the local TV cameras and the judges of the provincial science contest. One group was explaining the Seven Wonders of the Equator, which include disappearing shadows, water swirling down plugholes in different directions on either side of the line (not true in fact, though enthusiastically 'demonstrated' by several groups), weak gravity and high-intensity sunlight. These students were mostly ethnic Chinese, from an expensive private school, and they had prepared their project in English. 'The intensity of the sunlight is great richness, because from it we will make sun force,' explained one boy. Another elbowed him: 'Solar power, not sun force,' and they giggled.

I asked how much of Pontianak's electricity supply actually came from 'sun force'. 'Ya, almost none. We're just talking about potential,' said one of the boys. I suggested, half joking, that they go and speak to the Mayor about realizing that potential, about making Pontianak a model of energy efficiency. 'Yes, we will!' they yelled, in English. 'We are the new generation. We can change the world!'

I had company on this leg of the trip. I'd come across a blog, *Gangs of Indonesia*, and had written to its author Melanie Wood out of the blue to say how much I liked her work. During one of my pit-stops in Jakarta we met in a cocktail bar, a place humming with Indonesian yuppies stirring absent-mindedly at their pomegranate-with-vapours-of-fresh-ginger cocktails and stroking their iPads. We chatted for a while and I mentioned that I'd be leaving in two days' time for Kalimantan. 'I'll come with you,' she had said.

I looked her up and down. She was wearing a well-cut blouse, a short, navy-blue skirt, and elegant sling-back heels; I couldn't imagine her in a rusty bus with sick-bags swinging from the ceiling. I tried to explain how I travelled, but she was unfazed.

Melanie was a great travel companion; she was hardy, resourceful, cheerful and game for almost anything. And she was tall and blonde, with piercing blue eyes. Beside her I became almost invisible, hardly foreign-looking, even. That meant that Melanie took over as Pied Piper, followed around by gaggles of children, posing for the endless photos that are the tyranny of universal cell-phone ownership. I felt like I was on holiday.

Singkawang, which sits on the coast about four hours north of Pontianak, is one of the few towns in Indonesia where the majority of the population is ethnically Chinese. The whole town has a very Straits-Chinese feel to it; the buildings are mostly two-storey shop-houses with saloon doors, a colonnaded balcony on the upper floor and carved metal awnings providing shade below. It could be Singapore or Penang circa 1940, but for the tatty 1980s construction values.

The first evening in Singkawang, Melanie and I sat at an

outdoor cafe that specialized in a tea that looked a bit like rooibos, but was in fact made from a local variant of chrysanthemum, picked in the wild by Dayaks. Around us flowed a procession of young people on Vespas and Lambrettas. These beautifully restored scooters were the latest trend. Their riders wore retro helmets to match; the national law requiring full-face helmets was roundly ignored. Even brand-new Hondas had been dolled up to look 1950s.

I got chatting to Hermanto, the owner of the tea stall. He said Singkawang didn't get many Western visitors. 'The only thing we're known for is human trafficking!' he said cheerfully. I had indeed heard that the town was the hub of a huge mail-order-bride business; was it true? The brides, yes, he said. The trafficking, no.

The bride business started in earnest in the 1970s, when Taiwanese firms were busy turning West Kalimantan's trees into timber and plywood. Visiting businessmen realized that the Chinese women of Singkawang might make good companions for the many poorer Taiwanese men who had aged through their compulsory military service without being able to marry, and alerted the traditional matchmakers who still helped many Taiwanese parents find appropriate spouses for their children. The matchmakers helped couples to exchange letters and photographs; if they and their families agreed, the woman would go off to Taiwan. Hermanto said that most of the brides in those early days were in their forties – old maids, by Indonesian standards. 'Of course, some men pretended they were richer than they were, there were disappointments. But mostly it was win-win.' These days, Hermanto said, people still used matchmakers, but there were fewer bad outcomes. 'The candidates Skype each other, and flights are so cheap that the guy almost always visits to see if they get on.'

Newspaper stories that described these exchanges as 'trafficking' almost always quoted the same woman, Maya Satrini. Google told me she was a member of the Singkawang district AIDS commission, so I wandered down to see if I could find her in their offices. She wasn't there, but her colleagues had the same relaxed attitude to the bride market as Hermanto did. They saw the hook-ups between Taiwanese men and local women as not much different to internet dating. 'You pay a fee to a dating website, you pay a fee to the matchmaker; what's the difference, really?' said one woman.

The major difference is that the matchmaker's job is to ensure that the girl's family gets paid a bride-price. That's been the case in traditional Chinese societies for millennia, but in recent years it has been recast as 'selling' women. The suspicion of anti-trafficking look-outs is further aroused because matchmakers draw up contracts, often for three or five years. That means that if the relationship doesn't work out, the woman can come home without losing face, just as a migrant worker comes home after a two-year contract working as a housemaid in Malaysia. Unlike maids' contracts, though, these ones specify that any children of the union stay with the father.

'If she's from a poor family, getting married to one of those guys might be the best chance she has of helping her parents. Filial piety is still very much part of our tradition,' Hermanto had said. I was taken aback. It had never occurred to me that there might be poor ethnic Chinese families in Indonesia.

Some of the first written records of life in the islands that coalesced into Indonesia are written in Chinese. Traders from mainland China have been an integral part of the archipelago's economy for well over a thousand years, and they have contributed culturally too. The Chinese admiral Zheng He, a Muslim eunuch from Yunnan, was among those who introduced Islam to the ports of northern Java. But Indonesia's relationship with its Chinese immigrants has been fraught.

Many of the earliest Chinese immigrants were actually traders who had the doors to their home ports slammed on them by a Ming Dynasty emperor who banned private trade in the late 1300s. Unable to go home to China, these men settled in ports along the north coast of Java. They learned Javanese and married local girls. In the mid–1700s the local rulers of at least four cities in Java were of Chinese descent.

The Chinese also brought skills that local rulers needed. Princes and sultans, admiring the merchants' business acumen, often appointed them as harbour masters, customs officers and tax collectors. The Dutch East India Company, the VOC, followed suit. They used ethnic Chinese islanders to collect an unpopular rice tax that funded the company's many skirmishes with local sultans and princelings. The colonial government, wary of allowing the large 'native' population to grow rich, later gave the small Chinese minority a monopoly on opium dens, pawnshops and gambling houses.

The Dutch also sold the rights to run big businesses – mining gold in Kalimantan and tin in Sumatra, farming sugar in Java and tobacco and pepper in Sumatra – to well-established Chinese merchants. Rather than hire locals, these bosses shipped in hundreds, sometimes thousands, of workers from the Chinese mainland. This new wave of immigrants did not need to integrate as the traders had done. By the start of the twentieth century, there were over half a million people of Chinese descent in the Dutch East Indies, half of them outside of Java. Many of them lived in a bubble of Chineseness, speaking the language of their home province in China, recreating the dishes, the prayers and the marriage rites of their ancestors and working, working, working.

In Singkawang, Melanie and I stumbled on a ceramics factory that has an old-fashioned 'dragon kiln', a sort of humped tunnel eighty metres long, ending in a beehive-shaped furnace. The design, which the workers say originated in Guangdong province in southern China, is ancient, though this latest kiln was not built until the 1970s. Walking into the kiln, I saw hundreds of pieces all lined up, dipped already in glazes of indistinguishable rainy-day greys. Once there are 1,000 pieces ready to go, the door will be bricked closed, the kiln fired up and fed with logs. Twenty hours later the brown sludge will have brightened to oranges and browns, to greens and bright blues, and the pots, statues and ornamental dragons will be ready for market.

In the back of the yard was a brick factory. A young man with the lanky build and fine features of northern China appeared from the banks of a small pond down below with a wheelbarrow full of newly dug clay. He kneaded it a bit, then hived off large chunks and slapped them down in front of two women who were standing at a table. Each took a handful of the clay, pressed it down into an oblong mould, dragged a metal blade over the top to smooth it off, then smacked the newly 'printed' brick down on the table. That would earn its maker sixty rupiah, about seven cents. The women said they could do between 300 and 400 day.

I had seen this brick-making once before, in South Sulawesi. There, the women making the bricks had hands made stumpy by leprosy. Sitting with them had been the factory owner, a pretty young ethnic Chinese woman in a pink tracksuit. That was the natural order of things in most of Indonesia. Here in Singkawang, it was ethnic Chinese women doing the work and earning less than two dollars a day.

I was shocked, in the way that a visitor in the colonial era would have been shocked to see a Dutchman cutting cane in the sugar fields. And I was suddenly very aware of how completely I had absorbed indigenous Indonesians' stereotypes about the *babahs*, as Chinese traders are sometimes called, though never politely. All Chinese are canny businesspeople, the stereotype holds, hard-working and deeply clannish. Though they are generous in supporting their own kind, they are always willing to wring an extra rupiah out of an indigenous Indonesian. As a result, they grow rich.

'I worked for the *babahs* for years', said an Indonesian businessman I had met earlier on my travels, in eastern Indonesia. 'I watched, I learned. Especially, I learned to work hard.' In the end, though, he felt there was a vacuum at the centre of their lives. 'Everything is only for money, money, money. From morning to night, money, money, money. Eat, money, sleep, money, die. But in the end, I wonder what for?'

The anti-communist conflagration of 1965 gave many indigenous Indonesians a chance to avenge the jealousy they felt for the hard-working, clannish Chinese on whom they depended for so many of the things they wanted or needed. Sukarno and the PKI had both been flirting with Beijing, ergo, any Chinese person must be a communist and therefore fair game. 'It was doubly unfair, because lots of the Chinese community here were refugees who fled China after the communists won the civil war in China in 1949,' said Hermanto, the chrysanthemum tea shop owner. 'Then they get accused of being PKI and . . .' He drew his finger across his throat.

The Chinese Indonesians that survived 1965 were roundly discriminated against. They were not welcome in the civil service, the military or the other institutions of state. Relatively well educated, they were pushed even further into the markets, shop-houses and small factories that *are* the private sector in most of Indonesia. They kept their heads down, worked hard, and strengthened kinship networks that they could draw on in dangerous times. These networks are really not so very different from the web of exchange which ties Mama Bobo into her vast extended clan in Sumba. Except that among Chinese Indonesians the medium of exchange is not buffalo but contracts and capital, and they are not slaughtered, but used to spawn more contracts and capital.

Like the Javanese princelings of the pre-colonial age, Suharto needed the capital and the commercial networks that the Chinese diaspora could provide. He handed out monopolies; in return, the Chinese Indonesian compradors underwrote many of Suharto's political operations. Indonesia got capital investment in export-led industries, and the Chinese got richer. Typically, though, what Suharto gave with one hand he took away with the other. He entrenched social discrimination against the Chinese; Chinese schools, temples and newspapers were closed down, and the ethnic Chinese were pressured into taking Indonesian-sounding names.

In the mid-1990s the Australian government published a book that included an eye-catching table showing that ethnic

Chinese controlled 80 per cent of the Indonesian economy. Much less eye-catching and always overlooked (including by me, in my reporting for Reuters on the subject), was footnote 17, which mentioned that the figures didn't include those bits of the economy that are controlled by state enterprises or foreign multinationals. A reworking of the numbers suggests that Chinese Indonesians owned just under a third of the nation's wealth, still eight times more that you would expect for a group that makes up just 3.5 per cent of Indonesia's population.

Their disproportionate wealth made Chinese Indonesians an easy scapegoat when the rulers of the day felt the need to allow people to blow off political steam; the first major assault on the Chinese community dates back to 1740. Looting and the systematic rape of Chinese women reached a peak in the chaos that led to the downfall of Suharto. Since then, many of the discriminatory laws of the Suharto era have been repealed, and Chinese Indonesians have begun setting up bilingual schools and drifting back to Confucian temples. 'It's got a lot better now,' one Chinese shopkeeper told me. 'By which I mean, I no longer live my whole life thinking: I wonder if I'll get through this year without my shop being burned down?'

In Singkawang, Melanie had assumed the role that the Reuters photographer Enny used to play. She sat on the back of our rented motorbike as I cruised around town looking for adventure, and poked me in the ribs when she saw something interesting. At one such poke, I skidded to a halt in front an old Chinese lady, her face framed by thick curtains of freshly made noodles hanging out on the dusty roadside to dry.

I greeted her, but she spoke virtually no Indonesian. Then I brushed off my rusty Mandarin and tried that. It worked; she brightened up instantly and became quite chatty. The noodle factory belonged to her son Ah Hui, she said, and she invited us in to look around.

It was like the seventh circle of hell. Under a single bare light-bulb, a huge machine that looked a bit like a mediaeval instrument of torture whirred and clanked. Into its maw, Ah Hui – skinny, shirtless, sweating – poured a crumble of flour, egg and water. Clank, clank, chug-chug–chug, whirr, shudder, *clunk*, bang, *boom*, clunk. It felt like someone was playing the drums on the inside of my skull. The machine burped toxic black fumes and suddenly all was silent. A bolt had shaken itself out of place. One of the teenaged workers fished around in the dough, extracted the bolt, put it back in place, and restarted the machine. Eventually a sheet of dough emerged and was wound, pressed, combined and rewound around a large stick, like a giant toilet roll.

Once the ridged shelves along the wall were loaded with toilet rolls, the mangles were changed for blades and the shredding of noodles began. A peculiarly beautiful Dayak boy in a battered red cowboy hat sat at the mouth of the monster machine. As it spat out noodles, he scooped them over polished wooden sticks and handed them off to a team of boys who hung them in the drying room next door. It was a big room with a skylight and many ceiling fans, all crusted with spider webs and soot. Dotted around the floor, invisible among the curtains of drying noodles, were rusty burners fed with gas from tubes that trailed across the floor; I became aware of them only when my bare feet drifted too close to the flames. The burners speed the drying process; the room was an inferno.

Beyond the noodle curtains, not a metre from the flapping door to the loo, a wooden hot tub full of noodles steamed over an open fire; once softened, they would be packaged up and distributed to the street vendors around town.

Though the business was started by his grandfather, Ah Hui was not optimistic about its future. His own son was only six. 'By the time he's old enough, he won't want to do this sort of work.' Ah Hui said that, already, all of his staff were Dayaks. 'Chinese kids, they ask for higher wages, and then they only stay long enough to learn the business. After that, they set up in competition with you.'

As we were leaving, Ah Hui's mother gave me a huge bag full of noodles. 'It's so nice to find someone who speaks Mandarin,' she said. 'Hardly any of you young folks do.'

Returning to the chrysanthemum tea shop, I mentioned this to Hermanto. His own father was a Mandarin teacher, he said. Though he kept some texts hidden in the roof of their house, after the killings of 1965 the teacher did not dare to contravene Suharto's policies; he did not teach his own son Mandarin. 'Mine is the lost generation,' Hermanto said. 'I feel like I've been cut off from my roots.'

Ethnicity and roots are issues that loom large over Kalimantan; sometimes they erupt into cataclysmic violence. The killing of the Chinese in 1965 was an anomaly: the enduring friction is between two quite different ethnic groupings, the Dayaks and the Malays, who both consider Borneo to be their ancestral home-land. Over a century ago the greatest of all adventure writers, Joseph Conrad, set his first novel in Borneo. 'The Malays and the river tribes of Dyaks or Head-hunters are eternally quarrelling,' he wrote in 1895.*

The Malays, spread across Sumatra, peninsular Malaysia and Borneo, established Sultanates in what became the larger trading centres of Kalimantan centuries ago. They grew rich by stock-piling and selling on exotica from the island's forests: hornbill ivory, rhinoceros horn, gold, indigo, camphor and the delightfully named dragon's blood, a bright-red resin used by apothecaries. These and other glories of the forest were collected and paddled down the rivers by Dayaks, the colourful forest-dwellers who featured so prominently in *Boys' Own Paper*-type stories of the late Victorian period. These stories tell of great, steamy rivers that snake lazily through lush and fetid jungles. Tattooed savages with distended earlobes and pointed teeth sit around on the verandas of their communal longhouses, sharpening darts for their blowpipes and biding time until their next headhunting raid.

Feared by the colonists and neglected by more recent regimes, the Dayaks have sat for much of the archipelago's history at

* Joseph Conrad, *Almayer's Folly*. New York: Macmillan and Co., 1895.

the margins of the state, permanently under-represented in the bureaucracy and politics. They were unable to defend their forests against Suharto and his cronies; hundreds of square kilometres of their homeland were fed into the jaws of Taiwanese plywood factories. And their traditional systems of tribal leadership, their adat, could not stand up to the onslaught of Suharto's 'one-size fits-all' structure of village government.

In the mid-1990s a small group of well-educated, urban Dayaks grew tired of being portrayed as savages and even more tired of seeing most government jobs go to the Malays, an ethnic group favoured by Jakarta in part because they were nice, civilized Muslims, descended from the sort of Sultanates that Suharto's people understood. This small group formed the Institute of Dayakology. They found staunch allies among international development fashionistas, who had recently begun to focus on protecting trees, tigers and exotic tribes, and who had persuaded the United Nations to declare a Decade of the World's Indigenous Peoples. Dayak leaders quickly became fluent in the rhetoric of indigenous rights. These days, the organization describes its core principles as 'Gender equality and justice, fraternity, freedom, human rights, democracy, openness, justice, togetherness and anti-violence, so that the process of marginalization, oppression, exploitation and the invasion of globalization can be stopped, so that the dignity, values and sovereignty of the indigenous Dayak community may be upheld.' The language is modern, but it gave voice to resentments that had been festering since Conrad's day and before. Nowadays, the real political battles are still between Dayaks on the one hand and Malays on the other. But a third ethnic group – the Madurese – have become stuck like a punchbag between the two.

Madura is a parched and crowded island off the north-east coast of Java where it is hard to scrape a living; the Madurese have a reputation for ferocity. No one would rent me a motorbike when I visited Madura, because a few days earlier an itinerant toy-seller ('an outsider, like you' – from West Java, it turned out) had been killed and his motorbike stolen. 'Imagine if it happened to you,' said a Maduran woman with a posse of three Hondas, which I was eyeing hopefully. 'You'd be dead, but me, I'd lose the bike.' Then, more seriously, she said: 'You can't trust anyone in this island. Not anyone.'

The Dayaks have skirmished with the Madurese since they first arrived in Kalimantan as transmigrants in the mid-1960s. Then in 1997 a group of Madurese men were rude to a couple of Dayak women. The ensuing quarrel exploded into a frenzy of killing that spread far and wide across the province. As many as 1,500 Madurese died and tens of thousands were left homeless and huddled in refugee camps.

I found in chatting to the women in the District AIDS Commission offices in Singkawang that the legacy of this violence makes for unlikely conversation. We started off talking about sex, a mundane subject for people who work with HIV. The chat flitted over prostitution, alighted briefly on alternatives to the missionary position and then buzzed around the anticlimax of marriage. We decided you could track a relationship by looking at a girl's underwear. If you're still in lacy matched sets, you either haven't made it to first base yet, or you're in love. There's a slow slide into matching-but-comfy, then the inevitable whatever-is-clean phase: the greying knickers that once were white paired with a red bra that has seen better days. 'Then you know you're well and truly married,' said Ibu Ibit, a Malay in her early thirties.

There's something utterly universal about this sort of girl talk. 'When I think of how much time I'd spend washing my hair,' Ibit said, laughing. 'Back when we were courting, I mean. It had to be all shiny, all fragrant, even though I knew perfectly well that I was *not* going to take off my jilbab. Now, if it's even a little bit cold, I look at my husband – ' she gives a slow sidelong glance, half wicked, half guilty – 'and I'm like: it's a bit chilly, darling. Shall we just leave bathing 'til the morning?'

And then the conversation drifted on, and somehow we were talking about the ethnic war of 1997. 'Everyone just went crazy,' said Olin, who was Dayak. She described her elder brother and his friends coming home one day holding a human heart which they had cut from an immigrant from Madura. 'They laid it out there in the yard and the elders were making us all eat,' Olin said. Warriors who eat their enemy's heart are said to become invincible. 'My elder brother had already eaten, and when I refused he was really angry, threatening me with a machete. Everyone was shouting, and insisting, and finally I swallowed a little bit.' Olin related this in an absolute monotone. 'Then I ran behind the house and threw up. I didn't stop throwing up for a week.' It wasn't until she followed someone's suggestion to eat a bit of dog that Olin's stomach settled.

I asked Ibit if she remembered anything about these 'Troubles'. 'Oh, we had our own Troubles,' she said, and told me of the copycat pogrom, in 1999. Ibit described her daily walk home from middle school in Tebas, a small town in Sambas about an hour north of Singkawang, where she grew up.

'I'd be on my way home from class and these guys, boys I knew, would be walking along the road swinging people's heads in their hands. Their favourite thing was to tie two heads together by the hair and throw them up over an electricity wire, so that they would swing there like a pair of shoes tied together by the laces.'

'If you looked scared, it got worse,' she went on. 'A teenager would yell: "Hey, you! Catch!" and they'd throw a severed hand at you. They seemed to find it really funny. It was horrible.'

Ibu Ibit related this completely flatly, as though it was horrible, but also somehow quite normal. The other women in the office shook their heads with a sort of disgusted resignation. Yes, that's how it was in those days. And then the conversation moved on and we talked about the best place in town to eat seafood and planned a visit to a brothel where Olin often goes to hand out condoms.

The Institute of Dayakology vigorously defended the first wave of this slaughter, saying that it was required by adat.* This was inconvenient for the international indigenous-rights movement. Underdogs are expected to rail against a patriarchal

* See Jamie S. Davidson, *From Rebellion to Riots: Collective Violence on Indonesian Borneo.* Madison, WI: University of Wisconsin Press, 2009.

state or an exploitative multinational, perhaps even to resist by throwing a spear or burning a vehicle or two. But they are not supposed to slaughter other landless peasants and eat their hearts in the name of indigenous traditions.

The violence of 1997 shocked the nation, and the Dayaks turned the attention to their own advantage. They demanded more political involvement and Suharto, still on the throne at the time but growing less sure of himself, quickly appointed Dayaks to several positions of local importance that had always gone to the Malays. This angered the Malays. Severed heads and cannibalism are not traditionally part of the Malay repertoire, and the group had never been in conflict with the Madurese, who are fellow Muslims. But when they lost their jobs, Malay tempers frayed. When a Madurese immigrant stole a chicken from a Malay, a fight broke out and three people were killed. Suddenly the Malays were running around beheading the Madurese and throwing severed hands at Ibu Ibit. At least another 500 Madurese died in 1999 and 50,000 left the Sambas region, including second- and third-generation immigrants who had no other home and who ended up in camps in the provincial capital Pontianak.

Though the Dayaks have continued to press their advantage through a decade of decentralization, they took note of the Malays' willingness to play dirty and have been increasingly willing to compromise with them. In Kalimantan as in many ethnically mixed areas of Indonesia, politics has become a process of political 'cow trading'. For every mayor or bupati, there's a deputy. Often, these pairings will run across ethnic lines, one a Dayak, the other a Malay. Even the despised Madurese now get a look-in. So many of them fled to Pontianak that they swelled into a voting block. When I visited the city in 2012, the mayor was Malay, his deputy Madurese.

Magnesium flashes of extreme violence are common in modern Indonesia. In the early Suharto years they tended to get stamped out very quickly. The violence in Kalimantan ran for longer because the military's support for the President had already grown threadbare. Then Suharto stepped down and the jockeying for power between the civilian old guard, Islamic radicals, the armed forces and local potentates began. Traffic accidents turned into local rampages, the forces that should have put out the flames fanned them instead, and thousands died needlessly.

The worst of the post–Suharto violence had been in the eastern spice islands of Maluku, some 2,000 kilometres south-east of West Kalimantan. The roots of that conflict go back centuries and are tangled enough for a book of their own, but to summarize very briefly: the Dutch colonizers favoured the Christians of the southern Moluccan islands over the Muslims of the sultanates to the north. The better-educated Christians maintained their lock on the bureaucracy until the mid-1990s. That was when Suharto, in one of his intricate political balancing acts, started wooing Muslims. 'Christian' jobs were given to Muslims. At the same time, immigrants from hard-working Muslim tribes in Sulawesi began taking over Maluku's markets from more laid-back local traders, and there was growing rivalry between criminal gangs that organized along religious lines.

It took one fight between a Christian bus driver and a Muslim passenger in January 1999 to put a match to the haystack.

The two sides set about needling one another, and though the jealousies that underpinned the conflict had nothing to do with faith, the battle lines were quickly drawn between church and mosque. Graffiti insulting Mohammad was scrawled on one wall of the provincial capital, Ambon, a picture of Christ was defaced on another. People who had no real interest in prayer tied on headbands – white for Muslims, red for Christians, almost as though they were going to a football match – and joined the fighting. In some areas of Ambon, seven out of ten young men were out of work; this impromptu Holy War was a way of venting frustration and developing a sense of purpose.

The army did nothing. The police did nothing.

Fighting broke out as far south as Tual and as far north as

Halmahera. By 2002 over 5,000 people had been killed and another 700,000 – a third of the entire population of Maluku – had been driven from their homes. Even in idyllic Ohoiwait, where I had spent Christmas on this trip, the Muslims had been run out of town. Though a decade later some were beginning to trickle back, many of the tidy collective gardens maintained by Mama Ince and her friends in the lower village are planted on plots first fertilized by the burning of a Muslim home.

Nowadays, the people of Maluku explain the violence as being the work of unspecified '*provokator*'. 'We've always got along just fine with our neighbours,' I had heard all over Maluku: in Ohoiwait, in Tual, in Banda, in Saparua, in Ambon. 'Yes, the Muslims/Christians had to leave the island, but we didn't want them to go.' In Banda, almost everyone I spoke to about 'the Troubles' told me that they personally had taken their Christian neighbours down to the port to see them off when they fled. 'I cooked for them specially, I gave them pillows for the journey.' The same script, word for word, from at least a dozen people. 'I cooked for them, I gave them pillows. We didn't want it to happen. We couldn't protect them against the *provokator*.'

Provokator is part of Indonesia's vast vocabulary of political obfuscation, a word whose meaning is left deliberately vague, usually because naming a problem more specifically would mean that the government might have to address it in some way. But in this case, everyone knew that *provokator* meant a radical Islamist group named Laskar Jihad which arrived from Java with the blessing of senior politicians from Muslim parties and the express intention of cleansing Maluku of Christians.

In fact, the *provokator* did not arrive in Maluku until more than a year after the Muslims of Ohoiwait had to flee their homes and the Christians of Banda went into exile clutching their neighbours' pillows. In the sixteen months of conflict before the Javanese jihadis even showed up, many hundreds, probably thousands, of people of both religions were hacked up or shot by neighbours, cousins, colleagues, schoolmates, customers who were also indigenous Malukans.

The violence in Maluku was billed as religious, that in Kalimantan as ethnic. But as with most conflicts, both were really about access to resources. And both were initiated by indigenous populations who believed that immigrants from other parts of the nation were getting a better deal in 'their' native land. While I travelled the country in 2011/2012, churches in Java were being burned because the Sumatran Bataks who worship in them were doing well economically, and Hindus in Sumatra were attacked because hard-working Balinese transmigrants had bought nicer motorbikes and built nicer houses than the Lampung locals.

'Indigenous' is a tricky concept in the Indonesian context. Despite having integrated into the coastal communities of Java in the 1300s and formed a democratic republic in Kalimantan more than 200 years ago, Indonesians with Chinese roots will never be considered indigenous, that's clear. But almost everyone else is indigenous to one island or another, and in the historical rhetoric, all of those islands joined together voluntarily to form a nation in which all citizens have equal rights. It's hard, then, to argue that the Dayaks are somehow more 'indigenous' than the Malays, of whom the hunter-gatherer Rimba in Sumatra are a subset, and who have been in Kalimantan for all of recorded history. Constitutionally, the Madurese – who are also indigenous to this unitary republic – should have the same right to live in West Kalimantan as anyone else. The Dayaks I met disagree.

The bus to Sintang, bang in the heart of West Kalimantan, had a hole in the windscreen, just in front of my nose. Radiating from it was a great, star-shaped fissure, sealed with plastic cement, though not well enough to stop the rain from dripping through. A sticker of Sukarno, cool in his black *peci* cap and shades, held together the most dangerous-looking edges of the crack. From higher up the windscreen, a buxom blonde naked but for a nurse's cap, a Red Cross bikini and Russian hooker shoes looked down on the President. There were no windscreen wipers, but a lot of water was shaken off the glass by the vibrations from a giant boom-box. The playlist was rock from my early teen years in which *Hotel California* featured prominently; odd, since the ethnic Chinese driver looked like he was fourteen years old. At one point the bus juddered to a halt. 'Rest stop', called the driver, though we had clearly broken down. I went to take my 'rest', and emerged from the bushes to see the driver lying on his back, sucking petrol through a rubber hosepipe, something to do with creating a siphon, he said when I asked, wiping his mouth on his sleeve. It worked, and we trundled off again. I hadn't had high expectations of the town we were headed for, thinking it would be an undistinguished little place, but I lowered them anyway.

In fact, Sintang is large, thriving, pulsing with new motorbikes and curiously devoid of public transport. How do poor people get around? I asked Danaus, a young Dayak civil servant whom we befriended in town. 'There aren't really any poor people in Sintang,' he said. Rubber and palm oil has put money into everyone's pockets.

Unusually for an Indonesian city, Sintang makes quite good use of its riverfront. The banks of the majestic Kapuas river are lined with restaurants and bars built up on stilts to avoid flooding; most of them have terraces over the water from which one can watch the sunset. Well, usually over the water; we arrived at the end of an unusually long dry season, when the river was at its very lowest. Most of the restaurants were now hundreds of metres away from the water's edge. Marooned on the sandbanks at impractical angles were boathouses built on platforms of massive logs. Their residents longed for the river to rise again, so that they could straighten out their lives.

Melanie and I spent disproportionate amounts of time in the high-and-dry restaurants; for all their political tensions, Malay and Dayak seem to have fused in the kitchen to produce an extraordinarily delicious cuisine. From the Christian Dayak side come giant river prawns, pork with crunchy forest fungus and lots of leafy things: fiddle-head ferns and bright pumpkin flowers, for example. The Malays add spices and give us creamy *jengkol* beans, tasting not unlike over-ripe Camembert, cooked with tomatoes and shallots. The two influences come together perfectly in a dish of thick chunks of fish, slathered with garlic, ginger, chilli and lemon grass, wrapped in a large, edible leaf with a slightly bitter tang, and stewed gently in a coriander sauce.

Melanie and I set out in search of a Dayak longhouse. On the provincial map, the area around Sintang is jungle. On the ground, it is oil palm. For mile after mile, evenly spaced trees rise from bare earth, their straight, grey trunks topped with a dense crown of spikes that block the sky. We bumped along through this monotonous landscape for a couple of hours. Finally, the jungle. That lasted about six minutes. Then a clearing, and a Dayak longhouse.

The longhouse was slightly forbidding: a wide, flat-bellied beast squatting on stilts, like a komodo dragon raised off the ground ready to strike. The side wall was a thicket of branches and split bamboo bound together with rattan, tipping outwards from floor to wood-tiled roof. Every fifty metres or so, a squonky ladder or a notched log worn slippery with the passage of feet ran from the ground up to an open doorway and was swallowed into the darkness. Green gumboots stuck out from the walls at odd angles, as though someone had been catapulted into the building head first and got stuck halfway.

It was eerily quiet. On either side of the end doorway, wooden statues fixed potential intruders with dead-eyed stares. One had the sense of being watched from behind the bamboo wall, but had no idea of where to direct one's gaze in response. There were people around, definitely; occasionally I'd hear a giggle and catch sight of a flash of colour crossing the dark gulf of the doorway, and I'd know that the children of the longhouse had spotted us, but they didn't show themselves. Melanie went to try and tempt them out with her camera – a love of posing for photos seems to be a universal trait in Indonesia.

I heard a thumping behind me. A man was crouched over the side of a plastic paddling pool, hitting a lump of earth with a stick. With each thud, a huge dragon tattoo rippled down his back, there were hundreds of tiny splashes in the water, and then a churning and bubbling. He was beating ants out of their lumpy nest to feed to the catfish in the water below.

Pak Anton has just come back after twenty years living across the border in Malaysia. He made more money there. 'But you spend it all too. In Malaysia you have to pay to fart. You work all the time, you never see your wife, you never play with your kids. What's the point, really?'

Nowadays, Anton said, it was almost as easy to make money on the Indonesian side of the border. You could grow rubber or oil palm and sell to the plantation companies. Or, like Anton himself, you could build modern, porticoed bungalows for other people who had made a fortune in rubber and who had no interest in living in a longhouse. That brought in around a thousand dollars a month, and no charge for farting. Or for many other necessities of life. 'Here, I can still go to the forest, slash open a plot, grow as much rice as I need. I can get fish from the river, I can pick vegetables on the mountainside, all for free,' he said. He was worried, though, about the environment. Between the logging of the Suharto years and today's rubber and oil palm plantations, Anton now had to go much further to find forest to slash open for rice. He was also anxious that fertilizer and pesticide from the plantations were polluting the rivers so central to Dayak life. He had stopped drinking river water, he said, and was farming catfish in case the river fish died out.

Anton invited me into the longhouse. It was split down the middle, half open, half walled off. Parading down into the distance on the walled side, twenty-eight doors. Each led to the living quarters of a single family; a bedroom and behind that a kitchen. The infinitely long open space was the collective living room.

It was a Sunday afternoon; people were resting from their labours in the forest-fields. Some women were weaving, using back-strap looms. Others did the elaborate beadwork for which this tribe is famous. One woman looped half a dozen cotton threads around her big toe for tension, then rubbed the threads with a big lump of forest beeswax for strength. After that, she picked minuscule glass beads one by one out of a vast multicoloured pile, threading them onto this string or that and plaiting them together in an elaborate sequence which gradually resolved itself into a classic Dayak motif.

A plump woman sewed palm leaves together to make a wide, conical hat that would protect her from the sun as she paddled off to her vegetable garden in the forest. These hats, variously decorated with panels of beading, crochet or embroidery, graced the walls of Kalimantan's longhouses along with deer antlers, painted sampan paddles and Guns N' Roses posters.

An old lady, her shrivelled skin elaborately tattooed, her elongated earlobes now liberated from their heavy brass rings, squatted on her haunches weaving intricate, lumpy baskets used to store betel nut. A man with no teeth was repairing spike-toothed fishtraps with fresh rattan while one of his grandsons ran about screaming and pretending to shoot things with a bow and arrow.

I asked the old fellow how many grandchildren he had. 'Lots.' He started counting them off on his fingers, then shook his head. 'Oh, I don't know. Lots. More than a sampan full.'

Anton introduced me to a group of men. One was a retired soldier; I teased him about a huge mural I had seen in Sintang which for several hundred metres extolled the virtues of the Indonesian army as development workers. In one section, soldiers were building a mosque and church, companionably side by side. There was an operation against gambling and alcohol, in which soldiers wagged their fingers at villagers, who knelt shamefaced with their hands raised. In the dust in front of them, a bottle rolled around and a fighting cock flapped his wings. To restore morale, we later have the soldiers and 'The People' drinking coconut juice together.

The former soldier grimaced: *dwifungsi*, the Suharto-era 'dual function' which allowed the military to act not just as a defence force but also as a political machine down to the village level, is deeply out of fashion these days. But he did say that, for most of his time in the force, this had been a peaceful area. 'Everyone thinks the Dayaks are so fierce, but it's just a way of putting us down. Really we hate conflict.'

I asked him about the conflict between Dayaks and Madurese in 1997: hadn't that been pretty violent? 'Oh, that's completely different,' he replied. 'That's not conflict, that's just the Madurese getting what they deserve.'

The reputation for back-stabbing, double dealing and ferocity that I found in Madura itself travelled with the Madurese as they began to settle elsewhere in Indonesia. 'A Maduran will come and ask if he can cut grass from around your coconut trees and you'll say fine, just don't take the coconuts,' the soldier explained. 'Later you'll find him sleeping in a field, and he's got a big basket of grass, but if you put your hand inside you'll find that it's only grass on top, underneath it's all coconuts. And there he is, sleeping in front of you with his mouth open, pleased with the trick he has played. Of course you have to kill him.'

Later that evening, Danaus – a young Dayak civil servant whom we had met in Sintang – dragged Melanie and me to a cultural dance competition in the district hall. The whole place fizzed with excitement; even the Bupati was there, wearing a shirt made of batik in a Dayak motif. The competition was in two parts, first Dayak, then Malay, the brief to come up with a modern reinterpretation of their cultural traditions. The winner of each faction would go on to compete in the provincial capital, Pontianak. The pride of the district would be at stake. 'Now you'll see the real Dayak spirit,' said Danaus.

In the first dance, a group of women in beaded dresses and broad, conical hats walked very slowly in circles, raising and lowering a stiff plastic doll. The blonde, blue-eyed baby bobbed between heaven and earth receiving blessings for an exceedingly long time. When eventually they trooped off, I clapped weakly and wondered how many competitors there were. Danaus looked embarrassed. 'They didn't understand that they were supposed to do something creative,' he mumbled.

Then an explosion of sound. A young man whooped past my ear, banging a gong. Drums crashed all around; whistles squealed above and an instrument which seemed to be a cross between a violin and a didgeridoo wailed plaintive below. From the side doors, a group of young men, naked but for their loincloths, burst on to the stage, muscles rippling under tattoos. They leapt on one another's shoulders, balanced on one another's thighs. Danaus perked up.

Within minutes, their tattoos melted in rivulets down their bodies. Loincloths began to slip, revealing cycling shorts below. Danaus's pleasure wilted; these 'Dayak warriors' were extemporizing on moves taken from Malay dances. The crowd was clapping and shrieking its support but Danaus just shook his head. 'They might not know anything about their own culture but the judges will,' he said. 'Mixing Dayak and Malay – that's fatal.'

After a few more troupes of Dayak dancers had done their thing, Danaus announced that we were leaving. We'd just watched a group of girls leaping about with flaming oil-lamps balanced on their heads, while bare-chested warriors with hornbill feathers stuck in their hair assaulted a cubicle built of white sheets. This was a celebration, Danaus had said, of the practice of locking girls away from puberty until their Prince Charming, their One True Intended, bashed down the door. Despite myself, I was rather enjoying watching these groups of urban youngsters pour their enthusiasm into reinterpreting a culture that they would have been horrified to be subjected to. I said I'd stay for a bit longer, but no. 'It's only the Malays now,' Danaus said, 'and there's someone I want you to meet.'

It was 9.30 on a Sunday night, but Danaus was determined to take me to meet his mentor, Pak Askiman, who had recently been appointed head of the district public works office. We waited for a while in a reception room painted bright green with orange cornicing; it was lit by a chandelier that looked as though it had hunched its shoulders up to fit into the narrow space at the top of the stairs. A large tank full of exotic fish occupied one wall; the others were graced with paintings of wild horses stampeding through mountain streams.

After a little while a flunky came in and said: 'You can go up now.' Instead of climbing past the chandelier we banked off to the right into a vast new wing, less than half built but perhaps three times the size of the original house. After three floors of cement dust we spilled out into a cavernous games room, railed in with shiny chrome bars interspersed with the Mercedes logo. A group of men sat around a ping-pong table, smoking, drinking coffee and paying court to Pak Askiman. They were talking about flip-flops.

It was a subject I was up to speed on. While I was below decks on a Pelni ship a couple of months earlier, someone had switched on the television. The sound was poor and the image was a snow-storm of static, but it seemed we were looking at a mountain of flip-flops. The mountain sprouted from a bustling crowd, and it seemed to be growing. We speculated about what was going on. 'Modern art,' suggested one fellow passenger. 'It's a protest against made-in-China' said another. 'Hah!' retorted a third. 'If everyone joined that protest, all of Indonesia would be barefoot!'

In fact, a fifteen-year-old boy had been arrested because he had stolen a pair of flip-flops which happened to belong to a policeman. The cop's first reaction was to beat the boy up. The boy's mother reported the policeman for brutality. That angered fellow cops, who arrested the boy. Now he was facing five years in prison. Meanwhile, people accused of stealing tens of millions of dollars were bribing judges and getting off scot-free. At worst, the bigger criminals were sentenced to just a year or two. Flip-flops quickly came to symbolize Indonesians' disgust with the arrogance of the law.

Fuelled by waves of sweet coffee, we sat around Pak Askiman's ping-pong table solving the problems of the world until late into the night. There was a lot of talk about mob 'justice' as a substitute for proper law enforcement. Pak Askiman laid the blame for Indonesia's putrid legal system on the Dutch, who made different laws for different people.

In the early colonial years the government of the Netherlands East Indies had not bothered much with justice at all. As long as commercial transactions were safely subject to Dutch law, they saw little reason to interfere in the various systems of adat that governed how most people lived. Over time, these adat laws were codified. Dutch scholars collected adat laws the way Alfred Wallace collected beetles, capturing them live, cleaning them up, pinning them down between the covers of forty volumes and then classifying them into nineteen broad systems.

By the end of the nineteenth century the Netherlands East Indies had several overlapping legal systems. The first, a Western legal code that defended the rights of the individual and required qualified judges, was reserved for Europeans. Then there was indigenous law. 'Natives' went to one of three courts. Issues related to sharia law were heard in Islamic courts. Adat courts governed by local luminaries were for matters of marriage, inheritance and so on. For criminal cases, there were shadow native courts staffed mostly by bush lawyers with no proper legal training. 'Foreign Orientals' – mostly Chinese but also Arabs – were considered 'natives' except when it came to commercial law, when they turned European.★

Final appeal on cases that went through these native courts was heard by the European courts, effectively subordinating the local judicial system to the state.

'We still have three laws, just like in colonial times,' snorted Pak Askiman. 'Nowadays, senior officials like me are the equivalent of the Dutch class, businessmen have swapped in for the Chinese, and ordinary folks have taken the place of the "natives". How

---

★ The classification system was incredibly complex, and shifted over time. Indonesian wives of Europeans and their children became European. Illegitimate children were European if the father acknowledged them. In addition, 'natives' could qualify as honorary Europeans at the whim of the Governor General; these people were called 'Government Gazette Europeans'. Following pressure from a newly assertive Tokyo, all Japanese were accorded 'European' status in 1899.

the hell can you run a country properly when the law depends on your class?'

When I repeated this to a lawyer friend, she laughed. 'It doesn't depend on your class, just on your wallet. You know how it is here, justice goes to the highest bidder.' In surveys of corruption, two-thirds of Indonesians rate the Attorney General's office as 'dirty' or 'filthy'. Only political parties and the national parliament are considered more corrupt. Recently, the relatively independent Commission for the Eradication of Corruption (KPK) has arrested several judges in the corruption courts for taking bribes to throw out charges against the accused. Judges find it easy to acquit defendants because prosecutors have taken bribes to prepare a case full of loopholes. And they are very bad at policing their own system. The KPK had to step in because a Judicial Commission set up to clean up the courts has been so hopeless. The most recent data show that in 2008, it received 1,556 reports of misconduct by judges. The commission investigated 212 cases and referred twenty-seven cases to the Supreme Court, which did not act on any of them.

The Dutch left a deeply flawed legal system, certainly. But Indonesians, whose independence-era leaders were often lawyers trained by the Dutch, have done little to change it. They more or less adopted the 'native courts' side of the colonial legal system wholesale, complete with poorly trained prosecutors, a criminal code written in a language that only a tiny handful could speak and designed by the colonial state to keep native subjects in their place, and a habit of being dictated to by a ruling class that stood above a court of law.

Nowadays, there are three times as many Indonesians as there were in the early 1950s, but only half as many court cases. The distrust of law enforcement starts long before anything gets to court, with the police. Over six in ten Indonesians think that the police are corrupt or very corrupt. So Indonesians often take the law into their own hands. People get beaten to death by angry crowds because they have been caught stealing a chicken, because they lost control of their car and knocked over a pedestrian, because a jealous neighbour has accused them of witchcraft. If one of these incidents happens to involve someone who thinks of themselves as 'indigenous' and someone who is thought of as an 'immigrant', a tiny incident that ought to be resolved at the police station or the magistrate's court can turn into a minor civil war that costs hundreds of lives. With alarming frequency, mobs are turning on the police themselves. As I write this, in late March 2013, the newspapers tell of a sub-district police chief who was beaten to death as he led the arrest of a bookie who was running a gambling racket. Crowds closed in on the arresting cops after the bookie's wife accused them of being buffalo thieves. This was one of thirteen incidents in which mobs attacked the police in the first three months of 2013 alone. As long as Indonesians believe the police and courts are rotten to the core – 'Report the theft of a chicken and lose your buffalo,' the Javanese saying goes – mob justice will continue to rule.

Map L: Java, Bali and Lombok

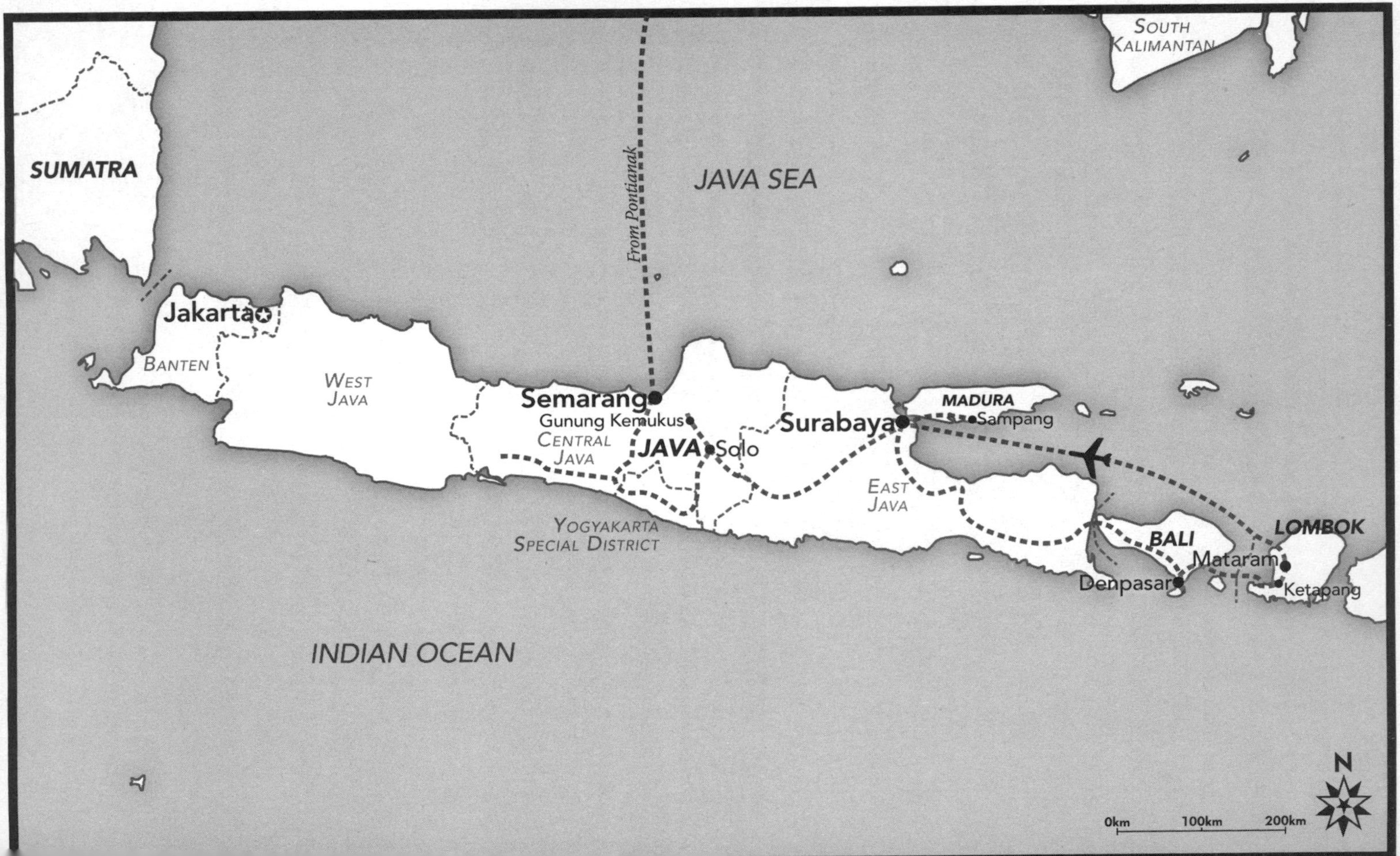

12

Faith Healing

Throughout my journey, I got my fix of world news by reading online newspapers in the internet cafes that are a relatively new addition to the townscapes of Indonesia. They sit below the ubiquitous cell-phone towers, close to the harbour or the bus station, perhaps shouldered in next to a nasi Padang restaurant. Generally, they are small shops furnished with cubicles that rise to waist height. About eighteen inches off the ground, often on an upturned crate, sit computer screens. Adolescents litter the floor behind the consoles. Girls are usually in gaggles in a cubicle, squeezing in front of the web-cam, then posting the pictures on Facebook. Boys are more often alone, doing on-screen battle with racing cars or dragons. Once or twice over the course of the year I saw people on Wikipedia, clearly doing their homework. But for most young Indonesians, the internet is pure entertainment. This is reflected in the language. To go online is *main internet*: to 'play (on) the internet'. Usually, there's a teenage boy with bad skin sitting up at a real desk playing computer games, acting as DJ for music that thuds from the wall-mounted speakers, and collecting money as people leave.

I attempted to zone out the music, the giggling and the *Zap! Pow!* sound-effects of the online gamers as I read the papers and tried to keep up with what was going on in the world. I was interested, too, in what foreign reporters were saying about Indonesia. 'Indonesia's Rising Religious Intolerance', read a fairly typical headline in the *International Herald Tribune*. 'Indonesia hit on rise in religious attacks', said the *Financial Times*. 'Rising religious violence "ignored" in Indonesia', thundered the *Sydney Morning Herald*. The stories quoted the Setara Institute, which tracks religious freedom in Indonesia, and which documented 264 attacks on religious minorities in 2012. They told of the construction of churches blocked, of 'deviant' Muslims beaten and killed and their mosques burned to the ground, of atheists jailed. They harked not very far back to the bombs in a Bali nightclub that killed over 200 people in 2002, and the Marriott Hotel bombs in Jakarta in 2003 and 2009, in which nineteen others died. Islamist groups were proud to claim these attacks as their own work.

Many learned volumes have been written about the various flavours of Islam within Java and of other religions across the archipelago, many finely honed reports have dissected the relationship between Islam and politics in the Middle East, Indonesia and elsewhere in the world. The entrails of terrorist networks have been pulled out and chewed over, the bloodlines of extremism have been run through the sequencers. Some see an Arab invasion in progress, others a revival of indigenous forms of faith.

And yet in close to a year of travel, including in areas such as Aceh and South Sulawesi that have in the past fought for an Islamic state, I had heard people talking about religion only in the most mundane terms, as an immutable fact of life like food or sleep. Religious labels were occasionally stuck on to paroxysms of violence such as the war in Maluku, but after the fires had been put out, most people acknowledged that people had been fighting about money, jobs and political power, not faith.

People usually asked what religion I was, of course. To many foreigners the question seems intrusive, it treads on something that we think of as a private matter. But in Indonesia, religion is an inherent part of one's identity. Since Suharto's day, every citizen has had to state their religion on their ID card. 'Belief in One God' is the first precept of the state philosophy, Pancasila. One can't be a Godless communist if one has a religion.

In Suharto's day, Indonesians could pick from a menu of five religions: Islam, Hindu, Buddhist, Protestant or Catholic. Nowadays, they can also choose to be Confucian. There's no room for the hundreds of locally specific beliefs like Mama Bobo's Marapu religion in Sumba; those faiths have been redescribed as adat, and people who practise them have superimposed the 'religion' that fits best with their history and dietary traditions. No group that celebrates its true religion by feasting on pigs and cattle could be Muslim or Hindu, for example, so Mama Bobo's ID card reads 'KRISTEN', which is shorthand for Protestant.

The one thing you absolutely can't be as a good citizen is an atheist, which is what I am. I have every respect for other people's faiths; I just don't happen to have one myself. Sometimes, once I had become friends with someone that I had met casually on the road, I'd confess to some of the other lies I told in introductory chit-chat. Actually, there's no long-suffering husband in Jakarta. In fact, I'm not on long leave from my job at the Ministry of Health. But I never, ever admitted to being Godless. To most Indonesians that would simply be incomprehensible, like saying I didn't breathe.

And so I would profess the faith of my parents and say that I was Catholic. When I told people in heavily Muslim areas this, they would sometimes say 'never mind', as though not being Muslim was some kind of slightly embarrassing handicap. But they'd invite me home to stay anyway – it wasn't a source of exclusion or discrimination.

Indonesians certainly live the rituals of their chosen religion more than most people do in Europe – many people routinely wear badges of their faith, a jilbab or peci cap on the head perhaps, a cross or a Buddha amulet around the neck. There is also an awful lot of collective praying at the mosque, the church, or the temple. I went to church more often on my Indonesian travels than I had in many years, and I also sat in quiet corners and listened respectfully to many sermons in mosques. It was simply expected, part of fitting in.

The most entertaining service I had been to on my travels

was surely at The ROCK, a famous Mega-Church in Ambon, the capital of Maluku province. The Representatives Of Christ's Kingdom can listen to their own radio station while waiting to hand their car over to the church's valet parking service. I had visited not long after Christmas 2011, and found a cavernous, deliciously air-conditioned building festooned with flashing fairy lights, Immanuel banners and tinsel. A good half hour before the service – the second of four that day – the stalls and the balcony level were both heaving, and people were being directed to the overflow room to watch the service on a giant screen. We had a big screen of our own in the main hall, as well as several television monitors. All of them were counting down the minutes and seconds until the start of the day's worship.

I spent some time admiring my fellow worshippers. The men were in suits or wearing batik or ikat shirts in ostentatious silks. The women tottered on six inches of royal-blue suede or diamanté platforms, here a cute sleeveless cocktail dress, there a gold flounce tight over the rump. But I had time, too, to look at the flyer I had been given as I came in. In Ohoiwait and the other towns in which I'd been to church we always got an Order of Service, with all the readings and prayers helpfully printed out. At The ROCK, the flyer said only:

Matthew 28: 18–20★

Then, in English:

Bless the City
Change the World
Breakthrough
Building Family Values
Atmosphere

★ The verses are a call to proselytize, and to obey.

The other thing on the flyer was a bank account number for donations, though we were also all given envelopes, and there were see-through collection boxes at every exit of the hall, many of them already half filled.

The screen ticked from 09:59:59 to 10:00:00. Magically (since in twenty-five years I have never known anything start on time in Indonesia) the stage filled with choristers and the hall filled with praise. Mostly, people were belting out the words that popped up on the giant karaoke screen in front of us, but by the end of the first hymn some of my neighbours were already swaying, clapping and speaking in tongues, the tears streaming from ecstatic eyes.

After a few hymns, the choir melted away. It was replaced by a fresh-faced preacher with Boy Band hair wearing a puce silk tie. He was bringing Jeeeeezus to our lives. *Amin!* To our families. *Amin!* To our political leaders. *Amin! Amin!* To Indonesia. *Amin!* To our small, neglected and isolated islands. *Amin! Amin!* He started to up the tempo, then began to crack jokes about the state electricity company, PLN. 'They say 2012 will be a year of darkness, and if you stick with PLN it certainly will be. Because only *Jeeeezus* shines his light every day of the year!' Laughter, but also diligent note-taking. Though he kept the stand-up comedy going for over an hour, he managed to say only two things: 1) it is our duty to spread the name of Jesus, and 2) if we wait patiently Jesus will fulfil our demands.

At 11.55 on the dot, he wrapped up with a quiet 'Amin'. There was one more rollicking hymn, and then, two hours to the second after the service started, it was all over and everyone tottered and flounced out to the hall.

I'm sure the whole format comes off some shelf in the American Bible Belt. And just like those faraway Mega Churches, the message was not of social engagement but of personal gratification. Nothing, but nothing was required of the congregation beyond the filling and depositing of envelopes. In the capital of the third poorest province in Indonesia there was not a whisper about equality in the eyes of God, not a mention that corruption

was a sin against which we might unite, not the slightest suggestion that the Representatives of Christ's Kingdom might help
one another or anyone else. The tears, the speaking in tongues,
this great outpouring of religious fervour was all about being
entertained as we waited patiently for our next pair of royal-blue
suede shoes.

Islam, too, had for several years been putting entertainment
value ahead of social engagement, at least among the middle
classes. When I lived in Jakarta I used to keep an eye on the
schedules of celebrity preachers as a routine part of planning my
movements around town. If Aa Gym – young, good-looking,
turbanned – was speaking in a posh South Jakarta hotel, Mercedes
and BMWs would be lined up around the block, disgorging
richly groomed women in Hermès jilbabs and Manolo Blahnik
shoes and causing a traffic jam that might last for an hour.

Abdullah Gymnastiar, aka Aa Gym, fell out of favour with
his adoring female congregation when he lied about taking
a second wife, but there have been plenty of other turbanned
preachers to take his place. Their recipe is more or less identical
to The ROCK's: take two parts entertainment, blend in one part
demand for funding, season with audience participation and
cook up into a promise of dreams delivered.

This dish can be served up on all sorts of platters. Islamic
televangelism is such big business that some stations run talent
shows to find new faces: last year's winner of one show, an eight-
year-old girl, was booked solid for sermons through the fasting
month. A Texan convert to Islam named Craig (Abdurrohim)
Owensby, who used to be a Mega Church preacher in Jerry
Falwell's fold, has made a fortune in Indonesia by working
with Aa Gym and other popular televangelists to deliver daily
doses of the Koran and accompanying preach-bites by text
message.

Koran-reading contests are as popular in Indonesia as visits
by Manchester United's touring team. When I was in Sumatra,
just before I went into the shrinking forest with the Rimba, I
was invited to one of these extravaganzas. For a whole week,

the Muslims of Jambi province had flooded the city of Bangko to witness their local celebrity chanters compete for a place in the national Koran-reading championships. Crowds of families, parties of schoolchildren, courting couples swirled around the fairground where the competition was held. Some peeled off to buy popcorn or candyfloss, to ride on the bumper cars or to check out the booths promoting the glories of Jambi's various districts. But most of the crowd was transfixed by the main event.

At one end of the central square, the current contestant knelt behind the Holy Book on a raised dais, surrounded on all sides by Plexiglas – a little air-conditioned pool of soundproofing in the steamy sea of fair-goers. Beneath, people strained to see her, to judge her composure and any other visible attributes of her piety. The singer's image was also relayed on a vast digital screen in the middle of the fairground, like a simulcast from the Royal Opera House into London's Trafalgar Square of a summer evening, without the champagne. Here, though, the audience was more engaged; there was much opinionated discussion of the contestant's voice, which blasted out of loudspeakers all around the square. 'It's the biggest social event of the year,' said Ira, who had invited me to the competition.

Many of Indonesia's televangelists have no religious training to speak of – one of the most popular started out as an actor in a religious-themed soap opera. And indeed many of them behave more like entertainers than like clerics. The Indonesian Broadcasting Commission reports a stream of complaints from traditional keepers of the faith who accuse celeb preachers of being more salacious than holy.

Middle-class women, the sort of women who have jobs in banking or PR and children in private schools, seem especially likely to enjoy this fare. Jilbabs have become an astonishingly complex fashion item among the richer set – is it okay to accessorize a Dior headscarf with a Chanel pin? Elaborate head-dresses layering a cone of purple silk over a sweep of lilac gauze are now quite the norm in workplaces where, when first I lived in Indonesia, most women went bare-headed. Indeed at every level of society, more Indonesians are manifesting the symbols of piety now than when I arrived in the late 1980s.

The boom seems to have started with the loosening of the bonds of national unity of the Suharto years. By the time I went back to Jakarta in 2001 to work in health, I noticed more of my Muslim friends and colleagues praying five times a day, fasting over Ramadan and dressing like Arabs; more of my Christian friends wearing crosses and going to church. Election rallies around the country started with a prayer (though many covered their bases with lewd dangdut dancing as well). Even workshops in which we taught prostitutes to distribute condoms to their peers began with a little religious blessing.

Keeping tabs on the sex trade had been part of my job at the time. Every now and then I'd get on my bike and negotiate the clogged highways leading to Jakarta's port area, then thread my way through to the tumbledown red-light districts beyond, just to see what was going on. I usually went around lunchtime; before that there was no one around, but if I waited until mid-afternoon the dangdut music would be shaking the wooden walls of the brothels and it would be hard to chat.

One day I wandered down past the stalls selling condoms and antibiotics and found the lean-to brothels more deserted than usual. One of the girls offered me a coffee. 'Bad day?' I asked. 'It's Friday,' she replied. Of course, the Muslim holy day. 'All the clients are still at the mosque for prayers.'

I asked if she thought that sermonizing in the mosque might make clients think again about buying sex. She laughed. 'Why would it?' she said. 'They're not doing anything wrong.' She explained that if a client was particularly pious, he would take the time to perform a wedding ceremony before getting naked. 'Then we get on with the sex business, and an hour later he divorces me.' By following the letter of the religious law, she said, the client could claim still to be a good Muslim.

Today's commodified, by-the-book forms of religion are not driving social change in Indonesia. In fact, it's the reverse. Urbanization and mobility are diluting the tribalism and collectivist

cultures that underpin much of Indonesian life. Religion recreates
the comfort of a known universe; it is a visible badge of identity
which suits the need to clump together, so very pronounced
in clannish Indonesia. Modern Indonesians are signing up for
orthodox religions as never before.

In those parts of Indonesia that still live closer to their
traditions, religion actually puts the brakes on progress. Because
really, what's the point in thinking ahead, in making plans, in
working towards a different future if everything is in God's
hands? 'Around here,' said a friend who runs a dive lodge in a
part of the country as yet little touched by the modern world,
'planning is almost an atheist act.'

Almost exactly a year after I had set out on my eccentric voyage
around Indonesia, I took a boat from the equatorial city of
Pontianak in Kalimantan to Java. As I looked forward to the
last month of my travels, I started to worry about the mismatch
between what I was reading during my forays into internet
cafes and what I had found in my conversations with most
ordinary Indonesians. Had I missed some great upsurge of angst
about religious extremism? Sitting on deck, heading for the
island that is home to most Indonesians, I resolved that I would
make deliberate trips to places which had a religious flavour
to them, I would start to ask people what they thought about
'rising religious intolerance'. It was that resolution that took me
to the city of Solo, in the very centre of Java, a place known as
a hotbed of Islamic fundamentalism. The men accused of the
bombings in a nightclub in Bali in 2002 studied in Solo, for
example.

I found a city with a split personality.

At Solo's centre stands the *kraton*, the Sultan's palace. It's a whole
town-within-a-town. The solid white wall which surrounds it is
punctuated by elegant arched gates, painted pale blue. These lead
to the small family compounds of the Sultan's many retainers.
In the surrounding streets, pitched-tile roofs slope into pretty

verandas that are often graced with bougainvillea or passion vines. At the local coffee stalls, large tin kettles with stubby spouts bubble over charcoal fires; from them wafts the scent of ginger tea so typical of Central Java. The city also specializes in milk drinks, many of them concocted only to appeal to Indonesians' love for contractions and wordplay. I couldn't resist ordering a rather disgusting concoction of sweet ginger, coffee, syrup and milk whose ingredients – *JAhe MAnis, KOpi, siRUP, Susu* – can be contracted to *Jaman Korups*, the 'Age of Corruption'.

Outside the walls to the west is a maze of streets that smells quite different, of honey and paraffin. This is the batik quarter. Small back rooms are dotted with tiny woks balanced on pint-sized braziers. Into one of these, a woman will dip an instrument that looks a bit like a pipe. She fills the copper bowl of the pipe with warm beeswax, blows on the nib that protrudes from it, then patiently traces golden lines on to the white fabric in her lap. She's laying out the design, the first of at least fourteen steps in the torturous process of making a single sarong. Except for the electric light-bulb over her head, the scene could come from pre-colonial times.

Step out of the kraton walls to the east, however, and all semblance of gracious Javanese living evaporates. This part of town is positively Middle Eastern. There are two giant mosques in the Saudi style, practically side by side. I wondered that there were enough worshippers to fill them both, then realized that one was actually a hospital, built in the style of a mosque. Almost every shop offered something that smacked of orthodox Islam: pilgrimages to Mecca, or souvenirs from Mecca sold to pilgrims who had already been there, but hadn't been able to fit all the necessary presents for the family into their luggage and were in need of top-ups. There were Muslim hotels that didn't allow drinking or visits from unregistered guests; I went into a few of these to see if they'd give me a room, but all said they were full. There were schools teaching Arabic, and shopfront after shopfront filled with mannequins in jilbabs and full-length dresses. This part of Solo is about as orthodox Sunni as it gets.

And yet the city sits in a part of Java that for centuries had a very different religious sensibility.

Until the late nineteenth century, Islam in Indonesia was a localized affair. It was strongest in the big trading ports, places like Makassar in South Sulawesi and Aceh and the other ports of Sumatra. But in rural areas such as Central Java, the Islamic religion was little more than a veneer daubed over traditional beliefs in the spirits of volcanoes, rivers and village guardians.

Then the Dutch invested in ports and steam ships, and the pilgrimage to Mecca became popular. By 1885, visitors from 'Jawa' – a generic term for South East Asian Muslims in Arab records – were the largest pilgrim population in Mecca. These Hajis came home with a renewed enthusiasm for orthodox Islam, and new (and, for the Dutch, dangerous) ideas about pan-Islamic politics.

The newly returned Hajis wanted to purge their home religion of all the flavours it had picked up while stewing for centuries in the rich cultures of the islands. The superstitions and mysticisms, the rituals of planting, harvesting and village life that had fused with Islamic prayers and orthodoxies over the years – all these must be dispensed with in favour of a return to pure, Identikit Arab Islam. The reformers favoured rational interpretations of the Koran; they set up an important network of schools that focused firmly on teaching science and the secular skills needed in a modern state.

Their rationalism put them at odds with the home-grown Javanese Muslims, whose spiritual heirs I found at Gunung Kemukus, Kemukus Mountain, a small hill about an hour north of Solo, where worshippers pray at the grave of a Muslim saint revered for his business acumen. On peak nights (every thirty-five days, when the seven-day Islamic calendar intersects in a certain way with the five-day Javanese calendar) thousands of men wearing batik shirts and women wearing their best jilbabs stream up to the saint's grave on Gunung Kemukus, hoping for a helping hand with their finances. The day I was there was an off day, and there weren't more than a hundred pilgrims all evening.

Each of them bought a banana-leaf full of flowers, and a plastic container of holy water; together these would set them back 100,000 rupiah, about ten dollars. They knelt and mumbled their troubles to a Muslim cleric outside the shrine. They handed over the flowers – these were wafted over a brazier of incense and handed back – and an envelope full of cash, another 100,000 rupiah, which was pocketed. Next, they went into the little shrine which covers the saint's grave, prostrated themselves, sprinkled holy water, rubbed their flowers up and down the lozenge-shaped ends of the grave, and mumbled their troubles all over again, this time to the dead saint.

Then they emerged from the shrine, and looked for a stranger to have sex with.

It's this anonymous sex that seals the saint's blessing and restores people's business to health. 'Where there's a womb, there's God,' a Javanese writer told me when I expressed my surprise at the goings on at Kemukus. 'Sex and spirituality always go together.'

The local government at Gunung Kemukus appears to disagree. They have put up a sign, spotted over with mould but still legible, that reads:

A PLACE OF PILGRIMAGE AND RECREATION
NOT FOR DOING OTHER THINGS
(GAMBLING, BOOZE, AMORALITY)
SOCIAL EVILS TEAM, SRAGEN DISTRICT

The district council that put up that sign also issues licences to the bars that cling to the hill: Hot Lips, the thudding Sexy Karaoke Bar and dozens more besides. The saint has certainly proved a blessing to the owners of knocking-shops, and has fattened the wallets of the thousands of girls that work there on peak nights. The villagers who facilitate meetings and rent out rooms don't do badly either. One lady sidled up to me as I sat on the steps outside the shrine. 'You can sleep with the preacher if you want,' she nodded at the paunchy, grey-haired man in thick glasses, busy waving flowers over the brazier and squirrelling away envelopes. I tweaked my headscarf defensively and deferred as politely as I could.

'Well, how about his younger brother?' She shot her lips towards another of the gatekeepers, this one in a shiny batik shirt of gold and white. The man unpeeled his buck teeth and grinned at me. 'You can do it at my place,' the lady urged. 'No need to pay, just a donation for the saint . . .'

The supplicants at the grave were an ill-assorted lot. A college girl was being taken through each step of her first visit by an avuncular minder. An immensely fat woman in a sequinned black top and Lycra leggings pressed herself against a very dark young man with bus-station hair, new Monster Mash hip-hop shorts and incongruous knee-length socks in beige nylon. He shuffled himself uncomfortably away from her all-encompassing bosom and scattered more flowers. She shuffled after him. He shuffled off again. Together, they danced on their knees around the grave; finally, he came full circle to the cream patent-leather shoes that he had left at the door. He grabbed them and fled.

Outside the shrine I chatted with a regular visitor who had the look of a circus strongman and who gave his name as Budi. How did he square all this holy promiscuity with the teachings of Islam? 'It's different,' he said. 'Islam is something that exists here' – he put one hand on his forehead. 'Javanese culture is something that exists here' – he put the other hand on his heart. Then he patted his heart. 'This is the thing you can never lose.'

The split between head and heart led to an ugly political rift during Indonesia's formative years. The modernists set up political parties that aimed to unite Indonesia under sharia law, a worldview based on the life and writings of a man who had lived in a faraway desert thirteen centuries earlier. More rooted Javanese villagers – those who wove incantations to Allah together with their obeisance to local spirits – did not want to be homogenized in this way. They rejected what they saw as Arab-style Islam and its political parties, and sided instead with the nationalists and communists, the groups that supported the staunchly secular (and very Javanese) Sukarno. Religious differences were thus mapped on to political parties. And religion, and especially the particular brand of Islam one subscribed to, became something to fight about. The most spectacular fight came in 1965. The orthodox Muslims considered themselves morally superior to the more old-fashioned villagers. When the army encouraged the anti-communist bloodletting of that year, Muslim leaders in Java were at the forefront of the violence. By equating heterodox religious views with communism, they gave their young followers permission to kill those Java-style Muslims whose beliefs were less pure.

When the dust had settled back over the blood-puddles, Suharto engineered a divorce between religion and politics. His bureaucracy worked to 'enrich' the spiritual side of Islam; religious teachers were trained and supported, mosques became more accommodating to all-comers. The effect was to push Islam further into the lives of many millions of Javanese who had previously shown only the most desultory interest in their religion. Though some of the Javanese-flavoured Muslims who survived 1965 converted en masse to Christianity, the majority stamped 'ISLAM' on their ID cards and started going to the mosque more regularly. In school their children were newly exposed to more orthodox Islamic beliefs.

As it happened, the shift was well suited to the times; more and more Javanese were leaving their villages and drifting to the disordered world of the cities, places where the webs of exchange that had tied them to their neighbours and that supported their local belief systems did not exist. A homogenized, geographically deracinated, reformist Islam, one that they now shared with other Islamic communities outside of Java – the Acehnese, the Minangkabau, the Bugis – served their needs much better than a religion that depended on worship at the village shrine.

Curiously, Gunung Kemukus was one of the few places in Indonesia where no one asked my religion. Many people, on the other hand, asked me about my business troubles. One of them was the boy in nylon socks. I mumbled something about cash flow. He knew all about that, he said. He had bought into an ice-cream franchise, a sort of pyramid scheme, in Gresik on Java's north coast. Four of the six sub-agents had grown bored cycling around selling iced lollies and had simply given up, leaving Nylon Socks to pay the collective debt. In a few days' time he would owe twenty million rupiah, about two thousand dollars.

'I don't know what to do, aunty.' He looked really forlorn. He had read about the Gunung Kemukus miracle on Facebook – he took out his phone and showed me the post. 'But I can't find anyone to have sex with me.' I said that some of the other ladies at the shrine had seemed keen. 'Ya, they're all for sale. If it doesn't come from the heart, it won't work,' he said. He turned his dejected eyes on me. 'Please, aunty . . .'

Though places like Gunung Kemukus still thrive, Islam in Indonesia has homogenized into something more orthodox than it was when Suharto came to power. Saudi Arabia has been underwriting schools and mosques in Indonesia that teach Islam off a Middle Eastern template. The classic mosques of central Sumatra and Java, with their modest, three-tiered roofs in terracotta tiles that echo the shape of Indonesia's volcanoes and blend into its villages, are increasingly giving way to variations on the Middle Eastern style – domed, minaretted, ostentatious. The simple scarf-over-the-head that used to serve for a jilbab is losing out to elaborate constructions that leave no wisp of hair visible; some girls now wear jilbabs even before they can walk. A small but increasing minority of women are covering themselves completely, and in parts of the country such as Madura and South Sulawesi, it's now quite common to see men trooping off to the mosque not in traditional sarongs and skullcaps but in full-length robes and turbans.

None of this was deemed worthy of comment by the people I met on boats and verandas, on buses and in coffee stalls. Those people talked endlessly about corruption or the miserable state of the roads, the schools, the health services, but they never worried openly about any rise in religious fundamentalism. Among my middle-class friends in Jakarta, however, the apparent Arabization of Islam in Indonesia was a cause of great angst. They were concerned about two groups in particular. One was the Prosperous Justice Party, the PKS, a parliamentary party modelled on the Muslim Brotherhood in Egypt. The other was the Islamic Defenders Front, the FPI, self-appointed guardians of morality who like to descend on red-light districts and smash up licensed bars in the name of Allah.

I ran into a group of concerned friends quite by chance during one of my Jakarta pit-stops, in a cafe popular with the type of activist that can afford to pay a brick-maker's weekly wage for a cappuccino. One of the group was a photographer; he invited me to see his new show, commissioned by a friend who worked at the Alliance Française. Another, a young lawyer, told me she had just taken a job at the National Women's Commission. A friend who helps curate Jakarta's gay film festival was there too. They had gathered to plan a demonstration. It was to be a counterpoint to the Islamic Defenders Front, who were gathering their forces to demonstrate against a concert by Lady Gaga. The pop singer's mere presence in the country would, according to the FPI, turn young Indonesians homosexual.

The next day, on my way to the dentist, I stupidly chose a route which took me past the Hotel Indonesia roundabout in the centre of Jakarta. This large traffic circle flows around a central fountain from which rises one of Sukarno's triumphalist sculptures. This one, nicknamed Hansel and Gretel, portrays a young man and woman throwing their hands up in a gesture of welcome to modernity. The cobblestones around the fountain have become the beating heart of the city for political demonstrators; it's from here they can most successfully draw attention to themselves by clogging the arteries of the already traffic-choked city. I found the circle crowded with bearded men in long white dresses. Some were barking through loudspeakers, others held up banners reading, in English: 'GO TO HELL LADY GAGA

THE MOTHER MONSTER.' They had also recruited quite a few teenaged girls in jilbabs and provided them with posters that read, in Indonesian: 'YA ALLAH! PROTECT ME FROM THE TEMPTATIONS OF THE ACCURSED GAGA DEVIL.' Through a photo of the pop singer was a large cross, emblazoned with the words: 'Stop Importing Immorality to Indonesia.'

Cops were blocking off the street that led to my dentist's surgery, so I thought I may as well join the counter-demonstration for a while. I texted a couple of the friends who had been planning it, to ask which side of the circle they were. 'Didn't make it,' one texted back. 'Busy at work and so much traffic.' 'In the end I couldn't be bothered,' replied another. Later, I took some of my friends to task about this: if they were genuinely worried about 'rising religious intolerance' and the restriction of their freedom to worship and to live as they pleased, shouldn't they make the effort to battle the traffic and raise their voices against religious zealots like the FPI? 'It's not really about religion, though, is it?' replied my lawyer friend. 'The FPI are just paid heavies that politicians wheel out when they want to whip up votes or defend their business interests.'

Since Dutch times and possibly earlier, powerful men in Indonesia have made common cause with thugs and gangsters to achieve political ends. Universally known as *preman*, supposedly from the Dutch *vrijman* (or Free Man, in English), the gangsters command fear and a reluctant respect.* In exchange for doing dirty work for politicians, preman are allowed a relatively free hand in racketeering; they are up to their biceps in prostitution, gambling, drug-dealing and much else. Indonesia in the 2010s looks a lot like Chicago in the 1920s. Nationalist organizations such as *Pemuda Pancasila* (Pancasila Youth) openly admit to using violence for political ends. In the 2012 film *The Act of Killing*, Indonesia's former Vice President Jusuf Kalla tells a Pancasila

---

* The talismanic word *merdeka*, meaning liberty but also national independence from Dutch rule, appeared in a Malay-Dutch word list compiled in 1603 with the meaning 'Free Man'. It derives from Maharddhika, a Sanskrit word transposed by the Dutch as Mardijker and used to refer to freed slaves and their descendants.

Youth rally that preman are indispensible to do the work bureaucrats can't do. 'We need preman to open up the road. Use your muscle!' he says, on camera. 'Muscles aren't *just* for beating people up, though you do sometimes need to beat people up ...' Muscles rippled under orange and black military-style fatigues as Kalla's thuggish audience applauded that line.

Preman come in various flavours. Besides those in orange and black fatigues, you can find them in common-or-garden biker leathers and in the long-haired, tattooed variety. More recently, they have also begun to appear in turbans or knitted skullcaps, long white robes and straggly beards. I first saw one of these holy thugs at around midnight one night in 2002. I had stopped in to say hello to Eris, a friend who managed one of Jakarta's sleazier gay nightclubs; behind us, a group of transgender dancers were fluttering around in their tummy-control knickers, trying to get their false eyelashes pinned down before their dance show. One of the staff bounded in: 'They're here.'

Eris opened a drawer and took out an envelope. Soon, a young man with the trademark beard and long white robes appeared; he seemed completely unfazed by the ribald catcalls he got from the half-naked trannies. There was a quick *salaam alaikum*, Eris handed over the envelope, the holy man nodded, and then he was gone.

'God, they're just as bad as those leather preman who used to shake you down,' I said with a laugh. 'What do you mean as bad as?!' she said. 'They *are* the leather preman. It's the same guys. That's their new look.'

The gangsters who were shaking Eris down had joined the Islamic Defenders Front, the FPI. This group appeared in 1998 when the authorities needed a roving squad of civilians it could call on to counter the student protestors. Jakarta's police commander admitted to giving the FPI money and logistical support. In return, FPI-related groups kept student activists far away from the meeting that laid the ground rules for electing Suharto's successor. The Islamic warriors also attacked the office of the Human Rights Commission which was investigating military abuses in East Timor. The arrangement made for strange bedfellows, really. The armed forces have a delicate relationship with political Islam. On the one hand the staunchly secular but equally staunchly right-wing army sees Islamic groups as a bulwark against socialism. On the other, it frets that Islamists, if they grow too strong, could threaten national unity. In 1998 the generals were prepared to cut a deal with the FPI simply because they were less threatening than the secular student movement that wanted to put the military's human rights record under the microscope.

Now that the political landscape has settled, however, the FPI and similar organizations can't rely only on providing mobs to politicians in need. These days, they generate income by protecting public morality. They selectively smash up those bars, nightclubs and brothels that don't pay them protection money. A friend in the music business told me they demonstrated against Lady Gaga only after her promoters refused to pay them to provide security for her concert. But they do not choose their targets indiscriminately. They never vent their wrath on the porn industry, for example, because it is said to be controlled by the military.

The FPI were quick to spot the market opportunity presented by democracy: an increasingly mouthy, freedom-loving electorate might begin to stand up against the old-fashioned political thugs such as Pancasila Youth. But no one can speak out openly against young men defending Islamic morality; they could move in on protection rackets with impunity.

To me, the FPI and their like are not a sign of the Arabization of Indonesian Islam, but rather the exact opposite. They have taken over the well-established function of preman, and they sell their holiness to the highest bidder. What could be more Indonesian than that?

The Prosperous Justice Party, the PKS, has undergone a similar transformation. Spawned of Islamic study groups at the better secular universities in Indonesia, with help from people who had studied in the Middle East, this party seemed at first to have an ideology as well as a useful social programme. The PKS worked hard in inner cities; they organized against endemic corruption; they outdid the government in responding to floods and disasters, and they provided services to those neglected by the self-serving politicians of the day.

Formed only in 2002, the PKS won over 7 per cent of the national vote in 2004, securing forty-five seats in parliament. They supported a controversial anti-pornography bill, and did even better at the next election. Then a PKS MP was photographed watching porn on his tablet during a plenary session of parliament, and the goody-two-shoes image started to unravel. As PKS politicians joined the cabinet and became knitted in to Indonesian politics, they lost their fervour for reform. The former party chairman starred in a huge corruption scandal centred on efforts to manipulate beef imports.

The Muslim Brotherhood-inspired PKS, now referred to as the *Partai Kotor Sekali* or Very Dirty Party, has been thoroughly Indonesianized, its formerly idealist members woven tightly into the country's deeply transactional political system. Patronage is proving an effective way of taming religious extremism.

Still Indonesia's urban middle classes worry. They point to a rash of regulations issued by local governments implementing sharia or Islam-inspired laws as further evidence that the country's secular basis is being undermined. The mayor who defeated my friend Nazaruddin in elections in the east Aceh city of Lhokseumawe came out with a classic: a by-law forcing women to protect their modesty by riding side-saddle behind a man on a motorbike. Newspaper headlines and tweet streams in Jakarta buzzed with outrage for days. But in the villages and small towns in parts of the country where they are most commonly issued, these religious regulations are seen as no different from any other rules: a simple annoyance. When the young man who had squired me around the trendier coffee shops of southern Aceh had made me hide my jilbab-less head from the Religious Police, I had expressed surprise that they took their duties so seriously. 'Only towards the end of the month, when their salaries are running out and they want to fine people,' Reza had replied. Indonesians routinely point out that most of the sharia by-laws don't affect the people who make the rules. There's lots of telling women how to dress, but no cutting off the hands of officials who steal from public coffers.

Michael Buehler, a political scientist who tracked sharia regulations in the early years of decentralization, told me that most of the religious by-laws were not put in place by politicians from Muslim parties at all. Rather, it was the old crocodiles from the secular parties of the Suharto era who, seeking legitimacy and support in this new democratic age, had been busy writing sharia into legislation. The game was to suck up to the village-level preachers who were thought to be able to deliver the votes of their congregation. The secular candidates promised that if they got elected with the help of the clerics' followers, they would pass any sharia by-laws that the preachers drew up.

Lately, though, Michael had noticed a change, especially in the rapidly urbanizing areas of West Java. 'Sharia regulations on Islamic clothing are *so* 2002,' he joked. Candidates in local elections now tell him that buying off the clerics with promises of sharia laws no longer works in any but the most deprived areas. The middle classes now pay more attention to Facebook and Twitter than they do to Muslim leaders, one candidate had told him. Politicians who want to play the religious card now need to push buttons that light up the interests of individual voters.

The former Governor of Jakarta, Fauzi Bowo, obviously believed that he could push people's electoral buttons by appealing to religious bigotry. He and I were once neighbours; his official residence was a block away from my former home in Jakarta. In September 2012, at the end of his first five-year term, he was up for re-election. Pak Fauzi and his running-mate both claim to be Betawi, the 'native' ethnic group in Jakarta. Both are Muslim. Their opponents were both 'outsiders'. Though the candidate for governor, Joko Widodo (aka Jokowi) was Muslim, he was from Central Java. If anything, that gave him an advantage over 'native' Fauzi, since 36 per cent of Jakarta's population is ethnic Javanese, against 28 per cent ethnic Betawi. But Jokowi's running-mate was doubly an outsider: of Chinese descent, and a Christian to boot.

During the campaign, Fauzi Bowo's team was blatant: Muslims were not allowed to vote for non-Muslim candidates, they said. Voting for anyone but Fauzi would be a vote against God, one well-known preacher told his congregation while the candidate stood at his side. Under Indonesia's electoral laws, neither politicians nor clerics are allowed to attack their opponents on religious or racial grounds during campaigns. But Fauzi just stood there and beamed.

I happened to be in Jakarta on election day, staying in my old house. I walked out the door, past the Governor's house, and a minute later was at the polling station set up in the park for the voters of Menteng, a neighbourhood of Dutch-era villas and neo-classical McMansions. Draped in satin, and lit with energy-saving electric lightbulbs, the polling station was furnished with a fridge to keep the drinks cold. It was quite the party atmosphere; ladies dressed in their best silk batiks sat picking delicately at fruit plates while their husbands made important-sounding calls on their BlackBerries. Behind them, uniformed maids kept an eye on children who were racing about on pink scooters or playing vampire games on their iPads.

I chatted with one or two of my neighbours; they fulminated about the incumbent's 'black' campaign and talked confidently of a new era. Then I got on my motorbike and drove fifteen minutes to Tanah Tinggi, a neighbourhood referred to by many of its residents as a slum. In fact, it's an eclectic mix. There are ramshackle houses cobbled together out of stolen sheets of zinc bolted onto the sides of Dutch-era villas built for 'native' civil servants. There are proud new two-storey houses in lurid colours, the fruit of someone's hard work in another, better-paid province. There are tenements straight out of a Charles Dickens novel, except that in Dickens's time, there wouldn't have been so many used hypodermics lying around.

All life seemed to be here, in the two metres of rat run between the tenement blocks. The centre was an open drain, handy for brushing teeth over, slopping cooking water into, and letting your children pee in – the shared bathrooms were way down the alley, near enough to smell but too far to go just for a pee. Ibu Nining, a smiley blob of a woman swathed in yellow, invited me into her home. It was about two metres square, with a ladder up one wall leading to an upstairs of the same size. The room was stacked high with belongings: a flatscreen TV, two huge speakers and a karaoke machine, a rice cooker. A little volcano of plastic toys had erupted, strewing headless dolls across the available floor space. In the middle of the room hung one of those wonderful baby-slings set on a big spring, so that one can bounce the kids to their dreams with a minimum of effort. In it, a boneless two-year-old gaped in sleep. I sat in the doorway – there wasn't room in the downstairs space for buxom Nining, the baby and me as well as all the stuff. Yet seven of them live in this house; Nining, her husband, the baby and another four children ranging up to sixteen years old.

On the wall opposite was an election sticker that read: 'Good Muslims vote for Muslims.' Under it, someone had drawn a handlebar moustache, the symbol of Fauzi Bowo, who was sometimes called 'Tache.★ It was getting close to poll-closing time. I asked Ibu Nining if she had voted, expecting her to stick up an inked little finger, the universal sign of civic duty discharged. But no. 'What's the point?' she said. 'For poor people like us, it's all the same. It makes no difference who is in charge.'

I picked my way through the needles and slops to the nearest polling station to witness the vote count. The Tanah Tinggi polling station did not have a fridge, satin tablecloths or fruit plates. When it began to rain, officials rushed about moving the

---

★ 'Tache once ordered my colleagues to pulp several thousand AIDS prevention posters because he didn't like the photo of him we had used. 'My moustache is crooked,' he explained.

ballot papers out of the streams of water that poured though the holes in the tarpaulin roof. But they were all neatly outfitted in batik shirts, all strung about with the ID badges of officialdom, and all extremely diligent in their task.

They had borrowed a karaoke machine over which to announce the results. At all elections in Indonesia, the ballot box is unlocked in public and every ballot paper is pulled out and held up to the light so that everyone can see which candidate has been 'punched'. Out came the first ballot: 'Candidate Number 1: Fauzi Bowo!' the official declared. ''Tache! 'Tache!' shouted the Governor's supporters. One vote got chalked up on a white board. Witnesses from each campaign kept tallies too.

Out came the second ballot. ''Tache! 'Tache!' The first seven or eight votes were for the incumbent Fauzi Bowo. So playing the religious card does work in Indonesia after all; the thought made me sour. Then there was a run for the challenger Jokowi and his unacceptably Christian partner. It went on like that, swinging in blocks of four or five votes. Perhaps groups of friends or family who came together all voted the same way. As the official reached deeper and deeper into the ballot box, the two candidates were neck and neck. Finally, he came to the last paper, pulled it out, and picked the box up to show us it was empty, like a magician showing us his hat before pulling a rabbit out of it.

The result was seventy-seven votes for the challenger Jokowi, seventy-five for the incumbent Fauzi Bowo, with two votes spoiled. Like Ibu Nining, half of the people registered at this polling station had not bothered to vote. I rushed off to the next nearest post, where the counting was still going on. There, the religiously divisive incumbent was winning comfortably. And at the next post, and the next.

Overall, Fauzi Bowo had won in Tanah Tinggi, one of the most crowded parts of Jakarta, where 40,000 souls are crushed into two-thirds of a kilometre squared. The exit polls, on the other hand, had already declared Jokowi the winner in the city as a whole. There was a triumphalist air to the Twitter stream: ''Tache: See what happens when you try to play with religion!'

When I got back to the posh polling station in front of the Governor's residence, they were just unpinning the last of the satin skirting, and loading the stacking chairs into a catering van. I asked the lead official what the result had been across the three polling stations in our little park: 574 to 186. 'Who to?' I asked. He gave me a withering look. 'Who do you think? Not *him!*' He nodded his head towards Fauzi Bowo's house and then turned his attention to his walkie-talkie.

So Jokowi, the Reformer, had won three-quarters of the vote in Menteng, home to the Have Everythings who were doing nicely from the status quo. The people in the slums of Tanah Tinggi, on the other hand, had chosen Fauzi Bowo, a man who had steadily neglected the poor during his twenty years in the upper echelons of the Jakarta administration, the last five of them as governor. It is with these people, the uneducated and the underemployed, the mothers who spend time keeping their toddlers away from used syringes, the fathers who make a living recycling bottles picked out of the garbage of the villas in Menteng, that the religion card seems to play well.

This is in part because where the state fails, the mosque often picks up the slack. The preacher's door is open to his congregation twenty-four hours a day. He provides small loans for emergency hospital treatment, he writes letters to get children scholarships in school. These gestures have lost currency among the growing middle class, which can take care of itself. But in poor parts of town, and in very rural areas, they still create a web of loyalty that makes the preacher a powerful man among the powerless.

When the Islamic Defenders Front demanded that the government deny Lady Gaga entry to Indonesia, Coordinating Minister for Legal, Political and Security Affairs Djoko Suyanto ignored them. People who didn't like her could just stay away from the concert, he said. *Boom!* the FPI appeared in front of his office to protest. When a journalist called to ask for his comment, he replied by text message: 'EGP'. EGP, from *emang gue pikirin*, is teenage slang that translates roughly as: 'Like I give a shit'. I thought at the time that it was a pretty good reflection of most Indonesians' attitude to extremism.

Most Indonesians seem to zone out groups like FPI because they feel life is too short to spend time worrying about a handful of zealots. A very few, however, are *forced* to worry, because those zealots are threatening their lives. Mosques belonging to minority sects are being torched by other Muslims, churches are being threatened and atheists jailed.

After my surreal visit to the sacred sex mountain of Gunung Kemukus, I trekked on eastwards as far as Lombok, the island to the east of Bali. Staunchly Muslim Lombok calls itself 'The Land of a Thousand Mosques. It is home to a good few of gopping vulgarity: great purple pimples rising from the rice fields, flying saucers in lime green parked next to the market, roadsides positively spiky with newly erected minarets, some of them less than 500 metres from an existing mosque. Lombok is also one of an increasing number of places in Indonesia where members of the Ahmadiyah community have been evicted from their village. The Ahmadiyah are a tightly knit subset of Muslims who stick together, invest in education, work hard, and tend to succeed. They have been around since before independence – the composer of Indonesia's national anthem was an Ahmadiyah – but the zealots have only recently turned on them.

Some talk of the Ahmadiyah as harmless crackpots, a bit like Scientologists. But a fair number of people I met, including a midwife in Lombok, a bus driver in Surabaya and a cop in the East Java island of Madura, grew apoplectic at the mere mention of the sect. All rushed to tell me that they were apostates, spreading false teachings. What false teachings? I asked, over and over. 'They are just wrong. They are out to confuse the public. It's dangerous,' the midwife had said. No one could ever tell me how the Ahmadiyah's beliefs differed from their own.

In fact, the sect is stained in the eyes of the back-to-Medina Sunni purists by the original sin of its founder. Mirza Ghulam

Ahmad, a scholar in the British-India era, was a great self-promoter and declared himself a prophet. To Sunni purists, that's sacrilege. There has been no prophet since Mohammad; anyone who believes otherwise cannot call themselves Muslim. Compounding their error, the Ahmadiyah are pacifist, they reject the notion of physical *jihad* in favour of a Holy War waged by the pen. But most of the people who take exception to them don't even seem to know this.

Some years ago the villagers of Ketapang in western Lombok burned a community of around thirty Ahmadiyah families out of their homes; I decided to pay them a visit. I stopped at a school to ask directions to the village. 'You won't be welcome,' warned the kindergarten head. And she was right. Ketapang grows like a tumour off a side road in rural Lombok, self-contained, hostile. I parked my bike at the roadside and walked in. A wall of stares. Silence.

I found a coffee stall arranged under a spreading mango tree. Three young lads wearing football strip – Juventus, Barça and one I didn't recognize – were lying around playing with their cell phones. I ordered a coffee from the stall owner. She looked up from her grinding stone, then went back to smushing up chillies. I waited. She smushed. Someone else came in and asked for a Fanta; she served him straight away. Then she went back to smushing. I waited. After some minutes, one of the lads, with hair spiky enough to put your eye out, said something in the local Sasak language and she grunted and served me a coffee. I tried to start a conversation with the lads about football, but it was like pulling teeth. I moved on to the elections – various candidates for village head had strung their banners up between houses. Nothing doing.

All around the village it was the same. Everyone was monosyllabic, suspicious, guarded. One woman did answer my questions about the work she was doing: the whole village seems to subsist by making brooms out of bamboo poles and coconut fibre matting, an occupation that brings in 3,600 rupiah a day, about forty cents. But no one would talk about anything more general, like education, or corruption, or religion. And for some reason I just couldn't bring myself simply to ask: 'So, what happened to your Ahmadiyah neighbours?'

If the victors were this tight-lipped, I didn't hold out much hope of getting a good chat going with the victims.

Lombok's long-suffering Ahmadiyah community, it turned out, were the polar opposite of their former neighbours: effusively welcoming, though apologetic about their surroundings. They were living in a dilapidated government complex in Lombok's main city, Mataram, about twenty-five kilometres from their village. The 'Transito' had been built in the 1970s as a stopover for transmigrants from Java or Bali as they headed further east. Now, plywood peeled in great sheets off the ceiling and buckets on the floor caught the rain that dribbled through the roof.

The whole community lives in a single large hall, divided up by thick brown curtains which don't reach the ceiling. This makes two rows of 'houses', each about two metres by three metres. Ibu Nur, who had been especially welcoming, pulled back the curtain to show me her home as we passed. It looked like a cross between Ibu Nining's tenement in Tanah Tinggi and the refugee camp that I had seen after the mudflows in Ternate: plastic storage boxes stacked up against the wall, school uniforms hung from a raffia clothes line, a sleeping mat rolled neatly back so that the kids could do their homework on the floor.

She and her family had lived here for almost seven years.

Nur invited me to come to evening prayers; everyone was heading out the back of the hall to a tiny prayer room which was squashed in next to the communal loos. Kids jostled to get up under the roof; latecomers overflowed into the courtyard and prayed in the rain. There was no loudspeaker, no sermonizing. A community elder, Pak Syahudin, led the prayers. Everyone else followed, and that was that. After prayers, as we sat in the gathering dusk watching the rain plop through the roof, I asked jokingly whether this counted as one of the mosques in this Land of 1,000 Mosques. 'Hah! People here are so Holier Than

Thou, but it's what's on the inside that counts,' said Nur.

I asked why they thought the villagers of Ketapang had taken time out from making brooms to attack them. Nur and the other young women in the group put it down to 'social jealousy', a vague but ubiquitous term used in any situation where one community comes into conflict with some other group that is doing better economically. The Ahmadiyah had moved to the west Lombok village of Ketapang after being run out of the east of the island. They were better educated than the locals, they had better contacts and they worked harder. They got richer. It is the story of migrants all over Indonesia.

Pak Syahudin let them speak, then disagreed. For him, the spark was political. 'Eight times we've been hounded out of whatever village we were in. *Eight times.* And every single time it is after the visit of some political bigwig or other.' He mentioned a cabinet minister from the Islamic Moon and Star Party and a candidate for bupati from the PKS. Syahudin believed the attacks were deliberately provoked by people who thought there were votes to be gained by taking an uncompromising stance against a religious minority.

It's quite likely that religious bigotry does produce votes in very local elections, where prejudices are more easily manipulated. But it doesn't work at the national level. In the privacy of the poll booth, most Indonesians show no interest in being governed by people who want to mix politics and religion. In fact, support for Islamic parties, highest in the 1955 elections at around 44 per cent, has been on a steady slide since properly democratic elections resumed in 1999. In the 2009 elections, fewer than 30 per cent of voters opted for Islamic parties: the big three winners were all staunchly secular. And the opinion polls were predicting an even worse outcome for religious parties in 2014.

Despite this, the national government has recently done little to uphold the law and protect religious minorities. In 2011 over a thousand people attacked about twenty sect members in an Ahmadiyah mosque in West Java, killing three of them. Police arrested some of the mob. Then trucks of white-robed supporters with bullhorns started rocking up at the police station, threatening apostates and all those who support them. As a result, the police did not charge any of the attackers with murder. A dozen men were sentenced to a few months in jail for minor offences; the longest sentence went to one of the surviving Ahmadiyah members, for punching a man who came at him with a machete.

Sitting outside her miserable home in Lombok's Transito, Nur put the government's failure to protect minorities down to sheer cowardice. 'They're terrified of demonstrations. It's as simple as that.'

Some thirteen years into Indonesia's raucously democratic experiment, it was more or less a given that organizations such as the FPI would be on the streets in a flash if the government was seen to be defending heterodoxy. Jakarta might step in to protect religious minorities if it thought the electorate would take to the streets demanding religious pluralism, but that won't happen. Most Indonesians support the idea of religious freedom in general, but members of the great orthodox Sunni majority are not going to storm the barricades and confront a handful of fanatics who have shown that they are willing to maim and kill, just to defend the rights of minorities that they think are crackpots. They just don't care that much. Like the Coordinating Minister of Legal, Political and Security Affairs, most Indonesians don't really give a shit what other people believe.

Map M: Java

SUMATRA

JAVA SEA

INDIAN OCEAN

BANTEN

Jakarta

WEST JAVA

Cirebon

Pekalongan

Tinggarjaya

CENTRAL JAVA

Bandungan

Semarang

Solo

JAVA

Yogyakarta

Gunung Kidul

YOGYAKARTA SPECIAL DISTRICT

From Pontianak

Surabaya

Sampang

MADURA

Englishtown

EAST JAVA

Ijen Volcano

BALI

N

0km 60km 120km 180km

13

The Other Indonesia

I had been on the roads and high seas of Indonesia for a year before I arrived in Java (that's not counting occasional dashes through Jakarta, which is almost a nation apart). I had visited twenty provinces and all four of the biggest islands – Sumatra, Sulawesi and the Indonesian parts of New Guinea and, most recently, Borneo – as well as dozens of smaller islands, some too little even to appear on the map. By the time I had clambered off the boat from Pontianak, my thoughts about Java had been coloured over with the opinions that wash around all these other places. Java is a place of smooth, well-lit highways along which people in business suits drive sparkling SUVs to meetings where they will seal important business deals. In Java everyone gets a great education and has access to wonderful hospitals, although confusingly some of them are still rice farmers who work unreasonably hard to squeeze an incredible three crops a year out of their fertile soil.

The Javanese will be unfailingly polite, I was told by blunter tribes, it's always *inggih, inggih, inggih,* yes, yes, yes, but watch out because before you know it they'll have stabbed you with a *kris* dagger they had behind their back. They're not as open as us, not as friendly, said people from most other parts of Indonesia (even the unfriendly parts). It's because of the hierarchy thing.

I had arrived in Java at Semarang, which sits more or less dead centre along the north coast of the island. It was four in the morning when my Pelni boat from Kalimantan steamed in. We

345

lined up on the dock next to three much larger Pelni ships, two of which had also just arrived. It was pandemonium. There was the usual stampede of porters up the narrow gangplank just as passengers shoved and jostled their way down. This time, though, there was an added bottleneck caused by people bending over and taking off their shoes, rolling up their trousers, tucking their skirts up above the knees without losing their dignity too completely, hiking luggage up to shoulder height. Because every single gangplank stretched down on to a dock transformed into a small lake. Every passenger had to wade knee-deep through about ten metres of water to get to dry land. I asked one of the boat stewards what was going on. 'It's high tide, Bu,' he said. Twice in any given twenty-four-hour period, the docks of one of Java's biggest ports are under water. At least one of the notions that other Indonesians have about Java – 'Those Javanese get all the infrastructure' – lay puddled at my feet.

Semarang was once the largest port in the Netherlands East Indies, the place from which all the sugar, tea and coffee of the rich lands of Central Java began their trip to the kitchen cupboards of northern Europe. Now, it is one of the biggest industrial centres in Indonesia; its hinterlands bottle Coke and Pepsi, they make dolls and pharmaceuticals, furniture and clothing. Its port has been overtaken by Jakarta and Surabaya, but it is still the third largest in Java, an important hub for cargo as well as passengers. And yet it wasn't just the dock that was in need of repair.

Just after dawn I took a motorbike taxi into town. We ploughed through the muddy water that swirled about in potholes of indeterminate depth. In front of us, a high-school student on a bicycle hit a submerged rock, tottered and fell. When he picked himself up he looked like one of those blocks of vanilla ice-cream that has been dipped in a chocolate coating on one side, half white, half brown. A tear cleared a path through the mud on his left cheek.

Semarang is sinking, and the old colonial quarter, perhaps the loveliest in Indonesia, is sinking fastest of all – at the rate of twelve centimetres a year, according to Megaputri Megaradjasa, aka Ibu Jenny. I'd seen Jenny's name in the newspaper I was reading on the boat; she was organizing a festival to celebrate the heritage of Old Semarang, complete with a classic car parade and traditional games and foods. I'd missed the festival by a day, but I went for a wander around the Old City anyway. It was both glorious and sad. The most iconic building, the Gereja Blenduk or Church of the Dome, dates from 1753. It has been beautifully restored; at night it glows like a piece of amber, preserving the dreams of colonists past. The church, with its copper dome and colourful stained glass windows, stands proud between two clock towers which proclaim, morning, noon and night but in perfect unison, that it is nine o'clock.

Most of the buildings in the Old City were built in the late 1800s and early 1900s by the grand enterprises of the day − trading companies, plantations, banks, though there were government offices too. A few of them have been given facelifts. But these rejuvenated belles are pressed shoulder to shoulder with others that have been left to their tropical fate. A shutter flaps loose from an elegant, arched window in the facade of a building that stands as though intact. Through the window, we glimpse the gaping hole where the roof once was. Next door, a wrought-iron staircase spirals up into nothingness, its upper reaches gnawed away by rust. Grasses cascade out of broken drainpipes, trees burst out of cracks high in the walls of once splendid palaces of commerce, obscuring the ubiquitous signs: FOR SALE/RENT.

Around the decaying grandeur, life goes on. People have built tiny houses out of salvaged wood and broken tiles; they lean Gaudiesque against the crumbling wall of some long-forgotten government department. A small child stands patiently in a plastic bucket in the middle of the cobbled street while his father bathes him. Under a beautiful wrought-iron balustrade, a team of men unpack their pop-up restaurant, serving rich chicken soup to a stream of Chinese businessmen in SUVs; the street stall has its own director of parking.

Semarang was more beautiful that I had imagined it would be, and more neglected. I tracked down Ibu Jenny in Toko Oen, a coffee shop started by her family in 1936. She said she was pleased by the success of the festival, which she had arranged in part as an excuse to bring in people with expertise in heritage and preservation. She had not really known what to expect: 'There's a general feeling that we Indonesians are not so interested in history or heritage, especially colonial heritage,' she said. But all the events were packed.

The goal of Jenny's Oen Foundation is to get Semarang declared a World Heritage Site by 2020. When I arrived, she was chatting with a Dutch professor of conservation who had spoken at the conference. He was huge on every axis, with satisfactorily Mad Professor hair and the look of a man who appreciates a tankard of beer or two. He was also charming, erudite and informative.

When the VOC started building Semarang in 1678, the city was protected from flooding by a system of canals that still exists, but is no longer up to the job. The real trouble is much more recent, the professor said. To slake the thirst of a booming population and of all the factories that squat on the outskirts of town, Semarang has been pumping fresh water out from under itself. The sea was getting sucked in to fill the void, rising gently around the ankles of Semarang's residents, beginning in the Old City, which is closest to the shore. That sapped people's willingness to invest in restoring the old buildings. 'Good restoration is a huge investment,' said Jenny. 'It's hard to ask companies who own the buildings to put in all that money if their employees will have to swim to work.'

Who does own the buildings? I asked. Both Jenny and the professor rolled their eyes. Land ownership is always a complicated business in Indonesia, especially if it involves property that was Dutch-owned at independence. Many businesses just scarpered, some changed their names, others were nationalized but without any agreed transfer of assets. On paper, many of these buildings belong to companies that have gone bankrupt or have been subsumed by giant conglomerates such as Unilever. Even if they could be sure of keeping the floors dry, most firms would be loath to invest in restoring these buildings if there were any chance that ownership could be disputed.

How supportive was the local government of Jenny's conservation efforts? I asked. More rolling of eyes. The Mayor of Semarang was in jail in Jakarta; he had been convicted of corruption a couple of months earlier. 'With this government, there's only one priority,' said Jenny, miming putting money into her shirt pocket, 'and it is not preservation of the colonial city.'

The professor explained the only viable solution: they would have to build a 'polder', a sort of giant dyke, around the Old City and pump water constantly out of it. I thought of the stinking canals designed to protect Jakarta from flooding. Every year, tonnes of garbage pile up in the canal; every year, when the rains come, the garbage drifts down and blocks the flood-gates, rendering them more or less useless. Every year, the city floods. Any flood-protection system in Semarang would have to be pretty low-maintenance, and be able to tolerate high volumes of trash. 'It's fine, the technology can incorporate waste management,' said the Dutchman. 'It's fine, we can hire people to pick out the garbage before it clogs the drainage system,' said the Indonesian. In retrospect, Jenny's response seemed to be the more realistic of the two. Though infrastructure was certainly a great deal better in Java than it was anywhere else in Indonesia, it was still far below par. And it doesn't seem that Java's pool of cheap labour will run dry any time soon.

A friend in Jakarta put me in touch with her cousin Evi in Semarang. The family owns a chain of fast-food stores specializing in Es Teler, a drink/dessert/meal that dumps avocado, jackfruit, coconut juice and a variety of gelatinous, wormy and blobby things onto a mountain of shaved ice to form a curiously intoxicating sugar-bomb. Evi was going shopping for a couple of tonnes of avocados and a stock of palm sugar and wondered if I'd like to come along.

I was actually keen to spend a bit of time in a 'real' city. Despite myself, I wanted to go to a nice, air-conditioned mall where I could drink a cappuccino made with fresh milk and no sugar. I wanted to go to the movies, and to spend time in a decent bookshop. I wanted to sit somewhere with free, high-speed wifi, talk to my friends on Skype, tweet, write blog posts, and do all the other things that young Indonesians do in the big cities of Java. But I couldn't resist palm-sugar shopping.

A relative drove Evi, her husband and me out of the Old City and up into the hills. Posh spas, garden restaurants and colonnaded mansions gave way to neat middle-class suburbs. Then came a rash of more affordable estates, boxy row houses fresh from the modular plans of the developers. Beyond those were the warehouses and factories that were sucking Semarang dry and causing it to sink. After that we reached open fields, heaving with chillies and ginger, with tobacco and soybeans, with roses and eggplant. I hadn't seen anything like this anywhere else in Indonesia. It is the reverse of the chaotic 'shove a stick in the ground and throw a couple of corn kernels in the hole' approach of Adonara or Halmahera. There was not a weed to be seen. Crops were planted in careful equidistant rows. The fields were patterned like a woven ikat cloth; chillies were banked neatly up and interlaced with rows of cherry tomatoes; red roses faced off against pink and white. Not an inch of soil was wasted. But there was nothing industrial about it, either. Families of farmers were tending their own fields; they each decided what to plant and when, based on market prices and the amount of effort they felt like putting in. Those that worked hardest and made most money often set up as first-line wholesalers, buying up crops from other villagers and selling them on to factories in Semarang.

Ibu Sanna was one such. We went to meet her because Evi was thinking of working with her to wholesale ginger. Impeccably coiffed and made-up, wearing a dusky spandex top threaded with silver and not sweating a drop, she walked us in the midday heat through her fields of chillies, tobacco and ginger. She had recently been buying up ginger from other farmers as well, selling it on to Sidomuncul, one of the biggest manufacturers of Javanese traditional medicines, including *Tolak Angin*, a ginger- and honey-based tonic. In the same way that English speakers 'catch a cold', Indonesians are 'entered by the wind'. To avoid this *masuk angin*, they drink Tolak Angin, which literally means Refuse the Wind. I carry it around the world with me – along with Ibuprofen it forms the totality of my medicine chest – and I was curious to see where it was made. In Semarang, I had waltzed along to a Sidomuncul factory expecting to be able to blag my way past the guards and go and chat with the managers as I had everywhere else in Indonesia. I was turned firmly away, underlining the scale and professionalism of companies in Java compared with many I had stumbled into elsewhere.

The scale was a problem for Sanna too; she had contracted to deliver twenty-five tonnes of ginger a month, but wasn't always able to scrape together that much from local farmers. She didn't have the capital or the storage space to stockpile ginger so that she could be sure of delivering what she had promised, and in the end had given up the contract. Evi, one tier up in Indonesia's gently graduated ziggurat of a supply chain, wanted to buy up whatever Sanna could collect; she'd ensure the rest of the stock for giant consumers like Sidomuncul from other sources and her own stockpiles.

We'd come to see Sanna not just to discuss ginger but because she said she could take us to get good quantities of *gula aren*, the crumbly brown sugar boiled down from the sap of the aren palm *arenga pinnata*, a key ingredient in a really good Es Teler sugar-bomb. Ibu Sanna changed from her cocktail-party top into an even more elegant outfit, a full-length dress in cotton jersey top-ped with a matching jacket that hugged tight over her bust and flowed generously over her rump. It was a classic Javanese mix; unimpeachably modest, but undeniably sexy.

While waiting for Ibu Sanna to touch up her make-up, I wandered around her neighbourhood. Inside the houses, cell phones were plugged in to charge, and TVs were thinly covered by knitted doilies. But from the outside, the scene seemed not to have changed for generations. Rice, taro root and other unidentifiable starches were spread out to dry in plaited baskets balanced on the terracotta tiles above wooden or bamboo-weave walls. A red steel wheelbarrow looked jarringly modern leaning up against one of the village houses.

In another film-set village, we spotted a man walking along with a fat bamboo cylinder hanging off either end of a carrying pole that bounced over his shoulder. On one side he'd hung a full jerrycan. To counter-balance it on the other side he'd slung a jack-fruit, freshly cut with the large machete that was strapped to the small of his back. We followed him home.

This gentleman's bamboo cylinders and jerrycan were filled with sap which he had just collected from the aren trees. 'Try it, it's delicious!' he insisted. His wife dipped a glass into the tube. It came out filled with a viscous piss-coloured liquid in which floated a couple of dead bees and other unidentifiable detritus. She held it out to Evi, who looked queasy. I took the glass and drank. It was warmish, sweetish, undistinguished.

The gentleman we intercepted sold his sugar at 17,000 rupiah a kilo, but he had no stock. He directed us to a nearby village. There we found a beautiful girl in a red blouse sitting on a porch, brushing out her waist-length hair: it was a scene from a Zhang Yimou film. But as soon as she heard what we wanted, she lost her languor. She flicked her hair into a bun, and turned businesslike. Yes, she had sugar; yes, it was top quality. In the dirt-floored kitchen, the chicken that was scratching around under a huge bamboo bell-jar did not look at the chicken that was being plucked for the pot. We inspected the sap bubbling over a wood-fired stove. After six or seven hours it would be poured into bowls to set. We turned over smooth, firmly compacted cakes of sugar in our hands. Evi agreed that it was top quality. Could the girl rustle up fifty kilos of it?

Yes. And the price? Twenty thousand a kilo. No, said Evi, not the retail price, the wholesale price. Twenty thousand, replied the Girl with the Long Hair. Evi and Sanna both started in on her in rapid-fire Javanese, with Evi every now and then shaking her head and repeating in Indonesian, 'At that price, Jakarta won't take it.' She offered 18,000. The next step in the negotiation was obviously to make tea, fry up bananas, and go through a lot of polite chit-chat. I went for a walk around the village. The Girl with the Long Hair went off and collected fifty kilos of sugar from various households. They started weighing it up, suspending it in batches off a scale the like of which I had seen in many rural kitchens in Indonesia: a tilted rod, a large hook, and a sliding brass weight. The girl still insisted on 20,000 a kilo. Last price. No discussion.

Evi's husband began another complicated game on his phone. The cousin-driver smoked. All the wheeling and dealing, the polite chit-chat and hard-edged ultimatums came from the mouths of women. It mirrored what I had found in more domestic situations elsewhere in Indonesia: the people in formal positions of power – the bupatis, the village heads, the religious leaders, the shamans – were all men. But it was usually the women who actually decided how many buffalo would be slaughtered, which rice fields would be sold off, which of the children would go to college.

As the negotiations dragged on, I went for another walk, stopping to chat with a group of women who were peeling onions for Indofood, the makers of Indomie noodles. They were paid 500 rupiah a kilo, peeled weight – five cents. The quickest workers could do ten kilos in a day. When I came back, Evi's husband was loading the sugar into the car. How much did you pay? I asked Evi, in English. 'Eighteen, of course. Poor girl, she's never had a sale this big before, she doesn't know the difference between retail and wholesale.'

The margins of business here were every bit as slim as among the tuna fishermen in Northern Sulawesi. But in Java goods seemed to pass through even more pairs of hands, racking up a few cents each time. On the one hand, you might argue that these tiny margins illustrate the efficiencies of a competitive market. On the other hand, they might just reflect the fact that in Java, time (and thus labour) is valued at practically nil. The Girl with the Long Hair would make around five dollars for two hours of chatting, bargaining and frying bananas. Evi would make twice that before costs, which would be absorbed by piggy-backing this on our next mission, the avocados.

It didn't seem much until I did the maths on the onion ladies. They were earning fifty cents a day.

Earlier on my travels I had crossed paths with Ahmad Tohari, one of Indonesia's most famous writers. He had invited me to visit him at home when I got to Java. So from the avocado-growing area of Bandungan, I headed south-west towards Tinggarjaya, a small town in the Banyumas region of Central Java. By the time I reached him I was in shock.

Quite by chance, I had hopped on a bus run by the Efisiensi chain. There were no sick bags hanging from the ceiling. There were no chickens in the luggage rack. There were no cracks in the windscreen held together by stickers of reclining nurses bursting from their bikinis. In place of the bus lout with spiky mullet hair, Monster Mash shorts and Attitude was a smiling girl in a neatly pressed uniform who brought me a bottle of cold water and an individually wrapped bun filled with red bean paste. I had a comfortable seat all to myself, for the whole trip. If I wanted to watch the video that played on the drop-down screens overhead, I could use the earphones provided. Otherwise, I could enjoy the silence: no dangdut even. The bus stopped at designated times in designated places, all of which had rows of sparklingly clean loos. We didn't break down once, or go off-piste to visit the driver's auntie. And the whole journey, covering a couple of hundred kilometres, cost all of 50,000 rupiah, about a quarter of what I had paid in other islands to cover the same distance in a rust-bucket filled with sacks of rice and trussed-up goats. Java was definitely different.

I found Pak Tohari sitting with his grandson and a couple of young journalists on the veranda of his house. He was dressed for Friday prayers, in a simple sarong and a striped shirt. He

asked about my recent travels and soon I was telling him about
Pak Askiman, the forthright Dayak who ran the Department of
Public Works in Sintang and who had been less than compli-
mentary about Indonesia's Javanese rulers.

'The Javanese colonized us with their mentality,' the Dayak
had said. 'For them there is only one right way, and that is to do
whatever the boss wants, whether or not he meets your needs.'
The first task of decentralization, in Pak Askiman's view, was to
throw off this mentality. 'People will always try to please the boss,
of course,' he had said. 'But in our culture, we have a right to
expect something back.'

I asked Pak Tohari if he thought Javanese culture was really so
hierarchical.

He pointed to the road which ran in front of us. His wife's
mother grew up in this house, he said, and when she was a girl,
the adipati would sometimes pass by in his carriage. The adipati
was a sort of super-bupati. Though he was actually a glorified
servant of the Dutch, he behaved like a sultan. His carriage
would be preceded by retainers who would march along ringing
bells. 'When they heard the bells, everyone would have to rush
out of their houses and bow down at the side of the road. They
weren't even allowed to look at the adipati, they were forbidden
to raise their faces to the sun.' Pak Tohari shook his head in a sort
of disgusted amazement. 'That was in the 1940s, mind you. The
1940s!'

The writer spoke heatedly of the cancerous effect of this kind
of feudalism, which he said was most firmly entrenched in the
courts of Yogyakarta and Solo, further east. He pointed to the
language of the sultanate towns, with their fine gradations of
respect. The young journalists that were with us nodded sagely;
they were helping Pak Tohari with a magazine intended to
revive the much more egalitarian form of Javanese spoken in
Banyumas.

It dawned on me for the first time that 'Javanese' is almost as
slippery a term as 'Indonesian'. I had been throwing it around
too casually. I did make a distinction between the Javanese and

the Sundanese, who live in West Java, speak a completely different language, and even drink their tea without sugar. West of them again sat the people of Banten; they sold themselves around the archipelago as faith healers and these days do a roaring trade in penis enlargement. But I had always thought that pretty much anyone who spoke Javanese as their first language – most of the 73 million people who live in the eastern two-thirds of the island – could fairly be described as sharing 'Javanese culture'.

Pak Tohari set me straight. Banyumas culture is less snobby and hierarchical than the Yogyakarta/Solo brand of Javanese, he said. It was the two courts right in the centre of the island that had, over the centuries, infected the country with a crippling bowing-and-scraping, the writer believed, as well as an obsessive concern for form over substance. Once the sultans had become paid functionaries of the Dutch and had no real politics to occupy them, descendants of rival princes codified all of their historical rivalries into tiny variations in the way a dancer bent her fingers back, or in the colour of batik that a prince of a certain rank was allowed to wear.

I had encountered this concern for form way back in 1989, when Reuters sent me to cover the Sultan of Yogyakarta's coronation. Sukarno, who considered most sultans to be lackeys of the Dutch, had allowed their courts to fall into a coma after independence. But the Sultan Hamengkubuwono IX had stood up firmly for the republic against his Dutch paymasters, and his court had stayed very much alive. The beloved Sultan died in 1988; now his son was taking his place on the throne of the central Javanese city.

We had to wear court dress to get into the palace. When I emerged from my hotel room in a sarong and a long, fitted kebaya blouse, the Reuters photographer Enny was waiting for me. Her hair was swept up into a traditional bun, enlarged by a huge fake *konde* hairpiece hung about with jasmine flowers. She was wearing a sarong in a white and brown design typical of Yogya, and a brocade kebaya. The look would have been perfect Javanese lady of high society, but for the two huge Nikon cameras slung across the kebaya like ammunition belts. I laughed.

Enny, on seeing me, did not laugh at all. 'You can't wear that!' Apparently, the batik that I had chosen was from Solo, another central Javanese sultanate with a *kraton*, or palace, about an hour's drive away. It had split from Yogya in the late eighteenth century and they had been at their culture wars ever since. Wearing a Solo batik to a Yogya coronation would have been like going to a royal wedding in Britain wearing a pair of knickers on my head. I changed.

Tens of thousands of people crushed the streets of Yogyakarta to watch the new Sultan pass by. He was in a horse-drawn carriage garlanded with jasmine flowers and topped with a giant gilded crown. Above the carriage twirled a golden umbrella which is the Sultan's badge of office. Within the palace complex, his passage was preceded by a procession of faithful retainers in a succession of unlikely uniforms. There were musketeers in Smurf hats carrying colonial-era rifles, a troupe of red-jacketed drummers with Napoleonic tricorns, a phalanx of spear-carriers in black stovepipe hats. The palace women carried peacock-feather fans and marched in various permutations of breast-cloth, brocade and batik which doubtless spoke volumes about their status. (In earlier, more polygamous times, the Sultan would indicate which of his wives he wished to have 'serve' him on any given day by sending her a breast-cloth bordered with the triangular mountain motif.) A group of dwarves and albinos, and even one or two albino dwarves, formed part of the procession; they strutted along in truncated sarongs and shiny red fezzes, bare-chested, apparently adding to the Sultan's power.

The Sultan himself, a modern man who later chaired the Indonesian Chamber of Commerce and fancied himself a candidate for President of Indonesia, sat on a throne on a raised dais. He wore a black velvet jacket encrusted with golden threadwork and a long string of pearls. A huge starburst of diamonds glittered on his chest. He sat absolutely expressionless as hundreds

of courtiers prostrated themselves before him. The more aristo-
cratic were allowed to raise themselves to kiss his knee.

Now, a quarter of a century later, sultanates are being revived
across the land, part of the explosion of interest in local identities.
When the Sultan of Solo invited his neighbours from Yogya
over for a Kraton Festival in 1995, it was largely a local affair. In
2012 the sultanate of Buton in Bau-Bau hosted representatives
from 120 kratons around Indonesia. I had visited a few of these
'palaces' – most were dilapidated wooden buildings filled with
crispy photos of past glory. Comparing their incumbents to the
Sultan of Yogyakarta was like comparing some exiled Mittel-
European royal living in a bedsit in North London to Queen
Elizabeth II.

The Javanese writer Pak Tohari agreed completely with the
Dayak bureaucrat Pak Askiman about the legacy of all this sub-
jugation: a culture in which everyone seeks only to serve their
boss, and in which the unaccountable boss has only his own
interests at heart.

This has wormed its way into the language. *Asal Bapak Senang*
– 'As long as Father is Happy', usually shortened to ABS – means
that you never had to think beyond carrying out the instructions
of your superiors. And there's *belum dapat petunjuk*, too: 'I haven't
yet received my instructions.' I used to hear these phrases all the
time from bureaucrats in the Suharto era, when I was trying
to get information about some development plan or financial
deregulation package. Without orders from above, no one would
even talk about anything, let alone do anything.

Even the man who presided over this culture of craven obedience got fed up with it. In the early 1990s, Suharto launched
a campaign against the *'petunjuk'* culture. He instructed his Vice
President to instruct his civil servants to stop waiting around
for instructions, to take more initiative. I thought this would
make an interesting feature for Reuters. I called the Vice President's office, and asked his chief of staff if he could arrange an

interview on the subject. 'I'm afraid that won't be possible,' the chief of staff said. 'Why not?' I asked.

'*Belum dapat petunjuk, Bu*' – I haven't yet received instructions.

There seems to be a contradiction at the heart of Javanese culture. On the one hand, there's a fundamental egalitarianism in Javanese village life because everyone mucks in together to get as much rice as they can out of this crowded land. On the other hand, you have the extraordinarily hierarchical structure of power, everyone bowing in the service of their superior. Perhaps this explains a central political contradiction, too: the rapid growth of Indonesia's communist party in post-independence Indonesia, and the ease with which Suharto re-established political hierarchies after the backlash.

Pak Tohari was an observer of that backlash. His trilogy of novels set in 1965, published in English under the title *The Dancer*, was the first major work by an Indonesian writer to describe the turbulence of the time. Masquerading as the story of a pubescent *ronggeng* dancer who ministers to the libido of her many admirers, it actually addresses the military's role in the indiscriminate killing of alleged communists. I asked the writer why he thought the communists grew so popular, then were so utterly reviled.

'For the *wong cilik* [the 'little people'], well, no one else had ever tried to do anything good for them; many people were drawn to their promises of land reform, of education,' said Pak Tohari. But, he said, the communist PKI party was also very divisive. They persecuted Muslim preachers and vilified the Three Devils of the City (capitalist-bureaucrats, corruptors and fraudulent manipulators) and the Seven Devils of the Village (landlords, traders, middlemen, extortionists, bandits, money lenders and usurers). Tohari's own father was deemed a land-owning devil, although his one and a half hectares couldn't possibly produce enough to feed his twelve children.

By mid-1966 at least half a million Indonesians lay dead.*

---

* A pall of silence since then has meant that there has been no official reckoning of the number of dead. Estimates range from 200,000 to over one million. A

Some had been over-zealous communists. Others were just men who had looked sideways at someone else's daughter, women who had once embarrassed a pupil in the schoolroom, businesspeople who had refused a loan to the village drunk.

After the slaughter: silence.

'I waited and waited for the big names to write about what had happened,' said Pak Tohari. Nothing. Finally, he couldn't stand it any longer. 'I had seen people shot with my own eyes. I couldn't just keep quiet.' He knew he could not just wade in and write about politics. 'That's why I had to wrap it up in porn, in all that sexy *ronggeng* stuff. I didn't even introduce the violence until the end of the second book.' Hence the central figure of Srintil, a teenager who restores the self-respect of her village with her fame as a dancer in the titillating and culturally embedded *ronggeng* tradition. Her childhood sweetheart runs off and joins the army in despair when she starts to receive 'guests', as all such dancers did. Later, the young soldier is involved in the killing of villagers accused of being communists.

'Srintil was inspired partly by that woman over there,' Pak Tohari said, shooting his lips out to indicate a house across the road from his home. 'When she was young, she used to go around with a bullhorn shouting communist propaganda.' I asked how she had survived. 'She was very, very pretty.'

Still now, many Indonesians are reluctant to confront the carnage that brought Suharto to power. As recently as 2007, the Attorney General ordered that stocks of fourteen school textbooks should be burned because they didn't lay the blame for the events of 1965 firmly at the feet of the PKI.

In 2012, nearly five decades after the fact, the National Commission on Human Rights prepared a report which described the killings of 1965–6 as

---

careful review of these estimates is provided by Roger Cribb in his paper of 2001. See Robert Cribb, 'How Many Deaths? Problems in the statistics of massacre in Indonesia (1965–1966) and East Timor (1975–1980)'. In Ingrid Wessel and Georgia Wimhofer (eds), *Violence in Indonesia*. Hamburg: Abera, 2001, pp. 82–98.

a state policy to annihilate the members and followers of the Indonesian Communist Party . . . leading to murder, extermination, enslavement, forced removal, deprivation of liberty/arbitrary imprisonment, torture, rape, persecution and forced disappearance.

The Attorney General promptly rejected the report. His colleague, the coordinating minister for politics, legal, and security affairs, said the military had simply done what it needed to do to save the nation.

When I wondered at the savagery of 1965, Ahmad Tohari had said, 'Carnage is a sort of Javanese tradition,' and pointed to the character of Kumbokarno in the *wayang* shadow-puppet plays, a noble hero who fights with his wicked brother and gets killed. The *dalang*, the puppet-master, dismembers the character limb by limb. 'Then he rips his head off. And the crowd absolutely loves it, they're baying for it,' said Tohari.

The wayang is so frequently used by foreigners as a metaphor for all that is illogical or inexplicable about Indonesia that it has become a bit of a joke, an outdated cliché, like people making comments about the fog in London or cuckoo clocks in Switzerland. No Indonesian had used wayang metaphors anywhere on my travels, and I didn't expect real, live Javanese to do so either. But they do, quite a lot. The former bupati has been succeeded by his wife, you'll hear, but the husband is still the puppet-master, determining the course of events. People will use nicknames from wayang characters to refer to a new boss or a potential girlfriend, so that everyone will instantly know what sort of person they are.

After I left Pak Tohari, I stayed for a couple of days with a friend who had recently built a comfortable house at the edge of the rice fields in a pretty village outside Yogyakarta. Kharisma was telecommuting to a well-paid day job at a foreign-funded research institute in Jakarta, but on Sunday morning he trooped down with all the other men of the village – the farmers, the cop, the headman – to break rocks for a new drainage canal. I joined the women, serving up a communal lunch, then doing the washing-up. This was *gotong royong* in action, the sort of village-level co-operative work which both Sukarno and Suharto held up as the core of Indonesian life, but which is in fact deeply Javanese.

After Kharisma had finished with his communal labour, we went off to eat at a Thai restaurant, one of the many delightful places that had recently mushroomed out of the rice fields around the increasingly sophisticated suburbs of Yogyakarta. Kharisma had told me that the nearby region of Gunung Kidul, which he described as a desiccated 'pocket of poverty' in otherwise fertile Java, had been a PKI stronghold. The backlash had been concomitantly brutal.

I flagged down a bus that was headed in that direction, sitting next to a woman who was on her way home from her job as a hospital orderly. She introduced herself as Tini, and she invited me to stay with her in the Gunung Kidul village of Nidoredjo. It was the day of the annual 'Cleaning of the Village' ceremony, she said, which meant that the yearly wayang would be staged that night if I wanted to go along. Marvelling again at Indonesia's kindness to absolute strangers, I said yes. On the way to Tini's home, I noticed that many houses had zinc replicas of characters from the wayang guarding the corners of their roofs, often with the date of construction enshrined between them: 2010, 2012. Even in this pocket of poverty, newly built houses seemed to be ten a penny.

It was a busy evening. First, there were community prayers at the Blessed Virgin Mary grotto – the village had converted to Catholicism *en masse* in 1966. Then I was taken to the farmers' cooperative meeting, where around thirty men and two or three women sat in their best batik shirts being elaborately polite to one another as they reached agreement over fertilizer subsidies. Finally the village wayang. I felt like I had walked in to a Suharto-era film about the golden age of Javanese village life.

When we arrived at the wayang just after 10 p.m., it had only just started. A string of makeshift foodstalls lined the path down to an elaborate marquee over a solidly built stage. Across the far end was stretched a huge expanse of white cotton. In front of it hung a blindingly bright electric light, shaded from view by a carved mask-shade. Along the bottom of the screen was a shelf made of the trunks of freshly cut banana trees; into this were jabbed a hundred or more wayang puppets, arranged by height. The largest and most impressive were exiled to the outskirts of the screen; the puppets swept down in progressively smaller and more manageable versions towards the centre where the puppet-master sat. The buffalo-hide puppets were carved, right down to the patterns on their batik sarongs, then painted and gilded too. It seemed like a lot of work for something that was going to show up as a shadow.

But the audience was all on the puppet-master side, the side where you could see the nice, colourful puppets. So was the large group of uniformed musicians, each with a kretek drooping from his mouth, each staring into space as he beat out extraordinarily complex melodies on his gong or xylophone. Kneeling in a row behind the orchestra were four stout women, all the rounder for their bulbous, *Mikado*-style wigs. These were the singers, each accompanied by a capacious handbag out of which popped powder compacts and lipsticks, and tissues with which to blot delicately heaving bosoms. The women were well past their glory days, but their singing was splendid yet.

Didn't anyone watch from the shadow side any more? I asked the man I was standing next to. He laughed. 'When did you last go to the wayang?!' More than twenty years ago, I confessed. 'Wah! It's changed a bit since then,' he said. The audience started shifting in force to the other side of the screen when the wayang went electric. Before that, when the light came from a large, flickering flame encased in a lantern, it had been much easier to imbue the shadows with life (and also rather harder to show off any on-stage glamour). 'Now, the audience wants to see *everything*. It's all about the showmanship.'

This puppet-master, sitting dead centre, his dagger sticking prominently from the back of his sarong, was certainly a showman. By day, he was an architect, working mostly with engineers on infrastructural projects – he had built the new runway for the local airstrip.

The only thing happening 'on screen' was a loooooong conversation between a waspish character and his bulbous-nosed opponent. And yet there were sharp intakes of breath from the audience, laughter, collective sighs. The architect was embroidering new patterns onto well-worn stories; he held the village spellbound. Except for the children who lay asleep open-mouthed in their parents' laps, of course, and the people who were wandering around because they were hungry, or had run out of cigarettes, or just wanted to stretch their legs and see what was on offer at the food stalls.

I went to the other side of the screen, to see if anyone at all was watching the shadows. It turned out that this was where the 'committee' – the group of village worthies who controlled the budget for the show – gathered to enjoy the fruit of their organizational work. They were all men, dressed mostly in smart batik shirts and peci caps, but they had not been ushered into a front row of overstuffed sofas the way they would have been at an ersatz cultural ceremony in a part of Indonesia that was trying to rediscover its adat. In this village there was no obvious 'Big Man'. I tried to guess who was who, to discern the hierarchy that would have been made explicit at a state-sponsored event. I pegged one man for village head on the strength of his clothes; he wore a beautifully cut, Nehru-style jacket in midnight blue. The following day he came out of his shop to greet me with a tape measure around his neck. He was the village tailor.

On the screen there was a fight between two characters and their retainers. Then the shadows disappeared. The committee drained their cups of sweet coffee and got up. It was only midnight; the wayang used to run until dawn. Could that really be it?

Of course not. The men were simply shifting to the other

side of the screen to watch an interlude of singing and stand-up comedy. This interruption of the story was first introduced about two decades ago to keep audiences engaged. On this occasion a mock-stroppy man was remonstrating with a pretty woman who subverted the refined movements of Javanese dance, swaying and gyrating them into something much sexier. Her ankle-length kebaya gown was see-through over the arms and midriff, embroidered with flowers and sequins over the bust. She talked back, flirted, batted her eyelids; modest and cheeky at the same time.

There was a bit of rap in Javanese, and a lot of making fun of politicians and prominent villagers. Then the committee member I was chatting with started pointing at me, and I was hauled up on stage to be gently (?) ridiculed in a language I don't understand. I resorted to physical comedy, turning the comedian into my husband, railing at him for flirting with the dancer. Much exaggerated finger-wagging, much sulking and frowning; finally I gave a mock kick to his backside. I fled from the stage to general hilarity. The next day, walking through the village, I was everyone's best friend.

When I left, at about two, the show was still in full swing. Walking home through the silent fields, I heard the gongs of two other orchestras. The villages used to join together to bear the expenses of the annual wayang. But in 2012, things were apparently going so well in this pocket of poverty that villages decided they could afford to rival one another. 'They paid more for their orchestra, but we have the better comedians,' said Pak Wardi, the man who had pushed me on stage.

I saw Pak Wardi again the following day. I had been walking along the road when I spotted a shed full of women bent over some unidentifiable but obviously fiddly task. In front of each person, two giant nails were driven into a work bench. Between them ran a tight white thread; on the bench were little packets of something that looked quite disgusting, like human hair.

It was exactly that. With an implement that looked like a miniature Victorian button-hook, the women were hooking two hairs at a time over the thread, then pulling them tight against their neighbours. They were making false eyelashes from the sweepings from the floors of salons. Washed and treated sweepings, but still . . . When I asked if I could take a photo, one woman laughed and said, 'Ya, this is what stupid Javanese villagers do for a living.'

The factory, which worked on contract for a Korean firm, had only been open a fortnight. The workers were paid 392 rupiah – about four cents – for a pair of 'Number 5' model eyelashes. Because they were still in training mode, most were only able to piece together a dozen pairs a day. Those that passed the three-month probation period would then be eligible for a range of supplements, mostly linked to productivity. A really good worker who managed to churn out four times what the fastest woman was now producing could earn seventy dollars a month.

Pak Wardi from the wayang committee appeared as I was talking to the workers; he owned the eyelash workshop and the pink colonnaded house to which it was attached. But he was wearing the red and white jumpsuit uniform worn by the men and women who pump petrol at the national Pertamina gas stations. He and his wife invited me into the house for coffee. Sitting under an outsized portrait of founding father Sukarno, he told me his story. He used to own a fair bit of land, and a fleet of minibuses and taxis. Then he decided to run for the local parliament, as a candidate for the PDIP party headed by Sukarno's daughter Megawati Sukarnoputri. He lost, and the campaign bankrupted him. 'Now we're starting again from scratch,' his wife said. Working at the local petrol station, Pak Wardi had earned enough to buy the zinc roofing, plywood work benches and neon strip lighting for the eyelash workshop. In exchange for providing the space and recruiting and managing the staff, he and his wife would get to keep 3.5 per cent of the turnover. 'One step at a time,' he said. I admired him for it.

Pak Wardi is obviously a True Believer in the PDIP's nationalist platform, such as it is; he was disappointed that these days voters responded to money rather than ideology. 'The party rules don't even allow vote-buying,' he said. 'But if the others all play that game, we have to play it too whether we like it or not.' He shrugged. 'The system is rotten through and through, what can you expect?'

Here, at least, today's democratic Etc. seems to act as a social equalizer. Not necessarily in the traditional sense, of spreading power to those who would never otherwise have had a look in, but at least as a way of redistributing wealth, as a vehicle for social mobility in both directions.

For years, foreigners travelling in Indonesia could be forgiven for believing that the only phrase taught in school was 'Hello Mister'. It is a sign of great progress that even in the outer islands, I am now sometimes accosted with 'Hello Missus!' instead. If village children are to venture further, they generally have to draw strength from one another first. There's much giggling, shoving and egging one another on. Eventually, a child will break ranks and yell: 'Wossyonem!' before screeching at their own bravery and ducking back into the crowd. When I turn around and respond: 'My name is Eliz, what's *your* name?' there is pandemonium, and the kids run off screaming.

They are worlds away from the boys I met on the equator in Pontianak, who were going to a bilingual school and doing their science project in English. The language of international commerce is something many Indonesians devoutly wish to acquire and there are a growing number of bilingual schools in Indonesia's bigger cities, but they are still for the rich and the super-rich. For young Indonesians long on linguistic ambition but short on cash, there's *Kampung Inggris*: Englishtown.

I had heard about Englishtown from several young people I had run into on my travels: a village in East Java where everyone speaks English all the time. No one I met had actually studied there, but I heard tales of intensive English classes, of using English in the post office and the coffee shops, of boarding with English-speaking families. After my forays to the schizophrenic city of Solo and sex-laden Gunung Kemukus, when I was staying with a sugar farmer close to the city of Kediri, a young woman told me that I was less than twenty kilometres from this mythical place. I borrowed a motorbike and headed off through the sugar plantations towards Pare, where Kampung Inggris was said to be. Sugar gave way to rubber, then to rice fields. Every now and then, a brand-new housing estate would lurch up out of the fields. 'ISLAMIC VILLAGE' one declared itself, the English words emblazoned in gold on an imposing gatepost. Behind the gates lay a short strip of two- and three-bedroom row-houses painted a lurid custard colour. The gatehouse was roofed to resemble a mosque. A gardener, painting black and white stripes on kerbstones, chased off a goat who had wandered in from the fields next door.

The first sign that I might have arrived in Englishtown was an advertising banner: 'Mr Bean Laundry. The Wash Service. Dry Clothes (kering). IRoned clothes (sterika)'. In English, I asked the attendant if I was in Englishtown. She didn't understand. But as I drove on I knew I must be: every second or third house was decked with banners advertising English courses and promising all manner of benefits. This one, for example, from INTENSE, graced with a photo of an infant wearing language-lab headphones:

I ntegrate between science and spiritual

N umber you among INTENSE family

T each you how to speak English better

E nrich your vocabulary every day

N ecessitate you to practice your English in INTENSE dormitories

S how you the ways to learn English easily

E nglish is easy if you think it's easy

INTENSE IS COMMITTED 2 U

The Seruni Camp (The Developing Confidence Camp!) offered speaking and grammar courses plus a room with a bathroom, wifi and free health care, all for 200,000 rupiah a month, less than US$25. I ducked into the attached coffee shop. *'Cari siapa, Bu?'* asked the owner, who was whipping up milkshakes for a handful of students. 'Who are you looking for?' I answered that I was looking for a coffee, and a town where people were supposed to be speaking English even at coffee shops. She laughed, and nodded at her clients, a group of spiky-haired boys in their late teens. 'Ya, *they* have to speak English, Bu. I don't speak a word.'

The boys were indeed speaking English to one another, and not badly. They came from all over Java and Sumatra, and they said there were students from eastern Indonesia in Christian boarding houses. Many of them dreamed of getting a scholarship and studying overseas. Had they studied English at secondary school? 'This is Indonesia, Miss,' said a young man from Riau, in English. 'School for six years, and at the end only Hello Mister.' 'The teachers, they cannot speak English too,' added another student.

Here in Kampung Inggris they were doing better, though none of the teachers was a native speaker. 'Sometimes, we don't know if the teachers are right. Like, how can one word have so many meanings?' asked the boy from Riau. He gave the example of the word 'leeff', reeling off the Indonesian words for the green thing that grows on a tree, the act of abandoning a person or place, a verb indicating human existence and an adverb meaning immediately. I got the first three: leaf, leave, live. But immediately? 'You know, like when you're watching football. Leeff from Old Trafford.' Oh, *live*! Layve. I exaggerated the difference in pronunciation but they just pointed to the phonetics in their textbook, which did indeed give exactly the same sound for the four words.

When I went to the loo out the back, I found a little knot of girls in jilbabs. They had hiked their long skirts up their thighs and were squatting around a tub, peeling vegetables and gossiping about a Korean Boy Band. In English. The owner told me that she had set up this 'camp' just the previous year. 'Everyone was doing it; I thought why not give it a try?' By her count there were now 174 English schools in Kampung Inggris. It all started with Pak Kalend at BEC, she said.

BEC was a lot more than just a kampung house with a banner strung out the front. There's an imposing gateway in front of a sizeable mosque; behind that is a proper school complex. In the office, a young man with a wispy beard wearing a knitted Muslim skullcap jumped up to attend to my needs. Minutes later, Pak Kalend appeared. He was stout and moon-faced, with a flared nose and neatly clipped grey moustache. He grasped my hand warmly. 'How may I help you, dear Madam?' His English was courtly, correct. I said I had come to pay my respects to the founder of the famous Kampung Inggris. 'Dear Madam, please don't call it that. I did not set out to build a Kampung Inggris and as a matter of fact most people in the kampung don't speak English at all. Let us call it "*Kampung Kursus Berbahasa Inggris*".' More accurate, perhaps, but 'English language course town' doesn't have quite the ring of Englishtown.

Muhammad Kalend Osen settled into Indonesian to tell me his story. He was a Kutai Dayak, one of the few Muslim Dayak tribes, born in East Kalimantan. 'But I knew I didn't just want to stay in the jungle.' At the age of twenty-seven, with barely any education, he took himself off to Java and studied for a few years with a polyglot religious teacher. Then, only because the cleric was away, Pak Kalend started tutoring civil servants who needed to pass English tests. That was in 1977. Now, BEC takes in 1,600 students a year. 'So far, 19,000 people can speak English because of us.' Pak Kalend beamed with pride, but he is not a show-off. BEC stands for 'Basic English Course'. 'I call it that because that's what I know I can deliver. The basics. That's what I will answer for.'

The campus was buzzing with young people in tidy uniforms, all speaking English to one another. It was show-and-tell day; the students had made posters which they used to explain their lives to one another. When they spotted Pak Kalend the students would rush up, grab his hand and touch it to their forehead in a gesture of respect. They'd do the same to me – it made me feel very old – then they'd elbow one another aside, each trying to tell us their story. One boy, rather a talented artist, had drawn a self-portrait in the centre of his poster. Radiating off it like electrons around a nucleus were bubbles in which he put his parents, his home town, his high school. The final bubble contained a carefully drawn pile of red 100,000 rupiah notes, and the words 'My purpose is to become a business man.' He could hardly contain his excitement as he outlined his future. In clear, confident English, he said: 'Where I come from we have many mangoes. I will buy mangoes for cheap, and I will sell them for expensive.'

A couple of days earlier, politicians in Jakarta had mooted taking English out of the primary school curriculum to make more room for religious and moral instruction. I asked Pak Kalend what he thought of the plan. He laughed. Then stared at me. 'You *are* joking, aren't you? *Please* say you are joking.' I shook my head. The self-taught Dayak covered his face with his hands. Then he looked up with a slightly acid smile. 'Well, as long as they don't try to stick their oar in here and tell me how I should teach, it can only mean more profits for me.'

By the time I reached Indonesia's second largest city, Surabaya, by way of tobacco warehouses and volcanic sulphur mines, I was thoroughly disabused of the notion that the whole of Java had turned into a long series of strip malls and identikit housing complexes linked by smooth asphalt roads and populated by the much vaunted 'rising middle class'. The transformation is on the way, certainly. Some 80 million people now live in parts of Java that the government classifies as urban (using measures of electrification, asphalt roads, percentage working in non-farming jobs and access to services). But that still leaves 57 million in real, old-fashioned villages.

Much in Java still conforms to the descriptions given by the legendary American anthropologist Clifford Geertz as long ago as the 1950s. It is politically hierarchical, certainly, but the tradition of village-level collectivism remains strong in rural areas. And yet people seem to feel that this spirit of social solidarity is under threat, that it may not survive the pressures of the modern economy, much less the wholesale move to that other Java, the McDonald's, Indomaret, toll-road, gated-community Java that is gobbling up the island, bite by bite.

In other islands, almost every conversation turned eventually to the glories and vicissitudes of regional autonomy. In Java, where people did not feel the same euphoric liberation from Javanese colonialism, the dominant worry was that Java would turn into Jakarta, a monumentally selfish society in which no one worried about their neighbours or even their extended family, a place in which individuals did nothing but struggle to get a leg up over those around them.

The phrase that is universally used to sum up this horrific prospect is '*loe loe, gue gue*'. From Jakarta slang, it translates literally as 'you you, me me', what's yours is yours, what's mine is mine. In sentiment, the closest English equivalent I can think of is 'dog-eat-dog'. Every time I heard it, I was reminded of the political pow-wows of two decades earlier when Mohammad Mahathir in Malaysia, Lee Kuan Yew in Singapore and Suharto in Indonesia would wax lyrical about 'Asian Values'. Misguided Westerners could criticize the Asian leaders for stamping on individual rights, they implied, but what the visionary leaders of South East Asia were really doing was protecting a culture that put the good of the collective ahead of the good of the individual.

It is certainly true that Jakarta, with its flooding, traffic and millions of mostly grumpy inhabitants is a shining example of the way in which individual selfishness destroys the common happiness. Surabaya is about a third the size of Jakarta. It sits about three-quarters of the way east along the north coast of Java and has a huge port, a thriving industrial sector, and one of the biggest red-light districts in South East Asia. When I had last visited in the early 2000s, it seemed quite likely that the city would follow Jakarta on the road to perdition. While preparing for an HIV survey in the city, I spent my time counting rent boys along the riverbanks and wading through used condoms and smashed whisky bottles in a vast cemetery whose tombstones doubled as knocking-shops.

Now, a decade later, the riverside cruising areas have turned into well-lit, landscaped parks with free wifi throughout, and Surabaya is virtually litter-free.

It is hard for someone who has not visited Indonesia to feel the full impact of those last five words: Surabaya is virtually litter-free. It is hard, too, to explain just how pervasive garbage is in this country. It is one of the strongest red threads binding the nation, and it is woven from the detritus of the commercial brands that get micro-packaged into sachets and find their way into every kiosk in the land.

All that packaging makes for a lot of litter. At the end of my long boat trip up through the islands of south-west Maluku, when I had carefully consolidated five days' worth of rubbish into a single plastic bag, I asked the fierce cook on the cargo ship where the bin was. She looked at me as though I had grown a second head, took the bag of rubbish, and threw it into the sea. Another time, someone was telling stories of how strange foreigners are. 'I've even seen them scrunch up a cigarette packet, then put it in their pocket instead of throwing it on the ground!' he said, laughing. 'Imagine!' I reached into my pocket and pulled out: three empty sweet wrappers, the plastic seal off a water bottle, and some used bus tickets. This was so absurd that he had to call everyone else on deck to see it.

There's such an assumption of littering that some companies even use it to appeal to consumers. Frutamin, a brand of sugary water that comes in various toxic flavours and was until recently owned by Pepsi, is packaged in single-dose plastic cups which turn into pretty coloured flowers if you throw them on the ground and stamp on them just right. There's no point making old-fashioned tut-tutting noises when you see people throwing garbage on the roadside or into the sea; in most of Indonesia, people will just look at you blankly: what's your point?

Some of the world's prettiest beaches are, above the waterline, ankle deep in old flip-flops, leaking batteries, shampoo bottles, instant-noodle cups, old election T-shirts, rusting cans. Occasionally, especially in areas where NGOs like to congregate, you'll see a hand-painted sign: No Littering! Ten times out of ten, it will be half buried in the backwash of the disposable consumer culture at which Indonesia excels.

And yet the second biggest city in Indonesia is almost litter-free. I was so amazed by this that I went to the town hall to try and find out what was going on. 'Garbage? Sure!' Without another question, a friendly guard took me to the fourth floor, and presented me to Ibu Anis, a civil servant who knew all about garbage. I told her I had been struck by the city's cleanliness, and wanted to know about their policies. 'Let's start at the beginning, then,' she said. I clearly wasn't the first person to have noticed the transformation of the city.

In 2001, that heady time soon after Suharto lost his grip on the nation, Surabaya's dump was closed following mass demonstrations by its neighbours. Actually, the dump was there long before the residents. They moved in because there was a good road leading to cleared land. 'Then they started protesting about the trucks and the noise and the smell,' said Anis. 'You wanted to say well, you shouldn't have built an illegal house next to the dump! But what can you do?' With the dump closed, the garbage started to pile up in every corner of the city; there was no ignoring it. That made it easy to get a grass-roots movement started, Ibu Anis said. With help from Unilever's do-good funds, the city trained neighbourhood 'garbage cadres'. I raised an eyebrow at this: Unilever is one of the biggest producers of household and beauty products in Indonesia, and therefore one of the biggest producers of the shiny packaging that gets dropped in the canals. 'I know, I know. Ironic, isn't it?' said Ibu Anis. But the programme worked; there are now 40,000 volunteers around the city, each organizing recycling in their neighbourhood. Most have also taken on the task of greening their areas; even the narrowest backstreets of Surabaya are lined with murals of open green landscapes fronted with rows of potted plants and flowers.

There's also a large network of Garbage Banks, run by an NGO with the support of the city government. These are not just places to get rid of recycled materials, like London's bottle banks. They are real banks, with savings books, cash payments and interest rates. Individuals and neighbourhoods can sign up for an account. Their waste gets weighed and they get paid for it; 5,000 rupiah a kilo for clean plastic if they put it in their savings account, slightly less if they want to be paid in cash. The NGO then sells it on to recycling plants at 7,000.

I visited one of the Garbage Banks. A woman with a hunched back and only one tooth limped in with a sack of plastic bottles. She showed me her savings book; she had over 200,000 rupiah in her account. She would use it, she said, to pay her electricity bill. The Garbage Banks have brokered a deal with the state electricity firm so that people can keep the lights on with their garbage savings. The neighbourhood accounts are usually emptied a few weeks before the annual 'clean and green' competition, in which each little clump of city blocks competes fiercely to cover itself with orchids and glory. 'It's amazing how hard people will work to win a cup for the neighbourhood and to get their names in the paper,' Ibu Anis had said. The most energetic Garbage Cadres will be taken on a study tour to Singapore, a favourite source of new ideas for the current Mayor of Surabaya.★ Trained as an architect, Tri Rismaharini was one of only eight women among Indonesia's 500-plus heads of government. She was elected Mayor after heading the City Cleanliness Department.

Surabaya seemed to me like a city that had managed to preserve some of the better aspects of Javanese collectivism even while modernizing. *Loe loe, gue gue* was not, after all, the inevitable destination of the road to progress. But I notice that they had done it not with the tools commonly used by the Javanese rajas

---

★ The Garbage Bank idea originated in Yogyakarta. 'We'll steal good ideas from anywhere and improve on them,' Ibu Anis had told me when I visited her office. 'We're not proud.'

or the Dutch and Indonesian bureaucrats that inherited their methods. Surabaya did not terrorize the 'little people', did not threaten punishment or impose unenforceable fines on people who litter. No, the city did something singularly un-Indonesian. It worked through incentives, rewarding people for doing the right thing rather than punishing them for doing the wrong thing. And it showed that incentives can work at the community level.

Collectivist culture without the feudalism. Perhaps it should become Indonesia's next Etc.

Epilogue

I wended my way back to Jakarta by way of batik workshops and rice farms, knowing that I wouldn't be able to pack all the Indonesias I had wandered through into a single book, knowing too that there were thousands of other Indonesias still to discover.

At a farewell dinner in Jakarta (my umpteenth over the years) I turned up an hour late, wore a sandal tied on with purple ribbon, and answered my phone at the dinner table, listening patiently to an overweight transgender who had called from Tanimbar, 2,700 kilometres away, tell me how drunk she was. My (Indonesian) friends teased me about how 'Indonesian' I had become. I chose to take it as a compliment.

Right at the start of my trip a woman sitting near me on the deck of a ferry, trying to distract a screaming toddler, had pointed and told the child to give sweet granny a kiss. I had looked behind me, but there were no grannies there. The toddler had made for me, and given me a snotty embrace. *Sweet Granny?!* I had been appalled: I was a hard-drinking occasional smoker who could flirt at a bar in several languages and who was competitive even at yoga. Sweet Granny! But as the weeks and months of travel passed, I had settled into the rhythm of ordinary life in extraordinary places, a life that involved repetitive conversations, mindless tasks and an unaccustomed amount of public piety, a life that decidedly did not involve alcohol, cigarettes, or flirting with strangers. And I didn't mind it.

I waited for boats that were eighteen hours late with little more than a shrug. I watched women balancing jerrycans of water over their shoulders, on their backs and on their heads all at once, and never asked if they had considered making a wheelbarrow. When I did ask questions, I often settled quickly for the most common answer: *Begitulah.* 'That's just the way it is.' Over time, I grew to accept that there is a very great deal about Indonesia, the world and life in general that I will just never know.

Of some things, though, I have become more sure. On the way to the airport as I was leaving Indonesia after thirteen months of travel, the retired architect who drove my cab said he didn't think Indonesia could withstand the centrifugal forces of decentralization. The country was headed for break-up, he feared. A year earlier, I had begun to share his concern; now I nearly jumped down his throat in defence of the integrity of the nation that declared independence in 1945 and that has weathered so many Etcs since.★ The threads that bind this nation will not be easily dissolved.

The sturdiest of these threads is surely collectivism – village-based in Java, more clannish in much of the rest of the country, formalized nationwide through the giant web of the bureaucracy. Almost all Indonesians are bound into at least one important web of mutual obligation, often several. This provides many Indonesians with a quiet sense of security; daily life seems less anxious than in more socially fragmented nations. Faith (and the fatalism that so often shadows it) plays a part here too; there's little point being anxious about a future that is in God's hands.

Inevitably where personal networks count for so much, private and public obligations become tangled up, and the threads of collectivism get bound into stouter ropes of patronage and corruption. Though international observers rail at the cost of corruption in Indonesia, few give much thought to the role it plays in tying the archipelago's mosaic of islands and disparate peoples into a nation. In Indonesia's current Etc., patronage is the price of unity.

Citizens of a bounteous land, Indonesians are united, too, by

---

★ At independence that nation did not, of course, include Papua.

an extraordinary generosity of spirit, a tolerance of difference. They welcome strangers like me into their homes and their lives, they go out of their way to help people in trouble. Arguably, they can be *too* tolerant, too slow to take a stand in defence of larger freedoms against a minority of crooks, thugs or self-serving leaders. And when the tolerance breaks down, Indonesians throughout the islands have shown themselves capable of brutality on a grand scale. But the breakdowns are few, considering the country's diversity. No other nation has welded so much difference together into so generally peaceable a whole in the space of less than seventy years.

Like all Bad Boyfriends, Indonesia certainly has its downsides. The staff in the tourist office are spectacularly incompetent, it's true (and also utterly charming). The cops will try and shake you down for a bribe every now and then, without doubt (but they will also steal your bike back when you lose the key, and drive you to the locksmith into the bargain). The government makes a habit of announcing cataclysmic political changes with a minimum of preparation, certainly (though if the new Etc. doesn't work, they'll quickly come up with another – 'Nation-building by trial and error,' one retired general told me with a smile and a shrug). But Indonesia's upsides – the openness, the pragmatism, the generosity of its people, their relaxed attitude to life – are ultimately the more seductive traits, and the more important.

At the airport as I was leaving, I found a nice, clean, modern cappuccino bar, part of the JCO chain. To the left, a young man was frothing a flower pattern onto a mug of overpriced coffee. To the right, ten or twelve people waited to buy boxed sets of donuts to take to relatives in faraway provinces. 'I'll have two of the chocolate, and four of the cheese, then, no, wait, four chocolate, and . . . Hey, Budi, do you think Uncle Karma likes strawberry . . .?' The attendant put donuts into a box, took them out, put them in again. Behind Budi, the line grew.

I went up to the coffee guy, who had finished his froth-art and who had no customers, and ordered a large cappuccino. 'You have to join the queue, Bu.' But there is no queue. 'That queue over there,' and he pointed to the scrummage of donut-seekers.

I joined the queue. 'What do you mean the blueberry ones aren't included in the special price promotion? How many were there? Five? Okay, well take them out and give me two choco-crunch and three coconut instead.' It took me fifteen minutes to get back to the coffee counter. In that time the coffee guy did not serve a single other customer.

'You have to admit that it makes no sense at all, making me wait in the donut queue when I only want a coffee,' I said, as he made my drink. He smiled and nodded agreement.

'*Ya, begitulah Indonesia, Bu!*' he said: That's Indonesia! And he handed me a coffee with a beautiful heart pattern etched into the froth.

Acknowledgements

This book is the product of the kindness of many friends and, especially, countless strangers (a goodly proportion of whom eventually became friends). Some you have met in the book; the generosity of many others is unsung in the text but no less appreciated.

I am especially grateful to the many people in Indonesia who welcomed me into their homes and their lives. In roughly the order I imposed on their hospitality, I'd like to thank some of them, and apologize to many more whose names I never even knew. In Sumba: Mama Lakabobo and family; Delsi, Ira, Asi, Juli, Dewa Lado and their mother Paulina; Piter Tibu and family, Karel Nooijen and Rosa; Andre Graff and Koni, together with Lexi, Billy, Domi and Daris; Imam Ladoregitera and family. Elsewhere in NTT: in Detutsoko, Anton; in Adonara, Mama Paulina and family; in Boti, the Benu family. In Maluku: Harry in Kisar; Dedi Wijaya and all the Pengajar Muda in Saumlaki, the Notabulen family in Ohoiwait and Tual, Ibu Tina in Banda, Ibu Edith in Ambon. In North Maluku: Vera, Tesi and family in Weda and Lelilef, Rob and Linda Sinke at the unexpected and glorious Weda Reef and Rainforest Resort; Ibu Elizabeth, Jongky and family in Sangihe, Flora Tanujaya and family in Manado. In Jayapura: Bpk Freddy and family. In Aceh: Syahyuzar Aka and Reza in Langsa, Bpk Adam and family in Idi Cut, with special thanks to Hanafiah; Nazaruddin Ibrahim and all his campaign team in Lhokseumawe; Hamidah Abubakar, Yufrida and family as well as Asya in Tangse; Nina Rachmadani and family in Singkil; Fidel in Pulau Banyak. Elsewhere in

Sumatra: in Sidikalang, Samuel Sihombing and family, together with Lidya and the staff of Petrasa; in Payakumbuh Gus Sakai; in Harau Ibu Nelsi and family and in Jambi Ira Yurda, Mijak, Gentar and family. In Bangka Belitung: Ishak Holidi and Jumiran Susanto. In Sulawesi: Herto Sampelan and Zunaidi Tjinong and family in the Banggai islands; Dauda Sampelan, Amien Rais and Sultan La Ode Muhammad Djafar in Buton. In the city of Makassar: Lily Yulianti Farid and the staff of the delightful Makassar International Writers' Festival, Luna Vidya and everyone at Bakti. In Kalimantan: in Mandor, Feralina Hakim and family, in Singkawang, Emily Hertzman and Niyan, Olin, Ah Hui. In Sintang: Danaus and friends, Bpk Askiman. In Nanga Lauk: Annisa Novita Dewi (Vivi), Ibu Dara and family. In Java: in and around Semarang, Megaputri Megaradjasa (Jenny), Evi Nugroho and family, Ibu Sanna. In Tinggarjaya: Ahmad Tohari. In Yogyakarta: Kharisma Nugroho and family. In Ngidoredjo: Aloysia Inlastini (Tini) and family. In Kediri: Heri Nugroho and family, and his many friends, including Heri 2. In Pekalongan: Veronica Nugroho and family. In Trijaya: Anijuniah and family, including the always fabulous Tarwi DeGraff. In Bali: the staff of the Colony Hotel, Adolf Brown, David Fox, Lily Wardoyo and Farquhar Stirling. In Lombok: Spike and Felicity Cockburn, Ibu Sopie and the teachers of the Pesantren Al Halimy, Nurhidayati and the residents of the Transito centre in Mataram.

The companionship of Jerome Tadié in Sumba and Melanie Whitmarsh in Kalimantan and Java greatly enlivened all-too-brief parts of my travels. Thanks to Jerome for improbable champagne and to Melanie for glorious photographs, many of which can be seen in the e-version of this book.

I'm immensely grateful to Heidi Arbuckle for allowing me periodically to reoccupy my former home in Jakarta, and to Bhimanto Suwastoyo and Arya for giving me a second home. Bhim has done more than anyone over more than two decades to introduce me to the vagaries of my Bad Boyfriend; he continues to inspire me to explore and discover Indonesia, and I keep coming back for more. Thank you, Bhim. Very special thanks to

Steve Wignall and all the staff at Villa Beji Indah in Nyukuning, Bali for providing refuge and good cheer for unreasonably long periods.

In Jakarta, many people have contributed to my well-being and to my thinking, both recently and in earlier times, and I thank them all. Those who helped me with this project include Ienes Angela, Luwi Arifin, Adji and Asmoro Damais and their extended family, Vidia Darmawi, Rudi and Jenny Harmayn, Shanty Harmayn, Mas Karta, Aristedes Katoppo, Butet Manurung, Gourie and Ashok Mirpuri, Nikki and Nihal, Felicia Nugroho, Kharisma Nugroho, Enny Nuraheni, John Riady, Thamrin Tamagola, Evi Trisna and everyone at Indonesia Menggajar, Amir Sidharta, Juliana Wilson, Ibu Yanti.

Friends and kind strangers have answered questions and have read and commented on various parts of this book and it is much improved as a result; I thank them very much for their comments, and apologize for those instances when I have clung stubbornly to my opinions. I'm grateful to Bobby Anderson, Willem Bake, Sophie Campbell, Vaudine England, Andre Feillard, Jack Hanbury-Tenison, Keith Hansen, Rachel Harvey, Sarah Hawkes, Sonya Hepinstall, Bert Hoffman, Sidney Jones, Olivia Judson, Asmeen Kahn, Maarten Kok, Gwen Njoto Feillard, Ong Hok Chuan, Gray Sattler, Paul Schulte, Adam Schwarz, Made Setiawan, Daniel Suryadarma, Bob Templar and Liz Wrenn. Four people – one of whom I have never even met – have read every word of at least one version of this book, and have often been subjected to several versions. Their insights, comments and questions have enriched my thinking immeasurably. Infinite thanks to Ed Aspinall, Claire Bolderson, Michael Buehler and Andrew Wilson.

In Bangkok, where much of the writing of this book was done, I was given house and home by Nicola Bullard and Philippe Girault; many thanks. Several people tended generously to my sanity, among them Delia Bethell, David Cole, Peter Emblin, Jake Lucchi, Palani Narayanan and Cerissa Nyen. Ricky Catwell kept me smiling in London, too. Thanks to all of you.

This book has had many midwives. Thanks to Tracy Bohan at the Wylie Agency who provided calming good humour throughout. In the United States, I'm grateful to Alane Mason at W.W. Norton, who saw it through from conception to birth, as well as to Anna Mageras. At Granta in the UK, the events described in Chapter 10 notwithstanding, the book has been immeasurably shaped by the magic touch of Sara Holloway. It has passed also through the able hands of Philip Gwyn Jones and Sigrid Rausing, to land safely with Bella Lacey. Thanks to all of you, and thanks to other members of the team past and present, including Iain Chapple, Christine Lo, Brigid Macleod and Sarah Wasley. In Indonesia, John McGlynn has been admirable in his handling of this book, as well as of the incomparable Lontar Foundation.

Eric Olason drew the maps on a tight schedule; thanks. I am grateful to Gaetan Bernede, video editor and designer extraordinaire, and to John Wheeler and his colleagues at SPi Global, all of whom have contributed to the electronic version of this book. Thanks to Lilo Acebal for the illustrations that appear in the electronic version of the book, and for very much more. Ditto Susannah Fiennes, including for her author portrait, and Marit Miners.

Nicholas Little kept the home fires burning and made the project possible; for that as well as for friendship and laughter past and future I thank him. My parents have, as ever, been beyond supportive. It was from them that I learned to travel with an open mind and an open heart; I owe them a debt I can never repay. Finally, I want to thank my brother Mark. Without his constant, patient, good-humoured support, most of it given at unreasonable hours, this book would not exist. Indeed, I might not exist. I dedicate it to him, with all my soul.

Glossary

Adat	Traditions, cultures and laws specific to an ethnic group
Aduh!	All-purpose expression of astonishment, delight or dismay
Bapak	Father, a respectful term of address for an adult man
Batik	Patterned cloth dyed using wax-resist techniques
Begitulah	That's the way it is
Bu	*see* Ibu
Dangdut	Indonesian pop music
Dari Mana?	Where are you from? A ubiquitous greeting
Gamelan	A Javanese or Balinese orchestra
Ibu	Mother, a respectful term of address for an adult woman
Ikat	Patterned cloth that is dyed before weaving
Jilbab	A head-covering worn by Muslim women
Kebaya	A long, fitted blouse; formal dress for Javanese women
Kebun	Garden, plantation, farm
Keluarga Besar	*lit:* 'Big Family', clan
Kraton	A Sultan's palace, a court
Kretek	A tobacco and clove cigarette
Merantau	To travel in search of one's fortune
Ojek	A motorcycle taxi
Pak	*see* Bapak
Pancasila	Indonesia's amorphous five-point political philosophy

Peci   A fez-like cap worn by Muslim men
Pendatang   An immigrant from another island, or their
                descendants
Reformasi   *lit:* The Reformation. Refers to the post-
                Suharto era
Waria   A transgendered person
Wayang   Puppet theatre. Most frequently shadow-puppets

Resources and Further Reading

If you would like to see photos and videos of some of the people and events in the book (and some that didn't make it to the book), please check out the enhanced e-book. You should be able to buy it from the normal on-line retailers, but you can find full details of availability in different territories at http://indonesiaetc.com/ebook. Buying the enhanced e-book is a good way of helping Elizabeth repay the debts incurred during this project. If you don't have a tablet that can show colour pictures and video, you can see some of the videos and slide shows from the enhanced e-book at http://indonesiaetc.com/extras

References for most of the factual statements in this book can be found at http://indonesiaetc.com/references

What follows is a list of resources and further reading that many Indonesia specialists will find eccentric and all will find incomplete, but that contains some of the material I found most useful. It is arranged thematically. Several of the publications listed here are collections of essays; individual essays and papers are listed at http://indonesiaetc.com/references

If you wish to draw attention to any important resource you feel is neglected, please email info@indonesiaetc.com and we will consider adding it to the online resource pages.

Films

The Act of Killing (2012), directed by Joshua Oppenheimer. An extraordinary documentary showing how Indonesia has (and hasn't) processed the memory of the slaughter of 1965/66.

The Year of Living Dangerously (1982), directed by Peter Weir.

387

Based on the novel of the same name; old but still good.

Sang Penari ('The Dancer') (2011), directed by Ifa Isfansyah. Based on Ahmad Tohari's triolgy of novels published in English under the same name. In Indonesian, with subtitles.

Lewat Djam Malam ('After the Curfew') (1954), directed by Usmar Ismail. Recently remastered, this classic of Indonesian cinema shows the difficulty that some former revolutionaries had in integrating into post-independence Indonesia.

English language news and current affairs

The two major daily newspapers in English are the *Jakarta Post* at http://www.thejakartapost.com/ and the *Jakarta Globe* at http://www.thejakartaglobe.com/. Both can be read free online.

The weekly news magazine *Tempo* publishes an English-language edition at http://magz.tempo.co/. There is also an online portal for the Tempo group's digital news at http://en.tempo.co

Inside Indonesia, a thematic quarterly magazine, edited in Australia, is the place to go for thoughtful reporting by people who study Indonesia. It also publishes weekly in-depth articles on current topics at http://www.insideindonesia.org

Literature

The best source of Indonesian literature in translation is the Lontar Foundation: see http://www.lontar.org. They publish books on paper and electronically. They also maintain a digital library with archival material such as videos of interviews with major Indonesian writers. The digital library is available at http://library.lontar.org

Equinox also publishes some Indonesian fiction in translation: See http://equinoxpublishing.com/browse/fiction

There is a remarkable collection of literature related to Malaysia and the archipelago at the Melayu Library: see http://www.sabrizain.org/malaya/library. The books and documents are mostly out of copyright; they include some classics from the early colonial years. If you use this privately maintained resource, please consider making a donation.

Some Indonesian books I like (in English)
Farid, Lily Yulianti, *Family Room*. Translated by John H. McGlynn. Jakarta: Lontar Foundation, 2010.

Lubis, Mochtar, *Twilight in Djakarta*. Translated by Claire Holt. Singapore; New York: Oxford University Press, 1986.

Mangunwijaya, Y. B., *Weaverbirds*. Translated by Thomas Hunter. Jakarta: Lontar Foundation, 1991.

Rusli, M., *Sitti Nurbaya: A Love Unrealized*. Jakarta: Lontar Foundation, 2009.

Toer, Pramoedya Ananta, *This Earth of Mankind*. Translated by Max Lane. New York: Penguin, 1996. This is the first of the books that make up the *Buru Quartet*. I like the next two – *Child of All Nations* and *Footsteps* – as well.

Tohari, Ahmad, *The Dancer: a trilogy of novels*. Jakarta: Lontar Foundation, 2012.

Wijaya, Putu, *Telegram*. Translated by Stephen J. Epstein. Jakarta: Lontar Foundation, 2011.

Novels set in Indonesia
Conrad, Joseph, *Almayer's Folly*. New York: Macmillan and Co., 1895.

Conrad, Joseph, *Victory, An Island Tale*. London: Methuen & Co., 1928.

Koch, C. J., *The Year of Living Dangerously*. Melbourne: HarperCollins, 1978.

Multatuli. *Max Havelaar, or, The coffee auctions of a Dutch Trading Company*. Translated by Roy Edwards. London; New York: Penguin Books, 1987.

History and nationhood
The Digital Atlas of Indonesian History (http://www.indonesian history.info) by Robert Cribb is an invaluable source of information on just about everything relating to pre-colonial, colonial and modern Indonesia, including history, geography, ethnicity, religion and other social issues. Thanks to the Nordic Institute of Asian Studies, it is now easily available online.

The Melayu Library (http://www.sabrizain.org/malaya/library) provides a wonderful, freely accessible online library of historical documents relating to what is now Indonesia. This includes many accounts by early travellers, and a great gallery of maps.

General histories
Brown, Colin, *A Short History of Indonesia: The Unlikely Nation?* London: Allen & Unwin, 2003.

Ricklefs, Merle Calvin, *A History of Modern Indonesia Since c. 1200.* Stanford: Stanford University Press, 2002.

Taylor, Jean Gelman, *Indonesia: Peoples and Histories.* New Haven: Yale University Press, 2003.

VOC and Netherlands East Indies
Bown, Stephen R., *Merchant Kings: When Companies Ruled the World, 1600–1900.* Vancouver: Douglas & McIntyre, 2009.

Gaastra, Femme, *The Dutch East India Company.* Leiden: Walburg Pers, 2003.

Milton, Giles, *Nathaniel's Nutmeg: How One Man's Courage Changed the Course of History.* London: Sceptre, 2000.

Zanden, J. L. V., *The Rise and Decline of Holland's Economy: Merchant Capitalism and the Labour Market.* Manchester: Manchester University Press, 1993.

Nationalism, 1965, Modern Indonesia
Anderson, Benedict, *Imagined Communities: Reflections on the Origin and Spread of Nationalism.* New York: Verso, 2006.

Cribb, Robert B., *The Indonesian Killings of 1965–1966: Studies from Java and Bali.* Monash Papers on Southeast Asia 21. Melbourne: Monash University Press, 1990.

Cribb, Robert, 'How Many Deaths? Problems in the statistics of massacre in Indonesia (1965–1966) and East Timor (1975–1980).' In: Ingrid Wessel and Georgia Wimhofer (eds.), *Violence in Indonesia.* Hamburg: Abera, 2001, pp. 82–98.

Cribb, Robert B., *The Late Colonial State in Indonesia: Political and Economic Foundations of the Netherlands Indies, 1880–1942.* Leiden: KITLV Press, 1994.

Schulte Nordholt, Henk, 'Renegotiating Boundaries: Access, agency and identity in post-Soeharto Indonesia', *Journal of the Humanities and Social Sciences of Southeast Asia* 159, no. 4 (2003), 550–89.

Schwarz, Adam, *A Nation in Waiting: Indonesia in the 1990s.* Boulder, Colo; San Francisco: Westview Press, 1994.

Vatikiotis, Michael R. J., *Indonesian Politics Under Suharto: The Rise and Fall of the New Order.* London: Routledge, 2004.

Geography

Sutherland, H., 'Geography as Destiny? The role of water in Southeast Asian history.' In: P. Boomgaard (ed.), *A World of Water: Rain, Rivers and Seas in Southeast Asian Histories.* Leiden: KITLV Press, 2007.

Tomascik, T., and A. J. Mah, *The Ecology of the Indonesian Seas.* North Clendon, VT: Tuttle Publishing, 1997.

Wallace, Alfred Russel, *The Malay Archipelago: The Land of the Orang-Utan, and the Bird of Paradise. A narrative of travel, with studies of man and nature.* 2 vols. London: Macmillan, 1869.

Politics, the economy and the law

The Indonesian Bureau of Statistics (now rebranding as StatisticsIndonesia) produces data on a number of economic indicators. Narrative reports are sometimes bilingual, and tables almost always are. They have a useful English-language website at http://www.bps.go.id/eng

The World Bank makes data available in easily downloadable formats. It also produces in-depth reports on specific areas of economic and social growth, and – if you are good at reading between the somewhat rosy lines – a useful quarterly report on the Indonesian economy. http://www.worldbank.org/en/country/indonesia

The OECD (of which Indonesia was not, at the time of writing, a member) works with fewer political constraints and produces some excellent analyses of the Indonesian economy, available at: http://www.oecd.org/indonesia

Readings

Asia Foundation, *Local Economic Governance*. Jakarta: Asia Foundation, 2011. asiafoundation.org/publications/pdf/1027

Aspinall, Edward, 'Democratization and Ethnic Politics in Indonesia: Nine Theses', *Journal of East Asian Studies* 11, no. 2 (1 May 2011), 289–319.

Aspinall, Edward, and Marcus Mietzner, *Problems of Democratisation in Indonesia: Elections, Institutions, and Society*. Singapore: Institute of Southeast Asian Studies, 2010.

Aspinall, Edward, and Gerry van Klinken (eds.), *The State and Illegality in Indonesia*. Leiden: KITLV Press, 2011.

Buehler, M., 'Indonesia's Law on Public Services: Changing state–society relations or continuing politics as usual?', *Bulletin of Indonesian Economic Studies* 47, no. 1 (2011): 65–86.

Burgess, R., M. Hansen, B. A. Olken, P. Potapov, and S. Sieber, 'The Political Economy of Deforestation in the Tropics', *The Quarterly Journal of Economics* 127, no. 4 (2012), 1707–54.

Davidson, Jamie, and David Henley, *The Revival of Tradition in Indonesian Politics: The Deployment of Adat from Colonialism to Indigenism*. Vol. 5. Abingdon, Oxon: Taylor & Francis, 2007.

Harvard Kennedy School, *From Reformasi to Institutional Transformation: A Strategic Assessment of Indonesia's Prospects for Growth, Equity and Democratic Governance*. Cambridge, MA: Ash Center for Democratic Governance and Innovation, 2011.

Henrich, Joseph, Robert Boyd, Samuel Bowles, Colin Camerer, Ernst Fehr, Herbert Gintis, Richard McElrcath, et al., 'In Cross-Cultural Perspective: Behavioral Experiments in 15 Small-Scale Societies', *Behavioral and Brain Sciences* 28, no. 6 (2005): 795–815.

Holt, Claire (ed.), *Culture and Politics in Indonesia*. Ithaca, NY: Cornell University Press, 1972.

Lev, Daniel, *Legal Evolution and Political Authority in Indonesia: Selected Essays*. The Hague: Kluwer Law International, 2000.

Van Klinken, Gerry, and Joshua Barker (eds.), *State of Authority:*

The State in Society in Indonesia. Ithaca, NY: Cornell Southeast Asia Program Publications, 2009.

Religion

For analytical reports on religious violence or extremism, see the Institute for Policy Analysis of Conflict at http://www.understandingconflict.org; Human Rights Watch at http://www.hrw.org/reports; and the Setara Institute at http://www.setara-institute.org/en/category/category/reports.

Readings

Beatty, Andrew, *A Shadow Falls: In the Heart of Java.* London: Faber and Faber, 2009.

Buehler, Michael, 'Subnational Islamization Through Secular Parties: Comparing Shari'a Politics in Two Indonesian Provinces,' *Comparative Politics* 46, no. 1 (2013), 63–82.

Fealy, Greg, and Sally White, *Expressing Islam: Religious Life and Politics in Indonesia.* Singapore: Institute of Southeast Asian Studies, 2008.

Geertz, Clifford, *The Religion of Java.* Chicago: University of Chicago Press, 1976.

Picard, Michel, and Rémy Madinier, *The Politics of Religion in Indonesia: Syncretism, Orthodoxy, and Religious Contention in Java and Bali.* Abingdon, Oxon; New York: Routledge, 2011.

Wilson, Ian Douglas, '"As Long as It's Halal": Islamic Preman in Jakarta.' In: Greg Fealy and Sally White (eds.), *Expressing Islam: Religious Life and Politics in Indonesia;* [... Papers Presented at the 25th Annual Indonesia Update Conference held at the Australian National University (ANU) on 7–8 September 2007], Institute of Southeast Asian Studies, 2008, pp. 192–210.

Conflict and violence

By far the best source of detailed information on specific conflict areas in Indonesia are the reports of the Institute for Policy Analysis of Conflict (IPAC): http://www.understandingconflict.org

The International Crisis Group has useful reports archived on its website: http://www.crisisgroup.org/en/regions/asia/south-east-asia/indonesia.aspx

Human Rights Watch also produces occasional analyses of issues related to rights and conflict: http://www.hrw.org/asia/indonesia

Books and articles on cultural and political violence

Barker, J., 'State of fear: Controlling the criminal contagion in Suharto's New Order,' *Indonesia* 66 (1998), 7–43.

Davidson, Jamie S., *From Rebellion to Riots: Collective Violence on Indonesian Borneo*. Madison, WI: University of Wisconsin Press, 2008.

Raedt, Jules de, and Janet Hoskins, *Headhunting and the Social Imagination in Southeast Asia*. Stanford: Stanford University Press, 1996.

Van Klinken, Gerry, *Communal Violence and Democratization in Indonesia: Small Town Wars*. London: Routledge, 2007.

Wilson, I., *The Biggest Cock: Territoriality, Invulnerability and Honour amongst Jakarta's Gangsters*. Sydney: Murdoch University, 2010.

Conflict in Aceh

Aspinall, E., *Islam and Nation: Separatist Rebellion in Aceh, Indonesia*. Stanford: Stanford University Press, 2009.

Di Tiro, Hasan, *The Price of Freedom: The Unfinished Diary of Tengku Hasan Di Tiro*. Norsborg, Sweden: National Liberation Front of Acheh Sumatra, 1984.

Drexler, Elizabeth, 'The Social Life of Conflict Narratives: Violent antagonists, imagined histories, and foreclosed futures in Aceh, Indonesia', *Anthropological Quarterly* 80(4) (2007), 961–95.

Schulze, Kirsten E., *The Free Aceh Movement (GAM): Anatomy of a Separatist Organization*. Washington, DC: East-West Center, 2004.

Conflict in Maluku

Spyer, Patricia, 'Fire Without Smoke and Other Phantoms of Ambon's Violence: Media effects, agency, and the work of imagination.' *Indonesia* 74 (2002), 21–36.

Van Klinken, Gerry, 'The Maluku Wars: "Communal Contenders" in a Failing State.' In: Charles Coppel (ed.), *Violent Conflicts in Indonesia: Analysis, Representation, Resolution*. London: Routledge, 2006, pp. 129–43.

Index

398   *Indonesia Etc.*